Routledge & K. Paul, 1976.
3 3029 00786 2659

822
S534zs
1976   2775
              Shaw: the critical
                  heritage
                            c.1

SHAW: THE CRITICAL HERITAGE

THE CRITICAL HERITAGE SERIES

GENERAL EDITOR: B. C. SOUTHAM, M.A., B.LITT. (OXON.)
Formerly Department of English, Westfield College, University of London

For a list of books in the series see the back end paper

SHAW

THE CRITICAL HERITAGE

Edited by
T. F. EVANS

Deputy Director
University of London
Department of Extra-Mural Studies

ROUTLEDGE & KEGAN PAUL
LONDON, HENLEY AND BOSTON

First published in 1976
by Routledge & Kegan Paul Ltd
76 Carter Lane,
London EC4V 5EL
Reading Road,
Henley-on-Thames,
Oxon RG9 1EN and
9 Park Street,
Boston, Mass. 02108, USA
Set in Monotype Bembo
and printed in Great Britain by
Butler & Tanner Ltd, Frome and London
© T. F. Evans 1976
No part of this book may be reproduced in
any form without permission from the
publisher, except for the quotation of brief
passages in criticism

ISBN 0 7100 8280 0

CENTRAL

C. 1

General Editor's Preface

The reception given to a writer by his contemporaries and near-contemporaries is evidence of considerable value to the student of literature. On one side we learn a great deal about the state of criticism at large and in particular about the development of critical attitudes towards a single writer; at the same time, through private comments in letters, journals or marginalia, we gain an insight upon the tastes and literary thought of individual readers of the period. Evidence of this kind helps us to understand the writer's historical situation, the nature of his immediate reading-public, and his response to these pressures.

The separate volumes in the *Critical Heritage Series* present a record of this early criticism. Clearly, for many of the highly productive and lengthily reviewed nineteenth- and twentieth-century writers, there exists an enormous body of material; and in these cases the volume editors have made a selection of the most important views, significant for their intrinsic critical worth or for their representative quality—perhaps even registering incomprehension!

For earlier writers, notably pre-eighteenth century, the materials are much scarcer and the historical period has been extended, sometimes far beyond the writer's lifetime, in order to show the inception and growth of critical views which were initially slow to appear.

In each volume the documents are headed by an Introduction, discussing the material assembled and relating the early stages of the author's reception to what we have come to identify as the critical tradition. The volumes will make available much material which would otherwise be difficult of access and it is hoped that the modern reader will be thereby helped towards an informed understanding of the ways in which literature has been read and judged.

B.C.S.

Contents

Three Plays for Puritans (published 1901)

▸ *Man and Superman* (1902)

John Bull's Other Island (1904)

Mrs Warren's Profession (1894)

▸ *Major Barbara* (1905)

CONTENTS

The Doctor's Dilemma (1906)

John Bull's Other Island and Major Barbara (published 1907)

Caesar and Cleopatra (1898)

Getting Married (1908)

The Shewing-Up of Blanco Posnet (1909)

Misalliance (1910)

Androcles and the Lion (1912)

⁕ Pygmalion (1913)

CONTENTS

Heartbreak House (1919)

Back to Methuselah (1920)

Saint Joan (1923)

The Apple Cart (1929)

Obituary Notices and Tributes

Preface

Bernard Shaw wrote an immense amount and an immense amount was written about him and his work. He wrote novels, criticisms and many essays and articles on politics and other subjects as well as the plays by which he is best known and which, during his lifetime and since his death, constitute his greatest claim to our interest. With regret, therefore, I have turned away from Shaw the man or the politician or any other aspect of his many-sided personality, and, for the purpose of this volume, I have concentrated on the response to his plays. I have tried to illustrate the contemporary reaction to the plays as they appeared and I have given most space to notices and reviews in newspapers and other periodicals. I am conscious that my selection is a personal one. From the very large body of material that I have read, I have chosen those items that give a continuing picture of the changing and developing reaction to Shaw's dramatic work. Another editor might well have presented a different picture. If space permitted, it would be valuable to include more items from foreign sources, but I hope that those that are included and the information given in the Introduction will help any reader who wishes to repair the omissions.

The material is arranged in chronological order as far as possible or convenient. The work of a dramatist presents a special problem in this respect. Several of Shaw's plays were not produced until some years after they were written and it seems preferable to print the comment in chronological order rather than to adhere rigidly to the date of composition. Thus, for example, although *Caesar and Cleopatra* was written in 1898, I have deferred comments until 1907, the year of the first London production. Although tempted, I have thought it best to concentrate on the first productions of plays and to leave out comment on revivals. I have tried to make it clear in the headnotes whether it is the play in performance or the printed text that is being discussed. The word 'notice' is used for criticism of a performance and 'review' for comment on the text.

Acknowledgments

I am indebted to the following for permission to reprint copyright material: the *Daily Telegraph* for Nos 1, 3, 37, 46, 53, 74 and 109; Associated Newspapers Group Ltd for Nos 2, 8, 21, 24, 30, 52, 64, 67 and 75; the Trustees of the estate of William Archer for Nos 4, 9, 18, 26, 31, 40 and 94; the *Illustrated London News* for No. 5; the *New Statesman and Nation* for Nos 6, 10, 15, 23, 33, 47, 49, 65, 69, 71, 73, 78, 81, 107, 110, 128, 131 and 133; the *Aberdeen Journal* for No. 11; the *Guardian* for Nos 12, 99 and 130; Mrs D. M. Maxse for No. 13; Sir Rupert Hart-Davis for Nos 14, 22, 32, 42 and 60; for Nos 16, 25, 29, 51, 72, 88, 104, 114, 126 and 129, which are reproduced from *The Times* and the *Times Literary Supplement*; *Blackwood's Magazine* for No. 17; the estate of Arnold Bennett for No. 19; George Allen & Unwin Ltd and Little Brown for No. 27; M. B. Yeats and Miss Anne Yeats for No. 28; M. B. Yeats, Miss Anne Yeats and Hart-Davis MacGibbon Ltd for No. 101; Longmans for No. 34; the *New York Herald* for No. 35; the *Evening Standard* for No. 36; the London School of Economics and Political Science for No. 38; Times Newspapers Ltd for Nos 39, 77, 83, 89 and 118; the Society of Authors as the literary representative for the Estate of John Galsworthy for No. 45; the *Yorkshire Post* for No. 50; Oxford University Press for No. 54, an extract from *The Life of Tolstoy* by Aylmer Maude; the Estate of H. G. Wells for Nos 55, 112 and 121; the Society of Authors on behalf of the Bernard Shaw Estate for No. 56; I.P.C. Newspapers Ltd for No. 57; Faber & Faber Ltd for No. 59, reprinted from *The Critical Writings of James Joyce*, and for No. 91; the Trustees of the Estate of H. L. Mencken and Cornell University Press for No. 60; Oxford University Press for No. 62, reprinted from *English Literature 1450–1900*; *Harper's Weekly* for No. 63; the Trustees of the Estate of John Palmer for No. 70; Colin Smythe Ltd as publishers of the Coole Edition of Lady Gregory's Writings for No. 79; the *Observer* for Nos 80, 90 and 102; the *Birmingham Post* for No. 82; Ashley Dukes and Ernest Benn Ltd for No. 84; the Trustees of the Estate of Alexander Woolcott for No. 85; the *Stage* for No. 86; the New York Times Company for Nos 87 and 117; *Le Figaro* for No. 92; Dame Rebecca

West and the *Saturday Review-World* for No. 93; the Trustees of the Estate of Émile Cammaerts for No. 96; the Letters Trust for T. E. Lawrence and the editor, David Garnett, for No. 97; Macmillan and the Estate of Sir Winston Churchill for No. 98; the *Socialist Leader* for No. 100; the *Listener* for Nos 103, 119, 124, 127 and 134; the *Spectator* for Nos 105, 113 and 116; Mrs Sonia Brownell Orwell and Secker & Warburg and Harcourt Brace Jovanovich Inc. for No. 106; the Trustees of the Estate of Lady Keeble for No. 108; the *Irish Times* for No. 111; the *Atlantic Monthly* for No. 115; Hutchinsons for Nos 120, 122 and 123; *Die Neue Zürcher Zeitung* for No. 125, Mrs Olga Miller for No. 132, Frau Katia Mann for No. 134, and Dr Eric Bentley for No. 135.

It has proved difficult in certain cases to locate the proprietors of copyright material. However, all possible care has been taken to trace ownership of the selections included, and to make full acknowledgment for their use.

Of the many libraries where it has been necessary to spend long hours of fascinating exploration, I owe the greatest debts to the Newspaper Library of the British Library and the periodicals library of the University of London: I am deeply grateful to the Directors and staff for all their willing assistance. Miss Marion Fleisher of the *New Statesman* has been particularly helpful in the identification of unsigned material.

Of many friends and colleagues, without whose help, advice and guidance the work would have taken even longer than it did, I must mention first Stanley Weintraub of the State University of Pennsylvania. Himself one of the leading Shaw scholars in the world, he has never failed to answer without delay any call I have made upon his apparently limitless generosity. Frederick W. P. MacDowell of the University of Iowa and Jürgen Seefeld of the University of Zürich have directed me to material that I might otherwise have missed. In my own Department of Extra-Mural Studies of the University of London, past and present colleagues have been most generous in various ways: they include Werner Burmeister, Frances Glendenning, Susan Liddell, Ronald Mason, Elizabeth Monkhouse, Susan Whitehead and Nina Young.

Finally, my wife and four sons have performed various invaluable tasks, ranging from the secretarial to the menial. Their subtle blend of tolerance and occasional exasperation has been a source of great encouragement and also an ever-present warning against the dangers of allowing a consuming interest to become an obsession.

Introduction

Bernard Shaw's first play was produced in 1892 and his last in 1950,[1] two months before his death at the age of ninety-four. For nearly sixty years he was a prominent figure in the world of the theatre. The pattern of contemporary response to his work may be summed up as a progress from gradual recognition as an interesting eccentric to acceptance as a member of the dramatic 'establishment', but the progress was by no means smooth. His reputation grew steadily after a successful series of productions under the management of Harley Granville Barker and J. E. Vedrenne at the Royal Court Theatre, London, between 1904 and 1907. Despite setbacks during and after the First World War, he became a dramatist of undoubted world stature with the production of *Saint Joan* in London in 1924. In the later years of his life his powers declined. Nevertheless, at his death, he was unchallenged as the leading English dramatist of the century, and a master of prose style. Since his death, there has been no substantial change in this estimate.

As Shaw put it, 'the best authority on Shaw is Shaw'.[2] The development of the critical response to his work was the subject of continuing comment by the author himself in his voluminous correspondence. His attitude to the criticisms of his plays may be seen in the Prefaces to the published editions. He was rarely resentful, even when he thought that his plays had been unjustly treated, but wrote from a lofty standpoint suggesting that, if anyone failed to recognise genius, the fault did not lie with the author.

The fact that Shaw was a dramatist gave a peculiar flavour to the critical response to his work. The majority of the notices of the plays were written within a few hours of the production or, at the most, within a few days. This may account for some unevenness, lack of polish and a hit-or-miss quality in many of the judgments. It also means that the opinions have a valuable spontaneity and are genuine first impressions. In addition, Shaw began writing for the theatre when he had already established a reputation as a journalist on political and similar topics, as well as in music and art criticism. Consequently, many critics found it difficult to judge his plays solely as plays in the orthodox sense and not as dramatised arguments. For this, Shaw was himself largely responsible. At the end of the preface to the first published version of his first play, *Widowers' Houses*, which appeared in book form in 1893, he asked expressly for the play to be judged 'not as a pamphlet in disguise, but as in intention a work of art, as much as any comedy of Molière's is a work of art, and as pretending to be a better play for actual use and long wear on the boards than anything that has yet been turned out by the patent constructive machinery'. He then went on to declare, half in earnest, but half in jest, that 'its value in both respects is enhanced by the fact that it deals with a burning social question, and is deliberately intended to induce people to vote on the Progressive side at the next County Council election in London'. Many readers and members of his audiences have always tended to take seriously the second part of this advice, while ignoring or forgetting the claims made in the first. Further features of Shaw's personality and writing that called forth a particular type of response were his humour and irony. These tones were closely connected with his belief that, because he was an Irishman, he looked at English life and habits with a specially clear vision that, in turn, enabled him to understand and present underlying truths with much sharper perception than mere natives could command.

PUBLICATION OF SHAW'S PLAYS

It is difficult to obtain full and accurate information about the publication of Shaw's plays. Constable & Co. Ltd of London, who were his publishers for many years, lost their records in the bombing during the war and neither they nor the Society of Authors, the trustees of the Shaw Estate, have been able to help. Some information is to be found in Shaw's letters.

The first play, *Widowers' Houses*, was published by Henry & Co. in 1893, as the first in a series of Independent Theatre Plays, edited by J. T. Grein. According to Shaw, in a letter of 16 April 1894 to John Lane, it was not advertised and only 150 copies were sold (Laurence, vol. I, p. 423). *Plays Pleasant and Unpleasant* were published in two volumes by Grant Richards in April 1898. Again according to Shaw, 1,240 copies of each volume were printed. The plays were published at the same time in Chicago by Herbert S. Stone, and Shaw was optimistic in thinking that sales would be greater in the USA. In fact, only 734 copies of each volume were sold. Shaw had much to say to

Grant Richards on the physical appearance of the books, the type, the binding, the advertisements, the sales policy and the author's royalties. *Three Plays for Puritans* were published in 1901, and 2,500 copies were printed. Shaw wrote savagely to Grant Richards that, in the first six months, 1,204 copies were sold, in the next six months 137, and in the third six months 80. Shortly afterwards, the publisher became bankrupt and Shaw's letters to him were at the same time sympathetic, scathing and amusing.

Shaw's long association with Constable began in 1903 with the publication of *Man and Superman*. Shaw was, in fact, his own publisher, making use of the commercial firm for office work and distribution. As is abundantly clear from his letters, he took the closest interest in every detail of the printing and marketing. *Man and Superman* sold 2,707 copies by the end of 1903. Shaw had great difficulty in finding an American publisher and, writing to the Macmillan Company in June 1903 (Laurence, vol. II, p. 333), he said that he 'should probably never attain a large popular circulation'. He went on to doubt whether 'from the purely business side' he was worth dealing with, as 'the necessary capital could always be invested in a book that would bring a larger return'.

In spite of these apprehensions, Shaw's plays appeared regularly and the sales were steady, if not immense. A limited Collected Edition of 1,000 sets was started in 1931 and in the same year there began also the publication of the Standard Edition, which gradually expanded to include, not simply the great majority of the plays, but much other work such as the music and drama criticism and the political and economic writings. The *Complete Plays* were issued in one volume by Constable in 1931 and the *Complete Prefaces* followed in 1934. Later, enlarged editions of each volume were published and both were issued at cheap prices by Odham's Press in association with a newspaper subscription scheme. Shaw contributed a special preface, in which he said that it was the first time that he had ever attached any condition to the perusal of his books except 'the simple ceremony of walking into a bookshop and paying for them'. His readers were now

in a position at once privileged and restricted. Privileged because you can read my plays at less expense than the readers of *The Times*. Restricted because you must begin the day or end the week by reading your favorite paper.

In July 1946, to mark Shaw's ninetieth birthday, Penguin Books issued a uniform set of ten volumes, nine of which were of plays. Of each volume 100,000 copies were printed and, in an unsigned review on 9 August 1946, the *Spectator* referred to the enterprise as 'unprecedented' and said that it 'ought to increase immensely the number of Mr Shaw's readers'. It added that 'in these books we have the foundations of the twentieth century'.

EARLY PLAYS

Shaw's first play, *Widowers' Houses*, was presented at the Royalty Theatre, London, on 9 December 1892. On 29 November 1892, the *Star* had published an 'interview'[3] drafted by Shaw, in which he purported to talk to a journalist about the play. The article was the first of many in which Shaw was to try to prepare the public for the novelty of his plays. The general tone of the article was flippant, and Shaw insisted that his play was 'nothing else than didactic'. On the playbill for the production it was described as an 'Original, Realistic, Didactic Play'. The Independent Theatre, which presented the play, could afford two performances only, and the production was not a financial success. Yet it aroused great interest and many of the critics rose to the bait, as they were clearly intended to do. Thus, the reviewer in the *Morning Post*[4] declared that 'original it is beyond all question, as we recall nothing like it in a long experience. It is also didactic and certainly realistic.' Some critics dismissed Shaw as a mere imitator of Ibsen with a gift for dramatising extracts from blue-books. An anonymous critic wrote in the *Athenaeum* (17 December 1892) that 'Ibsen has justly been charged with the greyness of his tints, and against the Scandinavian dramatists generally it may be urged that in reckoning up the ills of life they lose sight of the influence of hope; yet gloom so unbroken and hopeless as Mr Shaw depicts in his *Widowers' Houses* has not previously been exhibited on the stage.' William Archer, who had collaborated with Shaw in the original idea that later became *Widowers' Houses*, included in his notice of the play (No. 4) a full account of the genesis of the work, but concluded by saying that his friend had no gifts for the type of play that he had written. Shaw replied by emphasising his own knowledge of the economic situation and his amorous experiences, and he called Archer a 'sentimental Sweet Lavendery recluse'. In the *Speaker* (No. 6) A. B. Walkley said, as he was to do often in the future, that there were many merits in Shaw, but they were not the merits of the dramatist. In one of the shrewdest and most discriminating notices, H. W. Massingham wrote in the *Illus-*

trated London News (No. 5) that the production was 'a dramatic event of very considerable significance', chiefly because of what he thought the novelty of the play's type. He thought that Shaw was trying to show features of the society of the time in a way which no other dramatist had ever attempted.

Shaw's next two plays, *The Philanderer* and *Mrs Warren's Profession*, which were both written in 1893, were not performed until several years afterwards, the first through casting difficulties, the second because the subject-matter, professional prostitution, made it impossible for the Lord Chamberlain to license the play for performance. His next play, *Arms and the Man*, found a manager and a theatre soon after it was written, and it was first performed at the Avenue Theatre, London, in April 1894. The run lasted for fifty performances compared with the two of *Widowers' Houses*. Critics found it difficult to judge the play. Some condemned what they thought the incurable flippancy of the author, others deplored his tendency to concentrate on what they called the 'seamy' side of life. Among the latter was William Archer (No. 9) and Shaw appeared to have some of Archer's strictures in mind when he wrote a long article in the *New Review* for July 1894, with the title, 'A Dramatic Realist to His Critics'. In something of the same vein as that in which he had replied to Archer over *Widowers' Houses*, he asserted that he knew what he was writing about, whereas his critics had spent the whole of their lives watching plays, and their values, in consequence, were those of the stage rather than of real life.

Widowers' Houses had been published separately in 1893, but it was in 1898, with the two volumes of *Plays Pleasant and Unpleasant*, that Shaw's dramatic work first made an impact on the reading public. The volumes included seven plays in all; the 'unpleasant' plays were the first three named above and the 'pleasant' plays were *Arms and the Man*, *Candida*, *The Man of Destiny* and *You Never Can Tell*. Shaw's letters to his publisher, Grant Richards, show with what meticulous attention to detail he approached the task of making the plays readable. He emphasised that he required a departure from the custom of printing plays as if they were simply prompt copies for the theatre. It was his idea that the plays should be as readable as novels. Joseph Knight in the *Athenaeum* (No. 15) found that 'reading Mr. Shaw's plays is an agreeable and a perturbing task'. He said that the plays were 'quaint, whimsical, unreal, saucy, cynical, perverse, and a thousand things besides'. When *Three Plays for Puritans* was published in 1901 (the volume included *The Devil's Disciple*, *Caesar and Cleopatra* and *Captain Brassbound's Conversion*, all of which had been written between 1896 and 1899), several critics commented on the fact that Shaw's plays had not yet established themselves in the theatre. As it was put in the *Spectator* (in an unsigned notice, 13 April 1901), 'up till now they have only been put on at matinees or at suburban playhouses'. By this time Shaw had established himself in the theatre in another way. From 1895 to 1898, he wrote weekly theatre criticisms in the *Saturday Review*. This was an important episode in his career. As he wrote in 1906 in a preface to a selection of his dramatic notices, what he had written was 'not a series of judgments aiming at impartiality, but a siege laid to the theatre of the XIXth Century by an author who had to cut his own way into it at the point of the pen, and throw some of its defenders into the moat'. In spite of Shaw's campaign, in which he attacked both the conventional forms of Shakespearean revival and the fashionable play of society, it was still the view of many critics that his own plays, even if they included 'amusing and edifying dialogue' were, in the words of Arnold Bennett in the *Academy* (9 February 1901) (No. 19) 'decidedly not drama'.

THE ROYAL COURT THEATRE

The tendency on the part of critics to draw a distinction between such 'dramatic' qualities as the plays may have possessed and the arguments that they contained became even more marked when the successful seasons at the Royal Court Theatre began. Shaw's association with this theatre began when *Candida* was presented for six special matinées in April and May 1904. The play had previously been seen in provincial towns, and Oliver Elton had said in Manchester in 1898 that it ought to be produced in London (No. 12). The success of the matinées led to the famous Vedrenne–Barker season at the Court. This began with the production of *John Bull's Other Island* on 1 November 1904 (Nos 28–33). Reginald Farrer in the *Speaker* thought Shaw insincere and sentimental (No. 33) but the majority of critics were favourable. The play drew large audiences. Distinguished people, including many leading politicians, went to see it and Shaw's growing reputation was enhanced when a special Command Performance was given for King Edward VII on 11 March 1905.[5] The age of Bernard Shaw may be said to have begun. From then on, his plays commanded the greatest attention accorded to the work of any living dramatist. Argument about his ideas rather than discussion of his more obviously theatrical qualities tended to dominate the notices, but critic after critic, sometimes almost in spite of themselves, acknowledged the success of the plays, simply as stage spectacle and entertainment. Nevertheless, the comments of A. B. Walkley in *The Times*, despite warm appreciation of Shaw's treatment of the Irish and English characters, ended with the opinion, similar to that which he had expressed of earlier plays, that it was 'of course not a play but a thoroughly characteristic "Shavian" entertainment' (No. 29). On the other hand, Max Beerbohm, who had followed Shaw as dramatic critic of the *Saturday Review*, found in Shaw 'an instinct for the theatre' and thought that he could 'with perfect ease express his ideas effectively through the dramatic form' (No. 32). Beerbohm who was not, on the whole, a devoted admirer of Shaw, yet saw what other critics had missed: that Shaw's experience in political controversy and as a public speaker had enabled him 'to dispense with that form in which his thoughts can be pondered at leisure, and to make the best of that form in which they must be caught as they fly'. Among other critics who recognised in *John Bull's Other Island* qualities that had not previously been discerned, perhaps the most perceptive was E. A. Baughan who wrote in the *Daily News* (2 November 1904) (No. 30) that Shaw was 'an artist as well as a politician', added that 'he employed symbolism with the tact and delicacy of a poet' and, in his comments on the closing remarks of Keegan, came nearest to seeing what Shaw was really trying to say.

Man and Superman had been published in 1903, but it was not performed until October 1905. The book, which included very long prefatory material as well as the text of the play, led to discussion of Shaw's ideas even by critics who did not think that those ideas were being advanced seriously. The review in the *Spectator* (21 November 1903) is a good example. It began with the words, 'We have read Mr Shaw's book from beginning to end with some amusement; but never for an instant has it seemed to us that its author was in earnest.' When the play was performed, the majority of the critics paid less attention to the ideas. Gradually, it was coming to be realised that Shaw did possess the art of expressing himself in dramatic form. Some saw more deeply, and E. A. Baughan said in the *Daily News* (24 May 1905) (No. 24) that 'Shaw's play shows a quite surprising grasp of the mental outlook of his special audience', thus recognising his appeal to the intellectual section of the community. The critic of the *Morning Post* said that Shaw was 'the Beaumarchais of the social revolution, and though he was complaining a few years ago that no managers would take his plays, he will shortly be in firm possession of the West End theatres'.[6]

This may have been more than a trifle optimistic, if the fashionable theatre was in mind, but the numbers of performances of Shaw plays in the Royal Court Theatre repertory in 1904–7 was irrefutable evidence that the era of Shaw had arrived among those who considered themselves progressive in their theatrical taste. Of 988 performances in the Vedrenne–Barker season, 701 were of eleven plays by Shaw. The other 287 were of twenty-one plays by sixteen other dramatists. Shaw's plays were of higher quality and better box office than the others. At the end of 1905, almost exactly twelve months after the opening night of *John Bull's Other Island*, one more new major play was presented, *Major Barbara* (Nos 36–43). It is clear from a letter that Shaw wrote to the American actress, Eleanor Robson,[7] whom he was trying to persuade to play Barbara, that at least one manager of a fashionable West End theatre, Frederick Harrison of the Haymarket, had wished to present the play. Shaw remained faithful to the Royal Court. With the production of *Major Barbara*, there began to appear in the criticism of the newspapers and other periodicals a note that was later to be sounded very regularly: the suggestion that, while the new play had manifest virtues, it did not compare with its immediate predecessor. Shaw was greatly amused by this, pointing out with relish that almost exactly the same treatment was accorded to each new play as it appeared. *Major Barbara* incurred severe censure from the *Daily Telegraph* on account of what was called the play's 'desolating cleverness . . . that is purely destructive and never constructive'.[8] From a somewhat surprising source, Shaw's personal friend and Socialist ally, Beatrice Webb, came the comment that the play was 'a dance of devils' and that she was 'taken aback by . . . the triumph of the unmoral purpose' (No. 38).

Of the four dramatic critics who were now showing themselves the most serious students of Shaw, to judge from the care and length that their notices of his plays revealed, two, William Archer and A. B. Walkley, again found *Major Barbara* lacking in true dramatic qualities. Archer found the characters mere mouthpieces and the play itself verbose (No. 40). He compared it with *John Bull's Other Island* greatly to the disadvantage of the new play. Walkley repeated his favourite contention that Shaw, no matter how great his gifts, was no dramatist. The other two critics gave the play high praise. Desmond MacCarthy saw *Major Barbara* as a further step forward in Shaw's development, full of rich promise for the English drama as a whole. Max Beerbohm looked at, and dismissed, the idea that Shaw was no dramatist (No. 42). It was on account of some lines in *Major Barbara* that Shaw encountered some more of that opposition from respectable and conventional taste that he seemed at times deliberately to provoke. At the end of the second act, Barbara, in her despair at what she feels to be her total abandonment by those whom she has loved and trusted, cries, 'My God, my God, why hast Thou forsaken me?' Critics of differing views took exception to this and to the reference to thirty pieces of silver when Barbara speaks of betrayal to Bill Walker. When the play was published (with *John Bull's Other Island*) in 1906, Joseph Knight in the *Athenaeum* took a different view. He said that Shaw's method of challenging conventionally accepted ideas and points of view was for the advantage of readers and playgoers, 'for all such defiances of normal opinion set the playgoer thinking, and when once the playgoer starts thinking, there is the chance of a school of English drama coming into existence' (No. 49).

WIDER AUDIENCES BEFORE THE WAR

The Doctor's Dilemma was produced at the Royal Court Theatre late in 1906 and press reaction was far from unanimous. Desmond MacCarthy in the *Speaker*, on 24 November 1906, summed up the criticisms of the various papers and said that 'this play must surely have a strong, peculiar flavour to affect different palates so violently, making some critics grimace, some smile, and bringing tears to the eyes of others' (No. 47). The success of the Vedrenne–Barker season at the Court had persuaded the two managers to move to the West End of London in order to win greater recognition for their work. A lease was taken of the Savoy Theatre. Shaw had misgivings about the enterprise, but *Caesar and Cleopatra* was produced in 1907, after a trial tour in the provinces. Shaw had written the play in 1898 with the famous Shakespearean actor, Johnston Forbes-Robertson, in mind, but casting and other difficulties had prevented earlier production in London. The play had been a success in the USA and Germany where Shaw was beginning to be widely appreciated. In 1907, Shaw wrote, 'That Forbes-Robertson's Caesar should be famous in America before it has been seen here is a fact which speaks for itself on the subject of theatrical enterprise in London'. The Savoy production was not well received

(Nos 50–3). Several critics suggested that it ought to have been a musical comedy and it was compared with Offenbach's *Orphée aux Enfers*, Barrie's *Peter Pan*, and the type of frivolity in which the light comedian Seymour Hicks used to appear. Shaw was indignant at the reception given to the play and to the acting. He wrote to Forbes-Robertson's wife, Gertrude Elliott,[9] who played Cleopatra, and said that he was sorry 'that it was not possible to produce the play anonymously; for it is plain that the critics let their preconceived ideas of me get between themselves and the acting'. He said, as many playwrights have said of critics since, that 'they always hated the new stuff, even when they were trying their hardest to rise intellectually to the occasion. The consequence has been that every play of mine has had to begin by facing a unanimous and staggering attack from the Press, and has not become really successful until its revival'.

From the end of the Vedrenne–Barker productions at the Royal Court Theatre almost until the outbreak of the war in 1914, Shaw combined his writing of plays with a lively and spirited battle against the critics, teasing them repeatedly about their inability to understand either his opinions or his methods. In 1908, Shaw forestalled the critical reception of *Getting Married* in an 'interview' which he drafted for the *Daily Telegraph* before the play opened (No. 56). He asserted that his new play was his revenge on the critics. He declared that, following the rage and anguish with which the critics had greeted the 'discussion' that constituted the Hell scene of *Man and Superman* when it had been played at the Royal Court, the new play 'will be nothing but talk, talk, talk, talk, talk—Shaw talk. The characters will seem to the wretched critics to be simply a row of Shaws, all arguing with one another on totally uninteresting subjects'. Taking the hint, most critics were duly disappointed with a work that offered 'prolixity' and made the audience yawn. In truth, Shaw was now writing plays in which he departed from the conventional requirement of an orthodox 'story' to a greater extent than he had ever done before, and presented—the description that he gave to *Getting Married*—'a disquisitory play' or, as he called *Misalliance*, 'a debate in one sitting'. Before Shaw had finished *Misalliance*, he wrote to Vedrenne on 3 October 1909, saying that the play was to be 'nothing but endless patter; my bolt as a real playwright is shot'.[10] *The Times* critic said of *Misalliance* that it was 'the debating society of a lunatic asylum—without a motion and without a chairman'.[11] Max Beerbohm in the *Saturday Review* found that the 'debate' was not treated artistically (No. 60).

On the whole, Shaw's exchanges with critics were sufficiently softened by humour for the altercations to remain good-tempered, but his patience was severely tried by the official attitude that held up the public presentation of *The Shewing-Up of Blanco Posnet*; the reason given was the unconventional nature of the religious views expressed by Blanco Posnet. The play was refused a licence for public production in Britain by the Lord Chamberlain, and, after a battle, it was played first at the Abbey Theatre, Dublin, in 1909.[12] James Joyce saw the Dublin production and wrote a notice for *Il Piccolo della Sera*, Trieste, on 5 September 1909 (No. 59).

The ideas in Shaw's plays provoked great discussion, and what were variously taken to be severe attacks on marriage and family life in *Getting Married* and *Misalliance* respectively, as well as the supposed blasphemy in *Blanco Posnet*, gave rise to considerable controversy, but the plays did not succeed in the theatre. Thus, *Misalliance* failed to attract the public and ran for only eleven performances. Shaw was ahead of his audiences and often had to create them: one of the purposes of the prefaces was to publicise the plays. Later revivals of *Misalliance* were long runs. Ironically the next play that Shaw wrote, and one that was not designated as an entirely serious major work, proved to be the most successful of his career, judged solely by the number of performances in the opening run. This was *Fanny's First Play*, which ran for 622 performances. It was performed at the Little Theatre, London, on 19 April 1911, and Shaw chose to give it to the public under a cloak of anonymity, or the pretence of anonymity, thus fulfilling the wish that he had expressed about *Caesar and Cleopatra*. Few could have been misled for long. The play contained unmistakable clues to his identity in those passages where the play within the play was discussed by the dramatic critics, who were thinly disguised satirical portraits of prominent critics of the day. One line will illustrate this. It is when Vaughan (E. A. Baughan) says of the play, 'You can't deny that the characters in this play are quite distinguishable from one another. That proves it's not by Shaw, because all Shaw's characters are himself: mere puppets stuck up to spout Shaw. It's only the actors that make them seem different.' At another point in the play, Trotter (A. B. Walkley) remarks that, without wishing to do so, the critics find themselves always talking about Shaw.

At this time, that is in the years immediately preceding the First World War, almost everybody was talking about Shaw.[13] Although no longer engaged in the local government and other political activities that had continued to occupy much of his interest and energies in the years when he began to write plays, he was very prominent in many other fields of public interest and controversy, from presenting his views on the censorship of plays and the organisation of the theatre to making plans for the better running of the Fabian Society; in addition to writing plays he wrote such occasional pieces as prefaces —to his wife's translations of plays by Brieux or to a centenary edition of Dickens's *Hard Times*—and anonymous, but clearly identifiable, leading articles for the new weekly journal which he helped to found in 1913, the *New Statesman*. Religion was another subject on which he was always prepared to write and lecture, and the play, *Androcles and the Lion*, first presented in 1913, enabled him to combine religious discussion with childish romps in a way that E. A. Baughan said in the *Daily News* was 'curious and should be seen for that reason alone' (No. 64).

Shaw's last play before the outbreak of war in 1914 was *Pygmalion* (Nos 67–9). He had apparently gone out of his way to show his disregard for English audiences and English critics by allowing the first performance of all to take place in Vienna, where the play was produced at the Hofburg Theater on 16 October 1913. It was well received and the anonymous critic of the *Neue Freie Presse* said, on 17 October 1913, that the play 'has the power of stimulating thought in the audience, while entertaining them at the same time'.[14] The first English production at His Majesty's Theatre, London, on 11 April 1914, constituted a sensational event in more ways than one. The fact that Shaw's play was being presented at the fashionable West End theatre by the celebrated actor-manager, Sir Herbert Beerbohm Tree, with himself and the famous and controversial actress, Mrs Patrick Campbell, in the leading parts, emphasised that Shaw's progress to a leading position in the established theatre of the time was now complete. It is almost impossible, however, to assess accurately the critical response to the play itself because of the totally disproportionate amount of space, time and attention that was given to the use by Shaw, in a speech written for Mrs Patrick Campbell's part of the flower-girl Eliza Doolittle, of the word 'bloody'. This had been used on the stage before, notably by John Masefield; thus even this furore over Shaw was misguided. Some critics who might have been expected to give largely favourable comments on the play seem to have allowed the use of the adjective to affect them. Of these, E. A. Baughan in the *Daily News* thought *Pygmalion* soulless and, once more looking backwards, said that Shaw 'at his best . . . was capable of much better work, wittier, deeper and more stimulating. Even when his plays irritated one by their curious spiritual gentility they at least gave one to think'. Yet the controversy over the use of the word, which filled correspondence columns in many papers, undoubtedly attracted more people to the play. Tree tired of the play after three months and the run came to an end. He had made a profit of £13,000, and Shaw received ten per cent, on gross weekly takings of £2,000, thus achieving an unqualified success in the West End theatre. It was now the end of July 1914 and the war was to affect both the English theatre and Shaw's reputation.

LITERARY CRITICISM

Books about Shaw began to appear in the first decade of the century. The first was by the then little-known American journalist, H. L. Mencken. In the introduction to his book *George Bernard Shaw: His Plays*, published in 1905, Mencken commented on the growing interest in Shaw: 'Pick up any of the literary monthlies and you will find a disquisition upon his technique, glance through the dramatic column of your favourite newspaper and you will find some reference to his plays'. He gave especially high praise to *Man and Superman*. Holbrook Jackson in 1907, in the preface to his book on Shaw, the first published in England, deplored what he called 'the meagre acceptance of Shaw as a leader of thought'. He regretted 'the perpetual falling to pieces of critics of all orders at the instigation of each new preface from his pen', and he felt that there were intelligent persons whose brains were worthy of a better cause than that of accepting a mistaken popular view of Shaw. He saw Shaw in the same relation to his time as Swift and Carlyle to theirs, and found that Shaw's great contribution to the theatre was the introduction of philosophy to drama, while his great contribution to philosophy was the 'concentration of will into the energy of life'.

In 1907, also, Desmond MacCarthy published his book, *The Court Theatre*.[15] This consisted of a review of the Vedrenne–Barker season at the Royal Court Theatre, and MacCarthy wrote at the beginning about the influence of dramatic critics in educating the theatre-going public to an appreciation of new forms of play. He paid special attention to Shaw and said that 'his mission is not to glorify what is best in human nature, but to make men scrutinise their pretensions, their emotions and their conscience'. MacCarthy maintained that Shaw was having a great influence on his contemporaries and that he was 'an author of real significance'. In 1909, Shaw's friend and debating opponent, G. K. Chesterton, wrote a study of Shaw, and Shaw reviewed the book in the *Nation*, calling it 'the best work of literary art I have yet provoked' (25 August 1909). In a letter to Chesterton a little later (30 October 1909) Shaw showed himself less enthusiastic and said that 'a lot of it was fearful nonsense'. In general, Chesterton concentrated on Shaw as a philosopher and discussed the ideas in his plays, but failed to understand their essentially stage appeal. There was irony in the fact that Chesterton, who himself indulged to excess in paradox, should speak of Shaw's 'bleak and heartless extravagance of statement in certain subjects which makes the author really unconvincing as well as exaggerative'. Yet Chesterton warmed to Shaw as one who maintained gaiety in face of life and who helped to keep the modern age cheerful when so many made it the reverse. He ended his book with the resounding phrases: 'this shall be written of our time: that when the spirit who denies besieged the last citadel, blaspheming life itself, there were some, there was one especially, whose voice was heard and whose spear was never broken'. Shaw's position at the head of English dramatists was now being widely recognised. In June 1907, in an essay in the *Fortnightly Review*, St John Hankin, himself a dramatist whose plays had been performed at the Royal Court Theatre, wrote that 'Mr Shaw is indisputably the most distinguished living English dramatist. He is, in fact, the only dramatist of worldwide reputation whom we have' (No. 48). C. E. Montague, a leading critic for the *Manchester Guardian*, wrote in his *Dramatic Values* in 1911, that Shaw's 'serious thinking' was only ordinary but 'his wit is genius'. G. H. Mair in *English Literature: Modern*, in 1911, said that Shaw had founded a school of modern English dramatists (No. 62). One of the writers to whom he referred as having been influenced by Shaw, John Galsworthy, thought that Shaw was only 'ephemeral' but his work was 'serving a good contemporary purpose' (No. 45). Rupert Brooke (No. 44) and H. G. Wells (No. 55) were among other writers who commented favourably on Shaw at about this time. D. H. Lawrence also, while his admiration for Shaw was certainly qualified, wrote to his friend, Blanche Jennings, in 1908 to say that he had 'a passion for modern utterances'. He included Shaw's work in this category.[16] He said that he raved at Shaw but liked him because he was 'one of those delightful people who give one the exquisite pleasure of falling out with him wholesomely'. Later, in 1913, he wrote to Edward Garnett to say that he was 'sick of the rather bony, bloodless drama we get nowadays—it is time for a reaction against Shaw and Galsworthy and Barker and Irishy (except Synge) people —the rule and measure mathematical folk'.[17] An actress, who felt that Shaw's plays offered opportunities that were not to be found in the work of other dramatists was Lillah McCarthy, who created the leading female roles in several of Shaw's earlier plays and who was the first wife of Granville-Barker. In her memoirs, *Myself and My Friends* (published in 1933) she said that, if it had not been for such plays as *Man and Superman*, she would 'never have developed as a woman' (No. 108). One writer who found it impossible to agree with Shaw on literary 'art' was the novelist, Henry James (No. 58).

SHAW AND THE WAR

The First World War came at a central point in Shaw's career, not simply in respect of chronology. By 1914, his position among the most important dramatists then writing in any language could no longer be denied. He had shown himself both prolific and entertainingly successful in theatrical production. In addition, his published plays had aroused much serious attention. He threw himself with great energy into public argument about how the war should be prosecuted, and this led to inaccurate assumptions that he was opposed to the war. His activities caused great offence. This was not limited to those who knew him merely as a political figure. The Dramatists' Club, hardly a body that might have been expected to become embroiled in questions of national or international politics or of military strategy, agreed that it would be better for Shaw not to continue to receive the Club notices. This was a clumsy way of asking Shaw not to attend the Club. Shaw's fellow-dramatist, with whom he had always been on good terms, Henry Arthur Jones, was a leader of the movement to expel Shaw.[18] His strictures on Shaw's writings about the war tended, at times, to become hysterical, and extended to Shaw's plays as well. It was not surprising that the war years did not see many of Shaw's plays on the stage in London, although they were much performed in other towns. There was a long article on Shaw in the *Fortnightly Review* for March 1915. This was by John Palmer, and he gave it the provocative title, 'Bernard Shaw; an epitaph' (No. 70). The title was somewhat misleading because, while Palmer suggested that, in consequence of the writings about the war, Shaw's importance and influence were waning, he gave high praise to the dramatist. A younger critic, Dixon Scott, wrote a long article on Shaw in 1913 and this was published in book form in 1916 (No. 66).

FROM *Heartbreak House* TO *Saint Joan*

The idea that Shaw was finished as a serious artist gained strength from the silence that he imposed on himself as a dramatist during the war. When, in 1919, he published the book of plays on which he had been working for some years, the volume containing *Heartbreak House* and some shorter pieces, his friend William Archer said that 'ever since 1914 he has been practically out of action, and . . . now, when the cause of sanity and humanity needs every champion it can muster, he remains almost a negligible factor in the situation'.[19] Few other critics of *Heartbreak House* gave it higher praise than Archer had done (Nos 71–8). The general impression seemed to be that Shaw had fallen seriously out of touch. In the *Spectator*, an anonymous critic suggested that he had insufficient contact with other people and so could not draw convincing characters. He went on to call *Heartbreak House* 'a curious medley of harlequinade and London sermon, as bewildering in its way as Strindberg's *Spook Sonata*, without the eerie power of that distracted genius to grip the attention alike in eccentricity and commonplace' (25 October 1919). John Middleton Murry in the *Athenaeum* commented most favourably on the analysis of English society presented in the preface, but found the play itself 'half-procession, half-pandemonium' (No. 73). Not many critics did more than note in passing the fact that Shaw had tried to base his play on the Russian model that he found in Chekhov. Shaw had seen the Stage Society production of *The Cherry Orchard* before the war, and, according to one report, said that he felt like tearing up all his own plays and beginning again.[20] When *Heartbreak House* was presented on the English stage in 1921 (the first production of all was in New York in 1920) the unfavourable voices were again in the majority. Several critics commented on the tedium of the dialogue, and only Desmond MacCarthy praised the play highly, saying that it was 'perhaps (so far as the phrasing of the dialogue is concerned) even his best-written play' (No. 78). He spent more time than other critics in examining Shaw's attempt to catch the atmosphere of Chekhov, but concluded that Shaw's high spirits had seriously damaged the play. As *Heartbreak House* did little to advance Shaw's reputation, so, too, his next work evoked responses that were lukewarm at best. This was the massive *Back to Methuselah* (Nos 79–83). Shaw gave this play, five plays in one, the strange and daunting sub-title 'A Metabiological Pentateuch'. Again, this was presented on the stage for the first time in New York. When the text was published in England in 1921, it received careful study and some very long notices appeared. Much praise was given to the quality of the writing, in the long preface as well as in the play itself, but Shaw was thought to have been so sickened by material life, probably in consequence of the waste and destruction of the war, that he had turned to inhuman metaphysics. Some critics took up Shaw's hints of Manichaeism, and H. W. Massingham in the *Nation and Athenaeum*, beginning with comparisons of Shaw with Swift, ended by calling him 'a Christian heretic, a Manichee of the twentieth century'.[21] In the face of the reviews of the book, it is surprising that anyone was found to put the giant work on the stage. In 1923, however, *Back to Methuselah* was presented by Barry Jackson at the Birmingham Repertory Theatre. Critics saw a performance of sustained intellectual quality, but as drama, after the initial enthusiasm of the enterprise had worn off, *Back to Methuselah* led to yawns and empty seats. In London, some months later, there was a similar response. James Agate had found merits in *Heartbreak House* (No. 76) but he was rarely a warm admirer of Shaw. He had little sympathy with his political or social ideas, thought that he was too wordy, and deplored his habit of combining high thinking with low joking. He said that *Back to Methuselah* was 'a mystery and a mistake' and, in places, 'cheap' (No. 83). Arnold Bennett admitted that he 'went to sleep' on what was 'a most depressing night'. Desmond MacCarthy, reviewing the published play in 1921, said that it was 'not an artistic success' (No. 81); when he saw the play at a revival some time later in 1924 than the original London production, he wrote in the *New Statesman* that 'the superb merit of the play is that it is the work of an artist who has asked himself, with far greater seriousness and courage than all but a few, what is the least he must believe and hope for if he is to feel life is worth living.'[22] Dramatists, like many other artists, are notoriously fallible in their opinions of what is their best work. Shaw always said that *Back to Methuselah* was his masterpiece and it was this play that he chose when, in 1945, he was asked to select one of his works for the five-hundredth volume in the well-known series of reprints, the World's Classics, published by the Oxford University Press. He wrote a special post-script for that edition and said that 'Back to Methuselah is a world classic or it is nothing.'

Shaw had written to Mrs Patrick Campbell from Orléans in 1913 saying that he would 'do a Joan play one day' and suggesting a few scenes, including one of Joan's arrival in heaven, and referring to an incident when an English soldier gave her a cross of two sticks as she went to the stake. The play was not written until ten years later but it became his best-known work and the one to which many judges would give first place among all his plays. Once more, the play received its first production in New York (Nos 85–7). It was well received and Lawrence Langner wrote to Shaw on 9 January 1924, 'People are coming in droves to see Saint Joan, and it is a great success.' The public demand was such that the play was transferred to a larger theatre in March. Saint Joan was first presented in England at the New Theatre, London, on 26 March 1924 (Nos 88–91). A distinguished and popular actress, Sybil Thorndike, played the leading role and identified herself wholly with the character of Joan and with Shaw's own inter-pretation. The play ran for 244 performances. The critics of the daily papers competed with each other in praising the play and the pro-duction, the actress and the dramatist. Even A. B. Walkley who, astonishingly, condemned the play before seeing it, recanted after the first night (No. 88). In the weekly periodicals, considered judgment was less enthusiastic. Some critics complained of the length of the play and James Agate urged strongly, as did other critics on both sides of the Atlantic, that Shaw should delete the Epilogue, in which Joan returned to the world in the 1920s to find herself rejected as an awk-ward intruder, even by those who revered her memory and had recently canonised her (No. 89). Edmund Wilson in the New Republic[23] and Desmond MacCarthy in the New Statesman were among those who understood and defended the Epilogue. Some critics used super-latives of the play. Anne Doubleday wrote in Time and Tide that Saint Joan was 'a great poetic drama, the best thing Shaw has ever written'.[24] Desmond MacCarthy in the New Statesman found the most important feature of the play the skill with which Shaw showed that discussions or conversations could 'contribute to dramatic effect as directly as scenes of action'. When the text of the play was published in the following year, criticism tended to concentrate on the actual ideas in the play rather than upon the dramatic expression and presentation of the ideas. The reviewer in the Times Literary Supplement nevertheless echoed MacCarthy in saying that the play was 'a triumph in the adjustment of action to idea'.[25]

With the successful production of *Saint Joan* and its publication, Shaw reached the height of his fame. He wrote to Lawrence Langner after the London production, saying that 'everyone, to my disgust, assures me that it is the best play I have ever written'.[26] Shaw disliked honours and awards but he accepted the Nobel Prize for literature in 1926.[27] He did this conditionally. He was prepared to accept the award although he said that it puzzled him. He said that he presumed that it had been given out of a sense of relief because he had published nothing in 1925. He could not persuade himself to accept the money, as he thought it 'a lifeboat thrown to a swimmer who has already reached the shore in safety'. He proposed that the money be used to set up a fund to encourage Anglo-Swedish literary relations and this was done. At this point, although *Saint Joan* was such a success, Shaw felt that he had temporarily come to a halt in his dramatic work and he resumed his political writing. This, if not entirely abandoned since the war, had remained a lesser activity. When he took it up again, it was not in his former role as pamphleteer or publicist, but as the author of a textbook. The book was *The Intelligent Woman's Guide to Socialism and Capitalism*, written during the years following *Saint Joan* and published in 1928. Not surprisingly, its reception was mixed. Those unfavourably inclined to Socialism anyway could hardly be expected to admire the book and Socialists themselves were far from unanimous about it.

LAST PLAYS

Whether as a consequence of his work in *The Intelligent Woman's Guide* or simply because of a growing interest in the political situation of the time, the next play that Shaw wrote, his first for five years, had more directly political content than any of his other plays. Certainly in no major work before *The Apple Cart* had he looked so closely at the working of the British system of government. Shaw had been popular in many European countries since the beginning of the century and his appreciation of the close interest that the Polish theatre had always shown in his plays persuaded him to allow *The Apple Cart* to be performed for the first time in Warsaw in June 1929. In addition, it was thought that his witty treatment of political themes would have a special appeal for Polish audiences, and it proved a great success. *The Apple Cart* was then presented as the first play at the Malvern Festival, inaugurated in honour of Shaw by Sir Barry Jackson, and it was transferred to London in September (Nos 99–103). The play was well received on the whole, but there was sharp controversy about the political attitudes that some of the critics found in it. Ironically, it was the critics who would be expected to have least sympathy with Shaw's politics who found most to praise. Reviewers in such papers as the *Morning Post*[28] and *The Times*[29] referred to Shaw's command of technique; in the former, it was said of the first act that 'though nothing happens, the scene is essentially dramatic'. Christopher St John wrote in *Time and Tide* that 'if the Shaw Malvern Festival should become a permanent institution like the Shakespeare Festival at Stratford on Avon, it will be because Shaw is a good entertainer, not because he is a good philosopher'.[30] On the other hand, W. B. Yeats wrote to his friend, Lady Gregory, that he 'hated the play . . . it was the Shaw who writes letters to the papers and gives interviews, not the man who creates' (No. 101).

The Apple Cart caused Shaw to lose friends and admirers. When the play was published in 1930, he affected to be surprised at some of the criticisms and he tried to explain his political attitudes in a long preface. For some years afterwards, it was the conventional view that, with *The Apple Cart*, Shaw began to lose both his political sense and his dramatic skill, and many critics confused the two. Thus, H. W. Nevinson, up till then and, indeed, later, a great admirer of Shaw, wrote harshly in the Socialist paper, the *New Leader* (No. 100). He said that Shaw had not presented a fair balance of opposing forces, but had set a 'wise, considerate and thoughtful King' on the one hand against 'a gang of fools and knaves who represent the Cabinet' on the other. (Even if Shaw was thought to have distorted or misrepresented the political realities of the situation, there were some who thought that he had been more than usually prescient when, in a couple of years, the Labour government of Ramsay Macdonald collapsed in circumstances that bore some resemblance to those imagined in the play.)

None of the four full-length plays that Shaw wrote next after *The Apple Cart*—*Too True to be Good* (1931), *On the Rocks* (1933), *The Simpleton of the Unexpected Isles* (1934), and *The Millionairess* (1935) —added to his reputation. *On the Rocks* was a comparatively straightforward 'political comedy' but the other three were extravaganzas in style and technique and apocalyptic in tone. Shaw's disillusion with conventional politics at home and his preoccupation with the dictators abroad and the general deterioration of the international situation turned him to writing plays in an unorthodox style that combined a strong didactic streak with passages of farce and political satire. *Too True to be Good* impressed both W. A. Darlington in the *Daily Telegraph* and Charles Morgan in *The Times* (No. 104) as lacking form and not compensating for this by the 'memorable sermons, finely phrased' as Darlington put it. (It was not until 1965 that the play was appreciated, in a London revival, as being in the style of Samuel Beckett many years ahead of its time.) *The Simpleton of the Unexpected Isles* was not presented in London and it seemed that the long career of the dramatist had at last come to an end. By this time Shaw was almost eighty, but there were three full-length plays to come. Even if not on his own highest level, they were remarkably lucid and consistent with his developing thought. Alan Dent in the *Spectator* found *Geneva* in 1938 above the level of intelligence of the audience (No. 116). *Geneva*, a satire on the international political scene, with clearly recognisable caricatures of such figures as Hitler and Mussolini, proved popular enough to have a successful run in London in 1939, even though it excited lukewarm admiration from the critics. Shortly before the outbreak of war a history play, *In Good King Charles's Golden Days*, attracted more praise than other recent work and James Agate said that it embodied 'the re-affirmations of a great man' (No. 118), but Shaw's last full-length play, *Buoyant Billions*, first presented in Zürich in 1948 and at the Malvern Festival and in London a year later, was treated as little more than a late flicker of a rapidly fading genius. The Swiss critic who referred to the play as a 'repetition in a gentler key of familiar themes of the Irish Methuselah' (No. 125) was kinder than most.

Nevertheless, even if Shaw's later work was clearly not on the level of his earlier plays, he was still popular in the theatre, in revivals, both professional and amateur, and in two new forms of presentation. Shaw was interested in films from the early days of the development of the medium, and successful film versions of *Pygmalion* in 1938 and *Major Barbara* in 1941 brought his work before wider audiences. In addition, he showed great interest in sound broadcasting and gave many successful talks (No. 123).

LATER LITERARY ESTIMATES

During the inter-war years, Shaw's work gradually became the subject of more careful and detailed consideration. In 1932 H. W. Nevinson wrote in the *Spectator*, 'Wherever you go, you will find a controversy raging about Shaw. . . . In every civilised land I have heard the cry of "Shaw, Shaw, Shaw!" His fame is almost what is called universal.' From the large amount of critical comment in books and periodicals, however, as distinct from the immediate reviews of his productions, the general impression is of critics confronted with an author who resolutely refused to be labelled. Thus, Graham Sutton in the *Bookman* in March 1924, remarked that Shaw's detractors based their criticisms on diametrically opposed arguments: 'Half of them complain that Mr. Shaw is too serious, the other half that he is not serious enough.'[31] In a considered assessment, William Archer came to a less favourable conclusion than might have been expected. His article, 'The Psychology of G.B.S.', appeared in the month of his death, December 1924, in the *Bookman* (No. 94). He made a comparison between Shaw and Voltaire, but the estimate was entirely in favour of Voltaire. He summed up Shaw by saying that he could not think of anyone who had made 'so great noise and so little mark'. Yet this was about the time of *Saint Joan*, and other critics of this period spoke of Shaw as worthy of mention alongside Dr Johnson—Robert Lynd in the *Bookman*, December 1924 (No. 95); Thomas Hardy—Rebecca West in the *Saturday Review of Literature*, August 1924 (No. 93); Euripides—Herbert Edward Mierow in *Sewanee Review*, January 1928; and Molière—Émile Cammaerts in the *Nineteenth Century*, September 1926 (No. 96). In a long essay in the *London Mercury* in June 1933, Osbert Burdett made a comparison with Macaulay (No. 107). In the course of his article, Burdett quoted from *Autobiographies* by W. B. Yeats, in which the poet condemned Shaw for superficiality, saying that his writings were 'the brilliant mirror of a shallow time, a time dominated through fatigue by the falsehood of a monist materialism'. A similar approach, though directly related to the problems of dramatic technique, had been made by Ivor Brown in the *Fortnightly Review* in July 1930. He wrote on 'The Spirit of the Age in Drama' and argued that Shaw had won a victory in the theatre in that he had established the 'right' of the dramatist to ignore form and to write shapeless plays, if only his dialogue was brilliant enough, but that the example he set to other writers was a dangerous one. 'The new anarchy of construction', wrote Brown, 'is all very well when it liberates a Shaw; it is not at all well when it liberates the half-baked disciples of that master and the pretenders to a new gospel or a cosmic message.'

In the course of about forty years, therefore, some critics had returned to the view of Shaw the dramatist that had been taken by those who had seen *Widowers' Houses* as marking the arrival of a new and startling talent which was not that of a dramatist. In the 1930s, two leading literary critics made definitive statements about Shaw that were to influence a later generation of readers. T. S. Eliot, in 'A Dialogue on Dramatic Poetry', which was written in 1928 but which attained greater currency when it was published in *Selected Essays* in 1932, laid down in a brief utterance what came to be a widely accepted view, that Shaw had a poet inside him, but that the poet was still-born. The force of this dictum was partly, but not wholly, offset by the admission that Shaw was the greatest living prose stylist. Eliot's attitude to Shaw was influenced by dislike of his political opinions and of his personality.[32] He thought Shaw intellectually meretricious and therefore on a low level artistically as well. In spite of this, he confessed cautiously in his lectures on 'Poetry and Drama' (1951) that, in his use of vernacular prose for the speeches of the Knights in *Murder in the Cathedral*, 'I may, for aught I know, have been slightly under the influence of *Saint Joan*.' (Winston Churchill was opposed to Shaw's politics and he condemned his attitudes during the First World War; in 1929, nevertheless, he referred to Shaw as 'the greatest living master of letters in the English-speaking world' (No. 98)). The other estimate of Shaw in the 1930s that may be placed beside that of Eliot was 'Bernard Shaw at Eighty' by the American critic, Edmund Wilson (No. 115). This was first published in the *Atlantic Monthly* in 1938 and in the book *The Triple Thinkers*, in the same year. Much of it is concerned with adverse criticism of Shaw's political views and attitudes, especially with the deterioration that Wilson professed to find in Shaw's later years. He concluded by saying that whereas it 'used always to be said of Shaw that he was primarily not an artist, but a promulgator of certain ideas, the truth is, I think, that he is a considerable artist, but that his ideas—that is, his social philosophy proper—have always been confused and uncertain.' Wilson saw Shaw as a juggler who played with ideas in a way that came to fullest fruition in the writing of comedies for the theatre. In one of the best pieces of criticism of Shaw's later work, Edmund Wilson analysed *The Apple Cart* not, as most other critics had tended to do, simply as a debate, but in the terms of a musical composition. As Wilson put it, 'this music is a music of ideas—or rather, perhaps, it is a music of moralities'. The novelist and dramatist W. Somerset Maugham wrote in *The Summing-Up* in 1938 that Shaw 'has succeeded on the stage not because he

is a dramatist of ideas but because he is a dramatist'. Maugham's distaste for the drama of ideas as a form of play inclined him to under-
value this quality in Shaw. The literary critic, Cyril Connolly, writing
in the same year in *Enemies of Promise*, said that Shaw was not an artist.
He explained this by saying that 'much of his art consists in the plain-
ness of his writing for he is certain of the truth of his convictions and
the force of his emotions'.[33] This somewhat limited view of art may
have accounted for the lack of interest in Shaw in the intellectual
periodicals of the time. There are few references to Shaw in such
advanced literary and artistic magazines as T. S. Eliot's *Criterion*, F. R.
Leavis's *Scrutiny*,[34] Connolly's *Horizon* or John Lehmann's *New
Writing*. Younger writers and critics of the 1920s and 1930s, who were
concentrating on Joyce, Eliot and Proust, felt that Shaw had little to
offer them. A. L. Rowse wrote in the *Criterion* in December 1928 that
'after all, Shaw as an artist is likely enough to be outpassed by a good
half-dozen writers of our time in the memory of the future'.[35]

Other critics in the last twenty years of Shaw's life began to attack
his work on political grounds. The strongest attacks were from those
on the extreme Left, who thought that he had betrayed Socialism.
Christopher Caudwell wrote from a strong Marxist standpoint in
Studies in a Dying Culture (1936). He described Shaw as 'bourgeois',
'Utopian', 'social fascist' and 'the world's buffoon', and said that he
was 'helplessly imprisoned in the categories of bourgeois thought'. A
milder but still adverse comment on Shaw was that of George Orwell
(No. 106), but it is surprising that he said nothing about the actual
quality of Shaw's writing. In *Bernard Shaw: Art and Socialism* in 1942,
E. Strauss examined the relations between Shaw's drama and his
politics and found a tension in the plays that robbed them of their
power as social or political documents while enhancing their virtues
as drama. Another Marxist critic, Alick West, took for the title of a
study of Shaw published in 1949, the year before he died, the remark
that Lenin had made about him (and that Caudwell had quoted in his
book), *A Good Man Fallen among Fabians*. West maintained that Shaw's
Fabianism prevented him from seeing the correct political solutions,
but he could not deny that he had 'artistic vision'.

In the foreword, written in 1947, to *Bernard Shaw*, Eric Bentley
refers to the dearth of serious criticism of Shaw to be compared with
that which he found on two other modern writers, Henry James and
Kafka. He said that 'everyone has certainly had his say on Shaw, but
the say was casual without being tentative and vehement without

being solid'. Bentley is close to Edmund Wilson in emphasising the musical structures in the plays. He found Shaw, whatever his failures, to have succeeded in affirmation of the value of life, 'life with a blessing' against any idea whatever. There was valuable background material and some useful critical comment in *G.B.S. 90*, a compilation edited by Stephen Winsten in 1946 (Nos 122, 123). In the middle of the war there had been a great impulse to 'anecdotage' about Shaw, as opposed to criticism, with the publication in 1942 of Hesketh Pearson's 'biography', *Bernard Shaw: his Life and Personality*, in which the author had received great help from Shaw himself, who wrote or rewrote portions of the book. The book was sketchy, but it aroused great interest and it was supplemented in 1951, the year after Shaw's death, by a *Postscript* that included matter excluded earlier by Shaw or considered by Pearson inappropriate to repeat in Shaw's lifetime. The popular philosopher, C. E. M. Joad, wrote a book on Shaw in 1949, but this was found, some years later, to have been based very closely, even to the extent of unmistakable, if unacknowledged, quotation, on the actual text of Dixon Scott's 1913 assessment.

THE AMERICAN RESPONSE

In one of his early letters to Grant Richards, Shaw said that one indispensable condition for the success of his plays in book form was 'simultaneous publication in America' and added that 'there is much more to be made out of my name there than here at present'.[36] The figures for the sales of the volumes of the plays do not bear this out, but there is evidence to suggest that Shaw went further to becoming established as a dramatist in the theatre in the USA before the end of the nineteenth century than he did in England. Thus, *Arms and the Man* was presented successfully in New York in 1894, not long after the first London performance, and *The Devil's Disciple* was presented for the first time on any stage in Albany in 1897 (perhaps appropriately in view of the play's American theme and setting). The critical reception of the plays was mixed, but interest was great. Influential critics, such as Edward A. Dithmar of the *New York Times* and William Winter of the *New York Tribune*, both confessed themselves puzzled, but the latter thought that the spectator would enjoy *Arms and the Man* if he gave up trying to find meaning or purpose in it. James G. Huneker, who had read many of Shaw's earlier non-dramatic writings before he saw the plays, was much impressed by the quality of Shaw's writing.[37]

When he saw *Arms and the Man* in 1894, he found Shaw an improvement on Wilde, and he thought that *The Devil's Disciple* showed great advances in Shaw's stagecraft. After reading *Mrs Warren's Profession* and *Candida*, neither of which had then been seen on the stage, he said that they were 'plays written for the twentieth century' and found much to admire, including 'humor, beauty . . . and admirable technic'. Later, he thought Shaw a preacher rather than a playwright (No. 20). Richard Mansfield appeared in some early productions of Shaw's plays in the USA, and their success may partly be attributed to him,[38] but the real success of Shaw on the American stage began in 1903 when a young actor named Arnold Daly secured the rights in *Candida*, and the play was produced in New York. This production played for 150 performances and, with tours by Daly and other companies, *Candida* had been seen in most of the principal cities of the USA by the end of the season 1904–5. Daly also produced and acted in *You Never Can Tell* for a run of five months in New York in 1905. Shaw meanwhile tried, in vain, to persuade Richard Mansfield to follow his productions of *Arms and the Man* and *The Devil's Disciple* with *Caesar and Cleopatra*. In addition he wrote eloquent and persuasive letters to Mrs Mansfield, begging her to encourage her husband to appear in *Captain Brassbound's Conversion* and *You Never Can Tell*; the letters were not persuasive enough and Mansfield appears to have found the plays too demanding. The next step forward in the progress of Shaw's American reputation was the result of the appearance of an English actor, Robert Loraine, in *Man and Superman*.[39] Loraine had seen the play in London and become fascinated by it. Shaw gave him permission to produce it in America and, opening on Broadway on 5 September 1905, it started slowly but then began to play to large audiences. It broke attendance records in a way that was unheard of for a non-musical play. While the published book of the play was banned in the libraries of New York on the ground that it would pervert the morals of the young, large audiences went to the theatre to see the Life Force in action.

Within a few days of the opening of *Man and Superman*, the first production in America of another Shaw play brought the name of the dramatist into even greater if distorted, prominence. Arnold Daly decided to 'try out' *Mrs Warren's Profession* in New Haven, Connecticut, before opening in New York. The fact that the play had been refused a licence for public performance in England by the Lord Chamberlain added to public interest in the play, and the production was exceptionally well received. The subject of the play, professional prostitution, might have been expected to disconcert some members of the audience and critics, but it did not prevent serious and intelligent comment in the press. Thus, the local paper, the *Morning Journal and Courier*, said that what had been seen was 'a well acted and powerful drama, which had for its subject the present day hypocrisy of society'. Nevertheless, the New Haven Chief of Police informed the manager of the theatre that no further performances of the play would be allowed. When the play went to New York, opposition had been prepared. The papers vied with each other in the force of their condemnation, and to read the comments is to call to mind the celebrated *Schimpflexicon*, a selection of extreme critical reactions, compiled after the opening performance of Ibsen's *Ghosts* in London, from which Shaw quoted with glee in *The Quintessence of Ibsenism*. The *American* summed up the attitudes of all the papers with the opinion that the play was 'illuminated gangrene', but the notice in the *New York Herald* (No. 35), while condemning the play violently, did include a quotation from Arnold Daly's curtain speech in which he said that 'this play is not presented as an entertainment, but as a dramatic sermon and an exposé of a social condition and an evil which our purists attempt to ignore'. The Shaw movement in the USA tended to slacken in the years before the First World War and did not recover real momentum until the war had ended. The influential critic, John Jay Chapman, thought in 1913 that Shaw's treatment of humanity was 'crude and cruel' but said that he was 'a child of the age' (No. 63). While *John Bull's Other Island* reached the stage in 1905, *Major Barbara* was not seen in America until 1915. Mencken had detected a growing interest in Shaw, but it did not translate itself into a desire to put his plays on the stage. It is clear from comments by several writers that the name of Shaw was coming to stand for the treatment of controversial subjects in a witty if not always acceptable way. Carl Sandburg wrote to a friend in 1908, comparing Shaw with the English Socialist journalist and essayist, Robert Blatchford, and saying that 'S. is for the centuries, will be remembered with Diogenes and Epictetus. B. is for the decades.' Huneker in his later judgments continued to take a less favourable view of Shaw than he had shown in his notices of the earlier plays. For example, he wrote in 1914 that G. K. Chesterton was a 'much more gifted man than Shaw' even while he was picking out the inaccuracies in Chesterton's book on Shaw. In 1914, Huneker said that Shaw was 'a reactionary chock-full of old-fashioned notions and exuding sentiment and prejudice of the approved English variety'.[40] With a flash of prophetic inspiration he described *Pygmalion* as a mere comic-opera libretto, 'fairly begging for a musical setting' even though he thought it was weak in characterisation and 'piffling' in subject. He could not have foreseen the success of *My Fair Lady*, the musical play based on *Pygmalion* that met with such success forty years later.

In 1920, the Theater Guild of New York presented *Heartbreak House* for the first time on any stage.[41] This was the first world première of Shaw to be staged by the Theater Guild and it was followed by the first performance in the world of *Back to Methuselah*, the translation from the German, *Jitta's Atonement*, *Saint Joan*, *Too True to be Good* and *The Simpleton of the Unexpected Isles*. *Heartbreak House* was well received in New York and ran for almost five months. *Back to Methuselah* lost about $20,000 but Lawrence Langner, who presented it, thought the production an artistic and intellectual triumph. He wrote to Shaw in 1924 reproving him for failing to understand that the play 'was regarded as a great success, and not as a failure'. He explained that 'when you take into consideration that it ran for nine weeks in a small theatre, playing every night, you must appreciate that this was a magnificent achievement. . . . If we had had a theatre twice the size, there would have been a profit instead of a loss. . . . I am quite certain that if Goethe had seen *Faust* presented in parts one and two every evening for nine successive weeks, he would have stood on his head in amazement.' Practical considerations caused much discussion before *Saint Joan* was presented on 28 December 1923. There was a struggle between Langner and Shaw about cutting the play. Shaw resisted the suggested shortening and it is clear that the play held and fascinated the audience. Alexander Woolcott in the *New York Herald* (No. 85) wrote one of the most favourable notices. Such other well-known critics as Stark Young and G. J. Nathan left their readers in no doubt that Shaw had moved away from his customary methods in an effort to achieve sublimity and had failed. Gradually the efforts of Langner and his associates in the Theater Guild began to bear rich fruit. Langner's advice to his company, on financial as well as artistic grounds, was 'When in doubt, play Shaw.' During the 1920s and 1930s, the Theater Guild presented highly successful revivals of many of Shaw's plays in addition to the premières. At the same time, critical judgments of Shaw began to appear more frequently in magazines. These were mostly favourable, although one of Shaw's earliest American champions, H. L. Mencken, viewed him far less kindly in later years. In

1942, the *Saturday Review of Literature* devoted an issue to Shaw to mark his eighty-eighth birthday and this contained, among other tributes, a eulogistic editorial and a long article by John Mason Brown.[42]

OTHER FOREIGN RESPONSES[43]

In 1900, William Archer introduced an Austrian journalist, Siegfried Trebitsch, to the plays of Shaw.[44] Trebitsch was immediately convinced that Shaw was a genius, and his enthusiasm drove him to begin to translate the plays. Shaw welcomed and encouraged this; it was in the versions of Trebitsch that Shaw's plays arrived on the stage in Germany and there attracted actors and managers who took them to Scandinavia. Trebitsch translated three plays at first, *The Devil's Disciple*, *Candida* and *Arms and the Man*. The first to be produced was *The Devil's Disciple* in Vienna in February 1903. When *Helden* (*Arms and the Man*) was produced at the Deutsches Theater, Berlin, in December 1904, a German critic declared that Shaw had become 'a king of the German stage'. German interest in Shaw grew steadily before the First World War and after. *Pygmalion* had its world première in Vienna in 1913, and in 1932, according to one estimate, there were fifty-six productions of thirteen plays by Shaw in forty-eight cities and towns in Germany. German authors, from Thomas Mann to Bertolt Brecht, praised Shaw highly and Brecht wrote a tribute for Shaw on his seventieth birthday in 1926. The tribute was called 'Ovation for Shaw' and it first appeared in the *Berliner Börsen-Courier* on 25 July 1926. Brecht admired Shaw's intellectual attack on his audience and his 'contagious good humour'. He even said that he subscribed to Shaw's theory of evolution because 'a man with such keen intellect and courageous eloquence' deserved his confidence and because he had always considered 'the forcefulness of an expression more important than its immediate applicability'. In addition, Brecht, after seeing the production of *Saint Joan* by Max Reinhardt at the Grosses Theater, Berlin, with Elizabeth Bergner in the leading role, borrowed themes from *Major Barbara* and *Saint Joan* for his own play, *Saint Joan of the Stockyards*.

The impact created by Shaw's plays in other central European countries, such as Bohemia (later Czechoslovakia) and Poland was only little less powerful than that in the German-speaking countries. Prominent Czech political figures, such as Masaryk and Benes, were great admirers of Shaw. *The Devil's Disciple* was presented in Lwow in 1903 and, between 1903 and 1913, twelve plays by Shaw were produced in different places in Poland, from Warsaw to small provincial towns. One critic, A. Grzymala-Siedlecki, wrote of *Fanny's First Play* that 'in this work all the good sides of Shaw's genius shine out brightly; he refrains from those additions of doubtful taste which are enjoyed by audiences anxious to appreciate forced originality'. In Czechoslovakia, after the First World War, regular productions of Shaw in different towns led to the publication of an extended edition of his works by the State Publishing House.

Arms and the Man, presented in the version of Karl Mantzius, who also played the leading role of Bluntschli, was the first Shaw production in Denmark and it was in the same year, 1906, that Shaw was first presented in Sweden. In the first decade of the century several of Shaw's comedies ran in Stockholm for runs longer than the average for the city, but interest fell away. One critic wrote that 'Shaw was suddenly discovered to have been overestimated . . . a passing freak of fashion whom nobody need take seriously.' For a production of *Androcles and the Lion* in 1917, interest dwindled at such a rate that only one ticket was sold for the thirteenth performance. The award of the Nobel Prize for literature in 1926 resulted in some revival of interest in both stage performances and the printed plays, but it was not until after the Second World War that Shaw was fully rediscovered by the Swedish theatre. Some brilliant long-running revivals were presented at the Royal Dramatic Theatre in Stockholm, notably of *Captain Brassbound's Conversion* and *Man and Superman*. An additional impetus to Swedish interest in Shaw has been the great popularity of his plays in sound broadcast.

Shaw has never been so popular in France and the other Latin countries as in Germany and in Northern and Eastern Europe. In June 1904, however, the critic Maurice Muret wrote an article in the *Journal des Débats* with the title, 'De Nora à Candida'. He sought to show that *Candida* represented a rejoinder to Ibsen's plays, *A Doll's House* and *The Lady from the Sea*. According to Muret, *Candida* demonstrated the revenge of the traditionally ideal woman, that is, the wife and mother, over the 'new' ideal of the liberated and independent woman. *Candida* was produced in France in 1908 in a translation by a French Socialist, Augustin Hamon, to whom Shaw had given authority to translate his work, despite Hamon's own doubts about the adequacy of his English. Shaw reassured him by telling him that Madame

Hamon knew enough English to be able to help. The translation of
Candida was attacked, as were the Hamons' later translations, for not
possessing the sparkle of the original. Shaw began to attract the
attention of scholars and academic critics as well as of managers and
producers. The style of the French versions of Shaw's plays continued
to cause dissension and in 1925 the critic of *Le Figaro*, Robert de Flers,
wrote of Joan in the French production that she was 'denuded of all
verbal luxury, as poor in words as she was in garments, but so rich in
courage and faith' (No. 92). He added, however, that the later scenes
of *Saint Joan* reminded him of 'a Shakespeare more concentrated and
more co-ordinated'. The famous Italian dramatist, Luigi Pirandello,
gave his opinion of *Saint Joan* in a long article in the *New York Times*
(No. 87). He said that Shaw had come to believe less in himself and
more in what he was doing, and that the play, while possessing all the
best features of 'Shaw's witty polemical dialogue', was 'a work of
poetry from beginning to end'.

Shaw's work had many readers in Russia although, before the First
World War, few of his plays were seen on the stage. An edition of
his work in nine volumes was published in Moscow in 1910 and a
second edition, this time in ten volumes, was published in Moscow
and Saint Petersburg in 1911. There was an exchange of letters between
Shaw and Tolstoy. Tolstoy, in the last years of his life, found Shaw
unforgivably flippant on serious subjects, as shown in *Man and Superman* and *The Shewing-Up of Blanco Posnet* (No. 54). Shaw tried to
counter Tolstoy's criticisms by suggesting that there was no need to
excommunicate humour and laughter in the search for truth, part
of which was represented by the work of a creative writer. Tolstoy,
whose views on the function and purpose of art had, by this time,
settled into a far more rigidly didactic mould than even the author of
Widowers' Houses would have dreamed of, was not to be put aside.
A short time later, not long before his death in 1910, he spoke of the
dearth of good writers and added: 'There are none now unless, perhaps,
Shaw.' When the Soviet Union came into existence, Shaw was treated
with great respect, both as an author to be studied and as a dramatist
to be played in the theatre. This favourable attitude was no doubt
encouraged by the support that Shaw always gave to the Soviet state
and the admiration that he always professed for Soviet writers. It has
been calculated that 'between 1908 and 1942, there appear to have been
fifty-two separate editions of the plays'. There are records of many
performances, including thirty-eight performances of *Saint Joan* at the

Moscow Kamerny Theatre between October 1924 and January 1926, very soon after the first productions in the USA and England.

The Philanderer was the first of Shaw's plays to be translated into Japanese and a part appeared in the May 1908 issue of the magazine, Shijin (Poet). The literary journals began to include articles of Shavian interest, including reviews of Huneker's edition of the dramatic criticism and of Chesterton's book on Shaw. The Shewing-Up of Blanco Posnet in 1910 was the first play to be acted in a Japanese translation. In 1913, Shoyo Tsubouchi, who had translated Shaw's plays and written critical articles, published the first full-length study of Shaw in Japanese. Saint Joan was translated and performed very soon after it had appeared in the West.

OBITUARY AND CENTENARY TRIBUTES AND LATER DEVELOPMENTS

Shortly before the death of Shaw, a volume was published in the standard edition of his work with the title Sixteen Self-Sketches (1949). The appearance of these chapters of autobiography gave many critics the opportunity to write general reviews of Shaw's life, work and personality, even though they must have realised that it was more than likely that they might have to repeat themselves in a fairly short time. In one of the reviews, the Socialist journalist, H. N. Brailsford, said in the Listener (No. 127) that Shaw's glory was that 'after the neo-Darwinists, he brought back mind to the universe', and, making a comparison between Shaw's message in the speech of Lilith at the end of Back to Methuselah and some of the last words of Goethe, asserted that Shaw's guiding principle was that 'Salvation comes to him who never ceases to strive.' Shaw made a similar assertion, in relation to his craft as a dramatist, in the last piece of polemical writing that he published. Terence Rattigan, himself a dramatist, had written an article in the New Statesman on 'The Play of Ideas' (No. 128). Other dramatists contributed their views and, at the end of the controversy, Shaw was invited by the editor to submit a closing comment. In the course of his remarks (which appeared on 6 May 1950), Shaw united his concern for the Life Force, 'with its trials and successes and errors', with his own atavistic return as a playwright to Aristotle, Shakespeare, Mozart and the stage business of the great players that he had seen acting. Rattigan seemed clearly to be thinking of Shaw's plays when he wrote a letter to the paper the following week, 13 May 1950, to repeat his 'continued preference for plays in which the ideas have sprung from the characters over plays in which the characters have been created as mouthpieces for the ideas'. The suggestion that Shaw's characters were mere 'mouthpieces' figured in several of the assessments that followed his death on 2 November 1950. Some went so far as to say that Shaw's decline in his later years had meant that the plays written when he was past his best were mere propaganda, as compared with those works centred on character that he wrote in his prime, thus falling into the old trap of always praising the plays of the past at the expense of those of the present. Many of the obituary notices and articles were very uneven, spending far more time on the public figure or the private man, on the controversialist or the clown than on the writer or drama-tist. A leading article in the *Listener* a week after the death drew atten-tion to this:[45]

As for some of the epithets served up in Grub Street to describe this powerful thinker and man of genius, they have to be read in order to be believed; one can only hope that their authors had never read his books or seen his plays and had been told by the office boy that he was simply a great clown ... it is probable that Shaw was better appreciated in Paris and Berlin and even in New York than he ever was in London.

Ivor Brown in the *Observer*[46] made an attempt to foresee 'The Future of G.B.S.' He thought that 'the plays with most narrative value will outlast the discussion pieces' but praised the 'poetry' of *Heartbreak House* and said that the beginning and end of *Back to Methuselah* were 'deathless matter'. In a long unsigned article in *Time*, 13 November 1950, V. S. Pritchett said that Shaw was, in essence, 'a man of the eighteenth century, closer to Voltaire and Swift than to Marx and Morris'. Yet he found him a lesser artist than either Voltaire or Swift. 'A kind of middle-class gentility preserved him from the great disgust, the unspeakable horrors which greater imagination could grasp.' His prose, nevertheless, was a superb vehicle for the pamphleteer and the verbal wit was 'perennially irresistible'. In an article, 'Shaw Dead' in the Dublin monthly magazine, *Envoy* (No. 135), Eric Bentley echoed the *Listener* comments on journalistic reactions:

What I was reading made me sick. It was praise of Shaw, but what praise, and from whom! One would have thought the deceased was a bishop who had lived down his youthful wild oats by endearing himself to the best people in the diocese. Such mourning for Shaw was a mockery of Shaw.

Bentley's view of the obituary notices was probably directed at the opinions of Shaw the publicist rather than at the comments on the dramatist, for he said that the mourners forgave him for what he stood for 'in so far as it differed from what *they* stood for'. Public opinion in New York, Bentley added, took a striking form, for 'grasping the first occasion when Shaw was powerless to come back at them, the bourgeoisie brayed and Broadway dimmed its lights'. James Bridie, the Scottish dramatist, often thought to have been greatly influenced by Shaw, wrote in the *New Statesman* on 'Shaw as Playwright', one of the few to consider this side of Shaw at length (No. 131), and Sean O'Casey wrote of Shaw as a 'fighting idealist'.[47]

It was unfortunate that the centenary of Shaw's birth that was celebrated in 1956 followed so soon after his death. Insufficient time had passed for fully considered judgments to be given.[48] *The Times*, in an anonymous article from 'our dramatic critic', said that Shaw's reputation had not slipped perceptibly and 'it remains firm on the eminence assigned to it by the obituarists'. The article went on to suggest, however, that there were shifting clouds occasionally obscuring the eminence as, in the climate of the theatre at that time, symbolised by the uncertainties of Samuel Beckett's *Waiting for Godot*, the Shavian drama was unlikely to prove popular on the stage. In fact, the reverse was shown to be true. In the theatres of London and the provinces, as well as in foreign countries, Shaw's plays have been revived with both artistic and commercial success again and again, so that, more than once in the twenty years or so since the death, the phrase 'the Shaw Revival' has been used to indicate a whole shade of theatrical taste. Shaw is now firmly established in the 'classical' repertory of state and municipal playhouses in England and some other countries, notably Germany. *My Fair Lady*, the musical play based on *Pygmalion*, although striking conventional Shavians as an unfortunate travesty of the original, may have contributed to an enhanced interest in Shaw's other work.

In a centenary tribute, A. J. P. Taylor, the historian, said that Shaw was 'the greatest arguer there has ever been'; his article was, however, very unfavourable in its general attitude and Taylor contended that Shaw had nothing to say. On the same page of the newspaper in which Taylor's article appeared (*Observer*, 21 July 1956) was an article by the dramatic critic, Kenneth Tynan. Tynan found all sorts of fault with Shaw, but concluded that he was 'without doubt a great writer, greater than many whose emotional range was far wider and deeper than his'. Shaw's greatness, according to Tynan, lay in his having cleared the English stage of humbug and the English mind of cant. Gradually, in the years since the centenary, careful and scholarly examination of Shaw has developed. Much of this has been in the USA where, if Shaw is not such a quarry for detailed research and analysis as are, for example, James Joyce and D. H. Lawrence, he has been the subject of some works of value.

There have been long biographies and many books of reminiscences since his death, and several collections of letters have been published. The definitive selection of Shaw's letters, edited by Dan H. Laurence, is to be in four volumes. The first appeared in 1965 and the second in 1972. Dan H. Laurence has also edited a number of volumes of previously uncollected journalism by Shaw, and he has supervised the definitive Bodley Head edition of Shaw's plays that was published between 1970 and 1974. This has replaced the Constable standard edition and the volumes include, as well as the prefaces, many comments, 'interviews', and programme notes by Shaw, many of them printed in book form for the first time. In 1972, a massive concordance to Shaw's plays and prefaces was compiled by E. Dean Bevan of the University of Kansas. Unfortunately, it is based on the Constable standard edition.

In a long essay on Shaw in *Eight Modern Writers* (Oxford, 1963), the best all-round assessment to appear since his death, J. I. M. Stewart found Shaw to be 'more authentically an artist than a prophet', but saw in him also 'paradoxically, a surer grip of the religious than of the artistic character'. These comments emphasise the chameleon-like nature of Shaw's work that has so far eluded attempts at categorical identification. His combination, almost unique, of the dramatist and the publicist has ensured a continuing appeal for his plays, even when many of the controversies that excited him now seem out of date. The publication of the letters, which throw light on the plays and the thinking behind them and also on the circumstances in which they reached the stage and were published, is already leading to further valuations and estimates. It was Shaw's conviction that, just as he had stood on the shoulders of the dramatists and thinkers that had preceded him, so would his successors stand on his shoulders. Critics and scholars, who have so far failed to place him exactly, will find that his work presents a continuing enigmatic challenge.

NOTES

1 The last play, a series of sketches called *Farfetched Fables*, was first presented by the Shaw Society at the Watergate Theatre, London, on 6 September 1950.

2 Letter to Archibald Henderson, 30 June 1904 (Dan H. Laurence, ed., *Collected Letters*, II, 1898–1910 (1972), 425). Henderson had written to Shaw suggesting that he write his biography and hinting that he would have to rely heavily on Shaw for help (see Henderson, *George Bernard Shaw: Man of the Century* (New York, 1956), xvi).

3 The 'interview' is reprinted in the *Bodley Head Bernard Shaw*, vol. 1 (1970), 122.

4 *Morning Post*, 10 December 1892, 37596, 3.

5 The King, when Prince of Wales, is reported to have said after a performance of *Arms and the Man* that the author 'must be mad' (Henderson, 536).

6 *Morning Post*, 24 May 1905, 41494, 7.

7 Letter to Eleanor Robson, 21 June 1905, Laurence, II, 532.

8 *Daily Telegraph*, 29 November 1905, 15782, 7.

9 Letter to Gertrude Elliott, 4 December 1907, Laurence, II, 737.

10 Letter to J. E. Vedrenne, 3 October 1909, Laurence, II, 871.

11 *The Times*, 24 February 1910, 39204, 12.

12 See Lady Gregory, *Our Irish Theatre* (1914), chap. VI, 'The Fight with the Castle'.

13 For a full and detailed picture of Shaw's activities at this time see the opening chapter, 'Before The Deluge' in *Journey to Heartbreak*, Stanley Weintraub (New York, 1972, Routledge & Kegan Paul, London, 1973). This is a survey of Shaw's life and work during the war years, 1914–18, and gives much important information on the critical response to his plays during that time.

14 *Neue Freie Presse*, Vienna, 17 October 1913, 1.

15 MacCarthy's book was reprinted in 1966 by University of Miami Press. Stanley Weintraub edited the reprint and added an introductory essay. See Bibliography.

16 Letter to Blanche Jennings, 31 December 1908, Harry T. Moore, ed., *Collected Letters of D. H. Lawrence* (1962), 43.

17 Letter to Edward Garnett, 1 February 1913, Moore, 181.

18 See Doris Arthur Jones, *The Life and Letters of Henry Arthur Jones* (1930), 311.

19 *Nation*, 22 November 1919, vol. xxvi, 266. Archer's article was entitled 'Wanted, a new GBS'.

20 *Bernard Shaw: a Chronicle*, R. F. Rattray (1941), 201.

21 *Nation & Athenaeum*, 2 July 1921, 509, initialled review entitled 'Back to Manichaeism'.

22 *New Statesman*, 11 October 1924, reprinted in *Shaw*, 1951, 139.

23 *New Republic*, 27 August 1924, 380; reprinted in *Saint Joan: Fifty Years After, 1923–24 to 1973–74*, ed. Stanley Weintraub (Baton Rouge, 1973), 39.

24 *Time and Tide*, 4 April 1924, vol. 5, 14, 330.

25 *Times Literary Supplement*, 3 July 1924, 1172, 417.

26 Letter to Lawrence Langner, 28 May 1924, quoted in Lawrence Langner, *GBS and the Lunatic* (New York, 1963), 76.

27 See Henderson, 838.

28 *Morning Post*, 20 August 1929, 49044, 19.

29 *The Times*, 20 August 1929, 45286, 10.

30 *Time and Tide*, 23 August 1929, vol. 10, 34, 1022.

31 *Bookman*, December 1924, vol. LXVII, 399, 145.

32 See *The Literature of Politics* (1955), reprinted in *To Criticize the Critic* (1965), 136.

33 *Enemies of Promise*, reprinted in Penguin edition (1961), 18.

34 In a review in the *Spectator*, 1 April 1955, vol. 194, 6614, 397, with the title 'Shaw against Lawrence', F. R. Leavis defended D. H. Lawrence against what he took to be an improper comparison with Shaw that had been made by H. F. Rubinstein. He wrote, 'It is the automatism, the emptiness and the essential irreverence—all that makes Shaw boring and cheap; the emotional nullity that when, as in *St Joan*, he confidently invites us to respond to depth and moving significance makes him embarrassing and nauseating.'

35 *Criterion*, vol. VIII, 31, December 1928, 201.

36 Letter to Grant Richards, 8 November 1895, Laurence, I, 1874–1894 (1965), 698.

37 For a full account of Huneker's response to Shaw, see Arnold T. Schwab, *James Gibbons Huneker* (Stanford, Cal., 1963), chap. 13, 'Irish Tempers and English Reviewers', 139.

38 Letters to Mrs Richard Mansfield, 8 January 1897 and 10 December 1897, Laurence I, 717 and 829 respectively.

39 Winifred Loraine, *Robert Loraine* (1938), 75.

40 See Schwab, 172.

41 Lawrence Langner, *GBS and the Lunatic*, 20 ff.

42 *Saturday Review of Literature*, 24 October 1942, vol. XXV, no. 43, p. 6: reprinted in *Dramatis Personae* (1963), 103.

43 For the foreign response to Shaw, see Henderson, 903, Appendix 1, 'Shaw around the World' by Lucile Keeling, and the files of the *Shavian* and the *Shaw Review*.

44 See Siegfried Trebitsch, *Chronicle of a Life* (1953), 96 ff.

45 *Listener*, 9 November 1950, vol. XLIV, 1132, 489.

46 *Observer*, 5 November 1950, 8318, 4.

47 *New York Times*, 12 November 1956, sect. VII, 41, reprinted in *The Green Crow* (1957), 184.

48 In an article in the *London Magazine*, vol. 3, no. 12, December 1956, 53, Angus Wilson wrote on Shaw in a series, 'The Living Dead'. His article

included much adverse criticism but, in his concluding paragraph, he paid tribute to the gifts of humorous character-drawing in which Shaw had been taught by Dickens and Ibsen: 'Shaw at his best was the equal of his masters.' In his last sentence, he said, 'I find it difficult to believe that modern audiences would not be shaken by their crowded exuberance [that is, of Shaw's plays] which so often captures the very texture of life.'

Note on the Text

Wherever possible the material printed in this volume is given in the form in which it first appeared. Extracts from Shaw's plays and lengthy discussion of details of production and acting have generally been omitted. In addition, it has been necessary, with great regret, to shorten some longer articles and to include only those passages that make a particularly relevant or original critical comment. Omissions are clearly indicated.

The names of translators are given where known. The translations of Nos 92 and 125 are by the editor.

WIDOWERS' HOUSES

1892

Widowers' Houses, as explained by William Archer in his notice in the *World* (No. 4), was begun as a collaboration in 1884 and completed by Shaw alone in 1892. It was first presented by the Independent Theatre at the Royalty Theatre, London, on 9 December 1892 and a second performance was given at a matinée on 13 December.

1. From an unsigned notice, *Daily Telegraph*

10 December 1892, 11722, 3

J. T. Grein (1862–1935) was a playwright, critic and impresario, who founded the Independent Theatre of London in 1891. The object of this venture was 'to give special performances of plays which have a literary and artistic rather than a commercial value' (see No. 3).

Mr. George Bernard Shaw, in the speech with which he brought to a close last night's session of the Independent Theatre Society, to a certain extent 'gave away' Mr. Grein and his fellow enthusiasts. If there was one object more than another that the promoters of our metropolitan Theatre Libre set in the forefront of their programme at the commencement of their stage career, it was the fostering of the true, palpitating drama of modernity. This being so, the society's officials must have felt last evening like men who had cherished a serpent in their bosoms. Mr. Shaw's confession to an audience, who cheered and hooted him in factions, was frankness itself. He was delighted, he said, to hear his play, *Widowers' Houses* arouse tokens of disapproval; and he hoped in a very short time, the presentation of such a piece would be impossible. In other words, Mr. Shaw freely admitted that he had availed himself of the aegis of the Independent Theatre Society not to bring forward a symmetrical play of ambitious and elevating tendency, but to deliver a lecture upon 'the morality of the middle classes' in the matter of 'house knacking'—a lecture which he trusted would soon be vain and meaningless. This is all very well. but does this tend to the enriching of our dramatic storehouses with fresh, living and moving plays? Has Mr. Bernard Shaw misunderstood the society's object? Or is vitality a matter of no account in a drama? This, however, is perhaps a side issue which need not concern us too closely at the present moment. It would, however, make the position clearer if Mr. Grein and his friends would openly state whether they wish to welcome to their exclusive stage red-hot politicians with a topical lecture to deliver or dramatists with a play of general and lasting interest.

The above-noted avowal made last evening by Mr. Shaw clearly relieves us from the necessity of considering at length his 'didactic, realistic play' as a serious contribution to the catalogue of the contemporary drama. But the direction in which the writer's satiric shafts are aimed in *Widowers' Houses* may perhaps be indicated. In pungent and unsparing fashion the playwright holds up to scorn and hatred the morality, or rather the immorality, of those who batten on rents torn from the miserable occupants of slum-dwellings. No one could refuse to follow Mr. Shaw with sympathetic ear when he sets out on this crusade; for is not the evil of 'house knacking' a grievous and a crying one? But it is when the author tries to throw his righteous indignation into dramatic form that he courts the failure of his mission by the exaggerated terms of his homily. Mr. Shaw, we fancy, has pinned his faith a little too closely to 'the master' in the present instance. As an ardent admirer of Ibsen's methods, he has not scrupled to follow the doctrines of that writer to extremes and to hold up all his *dramatis personae* as entirely selfish and despicable. It is not the first time a sincere preacher has failed through putting his case too high; nor, we imagine, will it be the last. Mr. Shaw's system of play-building is indeed as faulty as the construction of the tenements under the system condemned by him. A moment's examination of the plot will make this clear. In the first place, we have the arch-proprietor of a score of fever-stricken slums, Mr. Sartorius. Dramatically, this figure is well enough conceived, and might be trusted to point the weightiest moral the playwright could desire, were his lead not followed with such persistency by his fellow puppets. Sartorius has a daughter, who dwells for awhile in blissful ignorance of the source whence comes her father's wealth. When she does know it, what is her line of action? We have been led to hope that the young lady, who does her love-making, as it were, in shorthand, may have a sympathetic heart. But no sooner is the daylight let in upon her father's unscrupulous livelihood than she immediately acquiesces in the position. So it is with her lover, Harry Trench. Certainly this gentleman's sensibilities rebel against the iniquity at first. No sooner, however, is it demonstrated to his satisfaction that his own income, as well as that of his prospective father-in-law, hangs upon the tumble-down rookeries whose occupants the grasping Sartorius is grinding to dust, than he too joins in the general approval. So, of course, does one Mr. Cokane, upon whose brow the legend 'Main chance' might well be imprinted. One was inclined to think that Mr. Shaw would really stay his hand when he came to deal with the destinies of the queerly-named rent-collector, Lickcheese, who in the second act of the play loses his situation because he pities the wretches under his hand, and refrains from giving the final twist to the vice. But the dramatist is implacable. It is a part of his mistaken plan to bring his curtain down upon a group of characters, all well pleased with the extortioner's rôle. And so even the discharged Lickcheese is made to harden his heart, to turn his coat, and to blossom forth as an aider and abettor of the very man whose grasping practices he has denounced. Most assuredly Mr. Shaw's scheme is consistent, but it is not convincing, and, like many another satire, it shirks its moral. Why, then, should the would-be playwright have attempted to bend the drama to his purpose, and so misused his materials? It may be inexperience; but we are rather inclined to think that the obstinate spirit of paradox which marks his critical essays has been allowed in the present instance to outweigh the earnestness and sincerity which, one would fain believe, underlie his pronouncement of strong political doctrines.

There was no lack of clever and diverting dialogue in *Widowers' Houses*. Mr. Shaw, except when he occasionally indulged in an inappropriate Gilbertian quip, gave unmistakable proof of his powers of writing crisply, naturally and wittily. That he has excellent ideas on the subject of characterisation was shown last evening by the opportunity which he held out to a young actor of marked ability, Mr. James Welch. Author and player between them contrived,

indeed, a portrait—that of Sartorius's recalcitrant creature Lickcheese
—which would not have discredited any modern drama. That Mr.
Welch is not already a well-known figure on the West-end boards
would be a matter for surprise were it not that the actor, like the
member of any other profession, must await his chance. Now that that
chance has come, managers have no further excuse for remaining blind
to the abilities of so thoughtful and artistic a player.

2. W. Moy Thomas, unsigned notice, *Daily News*

10 December 1892, 14568, 5

William Moy Thomas (1828–1910) was the dramatic critic of
the *Daily News*. Shaw was pleased with his comments on the play
and wrote to Charles Charrington on 14 December 1892, 'I have
established the fact that Moy Thomas is the greatest dramatic
critic of the age, and that Archer & Walkley are a pair of idiots'
(Laurence, *Collected Letters*, I, 372). On the same day he wrote to
Archer and said that 'I have come to the conclusion that Moy
Thomas (who sat it out again yesterday, every line) is the greatest
critic of the age' (Laurence, 373).

The hostile reception which Mr Bernard Shaw's dramatic satire met
with at the hands of a turbulent section of the audience at the Royalty
last night is greatly to be regretted; for the piece which, thanks to the
courage and energy of the Independent Theatre Company, has been
thus put upon the stage, is, in spite of a tedious and almost superfluous
first act, really a very remarkable production. *Widowers' Houses* is, of
course, not a romantic play; it is, moreover, not what is called a
'comedy-drama' and it has little in it to attract the spectator who is
looking for dramatic sensations. It is described by the author—if he is

responsible for the playbill—as a 'didactic realistic play', but those who
infer that this is only a Fabian pamphlet or a succession of Socialistic
tirades and rhetorical speeches, uttered by mere abstractions attired in
human clothing, will fall into a great mistake. On the contrary, it
exhibits many of the qualities which go to the making of a dramatist
of the first rank. Who, it may be asked, can be interested in a story
which aims mainly at setting forth the alleged iniquities of 'slum
landlords'? But *Widowers' Houses* does a great deal more than this. It
depicts character with a hand at once so subtle and so sure, and brings
out meanwhile the satirical aspects of their relations with so light and
easy a touch that it would be hard in these regards to name a recent
piece that could compare with it. The scene in the drawing-room of the
mansion of Mr Sartorius at Surbiton, in which this wealthy owner of
unwholesome 'tenement houses' discusses with his predestined son-in-
law, Dr Trench, and other friends, the very serious aspects of affairs
created by the disclosure in evidence before the Parliamentary Committee on the subject of the Dwellings of the Poorer Classes, is really
comedy of a very high order. Every person is here in his place as a
factor in the scene. Mr Sartorius, who finds it is time to acknowledge
that we live in 'a humanitarian age'; Dr Trench, who has thought of
renouncing the hand of Sartorius' ill-conditioned daughter but who
for certain cogent reasons, thinks better of it; Cokane, the latter's
smugly moral friend, with his unerring sense of propriety; and lastly
Lickcheese, the poor oppressed clerk, who, after being ignominiously
dismissed, has sprung into prosperity by blackmailing slum landlords,
promoting the Thames Iced Mutton Company, and trading in 'compensation' by purchasing property certain to be wanted ere long for
London improvements. Each speaks according to his kind, and the
result is a scene as diverting as it is clever in its satirical vein.

[Comments on details of the acting.]

In spite of the malcontents in the gallery, Mr Bernard Shaw (who had
been preceded by Mr J. T. Grein) made his appearance before the
curtain and claimed for his play the merit of being a true picture of
things that are 'going on in middle class society in London', adding
the expression of a hope that the time would come when such a play
would be to a London audience 'utterly unintelligible'. Mr Shaw
vouchsafed the further information that all the ladies and gentlemen
engaged had played that night gratuitously. That, he observed, was
'where the socialism came in', a remark which, by the way, was

received with groans by some persons in the gallery, who were possibly not well pleased at the prospect of the total abolition of wages when the Fabian Society have their way. The piece is announced to be given once more on Tuesday afternoon, but it is far too remarkable a work to be dismissed after a couple of performances.

3. J. T. Grein, from a letter to the *Daily Telegraph*

13 December 1892, 11724, 3

J. T. Grein took up the invitation of the *Daily Telegraph* critic (No. 1) to explain the policy of the Independent Theatre. He began by repeating the words of the first prospectus which referred to 'plays which have a literary and artistic rather than a commercial value' and went on to defend the choice of *Widowers' Houses*.

In the beginning there arose a complaint that English plays were neglected to make room for foreign ones, a perfectly unjust complaint, for the simple reason that no works of any literary and artistic merit were offered. The quantity was rich, but the quality of the poorest. Latterly, as our authors see that the Independent Theatre is a lasting and not an ephemeral affair, support has come from men who have hitherto kept aloof from the stage for want of an opportunity to obtain a hearing, for want of encouragement. Here are a few examples. On Friday I came forward with the first play of Mr. G. B. Shaw, whom I consider one of the most brilliant men of the day, and whose play, which I admire, was worth producing, even if it had tended only to convince the author in what way he grapples with the craft of play-writing, and what he has yet to learn. I think that, whatever may be the result of such an experiment, it is a step in the right direction to win such men as George Bernard Shaw for the drama, for I hold that there is more credit in a disputed success by a man above the average than in a triumph by a safe mediocrity. Mr. Shaw will be immediately followed up by others. . . .

I can only say in reply to your critic that, whether a man is a red-hot politician, or a faddist, or whatever one may call him, it matters not to me; he is welcome, and will find the doors of the Independent Theatre wide open to him so long as he is an artist.

4. From a notice by W.A., *World*

14 December 1892, 963, 14

William Archer (1856–1924), dramatist, essayist and dramatic critic, became a lifelong friend of Shaw. At the beginning of the article in the *World*, he describes how *Widowers' Houses* was conceived as a collaboration between Shaw and himself. He goes on to say that, despite his own fears that nothing would come of the proposal, Shaw determined to finish the play after a gap of seven years. Archer thought that the play showed Shaw's 'failure as an artist' but success in 'dramatising the blue-book'. Upon reading this article Shaw wrote to Archer on the same day saying, 'A more amazing exposition of your Shaw theory even I have never encountered than that *World* article. Here am I, who have collected slum rents weekly with these hands, & for 4½ years have been behind the scenes of the middle class landowner—who have philandered with women of all sorts & sizes—and I am told gravely to go to nature & give up aprioriizing about such matters by you, you sentimental Sweet Lavendery recluse. Get out!' (Laurence, *Collected Letters*, I, 373).

Partly to facilitate the labours of Mr. George Bernard Shaw's biographers, and partly by way of relieving my own conscience, I think I ought to give a short history of the genesis of *Widowers' Houses*. Far away back in the olden days, while as yet the Independent Theatre slumbered in the womb of Time, together with the New Drama, the New Criticism, the New Humour, and all the other glories of our renovated world, I used to be a daily frequenter of the British Museum Reading Room. Even more assiduous in his attendance was a young man of tawny complexion and attire, beside whom I used frequently to find myself seated. My curiosity was piqued by the odd conjunction of his subjects of research. Day after day for weeks he had before him two books, which he studied alternately, if not simultaneously— Karl Marx's *Das Kapital* (in French), and an orchestral score of *Tristan*

48

und Isolde. I did not know then how exactly this quaint juxtaposition symbolised the main interests of his life. Presently I met him at the house of a common acquaintance, and we conversed for the first time. I learned from himself that he was the author of several unpublished masterpieces of fiction. Construction, he owned with engaging modesty, was not his strong point, but his dialogue was incomparable. Now, in those days, I had still a certain hankering after the rewards, if not the glories, of the playwright. With a modesty in no way inferior to Mr. Shaw's, I had realised that I could not write dialogue a bit; but I still considered myself a born constructor. So I proposed, and Mr. Shaw agreed to, a collaboration. I was to provide him with one of the numerous plots I kept in stock, and he was to write the dialogue. So said, so done. I drew out, scene by scene, the scheme of a twaddling cup-and-saucer comedy vaguely suggested by Augier's *Ceinture Dorée.* The details I forget, but I know it was to be called *Rhinegold,* was to open, as *Widowers' Houses* actually does, in a hotel-garden on the Rhine, and was to have two heroines, a sentimental and a comic one, according to the accepted Robertson-Byron-Carton formula. I fancy the hero was to propose to the sentimental heroine, believing her to be the poor niece instead of the rich daughter of the sweater, or slum-landlord, or whatever he may have been; and I know he was to carry on in the most heroic fashion, and was ultimately to succeed in throwing the tainted treasure of his father-in-law, meta-phorically-speaking, into the Rhine. All this I gravely propounded to Mr. Shaw, who listened with no less admirable gravity. Then I thought the matter had dropped, for I heard no more of it for many weeks. I used to see Mr. Shaw at the Museum, laboriously writing page after page of the most exquisitely neat shorthand at the rate of about three words a minute; but it did not occur to me that this was our play. After about six weeks he said to me, 'Look here, I've written half the first act of that comedy, and I've used up all your plot. Now I want some more to go on with.' I told him that my plot was a rounded and perfect organic whole, and that I could no more eke it out in this fashion than I could provide him or myself with a set of supplementary arms and legs. I begged him to extend his shorthand and let me see what he had done; but this would have taken him far too long. He tried to decipher some of it orally, but the process was too lingering and painful for endurance. So he simply gave me an outline in narrative of what he had done, and I saw that, so far from having used up my plot, he had not even touched it. There the matter rested for months and years. Mr. Shaw would now and then hold out vague threats of finishing 'our play,' but I felt no serious alarm. I thought (judging from my own experience in other cases) that when he came to read over in cold blood what he had written, he would see what impossible stuff it was. Perhaps my free utterance of this view piqued him; perhaps he felt impelled to remove from the Independent Theatre the reproach of dealing solely in foreign products. The fire of his genius, at all events, was not to be quenched by my persistent applications of the wet-blanket. He finished his play; Mr. Grein, as in duty bound, accepted it; and the result was the extremely amusing and interesting evening of Friday last at the Independent Theatre. Even the most obstinate disparagers of that institution must admit that in this case, if in no other, it proved its utility and justified its existence. Here was an English play of unmistakable talent, ill-adapted for the regular stage, but eminently calculated to interest and entertain one, two, or three select audiences. The Independent Theatre provides the mechanism, which without it would be entirely lacking, for bringing Mr. Shaw into touch with these two or three theatres-full of intelligent playgoers, and offers to one actor, at least, an opportunity for distinguishing himself for which he might otherwise have waited year after year in vain. Who shall say, then, that the initiative and energy of Mr. J. T. Grein have been expended to no purpose!

No one is more heartily glad than I that my wet-blankets failed of their effect; yet I was not wrong in applying them. I did not foresee, or rather did not trouble about, Mr. Shaw's success as a propagandist; I did foresee his failure as an artist. Yes, failure! For though Mr. Shaw, with his unerring promptitude and felicity of retort, managed to save the situation in his concluding speech, he must not seriously run away with the idea that it was the political tendency of his play, or the ruthlessness of his satire on bourgeois respectability, that displeased the gallery. It was the imperfection of his stage-craft, the perversity of his character-conception, and the crudity of his character-drawing. Let him not reply that I cannot forgive him for writing a different play from that which I conceived. That play was contemptible; this one, with all its faults, is ten times better worth doing. I have long outgrown the *Rhinegold* stage of development; and the fact that Mr. Shaw instinctively put my precious plot aside proves that at that time he had already outgrown it and was so far ahead of me. The first act, in which some faint traces of my conception remain, is the one thoroughly dull and ineffectual portion of his play—though I must add, in self-defence,

that I had nothing to do with the character of Cokane, or the preposterous incident of the letter. In the second act, where Mr. Shaw
gets upon his own ground of economic theory and fact, he at once
becomes competent and entertaining. No reader of these columns need
be told that he possesses an unrivalled gift of lucid, witty, and attractive
exposition. In *Widowers' Houses* he displays in addition an unmistakable faculty for making political economy dramatically effective.
All the scenes in which Lickcheese is concerned are not only vivacious,
but genuinely dramatic. But for the farcical interpositions of Cokane,
they would be, as the play-bill puts it, at once didactic and realistic.
In dramatising the blue-book, in short, Mr. Shaw is astonishingly
successful; it is when he comes to telling his love story that his psychology and his stagecraft are alike found wanting. The fact is that
Mr. Shaw is himself too utterly unlike the average sensual man to have
any sympathetic comprehension of him. He conceives him theoretically
and satirically—deduces him by logical process from a set of Laroche-
foucauldian first-principles—instead of going direct to nature and
interpreting his observations by the light of inward experience. Where
he got his first-principles I cannot tell—no doubt they are to a great
extent hereditary—but some of them seem curiously at variance with
his own nature. For example, no reader of Mr. Shaw's novels can fail
to see that he conceives the world we live in as a very ill-tempered
world. The great emotions—love, hatred, reverence, jealousy,
revenge—play a very small part in it, sheer petty cantankerousness
plays a very large part. This theory, surely a rather gratuitous one,
provides the springs of action in *Widowers' Houses*. Everyone is ill-
conditioned, quarrelsome, fractious, apt to behave, at a moment's
notice, like a badly brought up child. This, no doubt, had a great deal
to do with the irritation expressed by the gallery, for nothing is so
contagious as ill-temper. I don't think Mr. Shaw fully realised the
general effect of snappishness produced by his dialogue; but it is clear
that he deliberately intended Blanche Sartorius for a vixen. Lest there
should be any mistake about it, he introduced into the second act a
scene of such childish crudity in the way of character drawing that I
search my memory in vain for any parallel to it. But apart from this
deplorable aberration, why should he have made Blanche a vixen at
all? It is all very well to steer clear of the ordinary sympathetic heroine,
but why rush to the opposite extreme? Mr. Shaw would only laugh if
I called it bad art; so let me say, what is equally true, that it is exceedingly bad argument. You cannot effectively satirise a class by holding

up to odium a grotesquely exceptional case. Mr. Shaw can scarcely maintain that vixenishness and cynical inhumanity of speech and action are among the characteristic traits of middle-class women—that Blanche Sartorius is a fair average specimen of the young lady who lives in suburban luxury upon her father's ill-gotten gains—yet he was bound as a serious artist, or, if he prefers it, as a competent dialectician, to give us a fair average specimen, and not to obscure his argument by assuming a monstrosity. The scene where Blanche, instead of expressing horror on learning the sources of her father's fortune, merely breaks out into a diatribe against poverty, is nothing but a piece of Gilbertian paradox robbed of its humour. The average Surbitonian damsel would have been loud in her sympathy for the denizens of the paternal rookeries, and would probably, by way of atonement, have given three more hours a week to her district-visiting for at least a month to come. There is nothing less realistic in its effect than to hold up the poor human soul, naked and shivering, for our inspection. We never see the human soul naked. Nature has wrapped it up in a decent integument of hypocrisies and self-deceptions; it is only by inference that we can strip it of its fur. Now it is the business of the realistic drama (and Mr. Shaw vaunts his realism) to lead us through appearances to realities; so that he who skips appearances to go direct to realities is no more a realistic artist than the painter who should depict the House of Lords in that undraped condition imagined by Teufelsdröckh. The same mistake vitiates the scene in which Sartorius retorts upon Trench. Ultimately, no doubt, Trench's indignation would have simmered down; he would have seen that he was not called upon to remake the world at his own expense, and he would have gone on pocketing his 700*l.* a year, with or without some little solatium to his conscience in the shape of charity. But even self-interest does not in three minutes upset the prejudices of a life-time. At 3.35 Mr. Trench is boiling over with indignation at Sartorius's misdeeds, and is prepared to make a very heavy pecuniary sacrifice in order to have no art or part in them; at 3.38 he is shrugging his shoulders and saying 'Kismet!' No, Mr. Shaw! Before you write your next novel or play, I beg you to add this to your list of first-principles: Even the bourgeois has his self-respect, however chimerical; he is very ready to blindfold it, but it is only in the last extremity of the struggle for life (and sometimes not even then) that he will kill and trample upon it. It is quite true, as Larochefoucauld says, that in the misfortunes of our best friends there is something not altogether unpleasing to us;

but that would not justify a playwright in making Pythias dance a hornpipe on hearing the news of Damon's bankruptcy. In Trench's instantaneous surrender in the second act, you have perpetrated a strictly analogous inconsequence.

If Mr. Shaw would or could divest his mind of theory, I think he would see that these lovers of his are not human beings at all. Can he produce any evidence to show that, even at Surbiton, passionate illusion is unknown in love, and that the young men and maidens of Thames Ditton spend their time in snapping each other's heads off instead of idealising each other? Truly, for a set of blood-suckers, Mr. Shaw's middle-classes are strangely bloodless. And he fails withal—partly by reason of his summary and paradoxic psychology, partly from other and subtler causes—to produce any illusion of real life. His world is without atmosphere; no breath of humanity, and least of all any *odor di femmina*, gets over the footlights. Therefore he gives his interpreters a peculiarly difficult task, and I prefer not to dwell upon their shortcomings. The one human being in the play was represented with singular ability by Mr. James Welch.

5. From a notice by H.W.M., *Illustrated London News*

17 December 1892, 2800, vol. CI, 770

This notice is almost certainly by Henry William Massingham (1850–1924), journalist, editor of the *Nation* from 1907 to 1923. This notice of *Widowers' Houses* was entitled 'A Realist Play'.

The production of Mr Bernard Shaw's play, *Widowers' Houses*, is a dramatic event of very considerable significance. The vital quality of the play is its freshness of type. It is neither tragedy nor melodrama, nor comedy nor burlesque. Mr. Shaw chooses to call it a didactic play, and it is this and something more. It is a study of modern life, purely ironical in conception, and almost completely realistic in workmanship. What Mr. Shaw has endeavoured to do has been to set society before us not merely in its surface aspect of love-making, intriguing, dinner-giving and eating, but in what he conceives to be the more vital light of the 'cash nexus.' He exhibits the modern lover, the modern father, the modern friend, the modern young lady as he believes them to be conditioned by the way in which they make their money and spend it. He gives us love-making without romance, friendship without sincerity, landlordism without pity, life as it is lived in the upper middle-class without charm. Now, it is quite allowable for his hearers to quarrel with this conception, to say it is unnatural, overstrained, false to the facts. But I cannot conceive how it can be regarded as improper material for a play. All Mr. Shaw is bound to do is to make his characters plausible, to give validity to their motives and consistency to his conception of their mutual relations. In a word, Mr. Shaw has put before us the Socialist criticism of life, and that may be quite as interesting, even supposing it is not quite as true, as the individualist or the merely conventional view. The English stage can be none the worse for a sincere attempt to exhibit life as the dramatist really believes it is being lived in London to-day.

[Outlines the story of the play.]

This is Mr. Shaw's play. Its moral is obvious, its didactic purpose is revealed from the raising of the curtain to its fall, its irony is at times a trifle too fine for its purpose and the shafts fly over the heads of the audience. But the reproach of slovenly construction or essentially uninteresting character does not lie against it. It reverses the conventional ending, the conventional set of characters, the conventional stage types: nevertheless it has a convincing method of its own. Its characters are drawn with perfect clearness, and in the case of the girl with specially minute, if a trifle malicious, art. And it gives the experiment of the Independent Theatre a new basis of original effort which one may very well hope to see developed.

6. A. B. Walkley, from an initialled notice, *Speaker*

17 December 1892, vol. VI, 155, 736

A. B. Walkley (1855–1926), dramatic critic and essayist, wrote dramatic criticism for several different periodicals before becoming dramatic critic of *The Times*, a post which he held from 1900 to 1926. He became a personal friend of Shaw, and *Man and Superman*, when first published in 1903, had for preface an 'Epistle Dedicatory' to Walkley. Walkley was never a wholehearted admirer of Shaw and, in a pseudonymous notice of *Widowers' Houses* in the *Star* on 10 December 1892 referred to Shaw's curtain speech, saying that he was 'an admirable speaker—and a detestable dramatist'. There was a softening of his attitude in later years (see Nos 29, 88).

The Independent Theatre has at length shaken off its xenomania and produced a home-grown play, *Widowers' Houses*, by Mr. G. Bernard Shaw. I hardly know which is the more remarkable birth of time, the play or the playwright. Mr. Bernard Shaw's name must be familiar to everyone who affects to keep abreast of the intellectual movement of the day. This is not the place to draw a full-length portrait, in the style of Hume or Macaulay, of Mr. Shaw. (Observe the modest implication that I could do this if I chose.) Indeed, not one portrait, but a whole galleryful would be required, for there are ever so many Mr. Shaws—

Uno Shawio avulso non deficit alter.[1]

You have Mr. Shaw the musical critic, and Mr. Shaw the novelist, and Mr. Shaw the Ibsenite exegete, and Mr. Shaw the Fabian, and Mr. Shaw the vegetarian, and Mr. Shaw the anti-vivisectionist—and now there is Mr. Shaw the dramatist. You perceive that I am trying to

---

[1] One Shaw torn away, another is not wanting to take his place. (The quotation is adapted from Virgil.)

assume an air of playful banter. But that is only to conceal my nervousness. The truth is, I am horribly afraid of Mr. Shaw and his merciless intellect. I know very well beforehand that the triumphant refutation of any adverse strictures I may have to make on his play will be the merest child's play for him. Like the unfortunate gentlewoman, reduced to crying matches for sale in the street, who sighed, 'I hope to goodness nobody hears me,' I can only trust that he will not see this week's *Speaker*.

Let me say, then, *sotto voce* and behind Mr. Shaw's back, that, from the playhouse point of view, *Widowers' Houses* is a singularly bad piece of work. The qualification is important, because there are several points of view from which the play will have to be regarded as a brilliant success. It is a scathing satire on the burgess mind. It is a pitiless exposure of the immoral aspect of rent and interest. It has the merit of bringing 'live' social and economical questions almost for the first time into the playhouse. It has very considerable literary qualities —the power of cogent argument, a terse and trenchant style, a really fine irony. But, for all that, it is a bad play.

It is odd, when you come to think of it, that one should have to apologise for considering a play as a play, and nothing else. But so it is. The political leader-writer, for instance, scorns any such consideration as shallow pedantry. 'We need not,' says one of that truculent tribe this week, 'discuss the questions how far a play which is primarily didactic is a perversion of the drama, or how far Mr. Shaw has succeeded in the dramatist's art. Cant about "art for art's sake" is not likely to trouble him. That may be left to a Cokane.' (By the way, Cokane, a character whom Mr. Shaw puts forward as a type of the conventional Philistine, half Podsnap, half Prud'homme, would be the last man to accept any artistic principle so esoteric as that of *l'art pour l'art*; but I am willing to make some allowance for the comprehensive ignorance of a political leader-writer.) Well, fanaticism about art for art's sake is one thing: it is quite another to insist that a work of art shall be judged by the conditions of that art and by the success with which it applies the methods peculiar to that art. Take a homely illustration—the apple. You may represent the apple pictorially, in which case it will be incumbent upon you to show its colour, its form, the smoothness and sheen of its surface. Or you may treat it scientifically, enumerate its pips, give it a family tree and a Latin label. Or, again, you may make it a literary theme, with graceful allusions to Mother Eve and Dame Venus and Sir Isaac Newton. But you must take your choice between these methods. It is of no use for the painter to say, for instance. 'See how I have suggested the literary qualities of the apple: here is Eve's serpent in the foreground, and there is Paris preparing to hand the apple to Venus,' and so forth. The answer to him is: 'Your business is to discover for me the pictorial qualities of the apple.' So it is with a play. If the playwright asks us to observe the skill with which he has treated the ethics or the sociology of his subject, we reply, 'That is all very well, but have you made the most of its dramatic qualities?'

Now, Mr. Shaw has not only failed to make the most of the dramatic qualities of his theme, he has failed to make anything of them, he has failed to discover them at all. Here is the case he has imagined:—A well-bred, well-intentioned young fellow discovers that the dowry of his intended bride is 'dirty money,' namely, the rents of some disgracefully neglected tenement-houses in a London slum. He will not touch this dirty money; and as the lady refuses to marry dowerless, (1) he breaks off the match. The lady's father, however, explains to him that his own income is part of these extortionate rents, being derived from a mortgage on the slum property; whereupon (2) he withdraws the epithet 'dirty' and, as he cannot consent to sacrifice his income or any of it, comes round to the conclusion that neglected slums and wicked landlords are essential features of the Cosmos. Then, having begun as a man of simple mind and honest instincts, he becomes more calculating and base than the wicked landlord himself; objects to improvements which the latter proposes, simply because of the consequent diminution of his own income. Finally, (3) as part of a shameful bargain (the particulars of which are neither here nor there) for swelling the amount of the 'dirty' money he is persuaded to renew his engagement to the landlord's daughter—and the play is at an end.

Whether this case is a real case, a true picture of life, or whether it is discoloured and distorted by Mr. Shaw's well-known views of the existing social and economic order, it is no part of my business to inquire. All that I care to point out is, that it contains at least three possible opportunities for drama, and that at each of the three Mr. Shaw breaks down. These opportunities I have indicated by numbers. At (1) we have a young couple who love one another after their own fashion (and a very odd fashion it is, by the way—a perpetual snapping and snarling, a cat-and-dog fashion, but still the dramatist wishes us to take it as quite sincere affection) suddenly parted. Here, then, we legitimately expect some show of struggle in the man's heart (we do not in the woman's, for she is represented as a shallow, hard creature, with no heart to speak of), we look for 'passion and duty coming nobly to the grapple.' But there is no struggle, no grapple. The jilting is made, as the French say, as simple as 'Good morning!' At (2) a still greater opportunity is lost. Here is a man whose character executes a right-about-face at a word—the mere word 'mortgage,' which suffices to turn hero into rascal. Mr. Shaw will say that is his point—scratch a middle-class hero and you find a rascal. Yes, but on the stage a mere scratch won't do. The playgoer wants these sudden revolutions explained, the way prepared for them, care expended upon bringing them into relief. When I find such a tremendous moral transformation effected in a moment, barely indicated by a hasty, 'I beg your pardon, I was mistaken" I feel that I have been baulked of my scène-à-faire.[1] As to (3) it is, to be sure, a delightful bit of irony, this 'happy ending' resulting from a disgraceful conspiracy among all the personages of the play, but it is not dramatic. I only see a number of people arguing round a table. Indeed, Mr. Shaw's people are not dramatic characters at all, they are embodied arguments. Mr. Shaw's premises may be sound and his logic impeccable, but that, I repeat, is not the point. The point is, what has he made of his dramatic opportunities? And my answer is—nothing.

[1] The obligatory scene at the climax of the 'well-made' play.

7. Oscar Wilde on Shaw's confidence

9 May 1893

Oscar Fingal O'Flahertie Wills Wilde (1854–1900), Irish wit and dramatist, in a letter to Shaw, appears to be ranking *Widowers' Houses* with his own *Lady Windermere's Fan* and *A Woman of No Importance* as the beginnings of a new 'Celtic School'. The letter is printed in *The Letters of Oscar Wilde*, ed. Rupert Hart-Davis (1962), 339, where a note by Hesketh Pearson is quoted to explain the numbering of the plays.

My dear Shaw, I must thank you very sincerely for Op. 2 of the great Celtic School. I have read it twice with the keenest interest. I like your superb confidence in the dramatic value of the mere facts of life. I admire the horrible flesh and blood of your creatures, and your preface is a masterpiece—a real masterpiece of trenchant writing and caustic wit and dramatic instinct. I look forward to your Op. 4. As for Op. 5, I am lazy, but am rather itching to be at it. When are you coming to the Haymarket?
Sincerely yours   OSCAR WILDE.

ARMS AND THE MAN

1894

Arms and the Man was first presented at the Avenue Theatre, London (later renamed the Playhouse) on 21 April 1894. It ran for fifty performances and, while well received on the whole by the critics, it lost money.

8. From an unsigned notice, *Star*

23 April 1894, 1928, 1

Enormously amusing, if slightly perplexing. Not fitting exactly into any ready-made category, but a nondescript, an amalgam of burlesque, farce and comedy. On the surface, little more than a joyous game of intellect and wit; beneath the surface little less than a profoundly serious criticism of life. A piece full of local color, and different locality from our own with a different scheme of color; and yet mutato nomine de te &c., in all essentials the personages are not remote and strange, but our neighbors (to save our self-love, I will not say ourselves) and familiar. Far better than *Widowers' Houses*, because the author has now learnt more of the playwright's business, he knows better now what can be got over the footlights and what cannot. Not that he has yet quite mastered the difficult technique of the stage. On that account, and for the still stronger reason that his train of thought, his mode of envisaging the universe, is peculiarly his own—that is, peculiarly unlike other people's—one does not always see what he is driving at. Even now, I admit I don't understand everything in *Arms and the Man*. But everything in it—even the things I didn't understand —exhilarated and delighted me beyond measure. My sides are still aching with laughter.

[Outlines story of play with comment on acting.]

The play kept the whole house in a perpetual roar of laughter, and the author received at the end a double call.

9. William Archer, initialled notice, *World*

25 April 1894, 1034, 22

Reprinted in *The Theatrical 'World' of 1894* (1895), 109.

Archer was at pains to point out that Shaw, thinking he had written 'a serious comedy, a reproduction of life as it really is' had, in fact, written a new kind of 'prose extravaganza'. In addition, Archer continued, he had concentrated on 'the seamy side' of life. Shaw replied to these criticisms in two letters dated 23 April 1894, reprinted in Laurence, I, 425–8, and in the preface which he wrote to the book of Archer's collected theatre articles. *The Theatrical 'World' of 1894.* He dealt at length with many critical attacks on *Arms and the Man* in an article, 'A Dramatic Realist to His Critics', in the *New Review* XI, July 1894, reprinted in *Shaw on Theatre*, edited by E. J. West, 1958, 18.

There is not the least doubt that *Arms and the Man* is one of the most amusing entertainments at present before the public. It is quite as funny as *Charley's Aunt* or *The New Boy*; we laughed at it wildly, hysterically; and I exhort the reader to go and do likewise. But he must not expect a humdrum, rational, steady-going farce, like *Charley's Aunt*, bearing a well-understood conventional relation to real life. Let him rather look for a fantastic, psychological extravaganza, in which drama, farce, and Gilbertian irony keep flashing past the bewildered eye, as in a sort of merry-go-round; so quickly that one gives up the attempt to discriminate between them, and resigns oneself to indiscriminating laughter. The author (if he will pardon my dabbling in musical metaphor) is always jumping from key to key, without an attempt at modulation, and nine times out of ten he does not himself know what key he is writing in. Here, indeed, lies the whole truth. If one could think that Mr Shaw had consciously and deliberately invented a new species of prose extravaganza, one could unreservedly applaud the invention, while begging him in future to apply it with a little more depth and delicacy. But I more than suspect that he conceives himself to have written a serious comedy, a reproduction of life as it really is, with men and women thinking, feeling, speaking, and acting as they really do think, feel, speak, and act. Instead of presenting an episode in the great war between the realms of Grünewald and Gerolstein, or in the historic conflict between Paphlagonia and Crim Tartary, he places his scene in the (more or less) real principality of Bulgaria, dates his action to the year and day (6th March 1886), and has been at immense pains to work-in Bulgarian local colour in the dialogue, and to procure correct Bulgarian costumes and genuine Balkan scenery. It is an open secret, I believe, that Mr Shaw held counsel on these matters with a Bulgarian Admiral,—a Bohemian Admiral would scarcely be more unexpected,—and that this gallant horse-marine gave him the hints as to the anti-saponaceous prejudices of the Bulgarians, their domestic architecture, their unfamiliarity with electric bells, and the mushroom growth of their aristocracy, which he has so religiously, and in some cases amusingly, utilised. But all this topographical pedantry proves, oddly enough, that ' 'e dunno where 'e are.' By attempting to fix his action down to the solid earth he simply emphasises its unreality. He is like the young man in *Pickwick*, who, having to write an essay on 'Chinese Metaphysics,' read up the articles 'China' and 'Metaphysics' in the Encyclopædia, and combined the two. Mr Shaw went to his Admiral for 'Bulgaria,' and to his inner consciousness for 'Psychology,' and combined the two in an essay on 'Bulgarian Psychology.' Why confound the issues in this way, my dear G. B. S.? Some critics have assumed, quite excusably, that the play was meant as a satire upon Bulgaria, and I should not be in the least surprised if it were to lead to a 'diplomatic incident' like that which arose from the introduction of the Sultan in *Don Juan*. Of course you really know and care no more about Bulgaria than I do. Your satire is directed against humanity in general, and English humanity in particular. Your Saranoff and Bluntschli and Raïna and Louka have their prototypes, or rather their antitypes, not in the Balkan Principalities, but in that romantic valley which nestles between the cloud-capped summits of Hampstead and Sydenham. Why not confess as much by making your scene fantastic, and have done with it?

Having now disentangled 'Bulgaria' and 'Psychology,' I put the former article aside as irrelevant, and turn to the latter. Mr Shaw is by nature and habit one of those philosophers who concentrate their attention upon the seamy side of the human mind. Against that practice, in itself, I have not a word to say. By all means let us see, examine, realise, remember, the seamy side. You will never find me using the word 'cynic' as a term of moral reproach. But to say of a man that he is habitually and persistently cynical is undoubtedly to imply an artistic limitation. To look at nothing but the seamy side may be to see life steadily, but is not to see it whole. As an artist, Mr Shaw suffers from this limitation; and to this negative fault, if I may call it so, he superadds a positive vice of style. He not only dwells on the seamy side to the exclusion of all else, but he makes his characters turn their moral garments inside out and go about with the linings displayed, flaunting the seams and raw edges and stiffenings and paddings. Now this simply does not occur in real life, or only to a very limited extent; and the artist who makes it his main method of character-presentation, at once converts his comedy into extravaganza. It is not Mr Shaw's sole method, but he is far too much addicted to it. His first act is genuine fantastic comedy, sparkling and delightful. Here he has set himself to knock the stuffing, so to speak, out of war; to contrast a romantic girl's ideal of battle and its heroic raptures, with the sordid reality as it appears to a professional soldier. He has evidently 'documents' to go upon, and he has seized with inimitable humour upon the commonplace and ludicrous aspects of warfare. Of course Bluntschli's picture is not the whole truth any more than Raïna's, but it presents a real and important side of the matter, the side which chiefly appeals to Mr Shaw's sceptical imagination. The great and serious artists—Tolstoi, Zola (for I am impenitent in my admiration for *La Débâcle*), Whitman in his *Specimen Days*, Stendhal (I am told) in *La Chartreuse de Parme*—give us both sides of the case, its prose and its poetry. Even Mr Kipling, who also has his 'documents,' has found in them a thing or two beyond Mr Shaw's ken. But for the nonce, and in its way, Mr Shaw's persiflage is not only vastly amusing, but acceptable, apposite. So far good. At the end of the first act we do not quite know where the play is coming in, for it is obvious that even Mr Shaw cannot go on through two more acts mowing down military ideals with volleys of chocolate-creams. But there are evident possibilities in this generous romantic girl and her genially cynical instructor in the art of war; and we hope for the best. Observe that as yet we have not got upon the ground of general psychology, so to speak; we have had nothing but a humorous analysis of one special phase of mental experience—the sensations of a soldier in battle and in flight. In the second act all is changed. Bluntschli, in whom the author practically speaks in his own person, without any effort at dramatization, has almost disappeared from the scene, and the really dramatic effort commences in the characterization of the Byronic swaggerer, Sergius Saranoff, and the working out of his relation to Raïna. At once Mr Shaw's ease and lightness of touch desert him, and we find ourselves in Mr Gilbert's Palace of Truth. The romantic girl is romantic no longer, but a deliberate humbug, without a single genuine or even self-deluding emotion in her bloodless frame. Sergius the Sublime has no sort of belief in his own sublimity, but sets to work before he has been ten minutes on the stage to analyse himself for the entertainment of the maid-servant, and enlarge on the difficulty of distinguishing between the six or seven Sergiuses whom he discovers in his composition. Petkoff and his wife are mere cheap grotesques, both more or less under the influence of the Palace of Truth. The major-domo, under the same magic spell, affords a vehicle for some of the author's theories as to the evils engendered on both sides by the relation of master and servant. And the most wonderful character of all, perhaps, is the maid Louka, who seems to have wandered in from one of the obscurer of Mr Meredith's novels, so keen is her perception, and so subtle her appreciation, of character and motive. All this crude and contorted psychology, too, is further dehumanised by Mr Shaw's peculiar habit of straining all the red corpuscles out of the blood of his personages. They have nothing of human nature except its pettinesses; they are devoid alike of its spiritual and its sensual instincts. It is all very well for Mr Shaw to be sceptical as to the reality of much of the emotion which passes by the name of love, and over which so much fuss is made both in fiction and in life. For my part, I quite agree with him that a great deal of foolish and useless unhappiness is caused by our habit of idealising and eternalising this emotion, under all circumstances and at all hazards. But it is one thing to argue that the exultations and agonies of love are apt to be morbid, factitious, deliberately exaggerated and overwrought, and quite another to represent life as if these exultations and agonies had no existence whatever. Here we have a girl who, in the course of some six hours, transfers her affections (save the mark!) from a man whom she thought she had adored for years, to one whom she has only once before set eyes on, and a young man who, in the same space of time, quarrels with the mistress about nothing at all, and, for no conceivable reason, makes up his mind to marry the maid. Such instantaneous *chassés croisés* used to be common enough in Elizabethan drama, and are quite the order of the day in Gilbertian extravaganza. In any more serious form of modern drama they would be not only preposterous but nauseous.

It is impossible, in short, to accept the second and third acts of *Arms and the Man* as either 'romantic comedy' or coherent farce. They are bright, clever, superficially cynical extravaganza. In the second act, there are some, not many, intervals of dullness; but with the re-appearance of Captain Bernard Bluntschli-Shaw the fun fully revives, and in the third act there are even some patches of comedy, in the author's finer vein. Pray do not suppose, moreover, from my dwelling on the pettiness and sordidness of motive which reign throughout, that the whole effect of the play is unpleasant. Mr Shaw's cynicism is not in the least splenetic; on the contrary, it is imperturbably good-humoured and almost amiable. And amid all his irresponsible non-sense, he has contrived, generally in defiance of all dramatic consistency, to drag in a great deal of incidental good sense. I begin positively to believe that he may one day write a serious and even an artistic play, if only he will repress his irrelevant whimsicality, try to clothe his character-conceptions in flesh and blood, and realise the difference between knowingness and knowledge.

10. A. B. Walkley, from an initialled notice, *Speaker*

28 April 1894, vol. IX, 226, 471

Walkley began by asserting that Shaw's 'fun' was not original but 'second-hand Gilbertism'. He then went on to try to analyse the qualities of the two writers.

Let us try and distinguish between Gilbertism and Shawism. . . . it turns upon a vital difference between two ways of regarding the current ideas of life and conduct. Mr. Gilbert never questions the validity of these ideals. He accepts them; his personages accept them, but do not act up to them. Gilbertism, then, consists in the ironic humour to be got out of the spectacle of a number of people hypo-critically pretending, or naively failing, to act up to ideals which Mr. Gilbert and his people hold to be valid. On the other hand, the very centre and axis of Mr. Shaw's position is that these current ideals are not valid; . . . he holds these ideals to be false; and his personages, beginning by accepting them as true, are driven by experience to perceive that they are not, that the world won't fit them, and that life cannot be fully and freely lived until they are discarded. Shawism, then, consists in the ironic humour to be got out of the spectacle of a number of people trying to apply the current ideals only to find in the end that they won't work. The difference between the two 'isms,' you see, is enormous. The one merely presents the old, and essentially commonplace, contrast between current theory and current practice; it seeks to demonstrate (and here is real cynicism) that man is bad because he cannot act up to his ideals. The other seeks to demonstrate (and here there may be wrongheadedness or false philosophy but, assuredly, no cynicism) that it is the ideals which are bad—bad, be-cause unworkable, obsolete, cramping—and that man cannot be good until he has ceased trying to act up to them. On the correctness of this theory of life, I take leave to repeat, it is no business of mine to offer an opinion. But it *is* a theory of life; and that is the stimulating, the fascinating thing about *Arms and the Man*. In the form of a droll, fantastic farce, it presents us with a criticism of conduct, a theory of life.

And now I think it is possible to see what Mr. Shaw is aiming at in those three odd personages—odd, until Mr. Shaw's theory of the falsehood of current ideals gives us the clue—Raïna, and Saranoff, and Bluntschli. The two first are idealists. Raïna believes in all forms of heroism, as delineated in the fancy pictures—heroic war, heroic young ladyhood, heroic love. Her chocolate-cream soldier dispels the first illusion, her own natural instincts expose the second, Saranoff's behaviour to Louka and, again, her own natural instincts destroy the third. 'I have told a lie,' she says at one moment in awe-struck tones; 'the second in my life.' 'Isn't that rather a short allowance, young lady?' replies Bluntschli. 'It wouldn't last me out a single morning.' She gasps. 'How did you find me out?' 'Mere common-sense and experience of the world, dear young lady.' If Raïna has been 'found out' —that is, if she has been to some extent a *poseuse*, only half-believing in her own idealism, Saranoff is on the other hand an idealist *pur sang*. He has the chivalric ideal. He is really brave—'In the charge I found I was brave; that, at least, is real about me'—and with a strong sense of honour, shown not only in his dismay at finding himself slipping, behind Raïna's back, into dishonourable conduct with Louka, but still more strongly, and indeed pathetically, in the catastrophe of his 'reparation' . . . to Louka. 'Damnation!' he exclaims, 'mockery everywhere! Everything that I think is mocked by everything that I do.' This, from the standpoint of Shawism, is the true tragedy of your idealist. Bluntschli (from the same point of view—remember that I am all along trying to explain Shawism, neither accepting nor rejecting it) is the real hero, the 'man' of the title: sincere, capable, practical, unaffected, who sees that the current ideals won't work and dismisses them *sans phrase*—or, rather, is blessed with a temperament which has never been able to accept them. One might go on to consider the others from this point of view—Louka, for instance, who might then turn out to be something else than the mere designing chambermaid she appears at first glance to be. But enough, I hope, has been said to show that this play of Mr. Shaw's is a very remarkable and almost— forgive the upholsterer's adjective—unique piece of work. And yet, even as I write the word 'unique,' I am tempted to delete it, for what, after all, is the lesson of this very new kind of farce but that of the old kind, from Molière down to Labiche; the injunction *naturam sequere*— due regard being had to the difference between nature as Mr. Shaw sees it and nature as Molière and Labiche saw it? But this strikes a vein of suggestion too deep for the fag-end of an article.

CANDIDA

1894

Candida was first presented by the Independent Theatre Company at Her Majesty's Theatre, Aberdeen, at the start of a provincial tour. There was one performance on 30 July 1897.

11. From an unsigned notice, *Aberdeen Journal*

31 July 1897, 4

To produce a play for the first time at this season of the year is always a risky experiment, but it was attempted last night at Her Majesty's Theatre with a fair measure of success. In *Candida* Mr Bernard Shaw works on familiar lines. A clergyman, with a charming wife whom he fails to understand or appreciate, as she at least would like to be appreciated: a lack-a-daisical eighteen year old poet, a bumptious father-in-law of the butterman type, and a female typewriter, are the chief characters, and with these materials it is easy to understand what sort of comedy is evolved. Of course the poet is madly in love with the pretty wife of the clergyman, talks a vast amount of high-flown nonsense about flaming swords keeping him from entering the kingdom and so forth, until the husband at last strikes a dramatic attitude and demands that his wife shall choose between them. Needless to say she does nothing of the kind. She sends the poet about his business, however, with a matronly kiss, and brings her husband to his senses with some practical observations on her usefulness to him in keeping his household in smooth working order. There are not a few smart sayings throughout the play, but on the whole it lacks robustness. A little more of the butterman and a trifle less of the poet would be a decided improvement.

12. Oliver Elton, unsigned notice, *Manchester Guardian*

15 March 1898, 8

Oliver Elton (1851–1945), author and critic, was a lecturer in English literature at Owens College, Manchester, from 1890 to 1900. He later became King Alfred Professor of English Literature in the University of Liverpool. The notice recognises in Shaw's play some of the qualities that had already won him a reputation as a critic, and recommends the play for production in London.

The Concert Hall, the scene of the Manchester Independent Theatre, is to disappear, and the Committee estimate that the performance of yesterday evening is likely to be the last they can promote. We hope that it is not so; that the mechanical or financial difficulty of finding a fit stage of operations will not be fatal; that the Manchester public will in future have the chance more than ever to encourage the presenting of plays that are for some reason unusual or adventurous; that the five pieces of Ibsen, *The Two Gentlemen of Verona*, *Love's Labour's Lost*, and *Candida* will find some sequel; and that we may often see, under the same auspices, companies as precisely matched to the high calibre of the dramas chosen as that which enacted Mr Bernard Shaw's play last night. We have throughout tried to meet the aspirations of the Independent Theatre Committee with criticism as searching as they ought to desire. If we have not always concurred in the promoters' own estimate of the performances, we have written, whether our criticisms were just or not, in the wish to further dramatic art in the city. Last evening's presentation we can only wish to applaud and celebrate.

Mr Bernard Shaw, who understands anything, would think it a high compliment to be compared to a Fool in Shakspere; but, as others might think it rude or unintelligible, we will not make the comparison. Inadmissible as much of Shakspere is to Mr Shaw the critic, Mr Shaw the dramatist is clearly and keenly alive to the supreme

70

effect of putting wisdom on the lips and the flashlights of irony in the hand of the jester, trolling and fanfaronading like a child. The weekly humour and paradox of Mr Shaw contain, we assure him, illuminations that make him eminent among dramatic judges. One character above all in *Candida* transfers something of this mixed critical manner to a tragi-comic personage. Whether or not *The Idiot* of Dostoieffsky inspired the creation of Eugene Marchbanks does not matter. The conception of a child-like creature, a poet, a boy of eighteen, got up to look like Shelley, not a man, femininely hectic and timid and fierce, who is the real chorus in the play and the final judge and searcher of hearts of his fellow-puppets, is hazardous; but it prevailed and triumphed. Mr Courtenay Thorpe need not have come on at first with a stuck and lackadaisical stare and he sometimes over-played. But he understood the part, and gradually the audience felt that he could not look otherwise to realise it. Mr Thorpe's voice and intelligence are very good; he had to act the real hero of the play. The Rev James Morell is a philanthropic 'Socialist' vicar, ever living up to his private picture of himself as melting a churchfull of his admirers with his eloquence. He is a variation of an Ibsen husband of the Helmer type. He arranges his household on theories of 'helpfulness' and fraternal service, which end in others doing most things for him. His curate, his typewriting lady secretary and others are blindly in love with him. This is part of the system, though he does not see it. His wife is attached, but in a highly different way, which the play has to unfold. She returns from an absence, bringing the 'boy' Eugene (who has been choked out of his miserable society home), apparently as a kind of fetching and carrying retainer. The first explosion comes when Eugene tells Morell something of what he, Morell, is; when he explains that he loves Morell's wife; that she is, mystically, 'His', because he and not Morell can understand her; and that Morell, who begins to throttle him in the pauses of his own rhetoric, is 'afraid of' him, Eugene. This is well; and Morell is enraged and half-shaken in his self estimate. Mr Charles Charrington has worked well with Mr Shaw in making the character of Morell very complete and formidably hopeless. We have never seen so persuasive a figuring of a hollow soul, ready with fresh and ever fresh reserves of phrasing drawn up from its wells. The accent, posture, and amphitheatrical manner in the crises of private life were all masterly; so was the sincerity of his bewildered rage, and his bitter clinging to his position as apostle and master. The only perplexity came at the end of the second act, when certain hopes were raised that Morell was after all, if by mere defensive egotism, to profit by the sight of his face as shown in the glass by Eugene, and even to turn the tables for a moment. But this may have been hardly consistent with the aim of the third and last act, which was to complete the portrait of Morell without mercy. Here was the opportunity of Candida. In a parade of marital confidence Morell has left her alone with Eugene for the evening while he went to make an oration. He comes back suddenly, and surprises Eugene with his head on Candida's knees. Eugene in his mystical manner explains the truth, that while barred by 'a flaming sword' from vulgar advances, he had all the happiness he desired, that of Candida's compassion, her comprehension of herself, her divine handling of his wounds, her goodness. All this part of the play was full of sallies and fitful side-intentions that make it hard to follow when heard, and therefore untheatrical. Once, when a red-hot poker in some way served as a symbol of chaste separation, a wild humour was half apparent. The end, after various hesitations, approaches when the two men invite Candida to 'choose between them'. Here is the crucial part; the playwright has landed himself in a kind of stalemate. He gets out of it by a device that nearly reminds us of the remark made in the play, 'How conventional you unconventional people are!' But it is convention at two removes. The obvious Adelphi plan would be for Candida to stick to her husband because she had promised in church to do so. The older romantic plan would be for her to assert her inner soul and go forth with the one man that can see into it, Eugene. One more double is requisite and sufficient for Mr Shaw. Its sentimental and dubious character is concealed by the ingenious conduct of the dialogue. She says, 'I choose the weaker'. Superficially this is the feckless boy and vagabond Eugene, and Morell, histrionic to the last, 'Accepts' her judgment. She then explains that the 'weaker' is Morell himself, whom she sees as he really is, but still, in a sort of maternal compassion, adopts. Eugene has understood; he rushes forth, 'the night is impatient' for him. She lets him go with a cruel text for him to remember, that she is fifteen years older than he, and that this difference will increase in meaning with time. 'When we are a hundred years older we shall be the same age', is the substance of his last retort. Then Morell embraces her, and curtain descends. The whole passage, we have said, strikes us as sentiment wrapped up in ingenuities, and it is some strain on belief that even Morell should welcome his reward with such rapture when receiving it as the corollary of his weakness from his direst critic, who has upset his whole theory of himself. Perhaps the playwright tugged impatiently at his motley and intricate knot. It has to be said, however, that Miss Janet Achurch played the difficult and sometimes indistinct part of Candida very well and in the only possible spirit, that of a serene clairvoyant, mistress of the whole position, disposing of a couple of children whose natures she explains to themselves and to each other. She has no passion for either, no commonplace conflict of love and duty. When they ask her to 'choose', she asks them to 'bid', as if in auction, what they can give her. She then makes her choice on the subtle principle described. Miss Achurch went through this piquant and abnormal situation with prefect naturalness and with an incisive deliverance of the points. A plainer and stronger part in a modern play of this type would be easily within her compass, and indeed has, by her performance of Ibsen's Nora, often been proved to be her forte.

The three leading personages were therefore very well played. So, in their degrees, were the others. Burgess, Candida's father, the North-country employer and honest, unconscious 'scoundrel' of high standing (scoundrel in the eyes of the Socialist parson), was admirably acted by Mr J. H. Atkinson, without any excess. Mr H. T. Bagnall did quite well as a curate, and Miss Edith Craig as a typewriter, and these were all the characters. *Candida* has been already played elsewhere in the provinces, though not often. It has yet to be heard in London, where it deserves no mean reception, especially if it is represented by the present company.

PLAYS PLEASANT AND UNPLEASANT

published 1898

Apart from the publication of *Widowers' Houses* in 1893, the appearance of the two volumes of *Plays Pleasant and Unpleasant* in 1898 gave readers the first opportunity of studying Shaw's work.

13. H. A. Jones, letter to Shaw

5 May 1898

Henry Arthur Jones (1851–1929) was a leading dramatist of the late Victorian and Edwardian periods. Shaw praised some of his plays warmly in *Saturday Review* articles. The two writers were on friendly terms, but they quarrelled during the First World War because of the violent objections of Jones to Shaw's views on the war. The following extract is from a letter of Jones to Shaw quoted in *The Life and Letters of Henry Arthur Jones* by Doris Arthur Jones (1930), 348.

I have read the plays with varied feelings—at times interested, here and there exhilarated, sometimes bored, sometimes, oftentimes provoked, but always with respectful attention. Much of them is not dramatic and would never be interesting in any circumstances to any possible audience, but there is a good deal that is very dramatic and would fail on our English stage because of the defective machinery now in use for conveying the author's meaning and design to our not over-intellectual audiences—by defective machinery, I mean those people from whose mouths our words issue in such a way that sometimes their purport is known, and occasionally a gleam of meaning is seen to be attached to them. And for this we ought to be grateful. There is too much of the journalist and pamphleteer in some of the pieces. Now, I am falsely accused sometimes of being a preacher—there never was a greater mistake—but you really do preach. I've said nothing of the constant jets and spurts of wit that are always dashing against our faces—that goes without saying in any and everything you write. I should like to talk over the plays with you when you have a day or two to spare—perhaps next month.

14. Review by Max Beerbohm, *Saturday Review*

14 May 1898, 2220, vol. 85, 651 and 21 May 1898, 2221, vol. 85, 679

Reprinted in *More Theatres* (1969), 21

Henry Maximilian (Max) Beerbohm (1872–1956) author and critic. Max Beerbohm, a half-brother of the actor, Herbert Beerbohm Tree, became dramatic critic of the *Saturday Review* in succession to Shaw in 1898. He considered Shaw 'the most brilliant and remarkable journalist in London' and felt himself inadequate to follow him. He confessed that 'of the literary quality in any play, I shall perhaps be able to say something, but I shall be hopelessly out of my depth in criticising the play itself'. It is clear that Beerbohm's attitude to Shaw was a compound of admiration, irritation and envy, but his criticisms of the plays are, on the whole, admirably detached assessments. Beerbohm's criticisms have been collected in three volumes, *Around Theatres* (1953), *More Theatres* (1969) and *Last Theatres* (1970). This review, which appeared in two successive issues of the *Saturday Review*, was not included by Max Beerbohm in the two-volume selection of his dramatic criticisms *Around Theatres*, which was first published in 1924.

In *A Christmas Garland* (1912) Max Beerbohm included 'A Straight Talk' which was a parody of Shaw's style in the form of a preface to *Snt George: A Christmas Play*.

I think it was Mr. Street who propounded an ingenious theory that the invention of printing had made serious and philosophical plays unnecessary, that one could learn far better from books than from the stage, and that the best thing for the stage to do was to be merely comic. But I hold that there is still some justification and some use for the dramatist-with-a-purpose. Though he may no longer be able to tell us what we did not know before, he can yet impress our knowledge in us more effectively than can any mere bookman: he can make us see our knowledge at new angles, and under new and more vivid lights. Nor is direct moral purpose always a fatal obstacle, but sometimes a very valuable incentive to dramatic art. In writing *Widowers' Houses*, *The Philanderer*, and *Mrs. Warren's Profession*, Mr. Shaw was, as he admits, impelled by a direct moral purpose. *A priori*, there is no harm in that. Whether the purpose that impelled him was morally sound is not a question which I have time to discuss. Whether it was quite genuine to him is a far more important point, and I am sure that Mr. Shaw is honestly firm in his convictions. Whether his convictions have helped him to write good plays, or have hindered him from doing so, is the point which most interests me and with which I propose to deal, taking *Mrs. Warren's Profession* as the test case, inasmuch as I think it to be the most considerable of the three works. Mr. William Archer has given us, through the *Daily Chronicle*, a long poem in which he declares this drama to be 'intellectually and dramatically one of the most remarkable plays of the age,' and Mr. Cunninghame Graham, coming upon us, rather suddenly, in the character of old play-goer, vows that in his opinion it is 'the best play which has been written in the English language in this generation.' But, as I have already suggested in these columns, there are some critics so advanced as to hold that a bad play is necessarily a good play, that (need I amplify the phrase?) there must be something very fine about a dramatist who defies the canons of dramatic art. There are also those who, confounding subject with treatment, and drama itself with the Sydney Webbs, believe that a serious theme is a touchstone of dramatic ability. An unpleasant theme, seriously treated, sends them into transports. Drag in the divorce-court, and they will solemnly credit you with immense talent for the stage. Drag in a brothel, and they will never have seen so great a play as yours. Mr. Shaw does not merely drag a brothel into his play, but makes it the play's basis. Let us be calm. Let us not be swept away on the strong wave of a genuine, but possibly mistaken, enthusiasm. My friends, let us consider the play as in itself it is.

[Outlines story of the play.]

I know well that, in giving a mere sketch of a play which one does not like, one is bound to do the play some injustice. I do not think that I have done any considerable injustice to *Mrs. Warren's Profession*, but I should like to say at once that the play is well and forcibly written, that the idea of it is firmly gripped, and that, obviously, the scenes are ordered by one who has some instinct for stage-craft. But no amount of stage-craft, and good dialogue and philosophic grip will enable a man to write a serious play that can be anything but ridiculous, unless the man can also draw human characters. If Mr. Shaw had been able to draw Vivie as a real girl, Mrs. Warren as a real woman, and Frank as a real young man, he might have produced a play which would have justified even the superlatives of Mr. Archer and the reminiscences of Mr. Cunninghame Graham. 'No conflict: no drama,' as he himself says in one of his excellent prefaces. To this formula I would add 'No sympathy: no conflict.' Conflict of a kind there is between Vivie and her mother, but as no one could feel any sympathy for the mother, even were she real and not a mere secretion of Shawism, nor for the daughter who is a mere secretion of Shawism and more utterly unreal than the most romantic heroine across the bridges, the conflict is not of that kind which makes a play effective, but is rather such a shindy as might be waged between a phantom pot and an imaginary kettle. Maupassant's Yvette was a tragic and a moving figure because she was a real girl, to whom the discovery of her mother's shame was really horrible. Mr. Shaw has declared that he thinks the scene in the second act between Vivie and her mother 'tremendously effective.' To whom, I wonder? As a matter of fact, it is not a scene at all. It is a fragment of a well-written pamphlet. Yvette tried to poison herself. 'That,' Mr. Shaw would say, 'was very silly and romantic of her. My Vivie goes out into the world to make a living for herself.' But that was the intention of Mr. Shaw's Vivie from the first rise of the curtain. The last fall of the curtain leaves her exactly as she was discovered. Nothing has been developed in her by the action of the play. Nothing has been developed in Mrs. Warren, nothing in Frank Gardner, nothing in any of the characters. Even unreal characters *can* be developed in a play. Even real characters *must* be developed; no development: no drama. Unreal characters, undeveloped, are no good at all. . . .

My readers may remember that I laid stress on the unrealness of the chief characters in his most ambitious play, *Mrs. Warren's Profession*. Well, I cannot admit that the chief characters in his other plays are one whit more real than Vivie Warren and her friends. They are, indeed, of precisely the same type. The men are all disputative machines, ingeniously constructed, and the women, who, almost without exception, belong to the strange cult of the fountain-pen, are, if anything, rather more self-conscious than the men. I am aware that there are inhuman persons in the world, here and there. One or two inhuman characters would not be amiss in a play. But the play that is monopolised by them can never be taken seriously. Does Mr. Shaw, like Mr. W. S. Gilbert, wish that any of his plays shall be seriously taken? For some of them, undoubtedly, that is his ardent wish, but, until he has been re-incarnated and has thoroughly re-written them, it will not be gratified. Moral purpose is all very well for a dramatist who, like Ibsen, can express it through the tragic or comic evolutions of realised human character. To a dramatist who cannot do that, moral purpose is a disaster; it forces him to burden himself and his puppets with a load which they cannot bear, a load without which they might be quite agile, effective and amusing. Mr. Shaw is not, as the truly serious dramatist must be, one who loves to study and depict men and women for their own sake, with or without moral purpose. When Mr. Shaw is not morally purposeful, he is fantastic and frivolous, and it is then that his plays are good. In farce, psychological reality is not wanted—it would be out of place, and *Arms and the Man*, and *You Never Can Tell* lose nothing and gain much, whilst *Widowers' Houses* and *Mrs. Warren's Profession* are ruined by the absurdity of their characters and situations. No one admires more heartily than I the keenness of Mr. Shaw's intellect and the absolute sincerity with which Mr. Shaw maintains and lives up to his convictions. Nor would any one be more heartily glad than I to see more intellectual force and more moral earnestness in the serious plays that are written for the English stage. But these qualities, without that human sympathy to which in the best dramatist they are always subordinate, are thrown utterly away on serious play-writing. Mr. Shaw's penetrating eye is of great use to him in satire or in criticism. He is one of those gifted observers who can always see through a brick wall. But the very fact that a man can see through a brick wall means that he cannot see the brick wall. It is because flesh and blood make no impression on the X rays that Herr Röntgen is able to show us our bones and any latch-keys that we may have swallowed, or fish-hooks that may have entered into our hands. Flesh and blood are quite invisible to Mr. Shaw. He thinks that because he cannot see them they do not exist, and that he is to be accepted as a realist. I need hardly point out to my readers that he is mistaken. To those who have read his plays I need hardly point out that, to all intents and purposes, his serious characters are just so many skeletons, which do but dance and grin and rattle their bones. I can hardly wonder that Mr. Shaw has so often hesitated about allowing this or that theatrical manager to produce one of his serious plays. To produce one of them really well would be almost impossible at any ordinary theatre. There is, however, one management which might attempt and be able to achieve the task. I refer to Messrs. Maskelyne and Cook.

Of Mr. Shaw's philosophy I need merely say that it rests, like Plato's *Republic*, on a profound ignorance of human nature. Just as the great idealist of Athens imagined that the equality of man to man, and of woman to man, would one day be not merely recognised but also established, so does our idealist of London believe that the tactics of Fabius are the one thing needed to ensure Socialism, Women's Rights and all the rest of his touching propaganda. Let him continue to believe so, by all means. But let him not imagine that, by writing dramatic representations of men and women as (perhaps) they ought to be, he is so far advancing his cause as to make any one believe in the possibility of his characters. In a word, let him write no more plays-with-a-purpose. Let him not be beguiled by Mr. Archer's contempt for *You Never Can Tell* and perfervid admiration of *Candida*. Mr. Shaw, as every one knows, is a man of inexhaustible wit and humour. Such qualities Mr. Archer is always ready to recognise in any writer, but he is never quite able to love them. He would rather see a man trying to be serious than succeeding in being funny. Extravagance and excess frighten him. He sees in them the constant menace to the talent of his friend, Mr. Shaw, and, like a hen with a duckling, his is never free from the stress of nervous anxiety. But let him cease to recall Mr. Shaw from the pond of farcical comedy. The critic's aim should be to encourage every writer to do what he can do best, what is most natural to him; not to implore him to persist in tasks which (be they never so superior) he will never accomplish. To every artist that form of art to which his own talent is best suited should seem the highest form of art. It is curious how often the artist is ignorant of his own true bent. To teach him his own true bent is the only service a critic can render him. Mr. Shaw has all the qualities which go to the writing of good farces. He may try, and try again, to be serious, but his nationality will always prevent him from succeeding in the attempt. When he writes seriously, he is always Paddy *malgré lui*.[1] A man should never be himself-despite-himself. He should be himself simply. I hope that in future Mr. Shaw will be Paddy, and leave the rest to chance. If he will do that, he has a great future in English drama.

[1] In spite of himself.

15. Joseph Knight, from an unsigned review, *Athenaeum*

28 May 1898, 3683, 703

Joseph Knight (1829–1907), was dramatic critic of the *Athenaeum* from 1867 until his death.

This review comments on the distinctive style of Shaw's stage directions in his effort to make his plays readable.

A vocabulary of adjectives might be employed in characterizing the contents of Mr. Bernard Shaw's two fantastically named volumes. They are, to begin with, amusing. Not one of the three 'unpleasant' plays comprised in the first volume, nor of the four so-called 'pleasant' plays constituting the second, belongs to that *genre ennuyeux*[1] outside of which, according to Voltaire, 'tous les genres sont bons.'[2] They are, besides, quaint, whimsical, unreal, saucy, cynical, perverse, and a thousand things besides. One thing more, they are mainly didactic. The author has a purpose of a sort, but scorns to stick to it. A Puck among dramatists, he leads you to a point at which you expect to be stirred, surprised, enchanted, you know not what; then, as the mood takes him, he whisks off, and leaves you listening to a derisive cachinnation behind the bushes.

The main purpose of the plays is satirical. Our author laughs at everything, himself included . . . His satire, Socialistic in aim, is chiefly directed against greed for money, but British Pharisaism, military ardour, scientific pretence, ecclesiastical hypocrisy, and other human qualities, affectations, or pretensions are lashed. Mr. Shaw possesses at least the courage of his convictions. In *Mrs. Warren's Profession*, which belongs distinctly to the 'unpleasant' plays, among which it is counted, he deals with a subject as unsavoury as dramatist, since the days of Dryden, has ever handled. . . .

In the prefaces to the two volumes Mr. Shaw expounds with

[1] Tedious category.
[2] All categories are good.

customary cleverness of paradox his views as to the relations between the player and the play, declaring that 'a skilfully written play is infinitely more adaptable to all sorts of acting than available acting is to all sorts of plays.' Born actors have, he holds, 'a susceptibility to dramatic emotion which enables them to seize the moods of their parts intuitively.' You must not expect them to grasp intuitively as well intellectual meaning and circumstantial conditions. For the sake of the actor, then, and for that of an English public noways addicted to the perusal of plays, Mr. Shaw furnishes such elaborate stage directions concerning characters and circumstances as have never previously been seen. The process is distinctly helpful to the reader, and should be so to the actor also. Mr. Shaw, however, who is plentifully endowed with imagination and grasp of situation, character, and dialogue, seems to have the vaguest notion of what can be realized on the stage. We have heard of a stage direction, 'Takes a cab and drives to the City,' and we have seen one in the work of a successful and brilliant dramatist, 'Sound of tumbrils [!] heard without.' We have here, however, apart from more elaborate directions, others such as these: 'In a stealthy, coldly furious whisper'; again, 'McComas's complexion fades into stone grey; and all movement and expression desert his eyes.' And again, the consciousness of the attitude towards himself of his two children goes through the father

with so keen a pang that he trembles all over; his brow becomes wet; and he stares dumbly at his son, who, just sensible enough of his own callousness to intensely enjoy the humour and adroitness of it, proceeds pleasantly.

Raphael is credited with having said 'Comprendre c'est égaler.'[1] The actor who can comprehend and carry out directions such as these will do more than equal, he will surpass not only his teacher, but all record. Reading Mr. Shaw's plays is an agreeable and a perturbing task. They will all of them bear reading twice, with the certainty that the mind will be stimulated afresh. Whether, however, it will be more stimulated or perplexed is a matter of doubt.

[1] To understand is to equal.

THE DEVIL'S DISCIPLE

1896

The Devil's Disciple was successfully presented in the USA and in suburban theatres in London before it was produced in the West End. The first British production was at the Prince of Wales Theatre, Kennington, on 26 September 1899, where it was given thirteen performances. The celebrated actor-manager, Johnston Forbes-Robertson, played the part of Dick Dudgeon in later productions but Shaw was reluctant to allow the play to be seen in the West End before he could be sure of a favourable reception. It was not presented there until 1907, after Shaw's position as a dramatist had been established in the Vedrenne–Barker seasons at the Court Theatre.

16. Unsigned notice, *The Times*

27 September 1899, 35945, 8

As a manager, Mr Murray Carson is open to one obvious objection. He appears to have insufficient belief in the efficacy of rehearsals. His recent production of *Richard III*, at Kennington was, at least on the first night, marred by this, and last night's production of Mr Bernard Shaw's play, *The Devil's Disciple*, laboured under the same disadvantage. But though there were times when the assistance of the prompter was required—and times, too, when that assistance appeared not to be forthcoming—and though some of the performers showed themselves almost painfully unfamiliar with the business of their parts, the evening was unquestionably an interesting one, and the verdict on the play as a whole decidedly favourable. Probably when the actors are more at home in their scenes the piece will go still better and produce a more harmonious and well-balanced effect.

The Devil's Disciple has been played frequently in America, and more than one London manager is supposed to have had thoughts of producing it, but hitherto, we believe, it has not been seen in England. Mr Carson is to be congratulated on his courage in giving it a trial. Not a little courage must have been required, for *The Devil's Disciple* cannot be called a sympathetic play. It is full of that mordant satire with which we are familiar in Mr Shaw's work and full, too, of that sense of insincerity, of mere posing which mars so much of it. Mr Shaw loves to poke fun at the world, at his audience, and at himself, and this attitude is quite inadmissible in serious drama. The dramatist must at least give the impression of being in earnest if his work is to hold the attention of a popular audience. But this is the very last thing that Mr Shaw does. At the most thrilling moments in his plays he will throw his situation to the winds in order to poke sly fun at his characters or his public. He will keep his plot waiting while he amuses himself with elaborating some scene which has only the slightest relation to it, if only it gives him an opportunity to air a paradox or dig respectability in the ribs. Thus a whole scene of *The Devil's Disciple* (and the most amusing scene in the play) was apparently inserted by Mr Shaw solely to give him an opportunity of satirising his *bête noire* the soldier. As a piece of stage fooling it was excellent and elicited the heartiest laughter, but its relation to the main interest of the drama was of the slightest. The fact is Mr Shaw's levity is uncontrollable. He is, seemingly, quite unable to take even his own work seriously. He sets out, apparently, with the intention of writing a drama of emotion, of sentiment even. For an act or two this mood lasts. Then he tires of his puppets, and finishes the play in a mood that is frankly whimsical and absurd.

The action of *The Devil's Disciple* takes place in America at the period of the War of Independence, and the play opens with a scene in which Richard Dudgeon, reprobate, arrives at his grimly Puritan mother's home to hear his father's will read. Good Parson Anderson and all the dour Dudgeon family are assembled, very far from pleased at having the black sheep in their midst. The will is read, Richard is found to be the heir, and in a scene of some dramatic intensity, marred by inefficient writing and, last night at least, by inefficient acting, he proclaims his negation of the creed of his family, and his allegiance to his master the devil. In the second act he is at Parson Anderson's, and the good man wishes to warn him of the danger he believes to be hanging over such a ne'er do weel from the English soldiers who are approaching the town. The rebellion of 1777 has broken out and somebody will probably be hanged by way of example. Having given his warning Anderson is called away, leaving Richard with his wife. The soldiers coming to arrest Anderson, mistake Richard for him, and Richard, in a moment of generosity, allows himself to be arrested in his stead. So far we have drama of a distinctly serious cast, and even of considerable intensity. But in the third act Mr Shaw has tired of his puppets and proceeds to make fun of them and banter with us. There is a Court-martial headed by an imbecile Major Swindon and a jolly, humorous General Burgoyne. Prisoner and Judges are delightfully lighthearted and absurd. The scene recalls the best things in *The Mikado*. We have several admirable jokes about the shooting of the British Army, the soldier's low order of intelligence, and the rest in which Mr Shaw's old paradoxes shine with renewed lustre, and finally the prisoner is condemned. In the last scene we see him about to be hanged. The 'Dead March' has played, the rope is round his neck, but Mr Shaw jests gaily on to the last, and finally somehow, anyhow, the play ends happily. Mr Carson's neck is saved and the house disperses in high good humour. As drama it is somewhat anarchic, but as an entertainment it is often delightful, and that is a sufficient excuse for Mr Shaw. The errors of taste which mar some of the scenes are regrettable, but students of *Plays, Pleasant and Unpleasant* are aware that Mr Shaw's taste is not always impeccable. On the whole he offends less in *The Devil's Disciple* than in most of his dramas. The acting generally was intelligent, and with more rehearsal might have been excellent. Mr Carson himself played Richard Dudgeon with great spirit and, in the third act, with considerable humour. Mr F. H. Macklin was admirable as Parson Anderson, the most sympathetic character in the cast, Miss Grace Warner as his wife displayed a good deal of tragic intensity, and Miss Bessie Hatton was good in the small part of Essie. But the most marked success in the acting was achieved by Mr Luigi Labiche, whose General Burgoyne was a most humorous and delightful figure. It is true that his part has really nothing to do with the main plot of the play, but on the anarchic principles on which Mr Shaw conceives his dramas this fact is of less importance than it would be in plays constructed on more orthodox lines. The reception of the play was decidedly favourable, particularly in the farcical scenes, and we are inclined to think that if Mr Shaw would give his mind to writing farces he would achieve a success which his more serious plays have hitherto failed to attain.

17. G. S. Street on Shaw as a new dramatist in an old tradition

1900

From a signed article, 'Sheridan and Mr Shaw', in *Blackwood's Magazine*, CLXVII, June 1900, 832.

George Slythe Street (1867–1936), author and critic, who later became Reader of Plays, began his article by saying that he had seen *The Rivals* by Sheridan and *You Never Can Tell* on consecutive days and this suggested certain comparisons. In his opening paragraphs he considered Sheridan, particularly in comparison with Congreve.

Mr Shaw has ideas. It might be thought from this remark that I propose to charge in his favour, but regretfully I am forced back upon criticism. Sheridan's weakness is his lack of ideas; Mr Shaw's weakness is his superabundance of them. Congreve's ideas come naturally from the play of his characters, and out of the fulness of his experience; Mr Shaw's ideas have to come in at all cost, and character and experience may go hang. It seems that in whatever he writes he must introduce his whole philosophy. It is an engaging and stimulating philosophy, on the whole, and a little of it here and a little of it there would be very well. But all of it everywhere at once is not well. In his plays, it has two bad effects. The first is that one seems to be listening to a lecture, a witty lecture, but not a play. The second is that it causes Mr Shaw to use his actors worse than dogs. To get an extra idea he will cheerfully sacrifice consistency of tone, and that is fatal to acting. In this *You Never Can Tell*, for an instance: a young woman, Gloria, is an ironical character, full of reason and philosophy and all that, and full also of human weaknesses. She is sympathetically ridiculous. But when a young man has kissed her on a slight acquaintance without her resistance, and her mother subsequently inquires what is troubling her, the curtain is rung down on her saying 'Shame!' and covering her face with her hands—an effect, so far as it goes, of tragedy, the outrage on maidenly delicacy permitted by unguarded weakness, the girl's hatred of herself, and so forth. For that moment, the farce, as a farce, goes to pieces, and the actress's comic effects and serious effects alike are spoiled. It is true in this case to say that Mr Shaw was to some extent saved from himself by the actress in question intelligently minimising the comic effects throughout, and so weakening the jar of the contrast; but Mr Shaw did not deserve that. In the best of his more serious plays, *Candida* and *Mrs Warren's Profession*, Mr Shaw commits the same sort of offence to bring off his contrasts, not of character so much as of theory and ideas, he sacrifices credibility and consistency all the time. Until this prepossession and exuberance are subordinated to the conditions of the playwright's art, Mr Shaw will not write plays which, simply as plays, will be excellent—until he is content that a theory shall not be stated unless it is natural to the given character to state it, and does not merely place it in the mouth of a character who is more appropriate to it than the others. But when this happens the excellent plays should arrive. He has a faculty of effective construction, both humorous and serious, and he understands how to oppose characters, if only (so to speak) he would let them alone. His dialogue is, I think, at present faulty. Intellectually, in intention, it is very good indeed, when the theories do not spoil it, but Mr Shaw's ear is inaccurate—his people speak out of their kind. The trick of making people talk naturally and yet with distinction, the crown of dialogue, is not indispensable—at least few dramatists have possessed it. But that the people should use their own expressions is a necessary condition of good plays. I thought *You Never Can Tell* Mr Shaw's best in this particular.

As a conscientious critic I have pointed out that Mr Shaw's abundance of ideas spoils his plays: I may add as a man that to me it is their great attraction. Moderately good plays do not amuse me, clever quips and flashes do amuse me. If Mr Shaw were to repeat *You Never Can Tell* for ever, I would go to see it in its latest form whenever it appeared. It is refreshing to be addressed from the stage as though one was an intelligent person. Hardly any one else so addresses one. Mr Jones has ideas, but they are the 'advanced' ideas of the last generation, the oldest-fashioned of all ideas. And as for the portraits of fashionable society, as the playwrights see it or wish us to see it, which form the bulk of our so-called comedies, firstly, I do not believe they are good likenesses, and secondly, they are neither comely nor interesting faces. Let Mr Shaw go on and prosper. Prosper? The audience at *You Never Can Tell* shouted with laughter all the time, and possibly some day the laughter will reach the ears of the managers. It is unlikely, but you never can tell.

However, regarded as dramatists, at present Sheridan has over Mr Shaw the advantages I have mentioned—that he wrote plays which are excellent as plays, that he had a distinguished style, and that he encouraged the players. But there is one resemblance which goes very far. The greatest writers of comedy could use normal characters and make them dramatic, entertaining, or what they willed. Sheridan was not one of them, and he was content to exploit eccentricity. Mr Shaw is not one of them (at present), and his eye is for eccentricity exclusively. He thinks it is not, as one of his characters would say, but it is. Even the characters he designs to be normal and a contrast to his eccentrics he makes eccentrically normal. Consequently in this respect— and it is most important—one's amusement in seeing his plays is just the same as one's amusement would have been in seeing Sheridan's if one had been Sheridan's contemporary. The sentimental schoolgirl in *The Rivals* is on precisely the same plane as the woman in *You Never Can Tell* who was 'advanced' in the sixties and believes herself to be 'advanced' still. Only Lydia Languish is gone from real life and in watching Mrs Clandon my mind strayed to Mr H. A. Jones. That is the added advantage of actuality. Lucky Mr Shaw!

CAPTAIN BRASSBOUND'S CONVERSION

1899

Captain Brassbound's Conversion was written by Shaw with Ellen Terry in mind for the leading part of Lady Cicely Waynflete but, in the first production, by the Stage Society for a single performance at the Strand Theatre, London, on 16 December 1900 (repeated at the Criterion Theatre on 20 December) the role was played by Janet Achurch. Ellen Terry did not appear in the play until it was produced at the Court Theatre in 1906.

18. William Archer, notice, *World*

26 December 1900, 7382, 25

Archer comments on the failure of managers to realise how successful Shaw's plays would be if presented in the commercial theatres.

This is not the occasion for a detailed criticism of *Captain Brassbound's Conversion*, an 'Adventure in Three Acts,' by Mr. George Bernard Shaw. The Stage Society production of the play was in many respects meritorious; but both in mounting and in acting it fell a good deal short of that even completeness which is necessary to give such a piece its full effect. I prefer, then, to await another opportunity, which surely cannot be long delayed, for discussing the individual merits and defects of the comedy. For the present, I shall merely ask again the question that seems to me more inexplicable each time a play of Mr. Shaw's is performed: why is it that the West-End managers leave these irresistibly delightful pieces to Independent Theatres, Stage Societies, the suburbs, the provinces and America, instead of competing for the honour and profit of being the first to set in motion the inevitable Shaw 'boom'? Mr. Shaw has now produced four plays, *Candida, You Never Can Tell, The Devil's Disciple* and *Captain Brassbound's Conversion*, every one of which, produced in the right way and by the right people, has a big money success in it; but none of our haughty managers will stoop to pick up the filthy lucre that is lying before their very noses. There is something admirable in their devotion to their cast-iron ideal of what a play should be. Mr. Shaw's work has certain peculiarities—eccentricities if you will—which conflict with that ideal; therefore they will have nothing to do with it. They will succeed by rule or fail by rule; they scorn to snatch success by methods which they do not quite understand. It is useless to tell them that audiences of every class simply revel in the ingenious and witty whimsicality of these plays, whenever they get a chance of seeing them. No—Mr. Shaw is a person who does not respect the conventional canons of dramatic authorship. You can never be quite sure whether, or how far, he is serious; and that is, in managerial eyes, an unpardonable sin. He mixes comedy with melodrama, philosophy with farce; and however delightful the mixture may be, the managers will not countenance any such hybrid product. Their attitude is noble, dignified, high-toned to a degree—but it is not policy, it is not business.

Though *Captain Brassbound's Conversion* is not by any means the best of Mr. Shaw's plays—though it oscillates fantastically between melodrama and extravaganza—though it sins against all sorts of rules and precedents and prejudices—the one incontrovertible fact remains that it is from first to last an intensely exhilarating, stimulating entertainment, the work of a thinker and a humorist who happens also to have a peculiar and original faculty for putting his satiric inventions in theatrical form. It is a draught of intellectual champagne, delicate enough for the most refined taste, yet not too 'dry' for the popular palate. Give it the ordinary advantages of a picturesque setting, thorough study and rehearsal, and the prestige of an established management, and the chances are twenty to one that it would draw all London. Put them even at five to one, and that is longer odds in its favour than can be claimed for the average West-End production; yet no manager is found to try the experiment. Mr. Forbes-Robertson, it may be said, has produced *The Devil's Disciple*. Yes; but he carefully refrained from giving it what I have called the ordinary advantages of a West-End production. He kept it pigeon-holed while he had a London theatre, and then produced it, unostentatiously, almost apologetically, in the country. How it has succeeded I do not know I read somewhere that at Kennington it drew much better houses than *Hamlet*, and when I went to see it at the Coronet Theatre, Bayswater, I found the house crammed and could not get in. It seems, then, that the provincial and suburban public found out for themselves what a delightful play it is, without the preliminary advertisement of a West-End production. Nevertheless the fact remains that Mr. Robertson put it to an unfair test. What would have been its success had it been given the chances that managers accord so lavishly to *Swashbucklers* and *Seconds in Command*? And what would have been the fate of *The Second in Command* had it been produced in the same half-hearted, hole-and-corner-fashion?

The reader probably thinks me absurdly dogmatic in predicting popularity for Mr. Shaw's work. It is proverbially impossible for any one to foretell with certainty the fate of any play. But please observe that in this case I am not merely backing my own judgment. I am basing my prediction, if so it can be called, on my observation of the unfeigned, unmistakable pleasure which these plays of Mr. Shaw's give to their audiences. 'Yes,' it may be said, 'to the special coterie-audience of the Stage Society!' Not at all; it happens that *Captain Brassbound* is the only play of Mr. Shaw's that I have seen presented at a coterie theatre. *The Devil's Disciple* I saw when it was produced by Mr. Carson before an ordinary suburban audience at Kennington; *You Never Can Tell* at a Strand matinée with nothing esoteric about it. In both these cases (in spite of obvious flaws in the acting) the enjoyment of the audience was as complete as at the Stage Society performance. That is the point which it seems impossible to make managers realise: say what you will of them (and they are open to any amount of criticism) these plays have been proved by actual experiment, and in the teeth of all sorts of external disadvantages, to be among the most *enjoyable* entertainments at present on the stage. Is it, then, so very rash to predict that there is a nice little harvest awaiting the manager who shall remove those external advantages and give the plays a reasonable chance?

THREE PLAYS FOR PURITANS

published 1901

Three Plays for Puritans, comprising *The Devil's Disciple*, *Caesar and Cleopatra* and *Captain Brassbound's Conversion*, were published in one volume in 1901. The publisher was Grant Richards, to whom Shaw wrote on 15 January 1905, reminding him that the agreement for publication of the volume 'was for 2500 copies only; and you have had that number printed.'

19. Arnold Bennett, review, *Academy*

February 1901

Arnold Bennett (1867–1931), later to be famous as novelist and critic, wrote this review of *Three Plays for Puritans* when he was still little known. The article appeared in the *Academy*, 9 February 1901, 127, with the title, 'George Bernard Shaw. An Enquiry'. Bennett later wrote plays himself but without great success. In *The Author's Craft* (1914), he made some comments about the ease of writing plays as compared with novels. This led to a correspondence with Shaw (see 'Arnold Bennett: Shaw's Ten O'Clock Scholar' by Kinley Roby, *Shaw Review*, XIII, September 1970, 96).

Upon the conclusion of the first performance of *Arms and the Man* at the Avenue Theatre, Mr. Shaw was called before the curtain by an audience of enraptured *dilettanti*. At the very moment of the author's appearance a lone man in the gallery gave utterance to a loud and inimical 'Boo!' Mr. Shaw nonchalantly raised his head,

> And with a look made of all sweet accord,

remarked, 'I rather agree with you, my friend.' It was an admirable instance of his impassive coolness under fire, his instantaneity of retort and his aptitude for saying what he does not mean. To these qualities Mr. Shaw owes much, if not most, of his popular reputation. He has finer qualities, the love of justice and the hatred of shams, but a popular reputation is not to be built on such characteristics; and had it not been for his extraordinary debating skill, Mr. Shaw, despite many excellences, would have remained to this day unappreciated instead of being as he terms it, a 'legend.' Mr. Shaw was a born debater, whether in speech or in writing. The dialectical *séances* in which he took part at Battersea used to provide one of the prettiest entertainments in London. Far too ambitious to leave nature alone, he has assiduously perfected a natural gift until it has become a formidable and not entirely unrighteous force in the country's intellectual life. The man who measures swords with Mr. Shaw is foredoomed to defeat. His cause may be good, but he will be beaten, and probably rendered ridiculous. One may say of Mr. Shaw, as Macaulay said of Burke: 'In a few scorching words he withered up the arguments of the unfortunate beings who dared to oppose him.' Only Mr. Shaw's words do not scorch, for he is neither an orator nor an enthusiast; they are cold as steel and they cut. The uncontrolled use of great power is always a severe trial of moral strength, and perhaps Mr. Shaw has himself somewhat succumbed to that victorious sword of his; perhaps he is now more its slave than its master. He has developed into a sort of intellectual bravo, a notorious duelist like Paul de Cassagnac, who goes about seeking insults. 'What! You contradict me? I beg you to step this way.' And the victim is led off to execution. There is, in fact, only one effective way of conversing with Mr. Shaw, and that is to assert baldly, to iterate, to reiterate, and absolutely to decline any semblance of argumentative combat.

We have said that he is not an enthusiast. The enthusiast is emotional, like the artist, and neither in Mr. Shaw's speeches nor in his works have we ever observed the slightest trace of emotion. His is a case of intellect almost pure. Every man has some sentiment, but Mr. Shaw has as little as a man may have. He is the indefatigable champion of social justice, not because he has a passion for social justice, but because he has an intellectual perception of it, because his aquiline eyesight instantly sees through all delusions, deceptions, and hypocrisies. His 'unquestioning faith in the power and validity of the intellect' (the phrase is Tolstoi's) is the most pathetic thing about him. Like Tolstoi's

Prince Andrei, 'the impossibility of expressing everything' seems never to have occurred to him, nor the doubt 'whether all that he thought and all that he believed were not vanity.' He has the arrogance which usually accompanies abnormal intellect. He scorns the entire human race, if not for one quality, then for another. His fellow-men will persist in feeling instead of thinking. Such fatuity is nauseous to him; it has, indeed, permanently soured him, so that he spends seven days a week in proving that he is surrounded by fools. And he is. His function—a function brilliantly and usefully fulfilled—is to depreciate human nature, to check its self-satisfactions, prick its bubbles, and drive it out of its paradises; and in this department of activity he is capable single-handed of the work of an entire epoch. One Shaw suffices. That is his *métier*. He thinks he has other trades. He calls himself a critic of the arts, and in particular, just now, of literature. 'Produce me your best critic,' he says in his apology for *The Devil's Disciple*, 'and I will criticise his head off.' Not in the least. Mr. Shaw might decapitate him with that sword, but he would not *criticise* his head off. The first attribute of the critic is sympathy, and Mr. Shaw has never shown sympathy with any of the arts. He has, we admit, explained with delightful and amazing skill the ideological side of certain art works which have an ideological side, such as Wagner's *Nibelung's Ring* and some of Ibsen's plays, but he finds nothing to say about those emotional qualities by virtue of which alone an art work can live. The august dithyrambic joy of a Berlioz in Beethoven or a Swinburne in the Elizabethans, the more sedate and intimate pleasure of a St. Beuve in George Crabbe or a Matthew Arnold in Heine: these are true criticism, but they do not argue, they state; they are the expression not of ideas but of emotions. Speaking of the immortal climax of *Antony and Cleopatra*, Mr. Shaw can only say: 'Shakespeare finally strains all his huge command of rhetoric and stage pathos to give a theatrical sublimity to the wretched end of the business.' He has the piercing vision of the young lady who on first beholding the west front of Westminster Abbey remarked that the clock had stopped. He always searches for the ignoble, never for the noble, and his gift of discovering it is preternatural. The major part of his judgments are worse than false; they are half true.

At the present time Mr. Shaw chooses to come before the world as a playwright. It is his innocuous hobby to be everything. He has been political reformer, novelist, art critic, musical critic, dramatic critic, vestryman—and still follows sundry of these vocations; but at the moment the stage looms largest in his view, and the *dilettanti* are excessively diverted by his *Three Plays for Puritans* (Grant Richards) being the third volume of his collected plays. In his *role* of Admirable Crichton Mr. Shaw succeeds as well at one thing as at another; and we have small doubt that he is as good a playwright as he has been a vestryman, or nearly so. His habit is to write elaborate prefaces, defences, and expositions for his plays. In his justification of *The Devil's Disciple*, the first piece in *Three Plays*, he states that he is a charlatan and a mountebank; but, of course, being after all human, he does not expect the reader to believe that. He also states that he is a 'dramatist of genuine vocation.' He proceeds to explain why he, a dramatist of genuine vocation, finds it necessary to be his own commentator. 'The reason most dramatists do not publish their plays with prefaces is that they cannot write them. . . . I write prefaces as Dryden did, and treatises as Wagner did, because I *can*.' Never was a more tragic blindness than this. The lamentable fact is that Mr. Shaw writes prefaces because he must; because he has so disdainfully neglected technique and the very rudiments of dramatic expression that he cannot say what he wants in the play itself, and is therefore obliged to botch it up with additions in the only medium which he really understands. To cover his own clumsiness he pretends that the reader or the hearer is a person of feeble or undeveloped mind who needs a guide through the marvellous subtleties of the Shaw genius. As the Clarendon Press issues a *Shakespeare for Schools*, so he feigns to issue a *Shaw for Asylums*. He talks at large of the philosophy and the tendencies of his plays when he should be employed in taking lessons from a competent dramatist—a dramatist who has learnt his business, not patronised it. In not one of Mr. Shaw's plays will the technique bear an instant's examination. A glance, for example, at *The Devil's Disciple* shows that after beginning the play in the usual manner in the first act, he begins it again in the second; the first act is wasted. The principal situation in the second act and the principal situation in the third are the tawdriest of venerable devices, disclosing absolute poverty of invention. Half the characters are useless to the action; and the whole affair, in essence, is an amorphous mass of melodrama and sheer sentimentality of the most British kind.

One might still be hopeful for Mr. Shaw's future as a dramatist, despite his present incompetence, if there was any hint in his plays of creative power. But there is no such hint. Neither a character nor a scene is realised: just as the author was never moved in writing them, so the reader is never moved in reading them. From end to end they are concoctions, in which everything is subordinated to the statement of an idea and the dazzling exchange of repartee. 'The drama,' he says, 'can never be anything more than the play of ideas'! That depends on what you mean by an idea. The De Goncourts once remarked that ideas were the curse of modern art, and they were right. Art, including dramatic art, it cannot be too often repeated, is a business of emotion, and the intensity and grandeur of its emotion are the measure of its greatness. Ideas! Mr. Shaw has often railed at Shakespeare because his ideas are so ordinary, his philosophy so obvious. Mr. Shaw is fertile of original ideas, he is a master of dialectics; his wit is unflagging, and he can shoot out damaging retorts like a Maxim gun. It would be strange, therefore, if he could not write amusing and edifying dialogue. He can. His dialogue is a continual feast; it reminds one of the old transpontine days at Battersea. But to cut it up into lengths and call it a play is simple effrontery. The dialogue is the mere exterior of a play, the part one does last, when the hard creative work is accomplished. Mr. Shaw's stage-pieces may be genius; careful critics have said so; but they are decidedly not drama. They might more correctly be called the Joseph's coat of a non-existent Joseph; fine raiment resembling a man until you poke it where the ribs ought to be.

The relation of this brilliant and wayward intellect to the general stolid public is a curious one. The public regard him as a sort of tse-tse fly, that will not leave them alone. Buzz! Buzz! That man Shaw again, stinging us, piercing our masks, oversetting our ideals, and making us highly uncomfortable! In many quarters he is looked on as an Enemy of the British Race, who ought to be exiled to St. Helena in keeping of some literary knight. But the public, great simple souls, do not know what is good for them.

20. J. G. Huneker on Shaw as 'a better bishop than a playwright'

May 1901

From a review of *Three Plays for Puritans* in the *Musical Courier* (New York), 15 May 1901, XLII, 22.

James Gibbons Huneker (1857–1921) was a leading critic of music and drama for several American periodicals, including the *New York Recorder*, for which he wrote a review of *Arms and the Man* in 1894, with the title, 'A Music Critic's Play'. He claimed to have introduced Shaw to America and before he became established as a playwright, Huneker defended him against attacks by other critics. In a chapter on Shaw in *Iconoclasts: a Book of Dramatists* (New York, 1905), Huneker wrote that the prefaces to Shaw's plays 'are literature, and will be remembered with joy when the plays are forgotten'. He later edited a selection of Shaw's dramatic criticisms.

It is the old Shaw masquerading again, this time behind the footlights. He is still the preacher, the debater of the Fabian Society, the socialist, vegetarian, lycanthrope and Irishman of the early days. . . . He can't be radical enough for me, for his admirers, for the tribes of persons he has educated to think for themselves. What I object to is using an art form—as a vehicle for instruction, for the dissemination of Shaw doctrines. . . . [He] has translated into Shawese the ideas of Ibsen, Fourier, Nietzsche, Wagner and other heroes of Continental thought. He is not himself either a profound or an original thinker. . . . His plays are sermons—clever, rollicking, crazy, sincere, witty, brilliant and perverse—withal sermons. . . . He is a better bishop than a playwright.

MAN AND SUPERMAN

1902

Man and Superman was written in 1901 and 1902. It was published in 1903. The play was first produced at the Royal Court Theatre on 21 May 1905 by the Stage Society. There were two performances, but the play was then presented in public by Vedrenne and Barker at the same theatre on 23 May 1905, for twelve matinées. All these performances were without Act III ('Don Juan in Hell').

21. G. K. Chesterton, review, *Daily News*

22 August 1903, 8

Gilbert Keith Chesterton (1874-1936), essayist, critic, poet and novelist, was a friend and adversary of Shaw. He was never close to Shaw in fundamental beliefs but greatly admired his wit and style. The feelings were reciprocated and this review is valuable as one of the earliest in which one of the two writers considered the work of the other. Chesterton's article, which was signed, with the title 'Man v The Superman', concentrated on some of the non-dramatic features of the play and the other material published with it. In his criticism of Shaw, Chesterton was always to return paradox for paradox and his sustained analysis of Shaw, *George Bernard Shaw*, which was published in 1909, impressed Shaw himself as the best 'work of literary art I have yet provoked' although he disagreed with many of the opinions and judgments that it contained.

I wrote last week some rambling remarks about how often scientific men treat from the outside, as oddities, things which they could treat from the inside as ordinary human tendencies. And, oddly enough, I find this very error in the best book that is likely to come out for some time, Mr Bernard Shaw's new play, *Man and Superman*. To attack the play would require a volume, and to praise it a library: I have no intention of doing either. It is concerned, as most people know, with the idea that a man and a woman marry, or should marry, chiefly to produce the higher type—the Superman. The hero is an anti-marriage philosopher, who is forced into marriage by the Life-force, and seems to me, I admit, to be simply doing artificially what most people do naturally. But I do not want to write about that now. The passage that reminded me of the scientists comes in the delightful 'Revolutionist's Handbook' at the end of the play. It is too long to quote, but the keynote may be given in the sentence: 'The modern gentleman who is too lazy to daub his face with vermilion as a symbol of bravery employs a laundress to daub his shirt with starch as a symbol of cleanliness'. Now, I should put this exactly the other way round. I should say that the same noble instinct to pay a ritual respect to others which we obey when we wear white linen might be seen in the savage when he paints his face a beautiful red. He thinks the gentleman a savage. I simply think the savage a gentleman. He says, 'Look at this vermilion and this starch. We have always been barbarous'. I say, 'Look at this starch and this vermilion. We have always been civilized'.

It is the same, of course, throughout the passage. Mr Shaw says that our medical cures are as much hocus-pocus as the old necromancy or miracle. I should say rather that most of our cures are what theirs were and professed to be, faith cures. He would think modern national feeling as brutal as that of a tribe: I should say the tribe had all the folly and all the heroism of a nation. But the real difference between us requires a broader statement.

I feel that in this fascinating and delightful play Mr Shaw has betrayed and embodied at last his one mistake. He has always prided himself on seeing things and men as they are. He has never really done so: as one might have guessed from his not admiring them. The truth is that he has all the time been silently comparing humanity with something that was not human, with a monster from Mars, with the Wise Man of the Stoics, with Julius Caesar, with Siegfried, with the Superman. But that is not seeing things as they are. It is not seeing things as they are to think first of a Briarius with a hundred hands and then see man as a cripple. It is not seeing things as they are to think first of an Argus with a hundred eyes and then look at the man in the street as if he were a man with one eye. It is not seeing things as they are to imagine a demi-god of complete mental clarity and then see all men as idiots. And this is what Mr Shaw has always secretly done. When we really see men as they are, we do not criticise, but worship; and very rightly. For a creature with miraculous eyes and miraculous thumbs, with strange dreams in his skull and a queer tenderness in his heart for this place or that baby, is really a stupendous and splendid thing. It is the quite arbitrary and priggish habit of comparison that makes us look down on ordinary things; not the facts of the case. It is the fact that every instant of conscious life is an unimaginable marvel. It is the fact that every face in the street has the incredible unexpectedness of a fairy tale. Mr Shaw, in the tone of this play, falls in some degree at least into the great weakness of his master, Nietzsche, which was the strange notion that the greater and stronger a man was, the more he would scorn common men. The greater and stronger a man is, the more he would feel an inclination to worship a periwinkle. That Mr Shaw finds democracy a failure, patriotism an imposture, love a debauch, chivalry a lie, family feeling a fiction, all this does not convince me (though there is a truth in all of it) that he has seen things as they are. But suppose I were to meet Mr Shaw in the street, and he did not see me because he was looking at his feet. And suppose as I drew near I heard him murmuring to himself, 'What are these two beautiful and industrious beings that I see always when I look at the ground, advancing, first one and then the other? What reason have they for serving me? What fairy godmother bade them come trotting out of elf-land when I was made? What god of the borderland have I to propitiate with fire and wine lest they suddenly run away with me? Let me erect an altar to the God of Legs'. Very likely Mr Shaw would run into a lamp-post. But I should know he was seeing things as they are.

And here comes in what is perhaps the most interesting of all the bewilderingly interesting things that Mr Shaw talks about in 'The Revolutionist's Handbook' appended to this play—the question of 'progress' – 'this goose-cackle about progress' as he calls it. He says that it is overwhelmingly probable that there has been no progress since the Greek age. Without going adequately into that side issue, I will admit it is highly possible that there has not. But then comes in the most interesting and abysmal difference between the deductions we draw. Mr Shaw says: 'Man as he is, never will nor can add a cubit to his stature by any of its quackeries'. Therefore, Mr Shaw infers, let us breed some bigger, braver, wiser animal with all speed, for the present condition is unbearable. I say 'If man will not progress he will stop as he is, in which state I find him very delightful'. This is not because I have any illusions about what he is. It is simply a matter of taste—like being fond of cats. But what Mr Shaw has to understand is that there is such a thing as being fond of humanity. Not wishing to make it better, like a Sunday school teacher. Not thinking it the only rational object of service, like a positivist philosopher. Not being sorry for its brute pains, like any decent man with a dying rat. But being powerfully and incurably fond of the old unaltered, fighting, beer-drinking, creed-making, child-loving, affectionate, selfish, unreasonable, respectable man. That is Christianity; that is democracy; and they can neither of them be failures, for they are purely spiritual and no one can reckon what difference they have made to the spirit. The whole issue is whether we see in this two-legged man a positive marvel or a negative result. Whitman loved him; Nietzsche detested him. Christ, when He was founding a Universal Church, chose, and that Church chose after Him, for its head neither the brilliant Paul nor the mystic John, but a fool, a boaster, a coward, a liar, a snob, a denier of the truth—in short, an ordinary man. And upon that rock He has built His Church, and the gates of hell shall not prevail against it.

It would seem odd to compare Mr Shaw to the meanest sort of Christian apologists. But this way of speaking of human improvement affects me very much in the same way as the attempts that the religious sometimes make to badger the sceptic into a faith in immortality. One set of people says, 'If there be a hereafter, we are lost'. Mr Shaw says, 'If there be no Superman, we are lost'. I beg respectfully, and without undue egoism, to state that I am not lost. I hope and think there is a future for the soul; I hope and think there is a future for the race; I hope there will be a Superman—it might be fun. But nothing will induce me to say that a child or a brass band or a baked potato are bad because there are not other things that would be good. If the Superman descends on us I think it will be while we are praising these things—while we are on the crest of the ancient ecstasies. And if he does not, I shall not lose much sleep. He may be impossible; that does not touch what interests me most. I am not impossible; that is sufficiently extraordinary.

22. Max Beerbohm, review, *Saturday Review*

12 September 1903, vol. 96, 329

Reprinted in *Around Theatres* (1953); 268. The review was published
with the title, 'Mr. Shaw's New Dialogues'.

Aristotle, often as he sneered at Plato, never called Plato a dramatist,
and did not drag the Platonic dialogues into his dramatic criticism. Nor
did Plato himself profess to be a dramatist; and it would need a wide
stretch of fancy to think of him dedicating one of his works to Aristotle
as notable expert in dramatic criticism. On the other hand, here is
Mr. Bernard Shaw dedicating his new book to 'my dear Walkley,' that
pious custodian of the Aristotelian flame, and arguing, with Platonic
subtlety, that this new book contains a play. Odd! For to drama Mr.
Shaw and Plato stand in almost exactly the same relation. Plato,
through anxiety that his work should be read, and his message accepted,
so far mortified his strongly Puritan instincts as to give a setting of
bright human colour to his abstract thought. He invented men of flesh
and blood, to talk for him, and put them against realistic backgrounds.
And thus he gained, and still retains, 'a public.' Only, his method was
fraught with nemesis, and he is generally regarded as a poet—he, who
couldn't abide poets. Essentially, he was no more a poet than he was a
dramatist, or than Mr. Shaw is a dramatist. Like him, and unlike
Aristotle, for whom the exercise of thought was an end in itself, and
who, therefore, did not attempt to bedeck as a decoy the form of his
expression, Mr. Shaw is an ardent humanitarian. He wants to save us.
So he gilds the pill richly. He does not, indeed, invent men of flesh and
blood, to talk for him. There, where Plato succeeded, he fails, I must
confess. But he assumes various disguises, and he ventriloquises, and
moves against realistic backgrounds. In one direction he goes further
than Plato. He weaves more of a story round the interlocutors. Suppose
that in the *Republic*, for example, there were 'Socrates (in love with
Aspasia),' 'Glaucon (in love with Xanthippe),' etcetera, and then you

have in your mind a very fair equivalent for what Mr. Shaw writes and calls a play. This peculiar article is, of course, not a play at all. It is 'as good as a play'—infinitely better, to my peculiar taste, than any play I have ever read or seen enacted. But a play it is not. What is a dramatist? Principally, a man who delights in watching, and can portray, the world as it is, and the various conflicts of men and women as they are. Such a man has, besides the joy of sheer contemplation, joy in the technique of his art—how to express everything most precisely and perfectly, most worthily of the splendid theme. He may have a message to deliver. Or he may have none. *C'est selon*.[1] But the message is never a tyrannous preoccupation. When the creative and the critical faculty exist in one man, the lesser is perforce over-shadowed by the greater. Mr. Shaw knows well—how could so keen a critic fail to detect?— that he is a critic, and not a creator at all. But, for the purpose which I have explained, he must needs pretend through Mr. Walkley, who won't believe, to an innocent public which may believe, that his pen runs away with him. 'Woman projecting herself dramatically by my hands (a process over which I have no control).' A touching fib! The only things which Mr. Shaw cannot consciously control in himself are his sense of humour and his sense of reason. 'The man who listens to Reason is lost: Reason enslaves all whose minds are not strong enough to master her.' That is one of many fine and profound aphorisms printed at the end of the book, and written (one suspects) joyously, as a private antidote to the dramatic tomfoolery to which Mr. Shaw had perforce condescended. Well! Mr. Shaw will never be manumitted by Reason. She is as inexorable an owner of him as is Humour, and a less kind owner, in that she does prevent him from seeing the world as it is, while Humour, not preventing him from being quite serious, merely prevents stupid people seeing how serious he is. Mr. Shaw is always trying to prove this or that thesis, and the result is that his characters (so soon as he differentiates them, ever so little, from himself) are the merest diagrams. Having no sense for life, he has, necessarily, no sense for art. It would be strange, indeed, if he could succeed in that on which he is always pouring a very sincere contempt. 'For art's sake alone,' he declares, 'I would not face the toil of writing a single sentence.' That is no fib. Take away his moral purpose and his lust for dialectic, and Mr. Shaw would put neither pen to paper nor mouth to meeting, and we should be by so much the duller. But had you taken away from Bunyan or Ibsen or any other of those great artists whom Mr. Shaw,

[1] It all depends.

because they had 'something to say,' is always throwing so violently at our heads, they would have yet created, from sheer joy in life as it was and in art as it could become through their handling of it. Mr. Shaw, using art merely as a means of making people listen to him, naturally lays hands on the kind that appeals most quickly to the greatest number of people. There is something splendid in the contempt with which he uses as the vehicle for his thesis a conventional love-chase, with motors and comic brigands thrown in. He is as eager to be a popular dramatist and as willing to demean himself in any way that may help him to the goal, as was (say) the late Mr. Pettitt. I hope he will reach the goal. It is only the theatrical managers who stand between him and the off-chance of a real popular success. But if these managers cannot be shaken from their obstinate timidity, I hope that Mr. Shaw, realising that the general public is as loth to read plays as to read books of undiluted philosophy, will cease to dabble in an art which he abhors. Let him always, by all means, use the form of dialogue—that form through which, more conveniently than through any other, every side of a subject can be laid bare to our intelligence. It is, moreover, a form of which Mr. Shaw is a master. In swiftness, tenseness and lucidity of dialogue no living writer can touch the hem of Mr. Shaw's garment. In *Man and Superman* every phrase rings and flashes. Here, though Mr. Shaw will be angry with me, is perfect art. In Mr. Shaw as an essayist I cannot take so whole-hearted a delight. Both in construction and in style his essays seem to me more akin to the art of oral debating than of literary exposition. That is because he trained himself to speak before he trained himself to write. And it is, doubtless, by reason of that same priority that he excels in writing words to be spoken by the human voice or to be read as though they were so spoken.

[There follows an examination of the characters of John Tanner and Ann Whitefield.]

We can no more be charmed by them than we can believe in them. Ann Whitefield is a minx. John Tanner is a prig. Prig versus Minx, with the gloves off, and Prig floored in every round – there you have Mr. Shaw's customary formula for drama; and he works it out duly in *Man and Superman*. The main difference between this play and the others is that the minx and the prig are conscious not merely of their intellects, but of 'the Life Force'. Of this they regard themselves, with comparative modesty, as the automatic instruments. They are wrong. The Life Force could find no use for them. They are not human enough, not alive enough. That is the main drawback for a dramatist who does not love raw life: he cannot create living human characters.

And yet it is on such characters as John and Ann that Mr. Shaw founds his hopes for the future of humanity. If we are very good, we *may* be given the Superman. If we are very scientific, and keep a sharp look out on our instincts, and use them just as our intellects shall prescribe, we *may* produce a race worthy to walk this fair earth. That is the hope with which we are to buoy ourselves up. It is a forlorn one. Man may, in the course of aeons, evolve into something better than now he is. But the process will not be less unconscious than long. Reason and instinct have an inveterate habit of cancelling each other. If the world were governed by reason, it would not long be inhabited. Life is a muddle. It seems a brilliant muddle, if you are an optimist; a dull one, if you aren't; but in neither case can you deny that it is the muddlers who keep it going. The thinkers cannot help it at all. They are detached from 'the Life Force'. If they could turn their fellow-creatures into thinkers like themselves, all would be up. Fortunately, or unfortunately, they have not that power. The course of history has often been turned by sentiment but by thought never. The thinkers are but valuable ornaments. A safe place is assigned to them on the world's mantelpiece, while humanity basks and blinks stupidly on the hearth, warming itself in the glow of the Life Force.

On that mantelpiece Mr. Shaw deserves a place of honour. He is a very brilliant ornament. And never have his ornamental qualities shone more brightly than in this latest book. Never has he thought more clearly or more wrongly, and never has he displayed better his genius for dialectic, and never has his humour gushed forth in such sudden natural torrents. This is his masterpiece, so far. Treasure it as the most complete expression of the most distinct personality in current literature. Treasure it, too, as a work of specific art, in line with your Plato and Lucian and Landor.

23. F. G. Bettany in an unsigned review, *Athenaeum*

26 September 1903, 3961, 422

The reviewer fears that Shaw's tendency to write at great length may incur the 'risk of begetting weariness in those he has been accustomed to exhilarate'.

Mr. Shaw's voice is that of 'one crying in the wilderness.' It is becoming that also of one who thinks he shall 'be heard for his much speaking.' In play after play he has satirized or libelled humanity, and in so doing he has contributed largely to its amusement, but in no perceptible degree to its amendment. This is doubtless as it should be, and his protests against the derision with which his professed desire to be taken seriously is greeted form part of his method. In *Man and Superman* he carries his theories to extremes, and incurs something more than a risk of begetting weariness in those he has been accustomed to exhilarate.

Having in mind the *Celestina* of Fernando de Rojas, with its twenty-one acts, Mr. Swinburne's *Bothwell*, Bailey's *Festus*, Victor Hugo's *Cromwell*, and some of the adaptations from Dumas père, we dare not describe *Man and Superman* as the longest of plays. We may not even pronounce it unactable, since it has been, the author tells us, 'publicly performed within the United Kingdom.' We will content ourselves, then, with calling it the longest joke on record, the most sustained composition that was ever written with the tongue in the cheek. Including the epistle dedicatory to Mr. Arthur Bingham Walkley, by whom the composition of the work is allegedly inspired, and 'The Revolutionist's Handbook,' mention of which is somewhat clumsily lugged into the action, the 'Handbook' itself forming an appendix or epilogue, *Man and Superman* occupies over 280 closely printed pages, a few of which advocate a species of fantastic Socialism intended for philosophy, while the vast majority consist of satire or banter of the kind popularized in Mr. Gilbert's *Engaged*.

Concerning the genesis of the book, Mr. Shaw tells us in the afore-mentioned epistle dedicatory—at the head of every other page of which Mr. Arthur Bingham Walkley's name is printed *in extenso*—that he wrote a play on the subject of Don Juan simply because Mr. Walkley asked him so to do, an example of affable acquiescence in suggestion that conveys a new and alarming idea of the possible responsibility of light-hearted demand. Don Juan, as represented in *El Burlador de Sevilla* of Gabriel Tellez, *Le Festin de Pierre* of Molière, or *Il Don Giovanni* of Da Ponte, has very little to do with Mr. Shaw's play, the only point of likeness to any of these being that during a portion of the third act Jack Tanner (who, as the mouthpiece of the author's cynical observations, stands for the author himself), Ann Whitefield, the heroine, and Octavius Robinson assume respectively, in the course of a sort of dream interlude, the appearance, and, in a burlesque fashion, the characters, of Don Juan Tenorio, Doña Ana de Ulloa, and Ottavio, and with the accession of the Devil (who may possibly come from Bailey or Miss Marie Corelli, but has a resemblance to Mendoza, a leader of brigands controlled by a syndicate) and a marble statue (in whom may be found intimations of Roebuck Ramsden, one of Ann's guardians), have a friendly gossip over the dulness of heaven and the comparative vivacity of hell. What is said in the course of the discussions which ensue is intended, apparently, to shock, but fails in its aim, being simply funny and frivolous.

[Quotes passages of dialogue from the Hell scene and elsewhere in the play and 'half-truths in the guise of epigrams' from 'The Revolutionist's Handbook'.]

Mr. Shaw is on familiar ground when he says that

'the lines put into the actor's mouth to indicate the fact that Hamlet is a philosopher are for the most part mere harmonious platitude which, with a little debasement of the word-music, would be properer to Pecksniff.

He occupies a new *terrain* when he confesses his disillusionment on such subjects as 'education, progress, and so forth.' It will be, however, a subject for regret if ever Mr. Shaw repents him in earnest of a flippancy which is better than much earnestness, and substitutes a world of fact for that of fantasy, over which his rule is absolute.

24. E. A. Baughan, initialled notice, *Daily News*

24 May 1905, 18465, 4

E. A. Baughan (1865–1938), was a leading dramatic critic of the time and appears, under the pseudonym of 'Vaughan' in the induction to *Fanny's First Play*.

With all his wit, quickness of perception, insight into character, and faithful yet humorous observation, there is something wanting in the composition of Mr. Bernard Shaw. He amazes one by the narrowness and, I am bold enough to say, the shallowness of his outlook on life. He is an anæmic idealist who has arrived at disgust through his idealism lacking human warmth and reality. A dramatist, after all, cannot express more than he knows or can deduce from his feeling and knowledge. Mr. Shaw, to judge from all his plays except *Candida*, has a singular and unenviable knowledge of women. He has seen a certain type, such as Gloria in *You Never Can Tell* and Ann in *Man and Superman*, and has seen her clearly; he has grasped some of the effects of the disproportion between the number of women and men in England, and from those accidental facts constructs a view of life which is only true in a parochial sense.

In *Man and Superman* he elaborates this idea, and makes woman the hunter of men. His Ann is deceitful, a coquette, at bottom a sensualist, a liar, and cruel withal. His John Tanner is a Don Juan, who is defenceless against the wiles of the man-hunter, because he has no illusions as to her character. He is also defenceless because he has no will or passions of his own, or anything but the gift of the gab. Another woman, Violet Ramsden, is cool-headed, calculating, selfish. A third, Ann's mother, is shrewdly weak, a woman who uses her weakness as a defence. Possibly such types exist, but Mr. Bernard Shaw cannot expect us to accept them just as characters, for the whole play has 'tendency' writ large upon it. And it is just here that Mr. Shaw shows his limitations of outlook, I had almost written his commonness of mind, for narrowness of vision is the mother of commonness, when humour comes to its interpretation. This is the more extraordinary because Mr. Shaw is far from being a man of common mind. But he cannot resist being humorous, and his humour often leads him into writing things which he must know are not far removed from the witticisms of the bar parlour.

That is the atmosphere of this *Man and Superman*. Mr. Shaw has dealt with the sex question just as if he were a suburban Don Juan who does not recognise in his successful adventures the effect of an over-population of women. There is actually a rather hideous chuckle in the play. Mr. Shaw has not been able to distinguish between the nature of women and the effect on it of a curious social accident. It is true that many women scheme to marry partly because there is not a man for each, but mainly because they have no other livelihood—or rather had not, for Mr. Shaw is growing rather old-fashioned. But it is not true of all women, nor is it true that they look on motherhood as the aim of their life, to be schemed for by dishonourable methods if necessary. That is purely a man's sentimental excuse for himself. It is always uttered and written by men; never by women. Nor is it true that the Home impels women to this course of action. Mr. Shaw is out in his psychology. One of the main faults of our home life in England is that instead of making girls seek a husband it makes them loth to leave its comfort and security. In nature the parent throws out its off-spring at the right moment. Mr. Shaw's home, if it had a general existence, would therefore be natural. Of course, all this is set forth with most entertaining wit, especially when that wit illuminates by pathos and is not employed to drive home Mr. Shaw's main thesis. If you forget that thesis you can have a highly diverting afternoon at the Court Theatre. Even on its questionable side Mr. Shaw's play shows a quite surprising grasp of the mental outlook of his special audience. He may even in time become the comedy writer for men and women who have the modern disease of mental and physical anæmia, for his John Tanner is the prototype of the modern man marred by the preponderance of women. Mr. Granville Barker is hardly the actor one would have chosen for the part, but he carried the thing through remarkably well. Miss Lillah McCarthy was a little artificial now and then, but she had to face the difficulty of conveying a side of Anne's character which is not expressed until the end. Mr. Edmund Gwenn's Henry Straker, a chauffeur who is an amusing product of the Polytechnic system, was quite the hit of the afternoon.

25. A. B. Walkley on *Man and Superman*

1905

Unsigned notice in the *Times Literary Supplement*, 26 May 1905, 176, 170: reprinted in *Drama and Life* (1907), 224.

Walkley examined Shaw's construction and showed how, in his view, the 'action-plot' of the play was 'often trivial and sometimes null'. He did not feel that it was his duty to analyse the 'idea-plot' and found 'the play as a play unsatisfying'.

It has been lately bruited abroad that Mr. Bernard Shaw is a somewhat lukewarm admirer of Shakespeare. If this be so, it is only one more illustration of the familiar gnomic saying of Euripides that there is no enmity so fierce as that of brother against brother. For Mr. Shaw and Shakespeare have at least one conspicuous bond of fraternal relationship; they both use the same stage technique. To Mr. Shaw as to Shakespeare organic plot-development is a matter of indifference, as compared with the systematic exhibition of ideas. They both ignore the *liaison des scènes*[1] with a splendid carelessness, and ruthlessly sacrifice imitation of external life to any passing velleity for propagandism. It is not the same propagandism, of course. Shakespeare's is the propagandism of current morality or beauty or sheer poetry; Mr. Shaw's is the propagandism of paradox or iconoclasm or sheer antinomianism. But the effect on the dramatic form is the same. Hamlet interrupts the action on the platform at Elsinore to expatiate on alcoholism, Gertrude keeps Ophelia's bier waiting in the wings while she gives a 'word picture' of a river bank, John Tanner brings everybody and everything to a standstill (always 'talking,' as Ann pithily puts it) in order to give forth so much of Nietzsche and Schopenhauer as Mr. Shaw has chanced to assimilate. Thus for the sake of something which may be very fine, but certainly is not drama, both dramatists cheerfully let the quintessential drama go hang. Neither of them is, for stage purposes,

[1] Linking of scenes with each other.

a man 'looking before and after'; they are both playhouse Cyrenaics,[1] living in the moment for the moment's sake. This identical result has arisen from very different causes. For Shakespeare there were the limitations and the licence of the platform-stage, together with a tremendous energy of creation which was perpetually driving him outside the bounds of drama. For Mr. Shaw there are his own limitations; he, too, is perpetually energising outside the bounds of drama, and if for a moment he gets inside them it is by a mere fluke. It is piquant to find identity of form so absolute with such a world-wide difference of content. No need, is there, to account for that difference? On the one hand a born dramatist, and that the greatest; on the other a man who is no dramatist at all. Let me not be misunderstood. When I venture to say that Mr. Shaw is no dramatist I do not mean that he fails to interest and stimulate and amuse us in the theatre. Many of us find him more entertaining than any other living writer for the stage. There are many things in his plays that give us far keener thrills of delight (we make a present of this admission to Mr. Sidney Lee) than many things in Shakespeare's plays. But that is because he is bound to be an entertaining writer in any art-form—essay or novel or play. All we mean is that when he happens to choose the play as the form in which he shall entertain us there is a certain artistic waste. There is waste, because Mr. Shaw neglects, or more probably is impotent to fulfil, what Pater calls the responsibility of the artist to his material. You forgive the waste for the sake of the pleasure. Nevertheless, in the interests of good drama, it is one's duty to be dissatisfied. We want a play that shall be a vehicle for the Shavian philosophy and the Shavian talent and, at the same time, a perfect play. Shall we ever get it? Probably not, in this imperfect world. We certainly do not get it in *Man and Superman*.

Had it not been for the typographical inconvenience of the arrangement one might draw up a balance-sheet of this play in two parallel columns. The left-hand column would display the action-plot. We use the term action, of course, in its widest sense, so as to cover not merely the external incident but the psychologic and, more particularly, the emotional movement and 'counterpoint' of the play. The right-hand column would give the idea-plot—that is to say, the more or less logical *nexus* of concepts in the author's mind which form the stuff, the

[1] The Cyrenaics were a school of Greek philosophers, founded by Aristippus of Cyrene, a pupil of Socrates. The Cyrenaics regarded pleasure as the only absolute good in life, but pleasures must be selected and this implies both intelligence and self-control.

real *raison d'être* of the play. Only by that method of sharp visual contrast could one hope to bring to light the masked interdependence of the action-plot and idea-plot and the curious way in which the one is warped and maimed in being made to serve as the vehicle for the other. We should, we think, have been better able to show by the method of parallel columns that the action-plot is well-nigh meaningless without the key of the idea-plot; that regarded as an independent entity it is often trivial and sometimes null; and that it is because of this parasitic nature of the action-plot, because of its weakness, its haphazardness, its unnaturalness, considered as a 'thing in itself,' that one finds the play as a play unsatisfying.

The idea-plot we are not called upon to criticise. In the playhouse a dramatist's ideas are postulates not to be called in question. Theories of Schopenhauer about woman and the sex-instinct or of Nietzsche about a revised system of conduct are most assuredly open to discussion, but not by the dramatic critic. His business is, first and foremost, with the action-plot. For that is what we *see*; it is in fact the play itself, in the sense that it is what is being played under our noses; it is the sum of all the direct appeals to our sensations, before we start the secondary process of inferring and concluding. Now what do we see on the stage of the Court Theatre? What is it that we are asked to accept for an hour or two as part and parcel of our daily human life? We see, first of all, a smug, bald-headed old gentleman who proceeds, *à propos de bottes*,[1] to spout the respectable middle-class Mill-Spencer-Cobden Liberalism of the mid-Victorian age. Then we see him vivaciously 'cheeked' by a youngish, excitable, voluble gentleman, who evidently stands for the latest intellectual 'advance.' The younger man tells us, by and by, that he is a product of Eton and Oxford; but some of us who think we know that product will nourish a secret conviction that he is really, like his *chauffeur*, a product of the Board School and the Polytechnic. He has steeped himself in those fragments of the newest German philosophy which find their way into popular English translations, and he spends his time—mark, the *whole* of his time—in spouting these precious theories. He does this, as he admits, because he has no sense of shame; to put it more simply, he is a young person of rather bad manners. We note—for in the theatre the most trivial detail that we *see* outweighs the most important philosophy that we deduce—that he wears a beard which in a few years' time will resemble Mr. Shaw's; and he has already acquired Mr. Shaw's habit (an apparently deliberate

[1] Without rhyme or reason.

piece of 'business,' and therefore one stands excused for mentioning it)
of combing his beard with his fingers. It is not unfair to assume that
there is as much of Mr. Shaw in Jack Tanner as there is of Shakespeare in Hamlet; and that (if Professor Bradley only knew it!) is saying
a good deal. Casually, this young man lets fall the remark that he is
descended from Don Juan. Why? What is Don Juan doing *dans cette
galère*?[1] That you soon discover when you are introduced to Miss Ann.
For Miss Ann is the new Don Juan, the huntress of men—no, of one
man (that is to say, no Don Juan at all, but for the moment let that pass),
the one man being Jack Tanner. Miss Ann means to marry Jack, though
he does not yet know it. What he does know (from the German) is
that man is the helpless prey of the 'mother woman' through the influence of the 'life force.' This Tanner expounds, in good set Schopenhauerian terms, to a sentimental young man, half engaged to Ann,
alleged to be a 'poet.' 'Alleged' is the word, because this young man's
profession of poet is, for stage purposes, a non-effective force. So far
as the play is concerned the 'poet' might just as well be a drysalter. And
thus it is that, busied as in the theatre we must be with the action-plot,
we are perpetually baffled and pulled up—wondering why Tanner is
descended from Don Juan and why Octavius is alleged to be a poet.
Also we wonder why Tanner lectures poor mild milksopish Octavius
about the devastating egoism of the 'artist man'—how the 'artist man'
is (apparently) the masculine of the 'mother woman,' how they are
twin creators, she of children, he of mind, and how they live only for
that act of creation, so that there is the devil to pay (examples from
literary history) when they happen to become man and wife. This, we
say to ourselves, may be all very true (for have we, too, not browsed in
the Dictionary of National Biography?); but why does Tanner say it
all, just at that moment, to the alleged poet but obvious barber's-
block Octavius? While we are thus racking our brain we are interrup-
ted by a new diversion. Octavius's sister (whom we have never seen or
heard of) is suddenly reported to have 'gone wrong.' Agony of Octavius; glaring reprobation of the 'respectable' types; and coruscation
of Nietzschean fireworks from Tanner. Conventional morality,
humbug! Is motherhood less holy—we beg pardon, less helpful—
because it is motherhood without 'marriage lines'? Etc., etc. (We say
'etc., etc.,' because the worst of Mr. Shaw's cheap German philosophic
baggage is that when you see the first article you know all the rest of
the set beforehand.) But stop; you may spare all trouble over the

1 In this galley (after Molière).

argument. For lo! it is a mistake, a false scent. Octavius's sister proves to be really and truly married. And the curtain of the first act descends upon a group cowering, as Tanner says, before the wedding ring.

Now this, the first section of the action-plot, is of course on the face of it a mere *pot-pourri*, a Caucus race, chaos come again. You have been immensely amused, Cyrenaically enjoying the moment for the moment's sake, but looking before and after (as you cannot help looking in the theatre) you have been disconcerted and *dérouté*.[1] What is the key to the mystery? The key is the idea-plot. Glance at that for a moment and you will see why Octavius is alleged to be a poet and why his sister is falsely alleged to be no better than she should be. (*a*) Fundamental idea: the irresistible power of woman over man in carrying out the aim of nature (or the 'life force') to make her a mother. (*b*) Development: partly in Ann's actions, mainly in Tanner's talk. And there, in that disproportion, at once you touch a dramatic weakness of the play. The properly dramatic development would have thrown all the onus upon Ann—we should have seen Ann energising as the 'mother woman,' and nothing else—and would have kept Tanner's mouth shut. But Mr. Shaw cannot exhibit, or can only feebly exhibit, by character and action; his native preference is for exposition by dialectic and ratiocination—*i.e.* by abstract talk; which is one of the reasons why you conclude he is no dramatist. (*c*) Corollary of the fundamental idea: if motherhood is nature's aim, then marriage is a detail—our morality which brands motherhood *minus* a wedding ring is false. Hence the 'false scent' about Octavius's sister's baby. (*d*) Antithetical question suggested by the fundamental idea: is there not a male counterpart to the 'mother woman'? Mr. Shaw hunts about. Yes, no, yes—it must be, the 'artist man.' Hence the alleged poetic vocation of Octavius, in order that Tanner may have a cue for haranguing him about the 'artist man' and the 'mother woman.' Not otherwise do they insert cues in 'musical comedies' when the time has come for a song or dance. That is one reason why 'musical comedies' are like Mr. Shaw's comedies—*not* comedies. If Mr. Shaw's play were a real play there would be no need to explain the action-plot by laborious reference to the idea-plot. The one would be the natural garment of the other; or rather the one would be the flesh of which the other was the bones. Octavius would be a real poet in the dramatic action (as is, for instance, the case with the poet in *Candida*); there would be no false alarm about Octavius's sister; Ann would exhibit Mr. Shaw's

[1] Confused, thrown off balance.

thesis 'on her own,' instead of by the help of Mr. Jack Tanner's lecture-wand and gift of the gab. In that way we should miss many diverting moments; but only in some such way as that could we get a real play.

We have left ourselves little space for Acts II and III. Fortunately little space is needed. For look again at the idea-plot and you will see that it soon exhausts itself, so that the action-plot, being as we have said a mere parasite of the other, is bound very rapidly to give out. Tanner can only continue to Schopenhauerize, and the moment of his falling into the lady's arms will synchronize with that in which the author is tired of his game and brings down the curtain. The so-called poet peters out; indeed, never existed. His sister is provided with an American husband. Why? *Vide*, once more, idea-plot. The super-chivalric American view of woman, being a contrast to the Schopenhauerian, obviously calls for mention. Hence Mr. Hector Malone. Hence also, indirectly, Mr. Malone senior, American millionaire and ex-Irish emigrant (opportunity for short *bravura* episode about wrongs of Ireland)—a character which—rare mischance with Mr. Shaw!—hovers on the outer edge of the tiresome. All that is left to be done is to emphasise in Ann woman's talent for lying (type-example: Raina in *Arms and the Man*), at the same time getting it neatly hooked on to the Schopenhauerian 'mother woman' theory. We must not forget two subordinate characters—Ann's mother, middle-aged, querulous, helpless in her daughter's hands, and the cockney *chauffeur*, the *fine fleur*[1] of Board School education, Henry Straker. These two small parts, from the point of view of genuine and fresh observation, are among the best things in the play. In them Mr. Shaw has been content to reproduce, instead of deducing. We wish he would more often fall a victim to the same weakness.

[1] Fine flower.

26. William Archer, notice, *World*

30 May 1905, 1613, 914

Every play of Mr. Bernard Shaw's is the result of a collaboration of three distinct personages: the dramatist, the philosopher, and the wit. The dramatist has almost always a bad time of it. He is a clever fellow: in *Candida*, in *The Devil's Disciple*, in parts of *Caesar and Cleopatra*, he did some capital work. But he is held in abject servitude by the other persons of the trinity; they conspire to outvote him at every point. When either the philosopher or the wit chooses to take the stage, the dramatist is simply nowhere. He cannot get a word in edgewise; and, what is worse, he cannot get a word cut out. The trouble is, of course, that he is not really a good dramatist. He has brilliant moments, but no staying-power, no self-assurance, no self-respect—otherwise he would not let himself be overborne in what ought to be his own peculiar domain. The most harmonious effect is produced when he retires altogether from the partnership, as in *John Bull's Other Island*, and lets the philosopher and the wit have it all their own way. In *Man and Superman* he makes a pretence of asserting himself, but it is quite idle. His colleagues stultify him at every turn; and the best thing we can do is to leave him altogether out of account, and regard the play, not as a dramatic representation of anything in nature, but simply as a fantastic allegory.

Of the remaining partners, the wit has always the last word; and this is just as it should be. As between the wit and the dramatist, we are bound, theoretically, to sympathise with the latter, and regret the usurpation which turns him out of his own house, so to speak. But as between the wit and the philosopher, there can be no doubt which ought to be the predominant partner. Mr. Shaw's philosophy can be picked up at any bookstall; his wit is unique, personal, priceless. The wit, in fact, is the man. To wish that he could subordinate it to dramatic consistency and truth is, after all, unreasonable; for it is simply to wish that he were not himself, but someone else. Let us be grateful for him as he is, and go to the Court Theatre and enjoy and applaud him. He is not, and he never will be, a great dramatist; but he is something rarer,

if not better—a philosophic humorist, with the art of expressing himself in dramatic form. It has taken me some time to arrive at this perception. Hitherto I have wrestled earnestly with Mr. Shaw to try to
make a serious playwright of him. *Candida* and some scenes in *Mrs.
Warren's Profession* awakened false hopes in me, and I strove, by a
judicious blending of flattery and insult, to foster the artist in him at
the expense of the humorist. It was a mistake, and I hereby renounce it.
The artist, at his best, was essentially inferior to the humorist. I was
labouring for the survival of the unfittest. Had I succeeded (a preposterous assumption) we should have been the richer by an inferior
Ibsen, the poorer by an individual, inimitable, irritating, tantalising,
incalculable, delightful Shaw. It would have been an unhappy exchange.

We see very clearly in *Man and Superman* one of the main reasons
why Mr. Shaw will never be an artist in drama. It is that his intellect
entirely predominates over, not only his emotions, but his perceptions.
Nothing either in the external world or in human nature has the smallest
interest for him except insofar as it fits into a theory. Nothing exists
for him save as matter for abstraction and generalisation. He has a keen
eye, and an amazingly retentive memory, for everything that he can
coax into a pre-existent mental pattern; but for things in their quiddity,
for character simply as character, and emotion as a fact of experience,
he cares not a straw. This is a repetition in other terms of what I have
so often said before—that Mr. Shaw is an incorrigible apriorist. In
this play he dramatises a purely metaphysical conception of Woman
as a man-devouring monster, relentlessly, perfidiously, indefatigably
executing the behests of a hypothetical Life-Force which bids her
subordinate everything to the continuance of the species. This myth,
for such it is, was invented, or rather popularised, by Schopenhauer,
and it usefully adumbrates a deep-lying truth. It might serve to inspire
a great philosophic poem—a *Pandora* to Shelley's *Prometheus*. But the
metaphysical truth becomes a glaring untruth when stated, as Mr. Shaw
states it, in terms of psychology. The Gulf Stream doubtless sets from
south to north, but do all the waves of the Atlantic therefore flow in the
same direction? No; the surface of the ocean is so buffeted about by
cross-currents and shifting winds that, though the fundamental bias
subsists, its effect on any particular wave is seldom appreciable. Now
the dramatist's business is with the visible billows, not with the un-
sunned depths, of the ocean of humanity. He must paint what can be
painted, what has form and individuality. By all means let the under-
currents be divined in his work, but not dragged to the surface. If he

insists on displaying them, and painting the ocean upside down, he produces, not a picture, but a map or diagram—a *Man and Superman*, in short.

In so far as Ann Whitefield is a credible human being at all, she is an ordinary minx, a little overdrawn. But the ordinary minx is not, as a rule, either consciously or unconsciously, intent on the continuance of the species—she is often very much the reverse. Ann differs from the ordinary minx in the fact that Tanner has lectured her into a sort of acceptance of his theory of her nature and function. She is a little vain of the part for which he casts her, and poses with some complacency as a mythological monster. She does not point out to him that if his theory be correct there is no particular reason why she should prefer him to any other equally personable male who can offer her a comfortable home. Her intense resolve that he, of all men, shall be her husband could no doubt be traced, by a competent psychologist, to numerous instincts and associations which, to the Life-Force, are matters of absolute indifference. But Tanner is no psychologist; he is, like Mr. Shaw, a pure metaphysician. Mounted on his Schopenhauer hobby, he lets it carry him, open-eyed, into a union he detests with a minx whom he despises, simply that Mr. Shaw may write 'Q.E.D.' where the ordinary dramatist would write 'Curtain.' If you want to see the Life-Force in operation, not in the metaphysician's allegoric puppet-show, but in the magic mirror of the poet-psychologist, you must go to the masterworks of Thomas Hardy.

I do not mean to say that there is no observation in the character-drawing of *Man and Superman*. Mr. Shaw could probably give chapter and verse for many traits in his study of the on-coming female and the recalcitrant male. He has observed and remembered whatever fits into his theory; the facts which do not dovetail with it leave no impression on his mind. A typical instance of this apriorism may be found in his return to his old thesis of the unreality of family affection. Mr. Shaw, in the days of his philosophic apprenticeship, conceived a low opinion of the family as a social institution. It became his cue to depreciate it by showing that it was not only an evil, but an hypocrisy; and ever since he has gone on observing the small minority of facts that tally with his preconception, and ignoring the overwhelming majority that contradict it. Family affection may be stupid, anti-social, retrograde; undoubtedly it is often the cause of much sorrow; but the man who denies that it is a reality, and one of the most potent forces in human affairs, simply proclaims the servitude of his vision to his will.

But to argue all the arguable points in *Man and Superman* would be to write a treatise as long as the volume to which Mr Shaw has given that somewhat fantastic name. After what I have said, it is perhaps unnecessary to add that I do not regard the play as a great work of dramatic art, properly so called. But an exceedingly amusing and stimulating entertainment it is beyond all doubt. Mr. Shaw uses the stage as a blackboard to illustrate his lectures on things in general; and not only is he the wittiest of lecturers, but the diagrams he draws on the board are marked by a vivacity of draughtsmanship that makes them, in their own peculiar way, very notable productions.

27. Bertrand Russell on Shaw as 'more bounder than genius'

1904

Extract from letter to Goldsworthy Lowes Dickinson, 20 July 1904: reprinted in *Autobiography*, vol. I (1967), 188.

Bertrand Russell (1872–1970), philosopher and author, was a friend of Shaw for many years. As is clear from this letter, he was not a whole-hearted admirer. He wrote at length about Shaw after his death in the *Virginia Quarterly Review*, vol. 27, Winter 1951, no. 1, and in *Portraits from Memory* (1956), 71. His comments were principally on Shaw as a personality but in the *Virginia Quarterly Review* article, he discussed the plays briefly and said that 'the final judgment upon Shaw will be, I think, that he was enormously useful as a reformer, but that his effectiveness as an artist was, to a large extent, temporary'. In *Portraits from Memory*, his summing up on Shaw was, 'one may say that he did much good and some harm. As an iconoclast he was admirable, but as an eikon rather less so.'

I think Shaw, on the whole, is more bounder than genius; and though of course I admit him to be 'forcible', I don't admit him to be 'moral'. I think envy plays a part in his philosophy in this sense, that if he allowed himself to admit the goodness of things which he lacks and others possess, he would feel such intolerable envy that he would find life unendurable. Also he hates self-control, and makes up theories with a view to proving that self-control is pernicious. I couldn't get on with *Man and Superman*: it disgusted me. I don't think he is a soul in Hell dancing on red-hot iron. I think his Hell is merely diseased vanity and a morbid fear of being laughed at.

JOHN BULL'S OTHER ISLAND

1904

John Bull's Other Island was originally written, in Shaw's words, 'at the request of Mr. William Butler Yeats, as a patriotic contribution to the repertory of the Irish Literary Theatre'. It was found to be 'beyond the resources of the new Abbey Theatre' and the first production was under the Vedrenne–Barker management at the Court Theatre, London, on 1 November 1904, for six matinées. It became one of the most popular plays in the repertory and King Edward VII attended a special performance on 11 March 1905.

28. W. B. Yeats, letter to Shaw

5 October 1904

William Butler Yeats (1865–1939), Irish poet, critic, dramatist and statesman, was a founder, with J. M. Synge and Lady Gregory, of the Irish Literary Theatre. His reactions to earlier work by Shaw had been mixed. In *Autobiographies* (1926), he wrote that he had listened to *Arms and the Man* on the first night in 1894 'with admiration and hatred. It seemed to me inorganic, logical straightness and not the crooked road of life, yet I stood aghast before its energy. . . . Presently I had a nightmare that I was haunted by a sewing-machine, that clicked and shone, but the incredible thing was that the machine smiled, smiled perpetually. Yet I delighted in Shaw, the formidable man.' He wrote to Lady Gregory on 12 March 1900, 'I saw Shaw today. He talks of a play on the contrast between Irish and English character which sounds amusing.' William Fay, of the Irish players, wrote to Yeats saying that the play was 'a wonderful piece of work' but he was doubtful whether it could be performed. When Yeats saw the production at the Court Theatre, London, he wrote to Lady Gregory on 7 November 1904: 'I have seen Shaw's play; it acts very much better than one could have foreseen, but is immensely long. It begins at 2.30 and ends at 6. I don't really like it. It is fundamentally ugly and shapeless, but certainly keeps everybody amused.' (*The Letters of W. B. Yeats*, ed. Allan Wade (1954), 442).

My Dear Shaw: I have been very long about thanking you for the play. I waited until I could give you Fay's opinion and Synge's. I sent the play to Synge the moment I had read it, and he went off to Belmullet, and neither wrote nor sent an address until yesterday. He sent the play back however through a member of the company he met on the way to Belmullet, and I sent it to William Fay, from whom I have heard this morning. I enclose his letter. Synge who is always rather languid in his letter writing tells me very little, except that he will tell me a great deal when we meet next week at rehearsal. Now as to my own opinion.

I was disappointed by the first act and a half. The stage Irishman who wasn't an Irishman was very amusing, but then I said to myself 'What the devil did Shaw mean by all this Union of Hearts-like Conversation? What do we care here in this country, which despite the Act of Union is still an island, about the English liberal party and the Tariff, and the difference between English and Irish character, or whatever else it was all about. Being raw people,' I said, 'we do care about human nature in action, and that he's not giving us.' Then my interest began to awake. That young woman who persuaded that Englishman, full of impulsiveness that comes from a good banking account, that he was drunk on nothing more serious than poteen, was altogether a delight. The motor car too, the choosing the member of Parliament, and so on right to the end, often exciting and mostly to the point. I thought in reading the first act that you had forgotten Ireland, but I found in the other acts that [it] is the only subject on which you are entirely serious. In fact you are so serious that sometimes your seriousness leaps upon the stage, knocks the characters over, and insists on having all the conversation to himself. However the inevitable cutting (the play is as you say immensely too long) is certain to send your seriousness back to the front row of the stalls. You have said things in this play which are entirely true about Ireland, things which nobody has ever said before, and these are the very things that are most part of the action. It astonishes me that you should have been so long in London and yet have remembered so much. To some extent this play is unlike anything you have done before. Hitherto you have taken your situations from melodrama, and called up logic to make them ridiculous. Your process here seems to be quite different, you are taking your situations more from life, you are for the first time trying to get the atmosphere of a place, you have for the first time a geographical conscience. (For instance you have not made the landlords the winning side, as you did the Servians in the first version of *Arms and the Man*.)

Synge who is as good an opinion as I know, thinks that 'it will hold a Dublin audience, and at times move them if even tolerably played.' He thinks however you should cut the Grasshopper, and a scene which I cannot recall, but which he describes as 'the Handy Andy-like scene about carrying the goose' and some of the Englishman's talk about Free Trade, Tariffs, etc. I asked him to make suggestions about cuts, as

I thought that our knowledge of local interests here might be valuable to you. I shall myself have one or two suggestions on details to make, but they can stand over. I have no doubt you will cut in your own way, but you may as well hear them. I had a theory when I was a boy that a play should be very long, and contain a great deal about everything, put in quite without respect to times and occasions, and that every man who played it should take the slice that suited him. I cannot say I hold that theory now, but there is something in it, the two parts of Goethe's *Faust* for instance, and the use all sorts of people make of them. To my surprise I must say, I do not consider the play dangerous. There may be a phrase, but I cannot think of one at this moment. Here again, you show your wonderful knowledge of the country. You have laughed at all the things that are ripe for laughter, and not where the ear is still green. I don't mean to say that there won't be indignation about one thing or another, and a great deal of talk about it all, but I mean that we can play it, and survive to play something else. You will see by Fay's letter that he is nervous about being able to cast it. I imagine the Englishman will give us most difficulty, but it will all be difficult.

I shall be in Dublin next week, and will talk the whole matter over with the company. It would be a help if you could let me know your own feeling about cuts. I will then have the play in my hands again and can go into detail.

Yours sincerely
W. B. Yeats

29. A. B. Walkley on
John Bull's Other Island

1904

From an unsigned notice in *The Times*, 2 November 1904, 37541, 6, reprinted in *Drama and Life* (1907), 219.

'It's all rot,' says Broadbent, the Englishman, of some speech by his Irish friend, Larry Doyle, 'it's all rot, but it's so brilliant, you know.' Here, no doubt, Mr. Shaw is slyly taking a side-glance at the usual English verdict on his own works. That verdict will need some slight modification in the case of *John Bull's Other Island*. For, in the first place, the play is not *all* rot. Further, it has some other qualities than mere brilliancy. It is at once a delight and a disappointment. It delights by its policy of pin-pricks. Mr. Shaw takes up the empty bladders of life, the current commonplaces, the cant phrases, the windbags of rodomontade, the hollow conventions, and the sham sentiments; quietly inserts his pin; and the thing collapses with a pop. Occasionally, he indulges in fiercer onslaughts with more formidable weapons. Like Johnson, after a certain conversation described by Garrick, he has 'tossed and gored several persons.' The play delights, again, by its able dialectic. Its interlocutors never shirk a point or swerve from it; every side gets a fair hearing, and though, in the end, all parties are dismissed with costs, you have a conviction that justice has been done. Englishmen and Irishmen alike get credit for their qualities as well as their defects. As an Irishman Mr. Shaw, perhaps, permits himself to tell us more than any English writer could venture to say about his country-men's weaknesses. There he speaks with authority. Add that Mr. Shaw has, for once, succeeded in depicting a natural and delightful woman. On the other hand the play is a disappointment because of its wilful, perverse disregard of anything like construction. It is written on the 'go-as-you-please' principle, without beginning, middle, or end. People wander in and out quite casually and say whatever happens to come into Mr. Shaw's head at the moment. A rivulet of 'story' meanders through a meadow of 'Shawisms' and trickles dry long before the curtain descends. There is no reason whatever why the play should end when it does—except that Mr. Shaw has had enough of it. We wish he had got tired a little sooner. Before the last act was over yesterday afternoon, our appetite for 'Shawisms' was sated.

30. E. A. Baughan, from a notice, *Daily News*

2 November 1904, 18291, 8

It would have been amusing, if it had been possible, to obtain a plebis-cite of the impressions which Mr Bernard Shaw's contribution to the Irish question made on the audience yesterday afternoon. I have no doubt very few took it seriously, for the tragedy of Mr Shaw's creative life is that his constitutional wit stands in his way. 'It's tommy rot, but it is so brilliant, you know', said his John Bull, as a comment on a long speech on Ireland and the Irish. That, with modifications, was probably the real feeling of those who laughed for nearly two hours and a half yesterday. The play is brimful of wit; it scintillates in every scene, and even tires the mental eyes. No doubt London will be told that *John Bull's Other Island* is essentially Shawesque. The author has written a formless piece of excellent fooling, with just an undercurrent of serious-ness. That verdict would certainly give an idea of the outside of the play. But behind all the wit and the broad humour I caught a glimpse of a Bernard Shaw in the white heat of seriousness. It was very pretty rapier work—the accomplishment of a master—but the rapier had no buttons. Yet it would not be fair to say that the play is merely a treatise on the solution of the Irish question. It is a drama in the sense that the characters utter opinions that are natural from their lips. Mr Shaw is an artist as well as a politician. Indeed, sometimes his sense of art seemed to me to condition his political views. You do not expect any conventional panacea for the sufferings of Ireland from Mr Shaw. He is essentially a destructive and not a constructive critic. In this play every idea and every thing is pierced by his rapier. He even makes a feint of turning his weapon on himself. He satirises the Liberal politician whose interest is purely sentimental, the Irishman who has lived long enough from Ireland to see the faults of his countrymen with clear eyes, and the Irish themselves, who are presented in a variety of types. But the slight love story, which at first seemed so vague and unnecessary that one rather resented it, gives, perhaps, the clue to Mr Shaw's real meaning—a pessimistic meaning, it must be confessed. Mr Shaw employed symbolism with the tact and delicacy of a poet. He has even given a version of the awakening of Brunnhilde by Siegfried. But what a Siegfried!

31. William Archer, notice, *World*

8 November 1904, 1584, 770

In this article, Archer shows that he had so far amended his previous opinions of Shaw as to find a trace of 'the poet within him' and to recognise *John Bull's Other Island* as 'a brilliant piece of dramatic literature'.

Someone showed me the other day a tiny pin-point of radium, restlessly coruscating, like a microscopic volcano; and I instantly saw in it—one of those parallelisms in which Nature delights—a physical image of the mental processes of Mr. Bernard Shaw. As a public-spirited citizen, he ought really to leave his brain, when he has no further use for it, to some scientific Institution; for it will certainly rank high in the scale of radio active substances. In *John Bull's Other Island*, at the Court Theatre, it throws off an incessant star-drift of glistening sparklets. Mr. Shaw has done nothing more original—nothing, to my thinking, more delightful. Some authorities, I see, pronounce his wit 'cheap.' Were it in the market, what price would they not pay, I wonder, for the fiftieth part of it! There are cheap things here and there, no doubt, for Mr. Shaw's self-criticism is none of the sternest; but you do not call a man a pauper because, amid a pocketful of minted gold, he happens to have two-pence halfpenny in bronze.

It is very easy to demonstrate that *John Bull's Other Island* is not a play. Compared with it, *Candida* and *The Devil's Disciple*—ay, even *Man and Superman*—are well-built dramatic machines. What little story it professes to tell is continually submerged in discussion, generalisation, fantastication. When the plot does come to the surface now and then, for five minutes or so, it proves to be one of those ridiculous stories of love at first sight and marriage the following morning, of which Mr. Shaw is so inexplicably fond. But even the ridiculous love story is delicious in its absurdity. The character of Nora is touched with a delicacy very rare in Mr. Shaw's portraits of women. It shows in him a remnant of pro-Hibernian sentiment which is human and amiable. Indeed, if we treat time as purely conventional, and substitute a week for every hour of Mr. Shaw's reckoning, the love story becomes no longer ridiculous, but a piece of excellent comedy. Then, again, the character of the Buddhist-Catholic Keegan is a real creation. It shows that Mr. Shaw, after all, is a son of the same soil which nourished Oliver Goldsmith. There is a real depth of thought and sincerity of feeling in Keegan which Mr. Shaw has scarcely attained before; and the thought and feeling are pleasantly aerated, not wantonly overfrothed, with humour. What could be better than this, for instance?—

NORA: I wanted to know whether you found Ireland very small and backward-like when you came back to it from Rome and Oxford and all the great cities?

KEEGAN: When I went to those great cities, I saw wonders that I had never seen in Ireland. But when I came back to Ireland I found all the wonders there waiting for me. You see, they had been there all the time; but my eyes had never been opened to them. I did not know what my own house was like, because I had never been outside it.

NORA: D'ye think that's the same with everybody?

KEEGAN: With everybody who has eyes in his soul as well as in his head.

In the whole part of Keegan Mr. Shaw gives momentary freedom to the poet within him—the poet whom, as a rule, he locks away in a secret cell, and never suffers to stir abroad save on condition that he shall keep on scourging himself with steel-tipped thongs of mockery.

But love and Buddhism are only trimmings to the play; the warp and woof are a keen analysis of Irish conditions and a genial caricature of English Liberalism. To some people, I fancy, the trenchancy of the caricature has been more apparent than its geniality, and they have bitterly resented the character of Broadbent. I confess I cannot understand this frame of mind. Even Broadbent can join in a joke at his own expense—if he happens to see it. There is probably better ground for resentment in the picture of Ireland, which, to those who think it unfair and untrue, must be all the more irritating for its vividness. But to me, whose business is to judge it simply as a piece of literature, it is entirely satisfying. Every turn of the dialogue—and it turns and twists with inconceivable nimbleness—presents a new facet of the problem, and gives one a new thrill of intellectual pleasure. 'All very well,' the orthodox critic may say, 'but what have all these political confabulations to do with drama?' I can only reply that each scene is, in itself, vitally dramatic, though it may lack that necessary relation to an organic whole which orthodox criticism regards as indispensable. For my part, when a theatrical performance gives me intense pleasure, in defiance of rule and canon, I do not argue myself out of my pleasure, but realise that the rules do not cover the whole ground. *John Bull's Other Island* is a thing by itself. I can think of no other play, English or foreign, with which it can properly be classed. If we must find a Polonius-pigeonhole for it, let us call it a philosophico-political prose extravaganza. But, label it how we will, it is a brilliant piece of dramatic literature. There is no other country in the world, I believe, where its qualities would have been so grudgingly recognised.

The acting was remarkably good, though the indisposition and consequent inaudibility of Mr. J. L. Shine rather let down some of the scenes. Mr. Louis Calvert was quite admirable as Broadbent—a comic creation of the first order. The gentle and humorous saintliness of Keegan was ably presented by Mr. Granville Barker, and Miss Ellen O'Malley was most delicate and delightful as Nora. I have no space to individualise the other characters, but must content myself with saying that almost without exception they were as good as could possibly be desired. The whole performance was taken a little too slowly; but it has doubtless been screwed up a bit by this time.

32. Max Beerbohm, notice, *Saturday Review*

12 November 1904, vol. 98, 2559, 608

Reprinted in *Around Theatres* (1953), 353.

Max Beerbohm defends Shaw's work against the 'usual parrot-cry: "Not a play" ', in a notice entitled 'Mr. Shaw at his best'.

Had Mr. Shaw been born in France, or in Germany, he would be at this moment the most popular playwright in Paris, or in Berlin. There is not the shadow of a doubt of that. As it is, he is becoming popular in Berlin. In New York he is popular already. Another decade will, with luck, see him popular in London. Meanwhile, I suppose, we must be grateful that his plays do manage to get themselves performed, some-how, somewhere, on the sly. During the past two weeks there have been some matinées of his latest play, *John Bull's Other Island*, at the Court Theatre. It seemed natural that the auditorium had not been warmed on the bitterly cold day when I found myself there. But the temperature made me feel rather anxious; for in England, a country whose natural breed is dullards, any intellectual activity—and it is only the actively intellectual persons who go out of their way to special matinées—generally carries with it some grave physical delicacy; and we cannot spare aught of such intellectual activity as is going on among us. A man might die worse than in seeing a play by Mr. Shaw. But it seems a pity that he should not live to tell the tale. Moreover, I am quite sure that if Mr. Shaw's plays were more seductively produced, they would appeal even to the dullards at large. In a warm theatre, within the regular radius for theatres, after nightfall—in fact, with just those cheerful commercial circumstances which are withheld from them—these plays would soon take the town. The dull middleman shakes his head, mutters some dull shibboleth, dives his hand into a pigeon-hole, and calls rehearsals of a new play which has nothing whatever to recommend it except its likeness to the present failure, and to the last failure, and to the failure before last.

The critics, for the most part, are scarcely less dull than the managers themselves. Over *John Bull's Other Island* they have raised their usual parrot-cry: 'Not a play.' This, being interpreted, means 'Not a love-story, split neatly up into four brief acts, with no hint that the characters live in a world where other things besides this love-story are going on.' In *John Bull's Other Island* there is a love-story. But it occurs only in the fabric of the main scheme. This main scheme is to present the character of a typical Englishman against a typically Irish background —to throw up the peculiarities of the Englishman by contrast with various types of Irishman and various phases of Irish life, and to throw up the peculiarities of Ireland by contrast with the invader. This scheme Mr. Shaw carries out in four long acts, two of which contain two scenes apiece. Not much actually happens in the play. The greater part of the play is talk: and this talk is often not relevant to the action, but merely to the characters, and to things in general. Pray, why is this not to be called a play? Why should the modern 'tightness' of technique be regarded as a sacred and essential part of dramaturgy? And why should the passion of love be regarded as the one possible theme in dramaturgy? Between these two superstitions lies the main secret of the barrenness of modern British drama. The first of them wards away the majority of men of creative literary power, who cannot be bothered to pick up the manifold little tricks and dodges which go to the making of what the critics call 'a play.' The second prevents playwrights from taking themes which would both invigorate their work through novelty and bring the theatre into contact with life at large.

Of course, I do not pretend that every good novelist could write a good play. There are essential differences between dramaturgy and any other form of literary work. My contention is that the dramatic instinct is no more rare than the narrative instinct, and that any man who has the dramatic instinct will, with a little practice, be able to write a good play. It is lucky for us that Mr. Shaw has not, like the vast majority of creative writers, been frightened away from the theatre. He has—though not, I wager, in a greater degree than many other men who dare only write novels—an instinct for the theatre, and he can with perfect ease express his ideas effectively through the dramatic form. None of our most fashionable playwrights could give him points in such technique as is really necessary. None is less amateurish in essentials. Mr. Shaw evolves his 'situations' with perfect naturalness, and brings his characters off and on, and handles a whole crowd of them simultaneously on the stage, without the least apparent effort. He has, also, this great natural advantage in the writing of dialogue: he can always express himself directly, in a clean-cut manner. He is a thinker, and often a very subtle thinker. But he is also a public speaker, accustomed to dispense with that form in which his thoughts can be pondered at leisure, and to make the best of that form in which they must be caught as they fly. From the stage, then, as from the platform, his thoughts never elude us. We never have to pause to consider what he meant in the last line. It is always well to read a play by him at leisure, when it is published as a book; for the thoughts in it fly too thickly for us to remember them all after a performance. But at the moment of its utterance his every thought flies straight to our brain. As his thoughts are, so (I apologise for the arbitrary distinction) are his jests. His humour always gets well across the footlights, even when the fun of the thing said derives nothing from the character of its sayer or from the moment in which it is said. Thus, when Broadbent, the English Liberal candidate in Ireland, talks to his Irish fiancée about the canvassing, and is met by her reluctance to talk to 'common people,' he cries 'Oh, but we must be thoroughly democratic, and patronise everybody without distinction of class.' That is not even a caricature of anything that Broadbent would say. It is just a critical conceit of Mr. Shaw's. It is, therefore, not stage-humour, in the strict sense. But it is stage-humour in so far as it is so delightfully simple and sudden—a joke which not a soul in the audience can miss. However, these detached jests are rare in Mr. Shaw's play. Most of the fun comes of a slight exaggeration on the things that the character actually would say. But Mr. Shaw has also the art of extracting a ridiculous effect from every scenic situation. Broadbent has been selected as candidate quite unexpectedly, and on the spur of the moment. His valet has not heard the news. 'Now, Hodson,' says Broadbent, 'you mustn't be standoffish with the people here. I should like you to be popular, you know.' 'I'm sure you're very kind, Sir,' says Hodson; 'but it don't seem to matter much whether they like me or not. I'm not going to stand for Parliament here, Sir.' 'Well,' replies Broadbent, dramatically, 'I am.' This passage is not excruciatingly funny to read. But it is, as any one with dramatic instinct can imagine, excruciatingly funny to hear. Again, I might describe for you, the scene in which Broadbent suddenly, by moonlight, makes his proposal of marriage, and is supposed by the young Irish lady to be intoxicated, and is by her converted to that uncomfortable belief, and led gently home by her; or I might describe the scene in which Broadbent drives away with a peasant's pig in his motor; but these descriptions would seem to me tame in comparison with the actual thing. There you have one of the tests of true dramatic humour: the inadequacy of pen and ink for a proper reproduction of it. Of all our playwrights Mr. Shaw is by far the most richly gifted with this humour. And of all his plays *John Bull's Other Island* is fullest of this humour. Yet none of our managers gloomily hovering around Portugal Street, will offer the play to a public against which the obvious (and self-made) indictment is that it goes to the theatre just to be amused.

'Just to be amused.' There is much besides amusement to be got out of this play (a fact which would, I suppose, form the manager's silly excuse for not producing it). Indeed, I think that none of Mr. Shaw's plays has so much serious interest. From all his plays one derives the pleasure that there is in finding a playwright who knows, and gives us, something of the world at first hand—a playwright who, moreover, has a philosophic view of things, and can criticise what he sees. Such displeasure as we have in Mr. Shaw's plays comes from the sense that Mr. Shaw is a little too sure of himself and his philosophy—a little too loudly consistent about everything to be right about most things. In this latest play of his, he seems to have mellowed into something almost like dubiety, without losing anything of his genius for ratiocination.

33. Reginald Farrer, from a notice, *Speaker*

19 November 1904, vol. XI, 184, 266

Reginald Farrer (1880–1920), author and critic, was a dramatic critic for the *Speaker* before Desmond MacCarthy became a regular contributor. His signed notice of *John Bull's Other Island*, from which this extract is taken, was entitled 'Salted Pap'. Farrer continued to take an unfavourable view of Shaw and said in a notice of *Man and Superman* (*Speaker*, vol. XII, no. 296, 3 June 1905, 232) that 'Mr Shaw leaves out life's good qualities, and then calls his fancy composition a portrait of the real world.' On 12 March 1906, he began a notice of *Captain Brassbound's Conversion* with an acknowledgment of Shaw's power to arouse interest: 'The amount of time journalists spend in writing about Mr Bernard Shaw is excessive. However, it has to be done; there is no getting away from him. No other writer's work promotes, so naturally, discussion. The public may be near getting tired of the subject; but I believe they still instinctively turn to see what he has been saying last and what can be urged for or against it. They cannot certainly be tired of anything he writes himself.'

It is never possible in this latest play to have any confidence in Mr Shaw's sincerity. His utterances, for one reason, are so entirely and solely destructive. For, when he has very wittily expounded the complete and valueless vileness of all our characters and institutions, the only alternative he has to offer us is the sloppiest pap of sentimentality. And it is not on a foundation of invertebrate emotionalism that a Shaka or an Issa can hope to regenerate this extremely faulty world. There must be some more virile idea; something, anything that appeals rather to reason than to the easy tears of comfortable, otiose compassion. Mr Shaw is a prophet showing the sham of everything actual; yet when, having listened faithfully, we humbly ask him what is next to be done, he has no resource but a torrent of fluid rhetoric. He, the keen and bitter satirist of things as he finds them, is, in reality, the merest, most innocent sentimentalist now living. For our life is one long compromise, and it is only an arrant sentimentalist, or a person of very tender years, who will quarrel with a compromise because it does not lead us direct to Utopia.

34. Francis Prevost on Shaw's growing reputation, *Edinburgh Review*

April 1905, vol. CCI, 412, 498

Henry Francis Prevost Battersby (d. 1949), journalist and author, wrote under the pen-name Francis Prevost.

In a long, unsigned article, Prevost reviewed the plays of Shaw that had been published up to the date of writing, including the recently produced *John Bull's Other Island*. Omitted passages examine the plays and other writings in detail. The article began with the observation that Shaw was more honoured outside his own country than within it, and commented that managers were reluctant to include the plays in their evening programmes and 'the common playgoer . . . has thus been debarred from forming an opinion of Mr Shaw's more recent work.' In the closing passage of the article, reproduced below, Prevost suggested that a 'fine' novelist had been absorbed in the playwright.

The misapprehension which at present separates the public of the theatre from Mr Shaw has been by him variously and vivaciously accounted for; so variously, indeed, that the reader may be pardoned for failing to realise why 'a reasonable, patient, consistent, apologetic, laborious person', as he describes himself, has gleaned so lean an armful from fields which have proved to other reasonable and laborious people a source of profit. It might seem ridiculous in dealing with a dramatist to preface an inquiry into the quality of his work by a question as to his social or political leanings, because the artist is commonly, and for the most part rightly, regarded as concerned rather with results than with causes, and as having no more constructive interest in morality than has a portrait painter in dressmaking. He is the chronicler of appearances, and though his production may be raw material for the moralist it is so only as authentic evidence to the fact.

But Mr Shaw is an artist of the other type. He is a dramatist because he is a moralist. For art's sake he would have nothing to do with art. He ranges himself beside the men with a message—with Blake, with Bunyan, with Micah the Morasthite. That would appear a very promising position from which to interest a public that worries itself considerably about the moral intent of art. Unfortunately, however, the public and Mr Shaw have different conceptions of morality. The dramatist's desire is to make things moral, the public's, to keep them so. The difference is disastrous when worked out in art. For while the public deems nothing needed by the social structure but the decencies of repair, Mr Shaw's thoughts are in the basement bent on abolition. Not that he is a mere iconoclast; he has a constructive scheme of his own, but it is one that necessitates rebuilding from the foundations. And inevitably this preoccupation of the mind's eye with an architecture of the future makes it a somewhat unsympathetic critic of the fabrics at present occupying the ground.

That is, so far as the popular estimate is concerned, his most obvious dramatic disability as a Socialist. He is interested in a new order of things; his public, in the old; and though his very sense of the necessity for that new order makes his trenchant commentary intellectually acceptable, his moral attitude, or as the public, having a different one, would say, his immoral attitude, is a source of occasional exacerbation, and his treatment of the emotions consequently suggests either a complete petrifaction of 'feeling' or a wanton and sardonic trifling with the susceptibilities of others. Not that Socialism as a constructive theory is directly responsible for more than the acute and humorous commentary which the plays offer on things as they are, since Mr Shaw never puts his own seriousness—which is a very considerable affair—into direct conflict with that of his public. His touch is always lightest where his convictions are most involved. . . .

The power of producing an impression of life which seems, and which is, more real than reality, may be counted Mr Shaw's supreme gift as a dramatist. He chooses the elements of his histories with such skill that the mere collision of character produces drama with the swiftness and certainty of a chemical reaction. And thus his plays have the disarming quality of seeming to write themselves. It is by this reaction also that he obtains the spontaneous freshness of his humour, which emanates as a natural issue of personality and position, and owes much of its effect to a combination of plausibility and unexpectedness.

He has, of course, an unusual gift for selecting the essence of speech, and contriving to pass it off as the most ordinary solution; so that his dialogue, in which there is scarcely an insignificant word, reads like any brightly trivial conversation, the simple outcome of the situation on the characters, and, for all its conciseness, its force, and often its brilliancy, hardly ever betrays a hint of the elaborate artifice, the telling intention. But behind the ability to write such dialogue is the far more important power of conceiving a theme possessing inherent energy of development, and peopling it with the essential intelligences for working out. It is this power that makes *Mrs Warren's Profession* so great a play, practically without dependence on a single theatrical device for heightening emotion. It is a play full of the common tragic possibilities, and they none of them 'come off'. Its intense interest is human, not histrionic. That is a simple explanation, but it is not one that can be offered for the effectiveness of one play in a hundred; and the only other plays of Mr Shaw's to which it completely applies are *Candida* and *John Bull's Other Island*.

Problem has ever been at the root of his work. No drama without conflict; no conflict without something to decide. All life worthy the name is a problem; and every play that would reproduce life must be either a problem or a platitude. A people that is unconscious of having problems to solve, that has outlived its interest in the interpretation of life, is beginning to be at the end of its intellectual resources. Senile decay is as surely indicated in a nation as in a man by a dull acquiescence in the immutability of things; and the literature of a waning race is almost always diverted from the great questions of conduct before it expires in aesthetic trivialities. Hence Mr Shaw's determination 'to accept problem as the normal material of the drama', and his understanding of drama as 'the presentation in parable of the conflict between man's will and his environment', are a pledge at least of vitality in his ideas, and vitality working itself out as creative philosophy is the supreme necessity to the art of the stage. . . .

Considering the difficulty of seeing Mr Shaw's plays on the stage, one must be grateful to his ingenuity in making them acceptable in the study. His reforming instinct, which does us no service in spelling and type-setting, works only for good in putting his scenes before us. His introductions and explanations often do more for us than the visible characters on the stage. Take this from a sketch of Mr Burgess, too long to give in full:

A man of sixty made coarse and sordid by the compulsory selfishness of petty commerce, and later on softened into sluggish bumptiousness by overfeeding and commercial success. A vulgar, ignorant, guzzling man, offensive and contemptuous to people whose labour is cheap, respectful to wealth and rank, and quite sincere and without rancour in both attitudes.

Could a presence and a life-history be put in fewer words? How excellent too is this impression of Mrs Whitefield as

a little woman whose faded flaxen hair looks like straw on an egg. She has an expression of muddled shrewdness, a squeak of protest in her voice, and an odd air of continually elbowing away some larger person who is crushing her into a corner.

Even in seating his people Mr Shaw gives us a helping of character, as in the contrast between Mrs Dudgeon, 'who assaults her chair by sitting down', and Titus Dudgeon, the man of gallantry, 'who sits down warmly between his own lady and his brother's'.

His stage directions, glorified into a gossiping Greek chorus, suggest how fine a novelist has been absorbed in the playwright; but drama is perhaps a safer harness for the reformer, since it keeps him all the way against the collar of effective expression, and saves him from that wayside loitering in ideas, whereby so many a traveller to Atlantis has lain down with his load. It is as a reformer we have here considered him, a voice crying in the wilderness of trivial work and mean ambition, a voice still hoarse with exhortation, still a little forced from having had to carry over the heads of a crowd.

Greater work than he has done he may yet do; but it must be conceived by a less contentious spirit and wrought in a serener air. He has done for us a deal of much needed preaching; but while it needs but the understanding of what men should not be to equip the Preacher, to the Pardoner must be discovered the deeper mystery of what they are.

MRS WARREN'S PROFESSION

1894

The Lord Chamberlain refused to issue a licence for performance of *Mrs Warren's Profession*. The Stage Society gave two private performances in 1902, but the first public production was in the USA, at the Hyperion Theater, New Haven, Connecticut on 27 October 1905. There was one performance but, although this was moderately well received in the press, further performances were forbidden by the police. When it was presented at the Garrick Theater, New York, on 30 October, the whole cast were arrested (and released on bail) on the charge of disorderly conduct. They were acquitted at the trial some months later. The notice from the *New York Herald* is a fair example of press reception of the New York production.

35. Unsigned notice, *New York Herald*

31 October 1905, 3

'The lid' was lifted by Mr Arnold Daly and 'the limit' of stage indecency reached last night in the Garrick Theater in the performance of one of Mr George Bernard Shaw's 'unpleasant comedies' called *Mrs Warren's Profession*.

'The limit of indecency' may seem pretty strong words, but they are justified by the fact that the play is morally rotten. It makes no difference that some of the lines may have been omitted and others toned down; there was superabundance of foulness left. The whole story of the play, the atmosphere surrounding it, the incidents, the personalities of the characters are wholly immoral and degenerate. The only way successfully to expurgate *Mrs Warren's Profession* is to cut the whole play out. You cannot have a clean pig stye. The play is an insult to decency because—

It defends immorality.

It glorifies debauchery.

It besmirches the sacredness of a clergyman's calling.

It pictures children and parents living in calm observance of most unholy relations.

And, worst of all, it countenances the most revolting form of degeneracy, by flippantly discussing the marriage of brother and sister, father and daughter, and makes the one supposedly moral character of the play, a young girl, declare that choice of shame, instead of poverty is eminently right.

These things cannot be denied. They are the main factors of the story. Without them there would be no play. It is vileness and degeneracy brazenly considered. If New York's sense of shame is not aroused to hot indignation at this theatrical insult, it is indeed in a sad plight.

[There follows a summary of the story of the play.]

Does not this literary muck leave a bad taste in the mouth? Does it not insult the moral intelligence of New York theater-goers and outrage the decency of the New York stage?

There was not one redeeming feature about it last night, not one ray of sunshine, of cleanliness, to lighten up the moral darkness of situation and dialogue; not the semblance of a moral lesson pointed. As Letchmere says of his family in *Letty*[1], 'We are rotten to the core', and the same might be said of the characters in *Mrs Warren's Profession*.

The play was well acted from a technical standpoint by Mr Daly as Frank, Miss Shaw as Mrs Warren, and others of the cast; but while that is ordinarily cause for praise in a performance, it constituted an added sin to last night's production, for the better it was acted the more the impurity and degeneracy of the characters, the situations and the lines were made apparent. There were a few slight excisions made in the play as written, but what was left filled the house with the ill odor of evil suggestion, where it was not blatantly immoral.

After the third act Mr Daly came before the curtain and made a speech in which he rather floundered as though he had forgotten what was committed to memory. He said that the play should only be seen by grown up people who could not be corrupted. Children might be kept to the old fashioned moral illusions, including Santa Claus and Washington.

'We have many theaters', he went on, 'devoted to plays appealing

[1] A play by A.W. Pinero, produced in 1903.

to the romanticist or child—New York has even provided a hippo-drome for such. But surely there should be room in New York for at least one theater devoted to truth, however disagreeable truth may appear.

'This play is not presented as an entertainment, but as a dramatic sermon and an exposé of a social condition and an evil, which our purists attempt to ignore, and by ignoring, allow it to gain strength. If Mr Comstock devoted half the energy and time to providing soft beds, sweet food and clean linen to the poor of New York that he does to the suppression of postal cards, we would have less immorality, for the logical reason that virtue would be robbing vice of its strongest features and attractiveness—comfort and health.

'It is a strange but true thing that everybody who has written to the newspapers, asking that this play be suppressed, has concluded the letter with the quaint statement, "I know the play should be suppressed, although, of course, I have not read the book". God has gifted these mortals with strange powers, indeed.

'If public opinion forces this theater to close and this play to be withdrawn, it will be a sad commentary indeed upon twentieth century so-called civilization and our enlightened new country'.

Then Mr Daly retired amid vociferous applause from the double distilled Shawites present and the speculators who had tickets for sale for to-night—if there is to be any to-night for the play.

MAJOR BARBARA

1905

Major Barbara was first produced for six matinées at the Royal Court Theatre, 28 November 1905.

36. From an unsigned notice, *Pall Mall Gazette*

29 November 1905, vol. LXXXI, 12683, 9

There is wit enough to make the fortune of half-a-dozen ordinary plays. The question is whether there is wit enough to save a three hours' discussion in the theatre. We doubt it.

[Comments briefly on the characters.]

There was, in short, the finest medley of 'high explosive' characters that Mr Shaw could imagine. And yet one got tired of them. One soon wearies of mechanical toys; their tricks once mastered, they cease to amuse. And so the play was not an eye-opener for long; and the whole of the third act did less to open eyes than to close them.

In one respect we think, and trust, *Major Barbara* may open the eyes of those who accept Mr Shaw as a prophet. In the midst of a play largely made up of gibes and pranks, came the words, 'My God, my God, why hast Thou forsaken me?' That Mr Shaw should use these words, perhaps the most awful in the world, betrays not only a freedom from creed but an utter want of the religious sense; it is impossible for Mr Shaw or anyone else to understand the world he lives in. In this play Undershaft declares with more justice than usual that religion is the greatest of all things, and further, advocates our 'scrapping' religion, which is not up-to-date, as he 'scraps' machinery in which there is the slightest flaw. Mr Shaw seems blissfully unconscious that what he really wants to 'scrap' is human nature, human nature as it is, has been for thousands of years, and is likely to be for thousands of years to come. We trust this crucial lapse, only the most serious lapse of many, will set people thinking, will prompt them to observe whether Mr Shaw, destitute of the religious emotion, is not destitute also of all those other emotions which make human nature what it is. If they will only do this, we think they will discover in Mr Shaw, a writer whose absence of feeling makes him a very unsafe guide. There will still be the amusing activity of his brain to admire and to be amused at, but a brain without a heart is never to be taken too seriously.

37. Unsigned notice, *Morning Post*

29 November 1905, 41656, 9

This adverse notice in a strongly Conservative newspaper upset Shaw and he regarded it as 'a virulent attack' (see Beatrice Webb's comment, No. 38). He wrote to the paper on 1 December and 2 December 1905, replying to the comments of the unnamed dramatic critic. Shaw's letters are reprinted in the *Bodley Head Bernard Shaw*, vol. III, 191, 192. In the editorial on 1 December, the *Morning Post* replied in turn to Shaw's first letter and defended its critic's strictures on what were considered Shaw's 'deliberate errors of taste'. Other correspondents expressed disapproval of features of *Major Barbara* in succeeding issues, some without having seen the play, but J. E. Vedrenne, who was jointly responsible for presenting the play, wrote to the *Morning Post* on 1 December, pointing out that the critic's remark about Shaw being content to leave his plays 'to dazzle the elect at matinees in Sloane-Square' was 'hardly fair' as Shaw's plays had been presented at the theatre since the beginning of September, in the evenings as well as on Wednesday matinées, and 'we are playing to the capacity of the house'.

Mr Bernard Shaw's plays are just the productions suited to special matinees like those by which Messrs Vedrenne and Barker are now attracting special audiences to the Court Theatre. The ordinary playgoer while recognising the undeniable cleverness of Mr Shaw's work finds himself so puzzled, and perhaps so annoyed, by its lack of straightforward intelligible purpose, its deliberate perversity, and its self-contradictory insincerity that he can derive from it little of the pleasure which he seeks in his visits to the theatre. He does not object to mordant satire in comedy if only he can feel sure what theory of life, of art, or of morality it is that is being satirised. He can put up once in a way with the absence of any serious appeal for his sympathy; but he does not like having his sympathy played with by *dramatis personae* who first rouse it and then hold it up to ridicule. He wants to know whether it is at the expense of his subject or his audience or himself that the witty dramatist is seeking to point a sally and raise a laugh. About this he never feels quite sure in the case of pieces like *Arms and the Man* and *Candida*, *Man and Superman*, and even *John Bull's Other Island*. So in spite of their admitted brilliance he is content to leave them to dazzle the elect at matinees in Sloane-square.

Criticism dealing from this point of view with Mr Shaw's latest dramatic experiment is ingeniously disarmed by the official definition of it as 'a discussion in three acts'. The 'discussion' of *Major Barbara*, as the piece is called, certainly promised plenty of lively interest of a certain kind, since one of its scenes was laid in a typical shelter of that Salvation Army in which its heroine holds rank as an officer. Moreover, there seemed to be assured interest of quite another order from the presence in the cast not only of players like Mr Louis Calvert and Mr Granville Barker, who have generally made their most artistic mark in Mr Shaw's creations, but of Miss Annie Russell, a charming young American actress whose too rare visits to us have been paid in association with dramatic effort as unlike *Major Barbara* as any effort well could be. For a few scenes this promise was fairly fulfilled, but in the end the fireworks which went up as rockets came down as sticks, and the light thrown out by them was seen to have been as fitful and misleading as that of fireworks generally is. The characters which had begun by being so entertaining with their extravagant talk ended by growing tiresome, and seemed to weary even their impersonators by the inconsistency of their pseudo-realism. Prominent amongst them is Andrew Undershaft, the millionaire manufacturer of torpedoes and aerial battleships, who believes in no remedy for the ills of society save force, as embodied in his instruments of murder and mutilation. Against his cynically expressed theories of truculence is pitted the more or less conventional religious charity of his daughter Barbara as practised by her in all sincerity under the banner of the Salvation Army. For a while it looks as though the triumph or at any rate the moral victory would ultimately rest with Major Barbara, who with her gentle firmness, her goodness, and her inexhaustible pity scores heavily in her dealings with ruffianism and imposture at the West Ham shelter, which she induces her father to visit. But unfortunately the playwright cannot make even this concession to what may be called an agreeable moral without a display of taste so distressingly bad that he merely pains those whom for a wonder he seems trying to please. It is bad enough when he makes one of the Major's slum converts refuse the offer of a piece of bread with the remark that he is satisfied with 'the peace which passeth all understanding'. It is worse—and it is so bad that we wonder at it escaping the notion of the censorship—when Major Barbara in her disappointment is allowed to exclaim 'My God! My God! why hast Thou forsaken me!' and to be answered by the ribald retort: 'What price salvation now?'

The cause of Major Barbara's distress is the determination of her superior officer to accept on behalf of the Army not only the £5000 of Bodger, the distiller, but also the £5000 of her own father, Andrew Undershaft. Poor Barbara cannot bring herself to take ill-earned money for a good cause, and she is illogical enough to doff her uniform and throw up her mission because she cannot get the matter settled in her way. So she is left lamenting in her shelter while the Army sets forth on its procession through the streets, headed by the burlesque figures of her lover—a Professor of Greek!—beating the drum, and her father playing the trombone. Mr Shaw, of course, is jeering at them all—at the Salvationists with their readiness to be imposed upon, and at those who help them in order to suit their own purposes whether personal, political or merely whimsical. And he keeps up his bitter gibes to the last. In accordance with her promise to her father that she will visit his death-dealing factory if he will visit her life-giving refuge, Barbara goes there, accompanied by her mother, her lover, her sister, and her prospective brother-in-law, all of whom have in their several ways expressed profound disapproval of the means by which Undershaft and Company have made their millions. They go to curse but they remain to bless. The model town created by the objectionable firm so impresses them by its decorum, its prosperity, and its admirable institutions that one by one they fall easy victims to the long-winded logic of the cynical capitalist. The professor of Greek decides to accept the partnership offered to him as Undershaft's son-in-law, and even Barbara herself is brought to think that the most fitting field for her missionary labours may be found amongst the operatives who are building up her father's fortune.

As has been said, the play drags a good deal towards its inconclusive conclusion, and its offences against good taste and good feeling are of a kind not to be readily forgiven. But against these defects are to be set the merits of much brilliant if unconvincing dialogue, of a great deal of rather brutal humour and of an interpretation which must really be pronounced admirable all round.

38. Beatrice Webb on *Major Barbara*, 'a dance of devils'

1905

Diary entries for 29 November and 2 December 1905, printed in *Our Partnership* (1948), ed. Barbara Drake and Margaret I. Cole, 314.

Beatrice Webb (1858–1943), with her husband Sidney James Webb, was the author of many books on social and economic problems. They were closely associated with Shaw in the early history of the Fabian Society and were personal friends. Beatrice Webb had found *Man and Superman* 'a great work', but thought that *John Bull's Other Island* showed 'derision unaccompanied by any positive faith or hope'. Her comments on *Major Barbara* show how difficult it was for her to appreciate Shaw's combination of flippancy and earnestness. The Webbs went to see *Major Barbara* with A. J. Balfour, the Conservative Prime Minister, and the first part of the extract is taken from the diary entry for 29 November 1905.

G.B.S.'s play turned out to be a dance of devils—amazingly clever, grimly powerful in the second act—but ending, as all his plays (or at any rate most of them), in an intellectual and moral morass. A.J.B. was taken aback by the force, the horrible force of the Salvation Army scene, the unrelieved tragedy of degradation, the disillusionment of the Greek professor and of Barbara—the triumph of the unmoral purpose; the anti-climax of evangelising the Garden-City! I doubt the popular success of the play; it is hell tossed on the stage with no hope of heaven. G.B.S. is gambling with ideas and emotions in a way that distresses slow-minded prigs like Sidney and me, and hurts those with any fastidiousness. But the stupid public will stand a good deal from one who is acclaimed an unrivalled wit by the great ones of the world.

December 2nd. To-day, I called on the Shaws and found G.B.S. alone in his study. He was perturbed—indeed, upset by the bad acting, as he thought, of Undershaft and generally of all in the last scene—and by a virulent attack on the play in the *Morning Post.* Calvert, he said, had completely lost his nerve over Undershaft—could not understand or remember his part and was aghast at what he considered its blank immorality. I spoke quite frankly my opinion of the general effect of his play—the triumph of the unmoral purpose. He argued earnestly and cleverly, even persuasively, in favour of what he imagines to be his central theme—*the need for preliminary good physical environment before anything could be done to raise the intelligence and morality of the average sensual man.* We middle-class people, having always had physical comfort and good order, do not realise the disaster to character in being without. We have, therefore, cast a halo round poverty, instead of treating it as the worst of crimes—the one unforgiveable crime that must be wiped off before any virtue can grow'. He defended Undershaft's general attitude towards life on the ground that, until we divested ourselves of feeling (he said malice), we were not fit to go the lengths needed for social salvation. 'What we want is for the people to turn round and burn, not the West End, but their own slums. The Salvation Army with its fervour and its love might lead them to do this and then we really should be at the beginning of the end of the crime of poverty'.

I found it difficult to answer him—but he did not convince me. There is something lacking in his presentment of the crime of poverty. But I could honestly sympathise with his irritation at the suggested intervention of the censor—not on account of the upshot of the play, but because Barbara in her despair at the end of the second act utters the cry, 'My God, my God, why hast thou forsaken me'. A wonderful and quite rational climax to the true tragedy of the scene of the Salvation Army shelter.

39. J. T. Grein, from a notice, *Sunday Times*

3 December 1905, 4313, 4

Now that he is acknowledged at home and abroad as the most original English dramatist of the day, Bernard Shaw can venture to do that which in others would prove fatal. He may convert the stage into hustings and argue *ad infinitum*. He may bowl over all conventions as to proportion and construction. He may—to put it tersely—render the drama subservient to his mental discipline. For he is Bernard Shaw and we, sensible of our inferiority, are willing listeners. Perhaps in later days, when Shaw will be quite certain that he has subdued England and that he is estimated at his proper value, he will vouchsafe us the generous clemency of a victor. He will then bridle his exuberance, chasten some of his parlance, and consider that three and a half hours of discourse, in which the world and all its works (to say nothing of heaven) are discussed, are beyond the cerebral digestion of common mortals— consider that by giving too much a great part of his abundance must pass by unappreciated.

Later on, too, Mr. Shaw may avoid the error which disfigured the last act of his first play, *Widowers' Houses*, and which now stains the finest act English drama can show: the second act of *Major Barbara*. In that act, which is a presentation of a Salvation Army shelter, of admirable, of powerful fidelity to life, a ruffian, otherwise drawn by a master hand, twice before our eyes smites a woman with his fist. That double act of brutality literally moved the audience to shudders. It was beyond all bounds of realism in art. It was ugly and revolting. Physical brutality of any kind which bears the stamp of truth is not only inartistic, it is antagonistic to the nature of every man and woman in the house.

Having entered this protest with all the candour due to a mind so lofty as Mr. Shaw's, there is no further reason for fault-finding. *Major Barbara* is not merely a play which in many stages reaches greatness, but it is a store-house of information on subjects which too rarely occupy the mind of a hurried community. If ever the purpose, the inner working, of the Salvation Army were brought before the eyes of the public, in candid *pro* and *contra*, this *tour de force* was achieved by Mr.

149

Shaw. Major Barbara—the woman Salvationist—is the spirit, the soul, the greatness of General Booth's gigantic achievement. And better than processions, better than sermons, newspaper appeals, and private letters of omniscient wiseacres, will it bring home to the hearer what is the actual state of the submerged, what is done to raise them, and what remains to be done in order to strike at the root of the question. There are still many people in England who deny that Shaw has heart, and they see in him but a clever jester. Let them go to the Court Theatre. I say, behold, and listen. They will find there the revelation of the real man—a man who knows the world better than dozens of philanderers who talk in the House of Commons on the basis of evident second-hand information. Nor does Mr Shaw plead a one-sided argument. In his discourses you see, mentally, the constant oscillations of the scales, the strenuous effort to establish balance between capital and philanthropy. The man in the street, as well as the man in the stalls, must use his intellectual machine under the domination of this colossal, this universal thinker. For thought breeds thought, and the effect is, resist as we may, introspective.

I need not expatiate on the story and the store of cleverness of the play. It would mean an injustice to Shaw and expose the critic to ridicule for the exhibition of another man's ideas in a diluted form. *Major Barbara* is a play to be heard, to be seen, to be read. It will raise discussion and arguments galore. We need such drama, and may well forgo troubling ourselves about details of construction and form. Shaw is the man to raise the English drama to that pinnacle of intellectuality which makes for good and establishes the claim of the theatre as an educational force.

40. William Archer, from a notice, *World*

5 December 1905, 1640, 971

Archer found *Major Barbara* to show signs of decline after *John Bull's Other Island*. He analysed the play on allegorical lines but thought it far too long. Shaw wrote to Archer on 1 January 1906, saying that 'Your article on *Major Barbara*, the worst you ever wrote, delighted me.' He ended his letter by declaring that 'It is a MAGNIFICENT play, a summit in dramatic literature' (Laurence, II, 599).

Mr. Shaw is taking his revenge on Messrs Vedrenne and Barker for having, in their production of *Man and Superman*, omitted the dialogue in hell between Don Juan, Donna Anna, the Commander, and the Devil. He has determined to prove to them and to all of us, that he can make a mere discussion 'as good as a play'. And he has unquestionably succeeded. *Major Barbara* is a fascinating entertainment. Its plot is a negligible filament of unconditioned fantasy, which neither Mr. Shaw nor anyone else takes seriously for a moment. But we are pretty well accustomed nowadays to dispensing with plot. Mr. Shaw's real daring lies in dispensing with character. There are no human beings in *Major Barbara*: there are only animated points of view. The personages are of exactly the same substance as the dream-figures in the aforesaid dialogue in hell. They are like so many shuttles, each loaded with a particular colour of yarn; and the author, sitting at the loom, sets them nimbly flying back and forth, and weaving, in their vivid interplay, the somewhat violent tartan of his humanitarian-Nietzschean life-philo-sophy. In some of the shuttles the colours are negative, mere background tints to throw the high lights into relief. These negative shuttles are labelled Lady Britomart, Stephen Undershaft, Charles Lomax, &c.—the philistines and simpletons, the unidea'd or one-idea'd personages, incapable of paradox or irony. The positive hues are given forth by the shuttles labelled Andrew Undershaft, Adolphus Cusins, Barbara Undershaft: Andrew and Barbara forming the extremes of the colour-scheme and Cusins a harmonising medium between them. The inter-texture of opinions thus produced is not, of course, a drama, and still less a consistent philosophy. But it is extremely amusing to watch Mr. Shaw busily plying his loom, and bodying forth, thread by thread, the criss-cross pattern of his intellect.

It is evident from his description of *Major Barbara* as 'a discussion in three acts' that Mr. Shaw deliberately intended the complete subordination of action to thought. But I do not think that he intended the unreality of the characters; and from the fact that they have come out mere hollow mouthpieces I believe we may deduce a technical lesson. Compare the play with *John Bull's Other Island*. In that admirable comedy, though there is a good deal of Shawesque mannerism in detail, yet we feel that several of the characters—for instance, Broadbent, Keegan, Barney Doran, Nora, and Aunt Judy—are credible human beings, with something more than mere theory in their views. Now, why was it that Mr. Shaw succeeded in giving life to his characters in the one play and made them in the other mere ventriloquist's puppets? I think it was because the story of *John Bull*, though so slight as to be almost non-existent, was credible so far as it went.

[Archer examines the plot and finds that 'the incidents are wholly incredible'.]

After all, a fit of exegetical inspiration descends upon me, and I begin to perceive the symbolic purport of *Major Barbara*. It is an autobiographical allegory. Barbara represents the optimistic socialism of Mr. Shaw's younger years, when he used to deliver a dozen lectures a week ('Bin talkin' ever sence, 'av you?' says Bill Walker), takes collections in his Jaeger hat (typified by Barbara's tambourine), and imagines that the proletariat could be guided to economic salvation by railway-arch oratory and Fabian Essays. For this amiable, transient Shaw the fundamental Shaw (to whom we shall come presently) cherishes a lingering affection; whence the elegiac tenderness with which Barbara is treated. Then there must have been a time when Girondin socialism (if I may so call it) succumbed to the wiles of capitalism; the time perhaps—though this interpretation I advance with diffidence—when Fabians began to blossom into County Councillors and to consort with Prime Ministers. At this point, I take it, the half-converted working man asked 'Wot prawce Fabianism nah?' and relapsed into economic darkness. Can it have been Mr. Shaw's own defeat in the County Council election that revealed to him the fatal error of the

Girondins and threw him definitely into the camp of Nietzschean Jacobinism? Be that as it may, Undershaft represents the Shaw of the present. The play is one long discussion between Barbara, or beneficence through love, and Undershaft, or beneficence through power; and to Undershaft Mr. Shaw resolutely gives the upper hand. He is an admirable figure. There is a passionate and even poetical conviction in many of his sayings that is intensely dramatic and thrilling. I wish I could quote his speech beginning 'Come, come, my daughter; don't make too much of your little tinpot tragedy', or any one of a dozen other deliverances that fall with the conclusive clang of the guillotine blade. But over the Shaw of the past and the Shaw of the present there hovers a third Shaw, the Shaw of the fourth dimension, typified in the Euripidean ironist, Adolphus Cusins. He is in love with Barbara and he is hypnotised by Undershaft; but he is not, like them, absorbed in the illusion of the scene; he is at once an actor in their comedy and a dispassionate spectator. His is the philosophic intellect which can get outside of Time and Space, shake off the tyranny of the categories, and criticise the frame of things from the standpoint of pure reason. In short, he is the fundamental contemplative Shaw, while Barbara and Undershaft represent superficial and provisional activities.

Whether this be Mr. Shaw's own reading of the allegory I am not much concerned to know. Is it not the mark of the great symbolic poem that each of us can read in it his own secret? Here, at any rate, my researches into the inner significance of *Major Barbara* must close. Let me add that, as a mere question of literary art, the play is too long. It could be shortened by half an hour or so without the sacrifice of a single idea, or even of a single quip. Mr. Shaw is in some danger of running to verbosity.

41. Alex M. Thompson, from a notice, *Clarion*

8 December 1905, 731, 3

Alex M. Thompson (1861–1948), journalist and dramatic critic, was co-founder with Robert Blatchford of the Socialist weekly *Clarion* in 1892. For many years, he was part editor. Shaw was a frequent contributor. In his long article on *Major Barbara*, which was entitled 'The Sur-Passing Shaw', Thompson began by wondering what Arthur Balfour, then the Conservative Prime Minister, thought about the play. He had seen him at the theatre with the scientist, Sir Oliver Lodge, while 'ex-raiding Premier Jameson' was also in the house. Thompson examined the play at length, telling the story in detail with frequent quotation and calling the character of Barbara 'one of the most lovable stage women, despite all her talk, that ever dramatist conceived'. At the end of the article, in the passage quoted, Thompson commented on the main value of Shaw's play and the nature of the audience to which he appealed.

Of course, it is not the poet's business to be explicit. 'The truest poetry is the most'—enigmatic.

Shaw gives his patrons furiously to think—which is already more than playgoers bargain for—and the lines are clear enough along which their thought is driven; civilised society's primary business is to cast all its obsolete creeds and moral codes to the scrap heap and apply itself with all its might—even at the cost of bullets, blood and social revolution— not to the making of 'good' men, but to the making of healthy, strong men, to the elimination of the fit from the unfit, to the evolution of the Superman from the supervacaneous.

Such, I take it, is the moral of the audacious propagandist drama which Shaw has established in Sloane Square, amongst the most swagger of Society's afternoon Funxions. *He* does not give his tracts to missionaries. He sells them at top price to the enemy's officers.

There were almost as many carriages and motor cars outside the theatre at the first performance as there are in the Mall on a Drawing-room day.

42. Max Beerbohm, notice, *Saturday Review*

9 December 1905, vol. 100, 2615, 745

Reprinted in *Around Theatres* (1953), 409.

In this notice, with the title 'Mr. Shaw's Position', Max Beerbohm reviews changing attitudes to Shaw's plays on the part of critics and the public, including himself.

It must amuse him, whenever he surveys it; and I hope he will some day write a comedy around it. It bristles with side-lights on so many things—on human character in general, and on the English character in particular, and on the particular difficulties that genius encounters in England, and on the right manner of surmounting them.

For years Mr. Shaw was writing plays, some of which, by hook or crook, in holes and corners, were produced. They were witnessed, and loudly applauded, by such ladies and gentlemen as were in or around the Fabian Society. Not that these people took their socialist seriously as a playwright. They applauded his work in just the spirit in which, had he started a racing-stable, they would have backed his horses. He was taken with some measure of seriousness by such of the professional critics as were his personal friends, and were not hide-bound by theatrical tradition. Here, they perceived, was something new in the theatre; and, liking to be in advance of the time, they blew their trumpets in their friend's honour. The rest of the professional critics merely sniffed or cursed, according to their manners. The public took no notice at all. Time passed. In Berlin, Munich, Vienna, and elsewhere, Mr. Shaw was now a popular success. Perhaps in the hope that England had caught an echo of this exotic enthusiasm, Messrs. Vedrenne and Barker ventured to produce *John Bull's Other Island*. England had not caught that echo. There was only the usual little succes d'estime. But, not long after its production, the play was witnessed by a great lady, who advised an august person to witness it; and this august person persuaded a person yet more august to witness it. It had been withdrawn, meanwhile; so there was 'a command performance.' All the great ladies, and all the great gentlemen, were present; also, several paragraphists. That evening Mr. Shaw became a fashionable craze; and within a few days all London knew it. The Savoy restaurant is much frequented by fashion, and by paragraphy; and its revenues are drawn mainly from the many unfashionable people who go to feast their eyes on the people who are fashionable beyond dispute. No large restaurant can live by the aristo-cracy alone. Nor can even a small theatre. Mr. Shaw 'pays' now because now the English middle class pays to see that which is seen and approved by the English upper class, and (more especially) to see the English upper class. Whether either of these classes really rejoices in Mr. Shaw, as yet, is a point on which I am doubtful. I went to see *Man and Superman* a few nights ago. The whole audience was frequently rocking with laughter, but mostly at the wrong moments. (I admit that Mr. Shaw's thoughts are often so profound, and his wit is always so swift, that to appreciate his plays rightly and fully at a first hearing is rather an achievement.) But it was obvious that the whole audience was very happy indeed. It was obvious that Mr. Shaw is an enormous success. And in the roundabout way by which success has come to him is cast a delicious light on that quality for which England is specially notable among the nations.

His success is not gratifying to the critics. To those critics who are incapable of exercising their brains, and who have always resented Mr. Shaw vehemently, it is of course, galling to find themselves suddenly at odds with public opinion—the opinion which they are accustomed to 'voice.' Having slated *John Bull*, and slated *Man and Superman*, they must have been in a fearful dilemma about the play produced at the Court Theatre last week, *Major Barbara*. Perhaps this, too, was going to 'catch on.' Would it not be safer to climb down, and write moderate eulogies? I suspect it was stupidity as much as pride that diverted them from this ignominious course. They really could not make head or tail of the play. They were sure that this time Shaw really had come a cropper—had really delivered himself into their hands. 'A success, are you? Pet of the public, are you? We'll see about that. *We'll* pet-of-the-public you. *We'll* etc., etc. The old cries—'no dramatist,' 'laughing at his audience,' and the like—were not sufficient, this time. 'Brute' and 'blasphemer' were added. In the second act of the play, Mr. Shaw has tried to show some of the difficulties with which the Salvation Army has to cope. A ruffian comes to one of the shelters in quest of a woman who has been rescued from living with him. A Salvation 'lass' bars his way, and refuses to yield. He strikes her in the face. The incident is not dragged in. It is necessary to the purpose of the whole scene. Nor has any one ventured to suggest that it is an exaggeration of real life. Nor is the incident enacted realistically on the stage of the Court Theatre. At the first performance, anyhow, the actor impersonating the ruffian aimed a noticeably gentle blow in the air, at a noticeably great distance from the face of the actress impersonating the lass. I happen to be particularly squeamish in the matter of physical violence on the stage. I have winced at the smothering of Desdemona, for example, when it has been done with anything like realism. The mere symbolism at the Court Theatre gave me not the faintest qualm—not, I mean, the faintest physical qualm: aesthetically, of course, I was touched, as Mr. Shaw had a right to touch me. And it seems to me that the critics who profess to have been disgusted and outraged must have been very hard up for a fair means of attack. Equally unfair, for that it may carry conviction to the minds of people who have not seen the play, is the imputation of blasphemy. Mr. Shaw is held up to execration because he has put into the mouth of Major Barbara certain poignant words of Our Lord. To many people, doubtless, it is a screamingly funny joke that a female should have a military prefix. Also, there is no doubt that Mr. Shaw's play abounds in verbal wit, and in humorous situations. But the purport of the play is serious; and the character of Major Barbara is one of the two great factors in it. With keenest insight and sense of spiritual beauty, Mr. Shaw reveals to us in her the typical religious fanatic of her kind. Sense of spiritual beauty is not one of the qualities hitherto suspected in Mr. Shaw; but here it certainly is; and I defy even the coarsest mind not to perceive it. (To respect it is another matter.) When Major Barbara comes to the great spiritual crisis of her life, and when she believes that all the things she had trusted in have fallen away from her, what were more natural than that she should utter the words of agony that are most familiar to her? That any sane creature in the audience could have been offended by that utterance, I refuse to believe. It was as inoffensive as it was dramatically right. And the critics who have turned up the whites of their eyes, and have doubtless prejudiced against the play many worthy people who have not, like them, had the opportunity of seeing it, must submit to one of two verdicts—insanity or hypocrisy. I have no doubt that of these two qualities they will prefer to confess the latter. It is the more typically British.

In that delicate comedy, 'Mr. Shaw's Position,' the parts played by these critics seem rather crude. There is a subtler fun in the parts played by some of the superior critics—the critics who were eager to lend helping hands to Mr. Shaw in the time of his obscurity. So long as he was 'only so high,' and could be comfortably patted on the head, they made a pet of him. Now that he strides gigantic, they are less friendly. They seem even anxious to trip him up. Perhaps they do not believe in the genuineness of his growth, and suspect some trick of stilts. That would be quite a natural scepticism. A great man cannot be appreciated fully by his intimate contemporaries. Nor can his great success be ever quite palatable to them, however actively they may have striven to win it for him. To fight for a prince who has to be hiding in an oak-tree is a gallant and pleasant adventure; but when one sees the poor creature enthroned, with a crown on his head and a sceptre in his hand, one's sentiments are apt to cool. And thus the whilom champions of Mr. Shaw's virtues are now pre-occupied mainly with Mr. Shaw's defects. The old torches are still waved, but perfunctorily; and the main energy is devoted to throwing cold water. Whereas the virtues of Mr. Shaw used to be extolled with reservations for the defects, now the defects are condemned with reservations for the virtues. Mr. Shaw, it is insisted, cannot draw life: he can only distort it. He has no knowledge of human nature: he is but a theorist. All his characters are but so many incarnations of himself. Above all, he cannot write plays. He has no dramatic instinct, no theatrical technique. And these objections are emphatically reiterated (often with much brilliancy and ingenuity) by the superior critics, while all the time the fact is staring them in the face that Mr. Shaw has created in *Major Barbara* two characters—Barbara and her father—who live with an intense vitality; a crowd of minor characters that are accurately observed (though some are purposely exaggerated) from life; and one act—the second—which is as cunning and closely-knit a piece of craftsmanship as any conventional playwright could achieve, and a cumulative appeal to emotions which no other living playwright has touched. With all these facts staring them in the face, they still maintain that Mr. Shaw is not a playwright.

That theory might have held water in the days before Mr. Shaw's plays were acted. Indeed, I was in the habit of propounding it myself. I well remember that when the two volumes of *Plays, Pleasant and Unpleasant* were published, and the ordinary dramatic criticisms in this Review were still signed G.B.S., I wrote here a special article in which I pointed out that the plays, delightful to the reader, would be quite impossible on the stage. This simply proved that I had not enough theatrical imagination to see the potentialities of a play through reading it in print. When, later, I saw performances of *Mrs. Warren's Profession*, *The Devil's Disciple*, and *You Never Can Tell*, I found, to my great surprise, that they gained much more than they lost by being seen and not read. Still, the old superstition lingered in my brain. I had not learnt my lesson. When *Man and Superman* was published, I called it 'Mr. Shaw's Dialogues', and said that (even without the philosophic scene in hell) it would be quite unsuited to any stage. When I saw it performed, I determined that I would not be caught tripping again. I found that as a piece of theatrical construction it was perfect. As in *John Bull's Other Island* so in *Major Barbara* (excepting the aforesaid second act), there is none of that tight construction which was in the previous plays. There is little story, little action. Everything depends on the interplay of various types of character and of thought. But to order this process in such a way that it shall not be tedious requires a very great amount of technical skill. During the third act of *Major Barbara*, I admit, I found my attention wandering. But this aberration was not due to any loosening of Mr. Shaw's grip on his material. It was due simply to the fact that my emotions had been stirred so much in the previous act that my cerebral machine was not in proper working order. Mr. Shaw ought to have foreseen that effect. In not having done so, he is guilty of a technical error. But to deny that he is a dramatist merely because he chooses, for the most part, to get drama out of contrasted types of character and thought, without action, and without appeal to the emotions, seems to me both unjust and absurd. His technique is peculiar because his purpose is peculiar. But it is not the less technique.

There! I have climbed down. Gracefully enough to escape being ridiculous? I should like mine to be a 'sympathetic' part in 'Mr. Shaw's Position.'

43. Sir Oliver Lodge on Shaw the revolutionary teacher

1905

From signed article, '*Major Barbara*, G.B.S., and Robert Blatchford', *Clarion*, 29 December 1905, 734, 5.

Sir Oliver Lodge (1851–1940) was a scientist and educationist, who became the first principal of the University of Birmingham. He developed a deep interest in religion as a means of uniting body and mind. His article, which he saw as a supplement to the notice by Alex M. Thompson (No. 41), commended the play warmly: 'I would say to all readers: "Go and see it, if you can get in." Would that there were some municipal or corporately-owned theatres, so that it could be exhibited to everybody for fourpence.' He analysed the play, paying special attention to the religious theme, and set Shaw's approach to the problems of society against that of the Socialist publicist, Robert Blatchford, joint-editor of *Clarion*.

The critics who accuse Shaw of the remotest approach to blasphemy do not know what they are talking about. It is true he does not admire the ethics of the Sermon on the Mount—or, rather, he thinks them ineffectual and inadequate—but the sympathetic insight with which he interprets them, in spite of disagreement, is beyond praise. His treatment of the Christian religion, while yet, apparently, wishing to replace it by something more conducive to worldly success and prosperity—is the outcome of high genius.

That second act is great, one of the finest pieces of dramatic art that has been seen for a long time. It is the making of the play, and it leaves one screwed up and tense with feeling.

The third act flattens it all out again, and is diabolically cynical. It preaches the doctrine that poverty is the only crime worth troubling about; that success and money are the things specially worth striving for; that the millionaire not only has this world and time at his feet, but seems likely to dominate eternity, too.

As a sarcasm, all this would be legitimate: the conclusion of *John Bull's Other Island* was warped, too, but whereas that was sarcastically warped, this is cynically warped. The author is deadly serious in both, no doubt; but the hideous gospel he seems to wish—or tries to persuade himself, rather against the grain, that he wishes—to preach is not a natural and artistic outcome of the first two acts: it is forced on by reason of a foregone determination. Plenty of good things in that third act, of course; but the second act deserved a better conclusion. Perhaps the third act was written first, and then was not modified sufficiently to get it into tune with the two earlier acts. Perhaps, after all, it is only the wealthy cannon-maker's gospel that is being preached to us; why should we take it as the gospel of Shaw himself? Shaw must have a better gospel than that in the future, and some day he will tell it us, but not yet. As yet, perhaps, it has not dawned clearly even on him. Society does not go to be directly preached at, except perhaps by blatant stage-millionaires; but it goes to realise the real social conditions, and to enjoy brilliant sarcasm poured out upon its foibles— foibles which it does not really love, and would, I expect, gladly be rid of, if it knew the way.

The background of misery behind the fair front of Society is more in the average mind than people wot of. To more people than would be expected, the existence of wholesale and crushing poverty, towards which they feel as helpless as a Czar, is an intolerable burden.

Most writers, when dealing with or depicting well-to-do luxurious people, excite in the back of the mind a protest against the ignoring of all the hard social conditions which make such a state of comfort and idleness possible. A moderate competence, without working for it, seems expected as the natural condition of existence by every one of any social grade; but it is an unwholesome condition. In nearly all Bernard Shaw's writings, however, the background of strenuous labour, of poverty and overwork, which constitutes the foundation of modern Society, is kept present to the consciousness all the time, is borne in upon the mind even of the most thoughtless: it is not possible to overlook it, and that is one reason why his writings are so instructive and so welcome.

It cannot be that the moral, or immoral, of that third act is the advocacy of shooting and active violence. That is not the way to get improved conditions. The governing classes can beat us at the shooting game easily enough. Our state is not that of Russia, nor are our grievances so deadly. G.B.S. himself once persuaded the mob not to go on another window-breaking excursion into the West End—he showed them that they would easily get the worst of that. Moreover, the more enlightened, beneficent, and perceptive spirit which is gradually working its way into the hearts of the rulers and the better-off classes would be nipped in the bud and frozen by violence. The revolution is going on silently and peacefully, but none the more slowly for that. Work by peaceable and legal methods, and trust to the goodness in the heart of humanity, even of well-to-do humanity—and they will learn in due time. They want to learn; and plays such as these of G.B.S. will teach them more in a twelve-month than violence and disorder would teach them in a century. The old order is changing, changing by sheer divine right of truth and reason. The change may to us seem slow, but it is sure; and the more unconsciously and quietly the change comes, the better and more permanent will be the results.

What an amazing lot of reforms are wanted. Come out of that 'environment', Robert Blatchford, and help. What is the use of preaching about the influence of environment? We will admit all that.

What you say is true enough. Of course, environment controls our actions; but who made the environment? We are not drifting irresponsible machines, that must take everything that comes along, without any steering power, we cannot help being dominated by environment, but we can alter our environment, we can choose our road, and so make our own surroundings, to some extent; else are we indeed 'bottom dogs'.

44. Rupert Brooke on Shaw's plays

1906–7

Extracts from letters in *The Letters of Rupert Brooke*, ed. Geoffrey Keynes (1958).

Rupert Brooke (1887–1915), poet, was attracted to Shaw by reason of his own Fabian Socialist leanings as well as his admiration for Shaw as a writer. In a later letter than those quoted here (to Edward Marsh on 10 December 1909), he wrote that *The Shewing-Up of Blanco Posnet* revealed 'the beginning of senile decay in that brilliant intellect'.

(a) From a letter to Geoffrey Keynes, 10 January 1906 (p. 38):
Shaw's play was highly amusing & interesting, & very brutal. I suppose you have seen it? Shaw is a terrible example of the effect of commercial socialism on genius . . . brilliant brute. He is like a public school career, amusing but utterly soul-destroying. There was one sentence in *Major Barbara*, a virulent attack on the ordinary public-school master, at which I applauded very loudly & suddenly from a prominent part of the house. They nearly turned me out.

(b) From a letter to St John Lucas, October 1906 (p. 62):
I am delighted to hear that you are going to *J[ohn] B[ull]'s other Island*. It is unspeakably delightful. The average of acting all round at the Court [Theatre] is exactly four times as high as at any other theatre in London. Each character is perfect. And the play itself is exquisite, wonderful, terrific, an unapproachable satire on everything. The man who acts Broadbent is a genius. The only weak part in the whole thing is the final ten minutes of the first act. I envy you having it before you.

(c) From a letter to Erica Cotterill, January 1907 (p. 74):
I have just read through *Plays Pleasant* again, & feel more certain than ever that *Candida* is the greatest play in the world.

45. John Galsworthy on the 'ephemeral' Shaw

1906

Extract from a letter to R. H. Mottram, quoted in Mottram, *For Some We Loved* (1956), 76.

John Galsworthy (1867–1933) was already well-known as a novelist when his first play *The Silver Box* was presented at the Court Theatre later in 1906. Shaw had helped to persuade him to become a dramatist.

We've been to see two Bernard Shaw plays, *John Bull* etc., and *Man and Superman*. The beggar riles me with his out-Williaming of William, but he's a witty dog and his work (ephemeral enough) is serving a good contemporary purpose. He is only irritating in his pretensions and personality.

THE DOCTOR'S DILEMMA

1906

The Doctor's Dilemma was first presented at the Court Theatre on 20 November 1906, for a run of nine matinées.

46. Unsigned notice, Morning Post

22 November 1906, 41963, 4

Mr. Bernard Shaw is interesting because he is original, that is to say, because he is a person to himself. He is amusing because he has an inexhaustible store of intellectual fun; he is annoying because on the whole he is unintelligible. Probably he would say that he is only unintelligible north-north-west, and that when the wind is in the east he can tell the Court Theatre from the County Council. His original mission was probably that of a prophet to reconstruct the world. For such a task it is indispensable first of all to get a hearing, and Mr. Bernard Shaw long ago divined that the best way to get listeners is to amuse or startle them. So he became a veiled prophet, posing as the public jester and trusting that his real purpose would be perceived through the mask by kindred spirits. He makes war upon convention and cant, upon respectability, upon all that society thinks vital to itself.

He has found the stage his best platform and with characteristic effrontery the first conventions that he throws to the winds are those of the stage. He classifies plays as pleasant and unpleasant and draws a full house under either description. The Doctor's Dilemma is decidedly unpleasant. It has set the teeth of the critics on edge. A doctor falls in love with another man's wife and in order to be able to marry her makes arrangements to insure that she shall become a widow. When that happens, however, the lady marries somebody else. This story, apparently, Mr. Shaw regards as of no particular importance. He uses it merely as a device to give his puppets the chance of talking. The puppets are mostly doctors who spend a great deal of time in discussing their profession in the scientific jargon of the day. Mr. Bernard Shaw has taken a great deal of trouble to study the recent progress of methods of cure for diseases caused by parasites in the blood, and he is unable to keep his learning to himself. This medical conversation is cleverly distributed between half-a-dozen doctors, so that the audience gets its scientific instruction unawares and feels that it is being taken behind the scenes of a learned profession. The husband to be got rid of dies on the stage with a good deal of conversation calculated to offend persons with a disposition for reverence. And when in the epilogue the doctor discloses his desires to the widow, that lady, when announcing that she has already taken a second husband, annoys the audience by not disclosing her husband's identity.

All this is a part of Mr. Shaw's method, which consists of a mixture of pinpricks and wit. There is no plan of securing attention better than that of consistently annoying your hearers, especially if you give them some compensation in the shape of an almost uninterrupted flow of epigram and paradox, in which Mr. Bernard Shaw is usually brilliant. For those who want a stimulus in the process of dissecting modern life and society, treating it as a boy treats his new toy, pulling everything to pieces and not being able to put it together again, Mr. Shaw's plays of the latest type are just the thing. But those who wish for the pleasure appropriate to the theatre should avoid them. This is the reason why the critics quarrel with Mr. Bernard Shaw. They go to the theatre expecting a particular kind of product. Mr. Bernard Shaw gives them something quite different, to which the canons by which they are accustomed to test the works submitted to them have no reference. The traditional function of the theatre (we avoid the word normal because we freely admit Mr. Shaw's right to use the theatre for any purpose he pleases) is to give the pleasure afforded by the spectacle of what is admirable in human life and conduct—tragedy by showing that a fine character will be true to itself, in spite of all the obstacles of life and death; comedy by appealing to the instinct of reality through the perception of its antithesis, the grotesque. By letting flow the sources of laughter and of tears, the dramatist accustoms us to feel rightly about the course of human life. When he has done with us, if he knows his business, we feel a sense of elevation and of content. Mr. Shaw produces no such effect. He plays on our heads not on our hearts, and the net result of all his manipulation of us is a universal note of interrogation. Probably he has his uses. He recalls the judgment upon

Mephistopheles passed in the prologue of Goethe's *Faust*—of all the spirits that deny the scoffer is the least objectionable.

Mr. Shaw's deliberate confusion of the functions of social destroyer and playwright does not prevent his putting a great deal of clever dramatic construction into parts of *The Doctor's Dilemma*. In the scene at the Star and Garter the complete change that comes over the doctors' opinions as one after the other of them explains that Dubedat has borrowed money from him was a delightful bit of exposition. The characterisation of the doctors was admirable throughout, and making allowance for the elements of caricature and exaggeration had a distinct relation to actual life. The dilemma which confronts the doctor is made improbable because the doctors discuss it together; yet it has some psychological justification. Ridgeon, the hero, though he knows that Dubedat is a scoundrel, thinks him so great an artist as to be worth preserving. The sophism by which he persuades himself to acquiesce in his death is that the wife's ideal ought to be preserved, which will be impossible if Dubedat survives. The death scene, realistic and unduly prolonged, which offended many susceptibilities, was generally felt to be dramatically ineffective. It jarred even on those whose sense of right was not shocked by the studied parody of things sacred put into the mouth of the dying man. Dubedat would know that his language would not ruffle a group of medical men; but Mr. Shaw knew that it would many among his audience. The epilogue made the impression of a harlequinade. The audience felt that the persons whom it had already got to know could never have behaved as the actors did, and the illusion of truth being gone the element of fun was gone with it. The net effect was well summed up by one of the audience, who having intensely enjoyed the first three acts said at the end that he could not tell whether he had enjoyed the play or not.

Needless to say that the company of the Court Theatre gave on Tuesday as perfect a presentment as could be of the characters and of the play.

47. Desmond MacCarthy, notice, *Speaker*

24 November 1906, XV, 373, 226

(Charles Otto) Desmond MacCarthy (1877–1952), literary and dramatic critic, wrote criticisms of Shaw's plays in the *Speaker* and the *New Statesman*. His criticisms were collected in *Shaw* (1951).

In this notice, written after the first performance of *The Doctor's Dilemma*, MacCarthy surveyed the press reaction to the play. Other notices by MacCarthy of *The Doctor's Dilemma* are reprinted in *Shaw* (1951), but this notice was not reprinted.

The Doctor's Dilemma is the most interesting play now running. The dilemma is this: Is a doctor, who can only take a limited number of patients, to save an ordinary honourable man or a rascal who is a genius?

Most people who see this play will be occasionally bored, shocked, and irritated, frequently amused, and sometimes they will find their attention rivetted with intensity upon the stage. They will leave with something to talk about, subjects for abuse, and matter for praise, and with a multitude of topics for dispute. For fear my account of my own impressions should fail in carrying conviction, I will quote first some of the opinions of other papers. Their want of unanimity is painful but interesting reading. However, when critics disagree go yourself and see, is a jingle containing sound advice to the playgoer.

The *Tribune* declares that the second act is 'the most brilliant thing Mr. Shaw has done. Up to the end of the fourth act the play is daring, original . . . admirable . . . The death scene is enormously clever in an uncanny fashion.' But the *Daily Mail* says that if Mr. Shaw wrote the play 'to prove that his sensibilities are so dulled that he can see nothing beautiful, nothing sacred, in the dying moments of a man, whose head is pillowed on the breast of a woman who loves him, he has succeeded.' The scene is described as 'offensive and theatrical.' The *Daily Telegraph*, on the other hand, calls it 'a very harrowing death scene' . . . 'pathetic and almost tragic'; and goes on to add that Mr. Shaw 'has paid a greater attention than it is his wont to pay to the process of construction.' Not so the deft and rapid critic of *The Times*, who complains that 'if it is not quite true that Mr. Shaw loses the thread of his play, it is more than usually marred by his foible of discursiveness,' and condemns the death scene as bad taste and cheap art, only interesting to the morbid. The *Westminster*, too, accuses the play of 'lack of form and precision of idea.' The *Standard*, however, assures us that we find Mr. Shaw 'almost timidly reclining on the more conventional props and stays of stage craft.' The *Globe* sums up by saying, 'Judged as a whole, the work is a piece of capital fooling, which the lover of wit, frolic, and unreason is bound to see. . . . Not in these things (*i.e.*, the plot and characters) consists the vital portion of *The Doctor's Dilemma*, but on the satire lavished upon the profession which is worthy of Molière' (*sic*). But to the *Daily Telegraph*, again, the play is 'at once remarkable and significant, not because it satirises doctors, not because it attempts to reveal the psychology of the artist, but because it puts before us a dramatist who can draw a vivid and true character in Sir Colenso and a loving woman in Jennifer Dubedat.' Alas, the *Pall Mall* differs on that point too: 'Mr. Shaw has not told his story in such a manner that we in the least care what becomes of his amusing puppets!' The *Daily Graphic* thought the play spoilt by vulgarity and want of feeling; but the *Daily News*. . . . Enough! There is evidently a something remarkable to be seen at the Court Theatre. Mr. Shaw seems to provide an entertainment which excites, interests, disappoints, enraptures, and offends everybody. Tastes differ; but this play must surely have a strong, peculiar flavour to affect different palates so violently, making some critics grimace, some smile, and bringing tears to the eyes of others. That must be the first assertion to make about it; an assertion which only a weekly critic, with an opportunity of reading what others have said, could announce with emphatic confidence. It is as a critic in the advantageous position of having been fortified by the anticipations of others, of having compared impressions with the opinions of others, modifying both where they were originally less just, that I claim a hearing for *The Speaker* in this Babel of judgments.

It is rubbish to say that the satire on doctors is as good as Molière. Mr. Shaw's satire is amusing and often witty, but it is essentially satire upon contemporary and temporary types. It will not keep the perennial freshness of Molière. Its point depends too much upon current fads and fashions, upon the frequency of operations for appendicitis and of experimental inoculation. It is not airy, permanent satire upon human ignorance and pretence; but hilarious, thumping, obvious fun, made at the expense of prevailing prejudices, very good of its kind, but over-done. One tires of Cutler Walpole with his one remark, 'A clear case of blood-poisoning. Let me remove your nuciform sac,' just as one tires of some character in Dickens who reiterates a telling sentence. Cutler Walpole is on the stage nearly all the time; he hardly says any-thing else. He would certainly be better away in the fourth act. His inevitable remark adds nothing to the death-bed scene, and his absence would lessen the unreality of the gathering of four distinguished physicians, only one of whom has any professional business there, at the death-bed of an impoverished artist.

The avoidance of such improbabilities is absolutely vital to the impressiveness of Mr. Shaw's plays. For the impression his plays enforce is always that real everyday life is far more startling, fantastic, and moving than life beglamoured by art or heightened by conventional treatment. 'You think,' he is always saying, 'that people in love or in extremity feel, speak, and behave in such and such a way. If they ever do speak and behave so, it is because they are imitating what they have read or what they think they ought to feel. I will show you what they do and say and feel when they forget all that; and what is more, though you will think I am laughing in my sleeve at you or trying to shock you, in the end you will be more thrilled and amused by nature, by men and women with all their lyricisms, their incongruous appetites, their predicaments, their self-deceptions and unconscious consistencies than by stage heroes and villains, whom you know in your heart are not real.' And sure enough he has taken the shine out of half the modern plays played in London, even for those who do not care for his own. Unfortunately nature has given him a talent too much. He is a born caricaturist, and in consequence he is always sacrificing reality, not at the altar of sentiment, but at the altar of the god of careless hilarity. Hence we have not had from him yet a perfect and splendid play. Since half of the characters are always recognisable caricatures, and the other half are revealed from a point of view that upsets expectation, the emotion roused by the former unfits the mind for feeling the sig-nificance of the whole situation. His great fault is that he has not artistic self-control; he is devoted to his idea; but he is equally in love with a good joke, and he is apt to sacrifice alternately the one love to the other; so that at one moment he cannot resist preaching and explaining the whole point of the action through one of the characters, or bursting out into lyrical declamations revealing the emotion, the religion, behind it all; while at another he mars the reality of a wonderful situation by a joke usually excellent in itself but far from worth the sacrifice. He tries to create in the spectator the balance of mind and emotion he respects by alternately touching him and making him laugh. Sometimes that succeeds—when the scene, rousing a mixed emotion of joy, sympathy, and contempt, is a crude one like Broadbent's courting and comforting of Nora Reilly in *John Bull's Other Island*. But frequently this cannot be done by a series of consequent shocks: for the emotion which ought to be roused by Mr. Shaw's situations is often too complex and delicate to be produced by such galvanic methods. The death-bed scene of the artist in this play is an illustration of what I mean. Mr. Barker (Dubedat) dies naturally; *The Times* has found fault with him for this on the ground that a death struggle untouched by artistic emotion is an unfair, unilluminating assault on the emotions. I venture to differ. It seemed necessary that we should feel the chilly, quiet, matter-of-factness of physical extinction, which strikes us as so terribly inconsistent with all that we know death means, at the very moment we are feeling pity for a man whose will is still ablaze and whose mind is clear and detached in spite of the creeping languor of death. Dubedat dies in a pose. He hoards his last strength and his last words to stamp an image of himself on his wife's heart which he knows is not the true one. Next to his immortality in his pictures, he values that reincarnation most. He keeps an interviewer in the room, in the hope that some faint reflection of himself, as he would wish to be remembered, may possibly be thrown also upon the great blank sheet of the public imagination. The cheerful and callous young ass of an interviewer conveys by a few words, after all is over, that he has taken away a grotesquely topsy-turvy idea, such as would have disgusted the dead man and made him laugh sourly enough. That is a telling piece of irony; but profounder still is the irony of the success of Dubedat's pose upon his wife; nothing can henceforth shake her conviction that he is a hero, a king of men. She turns to the doctors, who have let him die because they judged him unworthy, and appeals to them as though they were all standing together on the top of a mountain of transfiguration. Yet Dubedat has some of our sympathy. In this last scene he only obeyed the same instinct which drove him in life to create beautiful pictures. His last picture is painted on his wife's mind. He had no respect for truth, that is why the doctor, who decides that he shall die, has Mr. Shaw's sympathy. Mr. Shaw's quarrel with artists is that they are liars. If only he would quarrel with humorists on the same ground what magnificent plays he would write! But this fine scene is spoilt by the interruption of improbable jokes. We are made to laugh, or, rather, we are just distracted enough to grin a little, by the fooleries of Bonnington and the monomania of Cutler Walpole. Would that Mr. Shaw was more of an artist or less of a wit! It is exasperating! It is almost enough to make a critic write a play with a chorus of professional critics condemning a dramatist to literary extinction for want of artistic self-control in preference to some commonplace writer, who has no gifts to tempt him away from being permanently conscientious on the low level of his little best! But then, after all, it is Mr. Shaw himself who has in England, to-day, given us the most vivid glimpses of dramatic excellence by the light of which we manage to find fault with him.

The acting was so excellent that it requires another article to do it justice.

48. St John Hankin on the position of Shaw

1907

Edward Charles St John Hankin (1869–1909), was a writer of
satirical social comedies, two of whose plays, *The Return of the
Prodigal* (1905) and *The Charity that began at Home* (1906), were
first produced by the Vedrenne–Barker management at the Court
Theatre. In an article in the *Fortnightly Review*, 'Puritanism and the
English Stage' (December 1906) (vol. LXXX, ns 1055), he wrote
that 'A play may be a serious work of art and yet remain amusing.
. . . people laugh abundantly at the plays of Mr Shaw, though he
is almost our only "serious dramatist".' In an article on 'Mr.
Bernard Shaw as Critic' in the *Fortnightly Review* for June 1907
(vol. LXXXI, ns 1057) from which the following extract is taken,
he compared the reception given to Ibsen's plays with that later
accorded to Shaw's. The essays are reprinted in *The Dramatic
Works of St John Hankin* (1912), vol. III, 131, 149.

The impatience and hostility which the English dramatic critic of the
'nineties displayed to Ibsen's work finds a curious parallel to-day in
their attitude towards the later work of Mr Shaw. In each case, I
suppose, it is the novelty, the breaking away from old methods and
conventions, which they find so galling. The Athenians, according to
St Paul, always desired some new thing. The English dramatic critic,
on the contrary, is always craving for an old one.

. . . It is a pity that our critics have this rooted distaste for originality,
or, in fact, for ideas of any kind in the theatre, for I do not see how any
drama can be expected to get on without ideas. It should be the critic's
highest function, in fact, to welcome freshness or courage in a new
play and point out its merit to an undiscerning public, whereas in
London the public seems often to be more discerning than the critics,
and certainly less intolerant of originality or courage. If the public had
taken the average dramatic critic's view of *Major Barbara*, or *The Doctor's
Dilemma*, or *The Philanderer*, they would have refrained from visiting
those plays, and would have flocked tumultuously to *Three Blind Mice*.

We know, however, that as a matter of fact they did nothing of the kind. But though all the forces of Fleet Street cannot banish ideas from the theatre altogether, they can and do strangle them when they get there to the best of their ability. 'My brethren,' said a clergyman in an impassioned peroration, 'if you see in the heart of any a spark of grace, water it! Water it!' That is what the dramatic critic does. He waters the spark—and out it goes.

I am inclined to question very seriously the wisdom of the average critic's attitude towards Mr Shaw's later work, just as I question very seriously the wisdom of his attitude towards the work of Ibsen. It seems to me to show a curious ignorance of Mr Shaw's position in the dramatic world of to-day. Mr Shaw is indisputably the most distinguished living English dramatist. He is, in fact, the only dramatist of world-wide reputation whom we have. His plays are translated into foreign tongues and played in half the capitals of Europe. They are read and discussed and defended and attacked whenever men of letters are gathered together who take any serious interest in the theatre. These are things which it is useless to ignore. The man who has attained a position of this kind must be reckoned with. He cannot be dismissed as negligible or unimportant. The purely parochial success of a two-hundred-night run in a London theatre sinks into insignificance beside a reputation of this kind. The mass of our critics, however, seem quite unconscious of this, and attack Mr Shaw's new plays, as they appear, with a contemptuous impatience that they would never dream of displaying to those of Mr Grundy or Captain Marshall. Of course, this does no harm to Mr Shaw, whose position (like Ibsen's) is not likely to be affected by what Smith or Brown write of him. But I am not sure whether it does any good to the critical reputations of Smith and Brown.

JOHN BULL'S OTHER ISLAND AND MAJOR BARBARA

published 1907

49. Joseph Knight, from an unsigned review, *Athenaeum*

27 July 1907, 4161, 107

Joseph Knight began his article by wondering whether Shaw
'distrusted his own dramatic powers' as he could not publish his
plays without long prefaces. If Shaw's ideas should ever become
old-fashioned, his plays would die 'for it is only by the ideas which
they embody that Mr. Shaw's stage-works will live.' He went on
to enumerate some of Shaw's faults in construction and character-
drawing.

And yet, when all reservations have been made, we should have a
difficulty in over-rating the indebtedness of the English stage to this
Irishman; to him it owes, or may owe, its emancipation from various
tyrannies. Mr. Shaw is the playwright who has put new brains into the
theatre, and ruthlessly taxed the brains of his audiences. He it is who has
shown that it is possible to have an intellectual drama even in England,
and an intellectual drama that shall be amusing. He has removed the
reproach of dullness from the play which appeals to the mind, and has
helped to dispose of that pernicious heresy which holds that the office
of the theatre is to provide its patrons with an aid to digestion. What is
more, he has restored to the English drama its self-respect. Mr. Bernard
Shaw is one of the select and distinguished body of playwrights of
whom it may be said that their plays read as well as sound like literature. He has, in fact, while keeping his dialogue severely colloquial,
aided in annulling, temporarily at least, the divorce between our drama

and our literature, and thereby he has destroyed another fallacy—that which supposes that style, no less than brains, is an impossible thing in the modern playhouse. Above all, he has rid the theatre of its thraldom to conventionality. The curse of our drama for many a long day has been its slavish habit of imitation. A makes a little effort in the direction of originality, and straightway B imitates A, and C imitates B. Mr. Shaw has been consistently himself, and so we are conscious in his work of a fresh and vigorous point of view. It is no small matter that this enemy of sentiment has almost laughed out of court the silly, romantic conventions long in vogue as to the relations of the sexes, and has taught us how men and women really speak to one another under the influence of sex-emotion. It has been good—although not exactly pleasant—for the Englishman to learn that he is essentially a sentimentalist, though of course it is characteristic of Mr. Shaw that in his preface he should base his theories as to the real nature of Irishmen and Englishmen on two cases so wholly untypical of their respective nations as Wellington and Nelson. It is even for our advantage that Mr. Shaw should outrage our feelings of sympathy with life's failures by the brutal-seeming assertion that poverty is the greatest of social crimes. For all such defiances of normal opinion set the playgoer thinking, and when once the playgoer starts thinking, there is the chance of a school of English drama coming into existence.

CAESAR AND CLEOPATRA

1898

Caesar and Cleopatra, although written in 1898, was not presented in public in Britain until 1907, by which time it had been seen in the USA and Berlin. Shaw wrote in 1907 'that Forbes-Robertson's Caesar should be famous in America before it has been seen here is a fact which speaks for itself on the subject of theatrical enterprise in London'. The play was presented for the first time in Britain on tour at Leeds on 16 September 1907, where it was given three performances only. It was played at the Savoy Theatre, London, on 25 November 1907 for forty performances.

50. Unsigned notice, *Yorkshire Post*

17 September 1907, 18794, 5

The writer wondered whether for Johnston Forbes-Robertson to appear in such a play as this might not be 'a prostitution of his splendid talents'. It seems clear from this notice that, while Shaw was gradually becoming recognised as an important dramatist in the London theatre, taste in other parts of the country lagged behind.

Great as was the reception accorded to Mr Forbes-Robertson and Miss Gertrude Elliott last night on their most welcome visit to the Leeds Grand Theatre, there must have been very many among the unusually large audience present who followed with conflicting feelings the progress of the play with which the week's engagement has opened. That the opinion of Mr Bernard Shaw's out-and-out admirers was entirely favourable, there can be no doubt, but of the rest it would be difficult to speak definitely. Even those who went prepared for something unconventional in dramatic speech and action could not have helped but be startled if not shocked. We can well imagine the purist saddened even to indignation at the sacrilege perpetrated on the altar of antiquity when Caesar, roaming the desert alone, comes upon the extremely youthful Cleopatra, nestling in the moonlight between the paws of the Sphinx, and is invited to climb up so as to be out of reach of those terrible Romans. 'You funny old gentleman', says she; and he, in reply, 'why aren't you at home in bed' or words to that effect. And with this kind of 'chaff' Mr Shaw's 'history in four acts' is plentifully besprinkled.

Unquestionably *Caesar and Cleopatra* is an interesting play, and, still more interesting its representation. Perhaps it is a compliment to Leeds, too, that its first performance in this country should have been reserved for this city. It had a long and apparently a successful run in the States last winter, and its future course will doubtless be watched with curiosity by all playgoers. But if its production here is due, as stated, to the influence of the newly formed local Playgoers' Society, there will, we fear, be many inclined to think that that body has in this case done little to ensure the reputation it may be desirous of acquiring. And, similarly, there must be many whose judgment will lead them to regard Mr Forbes-Robertson's part and lot in such a production as, in some degree at least, a prostitution of his splendid talents.

The part of Julius Caesar, we are told, was expressly written for Mr Forbes-Robertson, and no one who knows his great qualities on the stage need be told that he not only looks the part of the great Imperator to perfection, but acts with all the dignity and force of which he is so thoroughly capable, and which his magnificent voice and elocution render so much more effective. But there are moments when even great Caesar's utterances become mere bathos on the lines laid down by Mr Bernard Shaw. The truth is *Caesar and Cleopatra* ought to have been presented as comic opera. Much of the satire is nearly as good as Gilbert's, and certainly it is not easy to resist the impression that the whole thing is nothing more than a huge joke at the expense of ancient history. In his playful way, the author, on the programme, refers possible critics to a host of historical authorities. That, however, counts for little. Passing acquaintance with an ordinary school textbook is enough to indicate the general drift. The period is that of the Alexandrine War—between 48 BC and 47 BC—when Caesar lands in Egypt after the death of Pompey, and puts the girl Cleopatra—she is in her 17th year—on the throne. The young Queen, impersonated with fine restraint by Miss Gertrude Elliott, learns from him how to be queenly, and her infatuation is returned. But above and beyond that dramatic intensity that marks certain of the situations, there is a feeling engendered that the dramatist has his tongue in his cheek all the while, and is simply using his puppets to point his satire at modern ways. Thus nearly every historical incident is turned, in greater or less degree, to account; and incongruous laughter follows. It is smart, in a way, and very entertaining; but it is hardly worthy of Mr Forbes-Robertson and the excellent company supporting him.

51. Unsigned notice, *The Times*

26 November 1907, 38500, 5

The suggestion made in the *Yorkshire Post* notice (No. 50) that *Caesar and Cleopatra* 'ought to have been presented as comic opera' was developed further by the *Times* critic (but without acknowledgment).

To see *Caesar and Cleopatra* is once again to regret Offenbach. None but the genius that set to lilting music the reckless wit of *Orphée aux Enfers* and *La Belle Hélène* could worthily 'score' this Shavian extravaganza. It may seem a far cry from Mr Shaw to Meilhac and Halévy and the other Second Empire librettists of Offenbach. But the truth is that, fundamentally, his method in *Caesar and Cleopatra* is their method. The essence of his 'history in four acts', as it is ironically styled in the play-bill, is the uttering of modern thoughts, modern slang, and 'topical' allusions of our own day by more or less historical persons of a remote age. We are aware that Mr Shaw has his own explanation of the 'modernity' of his characters. He puts forward a theory of history to demonstrate that the world in 48 BC was exactly like the world in 1907 AD, and accordingly that the only way of truly reconstructing Caesar and his contemporaries is by looking round upon our own contemporaries. And the answer to this, of course, is that there is no need 'to seek noon at fourteen o'clock'—no need, that is to say, to invent new (and quiet preposterous) theories of history in order to justify a formula of burlesque which is not merely its formula under Mr Shaw but also its formula under Meilhac and Halévy, and, for that matter, its formula under Scarron and the earliest pioneers in the field of burlesque. And so when we hear Cleopatra call Caesar 'old gentleman' and Caesar reply that he is merely middle-aged; or Caesar explaining, when the burning of the Alexandrian Library is in question, that 'I'm an author myself'; or directing the slaves who offer him Lesbian or Chian wine to 'bring me my barley-water'; or when we find a slave from Britain priding himself on his 'respectability', or remarking of a certain Egyptian marriage custom that it is not 'proper'; or when we hear the crowd of Ptolemy's courtiers shouting 'Egypt for the Egyptians'—why, then we say that 'Shavian here, Shavian there, we mind the biggin' o't' and that it is but the old, old burlesque producing its old laughs in its old way. And for the old way we want the old music.

Indeed, Offenbach would be a help to Mr Shaw in more ways than one. His tunes would fill up certain gaps, disguise certain *longueurs*, which were apparent last night in *Caesar and Cleopatra*, even though it had been docked of a whole act. There were conversations between Cleopatra and her maidens, or with Pothinus, or with Ftatateeta which were not a little tedious, and had much better have been sung. And, what is more, music would have gone far to atone for the total lack in the play of what children call 'story'. You wondered half the time what it was all about. There seemed to be no particular reason why Caesar should be here or Cleopatra there; no reason why they should be doing just what they did, or saying just what they said; no reason, indeed, why the play should not stop at any moment or go on for ever. All this *décousu*[1] would have mattered far less with Offenbach's orchestra to beguile the ear.

But then, of course, as by this time everybody knows, the *décousu* is Mr Shaw's way. He simply uses the play as a means of giving out to you everything that happens to come at the moment into his head. Well, fortunately, it is Mr Shaw's head, and the things that happen to come into it are generally amusing things. Nothing could be more amusing than the talk between Cleopatra and Caesar under the shadow of the Sphinx, or the scene between Cleopatra and her little brother-

[1] Rambling or disjointed material.

husband Ptolemy, or the utterances of the British slave Britannus, or the conversation between the Royal bodyguard and the wily Persian. But then Mr Shaw's way is also the way of the American Judge at his mother-in-law's funeral; he mingles grave thoughts with refined pleasantry. In other words, Mr Shaw must continually be reminding us that he is a thinker, he must ever and anon be profound—and as most of the thinking and all the profundity is allotted to Caesar, we fear Caesar occasionally, not often, but still occasionally, comes very near to being a bore. That was the greater fortune of Meilhac and Halévy; they were not Fabians or Shavians, but just men of the world and easy wits. But no matter. Mr Shaw must be allowed to exhibit his own temperament, and to write, as his Rufio was to govern Egypt, in his own way; and those who don't much care for the 'grave thoughts' can console themselves with the 'pleasantry'.

And perhaps, after all, Caesar, Mr Shaw's Caesar, was not quite so solemn in intention as Mr Forbes-Robertson makes him in fact. Our admiration for Mr Robertson's personality and talent is considerable and sincere; his dignity, his charm, the suave and sonorous grace of his utterance. But he is not, no he is not, brimming over with fun; we think he misses some of the humour of this Caesar, taking some of the irony in all seriousness, and generally aiming too steadily at an effect of impressiveness. The result is an occasional heaviness—as though he had said to his part, 'Caesarem vehis Caesarisque fortunam',[1] and his part had felt a little overweighted by so tremendous a burden. Nevertheless, it is an interesting, picturesque performance; and so, in a minor way, is Miss Gertrude Elliott's Cleopatra, a delightful childish Cleopatra as she should be, but not quite the little spit-fire, the little specimen of female ferocity in the bud, that Mr Shaw's Cleopatra, if we are not mistaken, is intended to be. Mr Ian Robertson is very diverting as the 'respectable' British slave. There was hearty laughter for the greater part of the evening, and a loud call at the end for the author, who gravely listened to Mr Forbes-Robertson's announcement that he was understood not to be in the house.

[1] 'You bear Caesar and Caesar's fortune.'

52. E. A. Baughan, from an initialled notice, *Daily News*

26 November 1907, 19250, 7

Baughan began his notice by wondering whether anyone could find 'the tomboyish tricks of Mr. Bernard Shaw amusing'. He thought the play 'dull and often downright foolish', but found it nevertheless not without merit. The notice has special interest for Baughan's suggestion that 'Mr. Shaw is not really a humorous man at all.'

With all those faults, however, I dare state that *Caesar and Cleopatra* is the most ambitious and, in some ways, the finest drama Bernard Shaw has written, for it certainly has moments of something like greatness. The failure of the comic side of the work must not blind us to its brief merits. This Julius Caesar, it is true, is only the prototype of all Mr. Shaw's other Supermen; but there is something noble in his composition, and in many respects the Roman conqueror is drawn according to the portraits which have come down to us. Shaw has made his Caesar great because he follows his will. He is without passion, unless it be for justice, and above all the petty promptings of passion. All this is in that fine speech before the Sphinx. 'My way hither was the way of destiny,' Caesar exclaims as a peroration: 'I am he of whose genius you are the symbol: part brute, part woman, and part God— nothing of man in me at all.' Mr. Shaw has never written anything finer than the beginning of this scene, and again when Caesar teaches Cleopatra how to be Queen, and, last of all, upbraids her for having started a blood-strife by the assassination of Pothinus. 'And so, to the end of history, murder shall breed murder, always in the name of right and honour and peace, until the gods are tired of blood and create a race that can understand.'

There is passion at last in this scene, and with the passion comes drama. I verily believe, looking back on an evening of pure burlesque and cheap jokes, that Mr. Shaw is not really a humorous man at all.

He jokes with difficulty, and does not appear to see that he himself is the real absurd person in the play. His witticisms have no real satire for they do not cut deep enough. If only a little more than mere intellect could warm his conceptions, he might be a great dramatist. But his imagination flags just when it should soar.

Caesar and Cleopatra is well put on the stage. The only important character is Caesar, and Mr. Forbes-Robertson plays him with finesse and a certain nobility of bearing. Miss Gertrude Elliott has not a light enough touch for a typical Shaw kitten, nor has she the lurking passion which should flash out as the girl gradually finds herself. From the rest Miss Elizabeth Watson's Ftatateeta and Mr. Percy Rhodes' Rufio stood out with some distinction. As a play of curiosity Caesar and Cleopatra should be seen. I wonder if the author, who was present, thought how much better he could deal with the same subject now.

53. From an unsigned notice, *Morning Post*

26 November 1907, 42279, 7

The personage of Caesar as drawn by Mr. Shaw appears to us to be a misfit. He is made to soliloquise to the Sphinx in a tone which is hardly credible of Caesar or of any other Roman of his day, and his magnanimity is explained away as mere calculation except in one fine passage, where he is made to express a modern doctrine on the subject. But the chief misrepresentation is that, whereas in truth Caesar was Cleopatra's lover, Mr. Shaw makes him treat her as a spoiled child, and gives no hint of passion on either side. It is difficult to believe that a piece like this can hold the stage after the attraction of curiosity has worn away, for it lacks the probability of character, which is more important than the accuracy of detail as regards dates and events. Such action as there is is irrelevant to the only possible vital theme, the spiritual relation between the chief personages. Mr. Shaw, of course, thinks otherwise, but the disquisitions which he has appended to his printed text to justify his reading are the best proof that it has no root in the poetical instinct. . . . No piece representing an ancient epoch has in our recollection been produced with better taste, and the performance is well worth a visit, though it does not produce the emotion which it is the dramatist's function to arouse.

54. Tolstoy on Shaw's lack of seriousness

1908

Leo Nikolaevich Tolstoy (1828–1910), the great Russian writer, was attracted by Shaw's plays but felt that he had too strong a desire to be original and to say unexpected things. Shaw sent him a copy of *Man and Superman* in 1908 and Tolstoy replied in a letter (undated, quoted in Aylmer Maude, *The Life of Tolstoy*, Oxford, World's Classics, vol. II, 461), from which the following extract is taken. The letter begins with specific comments on *Man and Superman*.

Shaw wrote to Tolstoy (on 14 February 1910) sending him a copy of *The Shewing-Up of Blanco Posnet*. He referred to Tolstoy's earlier criticism of him and ended his letter by asking, 'Suppose the world were only one of God's jokes, would you work any the less to make it a good joke instead of a bad one?' Tolstoy wrote back to say that he 'received a very painful impression' from the last words of Shaw's letter.

Dear Mr. Shaw, life is a great and serious affair, and all of us in the short interval of time granted us must try to find our appointed task and fulfil it as well as possible. This applies to everybody, and to you especially with your great gift of original thought and your penetration into the essence of all questions. And therefore, confidently trusting that I shall not offend you, I will tell you what seem to me to be the defects in your book.

The first defect in it is that you are not sufficiently serious. One should not speak jestingly of such a subject as the purpose of human life, the causes of its perversion, and the evil that fills the life of humanity to-day. I should like the speeches of Don Juan to be not the speeches of a vision, but the speeches of Shaw, and also that 'The Revolutionist's Handbook' should be attributed not to the non-existent Tanner but to a living Bernard Shaw who is responsible for his words. The second reproach is that the questions you deal with are of such enormous importance that, for men with such profound comprehension of the evils of our life and such brilliant capacity for expression as yourself, to make them the subject of satire may easily do harm rather than help the solution of these grave questions.

In your book I detect a desire to surprise and astonish the readers by your great erudition, talent, and cleverness. Yet all this is not merely necessary for the solution of the questions you deal with, but often distracts the readers' attention from the essence of the matter by attracting it to the brilliance of the exposition. In any case I think this book of yours expresses your views not in their full and clear development, but only in an embryonic state. I think that these views, developing more and more, will arrive at the one truth we all seek and towards which we all gradually approach. I hope you will forgive me if there is anything that displeases you in what I have said. I have said it only because I recognize your very great gifts, and for you personally have a most friendly feeling, and so I remain,

LEO TOLSTOY

55. H. G. Wells on Shaw's plays

1908

Herbert George Wells (1866–1946), novelist and publicist, wrote to Shaw (undated) in reply to a letter in which Shaw admonished him for his behaviour in a celebrated altercation in the Fabian Society of which they were both members (22 March 1908). Wells ended his spirited reply as follows:

We went to hear your play. I have always thought and spoken highly of your plays. They lack characterisation and modelling and the last act of *The Doctor's Dilemma* was disgraceful. But I know of no other playwright quite like you.

GETTING MARRIED

1908

Getting Married was first presented at the Haymarket Theatre, London, on 12 May 1908, where it ran for sixteen performances. It was not a failure but it did not attract a large public.

56. Shaw's revenge on the critics

1908

From an article in the *Daily Telegraph*, 7 May 1908, 16545, 7. Reprinted in the *Bodley Head Bernard Shaw*, vol. 3 (1971), 663.

A few days before the first performance, Shaw gave an 'interview' in the *Daily Telegraph*, from which the following extract is taken. Shaw seized the opportunity to poke fun at some of the more frequent criticisms of his plays.

'This play is my revenge on the critics for their gross ingratitude to us, their arrant Philistinism, their shameless intellectual laziness, their low tastes, their hatred of good work, their puerile romanticism, their disloyalty to dramatic literature, their stupendous ignorance, their susceptibility to cheap sentiment, their insensibility to honour, virtue, intellectual honesty, and everything that constitutes strength and dignity in human character—in short, for all the vices and follies and weaknesses of which Vedrenne and Barker have been trying to cure them for four years past'.

In face of such a cyclonic outburst, what could the overwhelmed interviewer do but murmur a few words of acknowledgement of the unsolicited tribute to the majesty of the Press, and inquire the exact nature of the revenge to be wrought by the new play?

'It is very simple,' said Mr Shaw. 'You remember *A Dream of Don Juan in Hell*, at the Court. You remember the tortured howl of rage and anguish with which it was received in the Press. Yet that lasted only 110 minutes; and it was made attractive by music and by the magically fascinating stage pictures contrived by Mr Charles Ricketts—a stroke of art which would have made a sensation in any other capital in Europe, and which was here passed over with complete unintelligence. Well, this time the 110 minutes of discussion will be stretched out to 150 minutes. There will be no costumes by Mr Ricketts, nothing but a bishop in an apron. There will be no music by Mr Theodore Stier or Mozart or anyone else. There will be nothing but talk, talk, talk, talk, talk—Shaw talk. The characters will seem to the wretched critics to be simply a row of Shaws, all arguing with one another on totally uninteresting subjects. Shaw in a bishop's apron will argue with Shaw in a general's uniform. Shaw in an alderman's gown will argue with Shaw dressed as a beadle. Shaw dressed as a bridegroom will be wedded to Shaw in petticoats. The whole thing will be hideous, indescribable—an eternity of brain-racking dulness. And yet they will have to sit it out. I see that one or two of them have been trying to cheer themselves with futile guesses at something cheerful to come. They are mistaken; they will suffer—suffer horribly, inhumanly—suffer all the more because when, at last, the final fall of the curtain releases them, and they stagger away to pen their maddened protest, and to assure the public that *Getting Married* is not a play, and not even a bearable experience, they will do so at the risk of being reminded by their editors that they said all this before—said it of *John Bull's Other Island*—said it of *Arms and the Man*, and of *Caesar and Cleopatra*—said it when they had plenty of fun, plenty of scenery, plenty of music, plenty of brilliant costumes; so that now, when their worst terrors have been realised and all the delights for which they were so grossly ungrateful have been taken away from them, the tale of their suffering will not be believed. Well, serve them right! I am not a vindictive man; but there is such a thing as poetic justice; and on next Tuesday afternoon it will assume its sternest retributive form'.

TOUCHES OF MERCY

'Then, will no concessions be made to human weakness?'

'Yes, a few. We shall not be altogether merciless. The curtains will be dropped casually from time to time to allow of first-aid to the really bad cases in the seats allotted to the Press. And Mr Harrison has very

kindly arranged with the authorities of the Charing-cross Hospital to
have an ambulance available in case of need.'

'Am I to understand that in order to revenge yourself on the Press
you have deliberately written a bad play?'

'Good heavens, no; there is nothing they would like better. I have
deliberately written a good play; that is the way to make the Press
suffer. Besides, you will please observe that the enterprise in which we
are engaged is not one to be fooled with. My play is the very best I can
write; the cast is the very best available in London; and, what is equally
important, the audiences will be the best audiences in London. These
audiences will enjoy the play and admire the acting keenly. But if we
are to please such audiences, we cannot please everybody. If you turned
a Tivoli or London Pavilion audience into the Queen's Hall and inflict-
ed Beethoven's Ninth Symphony on them, they would remember the
experience with horror to the end of their lives. That is what is the
matter with most of our critics—they are very decent fellows, but they
are Tivoli critics, and the Vedrenne and Barker authors are on the
Beethovenian plane. Hence, naturally, ructions! We appear to be
wantonly mocking and insulting the wrong people, when we are
simply doing our best most earnestly to cater for the right people.
There is not a single artist concerned in the production who would
consent to be made a party to any wanton eccentricity or tomfoolery.
The satisfaction of the people for whom we really work will be as keen
as the sufferings of the others will be hideous.'

THE PLOT

'Would it be indiscreet to ask you to lift a corner of the curtain prema-
turely, and give some notion of the plot of the play?'

'The play has no plot. Surely nobody expects a play by me to have a
plot. I am a dramatic poet, not a plot-monger.'

'But at least there is a story?'

'Not at all. If you look at any of the old editions of our classical
plays, you will see that the description of the play is not called a plot or
a story, but an argument. That exactly describes the material of my
play. It is an argument—an argument lasting nearly three hours, and
carried on with unflagging cerebration by twelve people and a beadle.
They are all honourable, decent, nice people. You will find the materials
for their argument in the Church Catechism, the Book of Common
Prayer, Mr Sidney Webb's Letters to *The Times* on the subject of the
birth-rate, the various legal text-books on the law of marriage, the

sermons and table-talk of the present Bishop of Birmingham and the late Bishop of London (Mandell Creighton), *Whitaker's Almanack*, *The Statesman's Year-Book*, *The Statistical Abstract*, the Registrar-General's returns, and other storehouses of fact and succulent stores of contemporary opinion. All who are intelligent enough to make these their daily reading will have a rare treat; but I am bound to add that people who prefer novelettes will have to pay repeated visits to the play before they acquire a thoroughly unaffected taste for it. If you would like me to go into the subject of the play in detail, I shall be delighted to do so.'

57. H. Hamilton Fyfe, notice, *World*: Shaw's 'dulness'

20 May 1908, 1768, 919

H. Hamilton Fyfe (1869–1951), author and journalist, was dramatic critic of the *World* from 1905 to 1910. The adverse nature of his notice forms an ironic reply to Shaw's remarks in the *Daily Telegraph* 'interview'.

I believe Bernard Shaw once declared, in answer to a query as to why he deliberately gave the majority of people the impression that he wrote with his tongue in his cheek: 'If I said what I mean seriously, I should be stoned.' In this, as in other matters, he took too extreme a view. He has in *Getting Married* said what he means very seriously indeed. But the audience at the Haymarket Theatre showed no inclination whatever to stone him. They merely yawned.

Various theories have been propounded by way of accounting for the tediousness of the piece. Some say it is dull because it isn't dramatic, because it is a 'conversation' (so the author labels it), and not a play.

But *John Bull's Other Island* was equally a conversation; that was delight-fully amusing and stimulating all the way through. Others are driven to the conclusion that Shaw wrote it as a trick upon the tiresome people who make him ridiculous by excessive adulation. Yet a third suggestion is that he intended it as an elementary essay in New Age propaganda among persons who have never thought about marriage at all. This would certainly explain the un-Shaw-like medley of stale argument and cheap jest which reduced an audience composed almost entirely of admirers to a state of annoyed, bewildered disappointment long before the piece came to an end. People capable of being entertained by the joke about a Nonconformist who called the Church of England the Scarlet Woman, and died of scarlet fever; or by a supplanted husband continually referring to his supplanter as 'the young man with a face like a mushroom'; or by the exquisite notion of a woman being in-troduced to a priest as 'Father Anthony,' and at once addressing him as 'Dad'—people who are amused by this music-hall knockabout style of humour would no doubt find Shaw's reasons for making divorce easier startlingly new, although, in fact, there is not one of them which has not been pointed out in innumerable articles, discussed at every intelligent luncheon and dinner table till most of us are tired of the topic, and orated about in Hyde Park every Sunday morning for the last forty years.

Each of these explanations is plausible, yet no one of them, I think, correct. So far as I can judge, after considering the piece from various points of view, Shaw has degenerated into dulness for the very simple reason that he is so tremendously in earnest. The commonest kind of bore is the man (or the woman) who becomes obsessed by a subject and is for ever harping upon it, convinced that it is of such importance as to insure everyone's interest in what he has to say about it. Shaw is obsessed by the subject of marriage. He plays round it, fascinated, like a small boy round the locked door of the jam cupboard or a wasp in a pantry where everything is securely covered up. He seems to feel that there is some ecstasy in life which he has not tasted. This is the third play in which he has tried to find out what it is. (The other two, of course, were *The Philanderer* and *Man and Superman*.) He is like a deaf man trying to explain the fascination of music. 'People go to concerts and operas,' the deaf man would say, 'for the pleasure of meeting one another, or in order to support managers and artists, or on account of the beauty of the women singers, or because they like to watch the odd movements of the instrumentalists.' It would never occur to him that they went to enjoy the music. So does Shaw, in writing about marriage, leave out of consideration the chief element, the only element which really matters—the element of Love.

Shaw can understand people marrying under stress of physical attraction, or because they want children, or because they amuse one another, or even for the purpose of bringing a play to an end. He is as far as ever from understanding that the compelling cause of nearly all marriages is that subtle compound of mutual tenderness and desire and comradeship which we call Love. That is the worst of Shaw as a dramatist. He is 'brainy' and so unemotional: so ignorant of the world and human nature and the forces which shape the destiny of man. That is why his plays will not survive beyond his own time. He is by far the wittiest and the most ingenious and, in a brilliantly shallow way, the most observant writer of his age, either in this country or any other. But there are things in life of which Shaw has no conception that almost any undergraduate could tell him about. Also he seems to be curiously unaware that there are any thoughtful, intelligent people in the world outside his own little set. When Father Anthony in *Getting Married* denounces all marriage as sinful, Shaw no doubt thought that this primitive Christian view would provide a piquant contrast against the 'ultra-modern' views of the Bishop who holds that, unless divorce is made easier, temporary marriages are bound to come; of Miss Grantham, who would like to do her duty to the State as a mother, but could not endure the degradation of cohabiting with a man; or of Mrs. Reginald, who would like to have a lot of husbands, each of a different kind. But really all these ideas belong almost to the same period. Miss Grantham is an early Victorian old maid, Mrs. Reginald comes out of Congreve, the Bishop merely repeats what all sensible people have thought for a hundred years past.

What the Bishop, with his solemn warnings to Prime Ministers, does not see, however, nor Shaw either, is that supposing divorce *were* made more easy, supposing temporary unions on George Meredith's lines became legal to-morrow, everything would go on almost exactly as it does now. The men and women who really want changes of partners get them as it is. A number of others think they would like them; but if they found they could get them, the possibility would be quite enough to convince them that they might go farther and fare worse. I have no doubt the divorce law will shortly be widened, but I cannot see that it is a matter to worry about one way or the other. Nor do I find other sensible people worrying about it, and that is the reason why sensible people found Shaw's immensely long and very earnest discourse on the subject wearisome and dull.

Hearing a Shaw play is like listening to an exceedingly clever person talking. There is no dramatic illusion, no development of character; but there is abundance of witty and suggestive talk. Yet, however well a person may talk, he will not talk equally well on all subjects, and on some subjects he is almost certain to be a bore, generally because he insists on taking them too seriously. This, I think, explains the failure of *Getting Married*.

58. Henry James disagrees with Shaw

1909

From a letter of 20 January 1909, reprinted in *The Complete Plays of Henry James*, ed. by Leon Edel (1949), 643.

Henry James (1843–1916), novelist and critic, did not have a very good opinion of Shaw. He confessed to an American friend in 1910, 'I do not think highly of Shaw. Wilde wrote a better play, I think, *Lady Windermere's Fan*. It is a distinctly good play, better than anything Shaw has written. Shaw has the sort of success that consists in being talked about, but I do not think him great' (quoted in Laurence, II, 828).

James had long had the ambition to be a successful playwright; a play *The Saloon*, adapted from his story *Owen Wingrave*, was rejected by the Stage Society in January 1909. Shaw wrote to James to tell him that the play had not been accepted and urged him to rewrite it. He declared that James had used his 'consummate art' to write a fatalistic play and that 'people don't want works of art from you: they want help: they want, above all, encouragement. . . .' James's reply, part of which is reproduced here, amounted to a firm rejection of Shaw's views about the nature and purpose of art.

I am ready serenely to answer you. I do such things because I happen to be a man of imagination and taste, extremely interested in life, and because the imagination, thus, from the moment direction and motive play upon it from all sides, absolutely enjoys and insists on and incurably leads a life of its own, for which just this vivacity itself is its warrant. You surely haven't done all your own so interesting work without learning what it is for the imagination to *play* with an idea—an idea about life—under a happy obsession, for all it is worth. Half the beautiful things that the benefactors of the human species have produced would surely be wiped out if you don't allow this adventurous and speculative imagination its rights. You simplify too much, by the same token, when you limit the field of interest to what you call the scientific—your employment of which term in such a connection even greatly, I confess, confounds and bewilders me. In the one sense in which *The Saloon could* be scientific—that is by being done with all the knowledge and intelligence relevant to its motive, I really think it quite supremely so. That is the only sense in which a work of art can be scientific—though in that sense, I admit, it may be so to the point of becoming an everlasting blessing to man. And if you waylay me here, as I infer you would be disposed to, on the ground that we 'don't want works of art,' ah then, my dear Bernard Shaw, I think I take such issue with you that—if we didn't both *like* to talk—there would be scarce use in our talking at all. I think, frankly, even, that we scarce want anything else at all. They are capable of saying more things to man about himself than any other 'works' whatever are capable of doing—and it's only by thus saying as much to him as possible by saying, as nearly as we can, all there is, and in as many ways and on as many sides, and with a vividness of presentation that 'art' and art alone is an adequate mistress of, that we enable him to pick and choose and compare and know, enable him to arrive at any sort of synthesis that isn't, through all its superficialities and vacancies, a base and illusive humbug. On which statement I must rest my sense that all *direct* 'encouragement'—the thing you enjoin on me —encouragement of the short-cut and say 'artless' order, is really more likely than not to be shallow and misleading, and to make him turn on you with a vengeance for offering him some scheme that takes account but of a tenth of his attributes. In fact I view with suspicion the 'encouraging' *representational* work, altogether, and think even the question not an *a priori* one at all, that is save under this peril of too superficial a view of what it is we have to be encouraged or discouraged *about*. The artist helps us to know this—if he have a due intelligence—better than anyone going, because he undertakes to represent the world to us; so that, certainly, if *a posteriori*, we can on the whole feel encouraged, so much the better for us all round. But I can imagine no scanter source of exhilaration than to find the brute undertake that presentation without the most consummate 'art' he can muster!

But I am really too long-winded.

THE SHEWING-UP OF
BLANCO POSNET

1909

The Shewing-Up of Blanco Posnet was written for Sir Herbert
Beerbohm Tree at His Majesty's Theatre, London, but was
proscribed by the Lord Chamberlain on the grounds of alleged
blasphemy. It was presented by the Abbey Theatre Company in
Dublin, which was outside the jurisdiction of the Lord Chamberlain. It was given fifteen performances. The play was not presented in the West End of London until 1921.

59. James Joyce on *Blanco Posnet* and Shaw the preacher

1909

Il Piccolo della Sera, Trieste, 5 September 1909.

James Joyce (1882–1941), Irish novelist, shows clearly from this notice, that he had no high opinion of Shaw. Unflattering comments on Shaw are to be found elsewhere in Joyce's work. His brother, Stanislaus Joyce, notes in *My Brother's Keeper* (1957) that James Joyce 'found the frank vulgarity of the music hall less offensive than the falsity of most of the legitimate drama of his day: Jones, Pinero, Sutro, Phillips (verse was always a mitigating circumstance), and most of all, Shaw'.

Joyce's article (entitled 'La Battaglia fra Bernard Shaw e la Censura'—'Bernard Shaw's Battle with the Censor') is reprinted in *The Critical Writings of James Joyce*, ed. Ellsworth Mason and Richard Ellman (1959), where there is a footnote in which Shaw is quoted as saying 'There was no exchange of letters between myself and Dublin Castle. The campaign was conducted by Lady Gregory and W. B. Yeats. I did not interfere.'

Dublin, 31 August

There is one gay week every year in the Dublin calendar, the last week of August, in which the famous Horse Show draws to the Irish capital a vari-coloured crowd, of many languages, from its sister island, from the continent, and even from far-off Japan. For a few days the tired and cynical city is dressed like a newly-wed bride. Its gloomy streets swarm with a feverish life, and an unaccustomed uproar breaks its senile slumber.

This year, however, an artistic event has almost eclipsed the importance of the Show, and all over town they are talking about the clash between Bernard Shaw and the Viceroy. As is well known, Shaw's latest play, *The Shewing-Up of Blanco Posnet*, was branded with the

197

mark of infamy by the Lord Chamberlain of England, who banned its performance in the United Kingdom. The censor's decision probably came as no surprise to Shaw, because the same censor did the same thing to two other of his theatrical works, *Mrs Warren's Profession* and the very recent *Press Cuttings*; and Shaw probably considers himself more or less honoured by the arbitrary proclamation which has condemned his comedies, together with Ibsen's *Ghosts*, Tolstoy's *The Power of Darkness*, and Wilde's *Salomé*.

However, he would not give up, and he found a way to elude the frightened vigilance of the censor. By a strange chance, the city of Dublin is the only place in all the British territory in which the censor has no power; in fact, the old law contains these words: 'except the city of Dublin.' Shaw, then, offered his play to the company of the Irish National Theatre, which accepted it and announced its performance just as though nothing were out of the ordinary. The censor was apparently rendered powerless. Then the Viceroy of Ireland intervened to uphold the prestige of authority. There was a lively exchange of letters between the representative of the King and the writer of comedy, severe and threatening on the one side, insolent and scoffing on the other, while Dubliners, who care nothing for art but love an argument passionately, rubbed their hands with joy. Shaw held fast, insisting on his rights, and the little theatre was so filled at the first performance that it literally sold out more than seven times over.

A heavy crowd thronged about the Abbey Theatre that evening, and a cordon of giant guards maintained order; but it was evident at once that no hostile demonstration would be made by the select public who jammed every nook of the little *avant garde* theatre. In fact, the report of the evening performance mentioned not even the lightest murmur of protest; and at the curtain fall, a thunderous applause summoned the actors for repeated curtain calls.

Shaw's comedy, which he describes as a sermon in crude melodrama, is, as you know, in a single act. The action unfolds in a wild and woolly city of the Far West, the protagonist is a horse thief, and the play limits itself to his trial. He has stolen a horse which he thought belonged to his brother, to repay himself for a sum taken from him unjustly. But while he is fleeing from the city, he meets a woman with a sick baby. She wants to get back to town in order to save the life of her child, and, moved by her appeal, he gives her the horse. Then he is captured and taken to the city to be tried. The trial is violent and arbitrary. The sheriff acts as prosecutor, shouting at the accused, banging the table, and threatening witnesses with revolver in hand. Posnet, the thief, sets forth some primitive theology. The moment of sentimental weakness in which he yielded to the prayers of a poor mother has been the crisis of his life. The finger of God has touched his brain. He no longer has the strength to live the cruel, animal life he had led before this encounter. He breaks out into long, disjointed speeches (and it is here that the pious English censor covered his ears), which are theological insofar as their subject is God, but not very churchly in diction. In the sincerity of his convictions, Posnet resorts to the language of the mining camp; and, among other reflections, when he is trying to say that God works secretly in the hearts of men, to the language of horse thieves.

The play ends happily. The baby which Posnet tried to save dies, and the mother is apprehended. She tells her story to the court and Posnet is acquitted. Nothing more flimsy can be imagined, and the playgoer asks himself in wonder why on earth the play was interdicted by the censor.

Shaw is right; it is a sermon. Shaw is a born preacher. His lively and talkative spirit cannot stand to be subjected to the noble and bare style appropriate to modern playwriting. Indulging himself in wandering prefaces and extravagant rules of drama, he creates a dramatic form which is much like a dialogue novel. He has a sense of situation, rather than of drama logically and ethically led to a conclusion. In this case he has dug up the central incident of his *Devil's Disciple* and transformed it into a sermon. The transformation is too abrupt to be convincing as a sermon, and the art is too poor to make it convincing as drama.

And may not this play reflect a crisis in the mind of its writer? Earlier, at the end of *John Bull's Other Island*, the crisis was set forth. Shaw, as well as his latest protagonist, has had a profane and unruly past. Fabianism, vegetarianism, prohibitionism, music, painting, drama—all the progressive movements in art and politics—have had him as champion. And now, perhaps, some divine finger has touched his brain, and he, in the guise of Blanco Posnet, is shown up.

JAMES YOYCE [!]

MISALLIANCE

1910

Misalliance, written in 1909–10, was first presented at the Duke of York's Theatre on 23 February 1910. It was produced as part of the Charles Frohman Repertory Season; neither the season nor *Misalliance* was a success and the play was given eleven performances only.

---

60. Max Beerbohm, notice, *Saturday Review*

26 February 1910

Reprinted in *Around Theatres* (1953), 562.

Max Beerbohm felt that Shaw had done less than his best work and been content simply to reproduce past characters, and stale ideas. His notice was entitled 'Mr Shaw's "Debate"'.

Very queer was its effect on me. As the evening wore on, the footlights receded, the audience vanished from around me, and though, far away, there the stage still was with people talking on it, and with me over-hearing them quite distinctly, I felt nevertheless that it was Sunday morning, and that I was walking along Praed Street, with a keen and unremitting north-east wind against my face. Keenly, unremittingly, from the road unswept in deference to the Sabbath, the wind drove into my eyes and mouth and ears dry particles of refuse. Bits of trampled paper careered wildly past me along the gutters. Orange peel and wisps of straw danced unholy measure. For all the wind's violence, there was a faint odour of staleness everywhere. I pressed on, wondering if the wind would ever drop, wondering that it had not yet blown all the dust and other remnants past me. But these seemed to be unending, and the wind permanent. It was with intense relief that I espied a hansom, and jumped in. . . . Only as I was driving away from the Duke of York's Theatre did I realise that all this was a parable, and not a fact. . . . The keen and unremitting north-east wind is, of course, symbolic of Mr Shaw's brain. The dust and other remnants stand for the staleness of the characters and the ideas which Mr Shaw here fragmentarily reproduces from his past work (in which they were so fresh). And Praed Street on Sunday morning is my hint of the cheerlessness of that resurrection, and of its distressing unloveliness. It does not include the unreality, the remoteness from human truth, that pervades the whole 'debate'. Let the fact that I have never been in Praed Street on Sunday morning stand for that.

There never was any reality in Mr Shaw's typical young men and women. (I except Ann Whitefield, in whom—though she was certainly not, as Mr Shaw claimed, 'Everywoman'—there was humanity enough). Mr Shaw has often explained that the critics' scepticism is because they are steeped in the conventions of the theatre and can't recognise a real thing when they see it. Well, speaking for myself, I deny that charge. The 'ingenue' and 'juvenile lead' of old-fashioned commercial drama have never imposed on me. They never have seemed to me to resemble the actual young men and women whom I have known. I see them as figments. And in that respect they do very closely resemble the young men and women of Mr Shaw. The difference is that they are pretty figments. Mr Shaw's are ugly. If a man invents, we prefer the result to be something better than life. We cannot understand a man taking the pains to invent something worse. In point of fact, a man never does consciously set himself that task. What he invents—however much worse it be than life—is either what he (by obliquity of vision) supposes life to be, or else what he would like it to be. Mr Shaw's young men and women are the more distressing by reason of the fear lurking in us that—Impossible! Mr Shaw is as distressed by his puppets as we are, and only by his righteous indignation against what he takes to be mankind is he enabled to go on with the task of fashioning them. When they were brand-new to us, their ugliness was atoned for by their brand-newness, and by the force and brilliancy with which they were presented. But now that we know them so well, and now that their creator just trots them perfunctorily out as figures in a debate that occasionally drifts into harlequinade and 'knock-about', these alternately impudent and whining young men, and these invariably priggish and hectoring young women, all of them as destitute of hearts as they are of manners, and all of them endowed with an equal measure of chilly sensuality, evoke in us a rather strong desire to see no more of them. Some comfort we take in our certainty that we shan't, at any rate, run up against them in the actual world.

[Some details of the characters and plot are discussed.]

I have said that these characters are perfunctory. Throughout the play, indeed, I had the impression that Mr Shaw had not done his best —that the work had been thrown off in intervals snatched from lecturing and speech-making and organising this or that. I wished he would have more conscience in organising his own art. I do not mean to decry his present fashion of writing 'debates' for the stage instead of plays. But a debate, to stand the test of the theatre, must be treated as an art-form. It must have some central point, and it must be progressive; must be about something and lead to something. *Misalliance* is about anything and everything that has chanced to come into Mr Shaw's head. It never progresses, it doesn't even revolve, it merely sprawls. Throughout the evening we are clutching at loose ends, all of which come off (though not in the slang sense); and we very soon grow weary of the pastime. So careless of his effects has Mr Shaw been that he repeats not merely from his previous plays, but from within the play itself.

[Some examples are given.]

To condemn a work of Mr Shaw's is for me a new and disagreeable sensation. I wonder if the fault is really all his. It is a mistake to suppose that in the things of the mind we are less apt to be inconsistent than in other matters. We know that a man may love a woman sincerely, and yet for no apparent reason, gradually or suddenly, cease to love her. Not less in his opinions about art is he at the mercy of inscrutable change. He may love this or that work, and then, without being able to give any satisfactory reason to himself, grow cold. Can it be that I . . . no! I have given very satisfactory reasons why I don't like *Misalliance*. . . . Praed Street, Sunday morning, and a not bracing, a blighting, wind.

61. H. L. Mencken on Shaw as 'a somewhat ridiculous crusader'

1911

Extract from a signed article, 'The New Dramatic Literature', *Smart Set*, August 1911. Reprinted in *H. L. Mencken's Smart Set Criticisms*, ed. W. H. Nolte (Ithaca, New York, 1968), 49.

Henry Louis Mencken (1880–1956), American journalist and author, editor of the *Smart Set* and the *American Mercury*, was one of Shaw's most enthusiastic admirers in America at the beginning of the century. In his book, *George Bernard Shaw: His Plays* (1905), he called Shaw 'a world-figure in the modern drama' and said that 'in all the history of the English stage, no man has exceeded him in technical resources nor in nimbleness of wit.' When he began to write regular dramatic criticism for the *Smart Set*, his view of Shaw gradually changed and, while he still admired the surface brilliance of Shaw's writing, he found little more than platitudes in the views and ideas that his work contained.

Another Irishman of parts—George Bernard Shaw, no other—comes before us with a new book of some four hundred pages, containing three plays and three long prefaces. In the case of *Getting Married* and *The Shewing-Up of Blanco Posnet* the prefaces are far more important than the plays. *Getting Married* shows, in spots, a plentiful cleverness, but elsewhere it shows mere smartness—and smartness, once its quality is reinforced by quantity, begins to grow tedious, like the kisses following the first dozen. As for *Blanco Posnet*, it is a somewhat cheap effort to shock the pious, in the course of which Mr. Shaw reveals the abysmality of his ignorance of spoken American. Where he got the dialect of his unearthy Westerners I don't know, but I venture to suspect some German version of the Italian libretto of *The Girl of the Golden West*. There remains *The Doctor's Dilemma*, an amusing and well-constructed piece, in which fun is poked at the medical fellows on the one hand, and that puzzling thing, the artistic temperament, is studied on the other. Shaw's hero is a great artist who is also a shameless scoundrel. To serve his art he preys upon all available game—his wife, his friends, mere strangers. At the very gates of success he falls ill, and eminent physicians are called in to wrestle with the bacilli which infest him. One of these physicians, the only one who can cure him, falls in love with his wife. What to do? Kill the scoundrel and get the wife, or save the artist and lose the wife? You may rest assured that Shaw neglects none of the opportunities that this amazing problem offers. The play, indeed, is the best he has done since *Man and Superman*.

But in the preface, in which he undertakes to dispose of medical experimentation, the brilliance of his rhetoric does not conceal the weakness of his cause. Not that he employs the old, old argument, depends upon the old, old false testimony, wrings the old, old tears. Far from it, indeed. With characteristic originality he seeks ammunition in the very latest discoveries of the pathologists—particularly in Sir Almroth Wright's discovery of opsonins and of the so-called negative phase in the process of immunization. But after reading fifty pages of his engaging paralogy, one suddenly finds at the end that it is mere nonsense, after all—that Shaw, like every other anti-vivisectionist, is merely a sentimentalist who strains at a guinea pig and swallows a baby. In brief, the wild Irishman sinks to the level of a somewhat ridiculous crusader. The trouble with him is that he has begun to take himself seriously. When he was content to write plays first and discuss them afterward, he was unfailingly diverting. But now that he writes tracts first and then devises plays to rub them in he grows rather tedious.

62. G. H. Mair on Shaw as the founder of a school

1911

George Herbert Mair (1887–1926), journalist and critic, included this assessment of Shaw in *English Literature: Modern* (1911), a volume in the Home University Library, 244.

In England men began to ask themselves whether the theatre here too could not be made an avenue towards the discussion of living difficulties, and then arose the new school of dramatists—of whom the first and most remarkable is Mr. George Bernard Shaw. In his earlier plays he set himself boldly to attack established conventions, and to ask his audiences to think for themselves. *Arms and the Man* dealt a blow at the cheap romanticism with which a peace-loving public invests the profession of arms. *The Devil's Disciple* was a shrewd criticism of the preposterous self-sacrifice on which melodrama, which is the most popular non-literary form of play-writing, is commonly based; *Mrs Warren's Profession* made a brave and plain-spoken attempt to drag the public face to face with the nauseous realities of prostitution; *Widowers' Houses* laid bare the sordidness of a society which bases itself on the exploitation of the poor for the luxuries of the rich. It took Mr. Shaw close on ten years to persuade even the moderate number of men and women who make up a theatre audience that his plays were worth listening to. But before his final success came he had attained a substantial popularity with the public which reads. Possibly his early failure on the stage—mainly due to the obstinacy of playgoers immersed in a stock tradition—was partly due also to his failure in constructive power. He is an adept at tying knots and impatient of unravelling them; his third acts are apt either to evaporate in talk or to find some unreal and unsatisfactory solution for the complexity he has created. But constructive weakness apart, his amazing brilliance and fecundity of dialogue ought to have given him an immediate and lasting grip of the stage. There has probably never been a dramatist who could invest conversation with the same vivacity and point, the same combination of surprise and inevitableness that distinguishes his best work.

. . . Mr. Shaw may be said to have founded a school; at any rate he gave the start to Mr. Galsworthy and some lesser dramatists.

63. John Jay Chapman on Shaw as 'a child of the age'

1913

Extract from signed article, 'Shaw and the Modern Drama' in *Harper's Weekly*, 19 April 1913, 57, 10.

John Jay Chapman (1862–1933), literary critic, poet and playwright. His article began with an account of *Fanny's First Play*, which he had seen in New York. After the first of the two passages quoted below, he told how a group of young girls, 'the graduating class from a fashionable school', had been sitting in front of him at the theatre and how 'every time a reference to adultery was made by the actors, the girls giggled in a knowing manner'. Chapman felt that the reaction of the girls to the play was a sign of the corruption and deception of youth at the time.

The article was prefaced by a brief editorial note in which it was stated that the editor did not endorse Chapman's views and added that 'we believe that he is mistaken in attempting to trace any connection between the indisputable popularity of Shaw's plays and the characteristics of an age which Mr Chapman believes to be increasingly corrupt.'

Shaw is a sincere playwright, and when we consider the fluffy mediocrity of the old plays, and of the old-style acting which Shaw's drama supplanted, we cannot help being grateful to him. He has revolutionized English acting. He has produced actors who, within their rather narrow limits, are as good as French actors. Shaw is a sincere artist;

he writes for himself and to satisfy himself. He has thus rediscovered one of the psychological secrets of art. The way to interest the world is for a man to write for himself. Shaw, as a man, is interested in the contrasts and incongruities of ethical theory which modern (perhaps all) life shows. His mind is satisfied when he has apprehended the irreconcilable conflicts in the world of morality. As an artist he is satisfied when he has successfully presented one or some of these conflicts. He really seeks nothing beyond this in his art; and yet the fact that he came into notice as a social agitator has left its heavy trace on his art; it makes him preach.

Whether it be preaching or poetry, however, Shaw's work has got him the attention of the world. Any group of educated people anywhere will be thrown into excited discussion by almost any bit of Shaw's work. This shows not only that Shaw is a very powerful and remarkable being, but also that his work bears a peculiar and vital relation to the passing moment. Some people think that Shaw's purpose is to amuse the fools and to bewilder the thinkers. My own belief is that Shaw wants merely to get heard of and to make money. Socialism and play-writing are his rattle. When he was young and poor, he agitated it loudly; and now that he is rich and famous he knows how to do nothing else except to work this rattle. You cannot say he is a man without a heart; he is the kindliest of men. But he is a man without taste or reverence. He does not know that there are things which cannot be made funny. He is a man in whose composition something is left out. You cannot *blame* him, any more than you can blame the color-blind. He is beauty-blind, and amuses himself with seeing what grotesques he can pick out of the carpet of life.

The objections to Shaw are thus seen to be not dramatic, but personal, and again, in a sense, not personal, but generic and of the age. Shaw's crude and cruel treatment of humanity—all done in the name of Fabianism (whatever that is), the somewhat loathsome touch of the social reformer who has worn off the fine edges of his feelings by contact with grossness (we find this touch sometimes in a certain type of clergyman), keeps sending chills of an unpleasant kind through a sensitive auditor, and chills of a very agreeable kind through the auditor who is deficient in human feeling or deficient in artistic experience. I suppose the fault of Shaw is like the fault of Ibsen. Ibsen is not content unless he has rasped our feelings. Shaw, to be sure, can laugh and is, to my mind, a thousand times a better man and better artist than Ibsen, who can only scowl. But Shaw has Ibsen's method. It was

Ibsen who first found out that the public was callous. Ibsen reasoned thus: 'If you want to give emotion to the average playgoer you must take a rusty blade from an old razor, attach it to a brick, and therewith suddenly shave off one of a man's toes. That is art'. Shaw has the same rake-and-saw theory. He cannot mention adultery (and it is his chief theme) without seeming to soil the whole of human nature in doing so.

In all this obtuseness Shaw is a child of the age, and his popularity depends upon this very crudity. If Shaw should touch human nature with the loving hand of, say, Molière, or present his characters in the transparent and pleasing atmosphere of sound-hearted humanity, his peculiar audience to-day would not understand him. He would lose his charm for his public; I say not for all the public (witness the charming plays that succeed) but for *his* public. Whatever *Hamlet* may have intimated to the contrary, *caviare* is what half the million wants to-day. We must have mustard at every course. We like the butter to be a little rancid, and humor seems flat unless it contains just a little tang of doubt as to the fundamental truth of virtue and honor. Such a public takes the romance out of its theater: and the loss is particularly visible in the romantic roles—namely, in the young characters.

... During the last thirty years, there has been a great demand in Europe for coarse literature, obvious, crude and bold, fitted for the appreciation of luxurious and materialistic persons, of ignorant persons, or fatigued persons. Now wealth joined forces with effete culture in search of sensation. The increasing demand for *piquancy* which such an audience implies, led to an ever-increasing grossness of concentration on the part of the artists. Wherever the relations of the sexes were concerned, this intensification led, of course, to pictures of female depravity at younger and even younger ages. It seems as if the limits of indelicacy had now been reached by this school of play-writing (unless childhood is to be attacked), and we may expect an emotional revival.

ANDROCLES AND THE LION

1912

Androcles and the Lion was first produced at the St James's Theatre, London, on 1 September 1913. It was given fifty-two performances.

64. E. A. Baughan on *Androcles and the Lion*

1913

Notice initialled E.A.B. in *Daily News*, 2 September 1913, 21055, 7.

Mr. Edward Sillward's lion acted Mr. Bernard Shaw off the stage at the St. James's Theatre last night. It was a most comic lion, and roared most realistically. The pain of the thorn, the joy when it is extracted by Androcles, and the gradual recognition of his benefactor by this Leo Shavianus when, by all the rules of the game, the Christian should have been eaten, were finely conveyed by Mr. Sillward. But that lion queered Mr. Shaw's characteristic gibes at the theatrical martyrdom of the early Christians.

All artists like to attempt the impossible, and I have no doubt Mr. Shaw took much delight in the writing of *Androcles and the Lion*. Would it be possible, he may have asked himself, to use the old fable as a basis for a semi-humorous and semi-serious criticism of Christianity? No dramatist but Planché, in the libretto of a pantomime, has ever touched the subject, because stage lions must be comic, and the story of Androcles is not essentially comic.

That Mr. Bernard Shaw has not succeeded is only another way of saying that he has attempted the impossible. He has actually shown some want of humour, or, perhaps, an insolent disregard of it, in expecting us to be interested in the ideals of the early Christians after the comic introduction of Androcles and his extraction of the thorn from the lion's paw. The fable would have had more force if there had been no lion and no Androcles. It is all very well to attempt to hang a meaning on Androcles' conquering of the savage beast by sympathy and kindness, the one Christian act, one may say, in the whole play, but it really will not do.

There are some fine things in the play, as when Lavinia, one of the leaders of the Christians, replies to a Roman captain's question, 'What is God?' 'When we know that,' she replies, 'We shall be gods ourselves.' There is an idea, too, in Ferrovius's apostasy because he finds that when he has to face the gladiators and should have died without a struggle, his old worship of the God of Mars is too strong.

Christianity cannot be until Mars is no longer worshipped. This Ferrovius is an interesting character, the prototype of all muscular Christians. There was humour in his allowing himself to be smote on both cheeks by a Roman exquisite and then insisting on teaching his assailant how Christian-like such humility makes a man feel. Up and down the fable was strewn many clever lines and amusing ideas, but the fable is one of Mr. Bernard Shaw's mistakes, and it was not surprising that such very heavy fooling mixed with serious ideas did not receive very enthusiastic applause.

65. Desmond MacCarthy, *New Statesman*

6 September 1913, vol. I, 22, 693.

Reprinted in *Shaw* (1951), 102.

Androcles and the Lion is the most amusing of Mr Shaw's religious plays.
He has written two religious dramas, *Major Barbara* and *Blanco Posnet*;
one farce, in which conversion is the main theme, *Fanny's First Play*;
and then he invented a new form, the religious pantomime. *Androcles
and the Lion* is the reverse of mediaeval in sentiment and doctrine, but
its nearest parallel as a dramatic entertainment is one of those old
miracle plays in which buffoonery and religion were mixed pell-mell
together. No contemporary playwright, except Bernard Shaw, could
write a religious pantomime (Chesterton alone among writers might
entertain such an idea), for no other dramatist believes so firmly in the
virtue of laughter, is so serious, and delights so much in knocking
serious people off their perch. He wants to move you; he cares more
about doing that than about anything else; but of all moods, in himself
it seems and in others, he distrusts the melting mood most. An English
audience has not as a rule sufficient emotional mobility to follow a
method which alternates laughter with pathos, philosophy with fun,
in such rapid succession. Consequently his plays generally divide an
audience into three sections: those who take in only the funny bits
(they are the majority, so his plays are popular), those who attend
chiefly to the religion and philosophy (some of whom dislike them or
are bored), and those who are irritated and puzzled by the two elements
being so thoroughly mixed together. Among the last are to be found
most of his critics. But no one can have appreciated a religious play by
Bernard Shaw *as a work of art* who has not, if tears come naturally to
him, cried, and then laughed so soon afterwards that he has forgotten
that he cried at all.

However often one may have criticised Mr Shaw, and I have done
so many times, it is exciting to do it again. One always feels as though
one was going to discover something new to say about him after
seeing his last play; the walk back from the theatre on such occasions

for a critic with a taste for his profession is a fine pleasure. What I am going now to say may not be new, but it was borne in on me with fresh force after seeing *Androcles*. Most of the critics of the play have spoken about his indiscriminate satire, his mockery of martyrs, his raising a cheap laugh by treating disrespectfully what is usually treated with reverence. In the more indignant of these criticisms there was something of that vulgarity and obtuseness which led the last Lord Chamberlain to ban *Blanco Posnet* as a blasphemous play. *Blanco Posnet* seemed blasphemous to the Censor because a horse-stealer, burning with the fires of conversion, did not express his feelings with conventional reverence. It is easy to understand a man, if he hates religion, feeling repelled by anyone in Posnet's state of mind, whether the zealot happens to be General Gordon, Wesley, or a horse-stealer. I can understand his disliking martyrs next worst to the people who make them. It is possible to hate religious zeal and be an exceptionally admirable man like Bradlaugh, Voltaire or Samuel Butler. But to allow good taste and convention to get between you and the recognition of the very thing you profess to and do reverence elsewhere, and then to call it blasphemous or mean is vulgar and inhuman. I am no theologian, but as far as I was ever able to make out what was meant by that mysterious sin against the Holy Ghost, so severely penalised that it really might have been more clearly defined, it was a deep, wilful, damnable unfairness to which this kind of obtuseness is certainly akin. My discovery about Mr Shaw was that his most striking merits as a writer spring from his being marvellously free from that obtuseness and all forms of spiritual snobbery. I do not mean that he sees everywhere what is most important, far from it; in some directions he seems to me quite blind, but whatever he does admire in human nature that he will see wherever it may be, and honour equally. Often he discovers it in situations and people where it is so buried in incongruities, or so smarmed over with bad manners and bad sentiments, that his recognition of it suggests to people that he is satirising the thing itself. In the case of this play many have apparently thought that because the meek little martyr, Androcles, is made to talk namby-pambily, and the gross, chaotic Ferrovius to parade his inward wrestings and bawl the phrases of a hot-gospeller, the dramatist was satirising the religion of these men. That is obviously a mistake—their tone, their sillinesses, yes, but not their faithfulness.

Ferrovius is explained with sympathetic insight. Lavinia says (it shocks him dreadfully for the moment) she would like to see him 'fight his way to heaven'—that is to say, to obey his instinct and use his temper, his masterfulness, and his sword. While into the mouth of the henpecked, inconspicuous Androcles is put one of those lines which summarise a character and delight a critic. He is too humbly pacific to fight for his life in the arena, too incapable of resentment, so he asks rather with the air of a tired man timidly excusing himself for taking a seat in a full waggonette, that he may be allowed 'to be the one to go to the lions with the ladies'.

There are four types of religious zealots represented, all of them fundamental enough to have existed in the second century just as they exist now. Androcles is the 'pure fool', the sort of little man who nowadays might go about in fibre shoes and an indiarubber coat to avoid using the skins of animals and drink almond milk with his tea. Yet in him burns a little flame of courage that no wind of misery or torment can make flicker. The drawing of his character is an instance of Mr Shaw's recognition of the qualities he admires in whatever character they may happen to be found. Ferrovius belongs to the type of 'born again', overwhelmingly manly, internally miserable, fighting parson, who sometimes gets into a scandalous mess to the horror of his flock, the amusement of the world, and his own scorching remorse. His religious life, apart from taking others by the scruff of the neck and compelling them to come in, is a continual struggle to acquire the Christian virtues of benevolence and submission and an inner freedom and peace. Born a servant of Mars and ignorant of himself, he has become a follower of Jesus of Nazareth. He, too, reveals himself in a sentence; he is terrified to think that he may betray his Master when he finds himself in the arena and give stroke for stroke. 'When I feel a sword in my hand I could as soon throw it away as the woman I love from my arms. Oh, what have I said? My God, what have I said?' He recovers confidence in himself by officiously exhorting the others to pray as they are hustled into the arena; but face to face with the gladiators the sudden glory of battle seizes him and he stretches out all six of them, to return again overwhelmed with remorse and shame. The delighted Emperor pardons all the Christians to commemorate such a feat of arms. He declares extravagantly that he will insist upon every man in the Pretorian guard becoming a Christian, and offers Ferrovius a place in it. Ferrovius, remembering perhaps Lavinia's words about fighting his way to heaven, accepts. His prayers and wrestling for the grace of Christian meekness have not been heard, and in the arena he has come to understand his own nature. 'The

Christian God is not yet', he mournfully concludes. 'I strive for the coming of the God who is not yet', is Lavinia's response to that.

Lavinia is the third type of martyr. She is the kind who goes to the stake with *nearly* the smallest possible amount of definite belief that she is, so to speak, in the secret of the universe. An after-life, a martyr's crown, mean little to her; purgatory and hell nothing at all. She is only certain of this, that the whole point of being alive and all satisfying happiness lie in obeying an instinct to identify herself with the will of the world which is thought of as divine, and that instinct prevents her from submitting, even by an act of formal recognition like dropping a pinch of incense on an altar, to a cult which stands in the way of her religion. The dialogue between her and the Captain of the Guard is one of the best serious passages in the play; it is quite short, but there is a great deal in it. He is rather in love with her, and he uses all the arguments that have been used against martyrdom to persuade her to sacrifice to Diana. He appeals to her scepticism, to her good taste as a lady and Roman (why make a pompous, hysterical fuss about a mere form), to her common-sense and self-respect (you're simply committing suicide and not even doing anything fine). To that last argument she has a reply which makes one think with that momentary intensity which often leaves a mark on one's permanent opinions: 'Death is harder for us Christians than for you.' She means *she* has something which she really wants to live for.

The fourth type of zealot is Spintho, who does not know what faith is. He is lashed on by his own misery and terror and lured by the hope of currying favour with superior powers. In a particular case he turned tail and was accidentally eaten by a lion; but he is the sort of creature who swells the ranks of every persecuted cause or religion and makes it all the harder for genuine people to fight or suffer for it. He usually attracts the almost undivided attention of persecutors who want to justify their conduct. As the centurion says while he is cuffing and shaking him, 'You're the sort as makes duty a pleasure.' Mr Shaw has omitted two other types of martyr: the man who goes to the stake with something very like a bad conscience (he is rare, but he is interesting and, I think, lovable), and the martyr who sacrifices himself because he simply thinks certain definite dogmas are true. Mr Shaw holds that such men do not face death for their creed. If this play were an historical drama this last omission would be a serious defect, but it is not, and I have, while discussing the thought in it, almost forgotten that it is a pantomime. Other critics, however, have described the fun, the inimitable lion, the Emperor, the call-boy of the Colosseum, who announces the next item on the programme in the familiar voice: 'No. 11. Lions and Christian women.' It was the thought and feeling in this delightful entertainment that needed further comment. Coming out from the theatre, I heard one man say to another: 'But what's the point to the whole thing?' 'Oh,' said his friend, 'it's a skit on plays like *The Sign of the Cross* and *Quo Vadis*. That's what it comes to.' I was jammed up close against them and I could not help saying: 'I think it would be nearer the mark to say that *The Sign of the Cross* is a skit upon it.'

66. Dixon Scott on Shaw's handicaps

1913

Extract from signed article, 'The Innocence of Bernard Shaw', *Bookman*, September 1913, vol. XLIV, 264, 239, and October 1913, vol. XLV, 265, 36. Reprinted in *Men of Letters* (1916), 1.

Dixon Scott (1881–1915), journalist and critic, regular contributor to the *Liverpool Courier* and the *Manchester Guardian*. In the first part of 'The Innocence of Bernard Shaw', Dixon Scott deplores what he calls 'the tyranny of technique over temperament' in Shaw, a contrast to the more usual line of criticism to the effect that Shaw's temperament prevented the fullest flowering of his undoubted literary gifts. Dixon Scott analysed Shaw's prose style in illustrative passages from the novel *The Irrational Knot* and other prose writing and said that 'for rapidity, poignancy, unanimity, promptness, an exquisite timing and adjustment of its parts, there is no prose to be compared with it in English'. He considered however that the very greatness of Shaw's gift as a prose stylist and the uses to which he put it prevented the development within him of the true artist. It was exactly 'Shaw's unsuitability for the rigid part of pedagogue' that made him adopt the rule so exuberantly. In the latter part of the article, quoted here, Dixon Scott applied his criticism to the dramatic work of Shaw. When *Men of Letters* was published, Shaw reviewed it in the *Nation* (17 February 1917, 682: reprinted in *Pen Portraits and Reviews*, 1932, 231, under the title of 'The Artstruck Englishman'). Shaw paid tribute to Dixon Scott's gifts as a critic but took issue with him on what he thought an unbalanced worship of style: 'to listen for a writer's message, even when the fellow is a fool, is one thing: to worship his tools and his tricks, his pose and his style, is an abomination'. He declared himself shocked by Dixon Scott's 'preposterous reversal of the natural relative importance of manner and matter'. Dixon Scott, in Shaw's opinion, failed to see that every man whose business it was to work directly on others 'must dramatize himself and play his part'. Because of his youth and immaturity, Dixon Scott thought such dramatic method merely a pose.

Nothing, then, could be clearer than that Mr. Shaw became a dramatist—not as a result of predilection—but simply because he was propelled into the part by circumstances. Once one realizes that, one also sees the huge unlikelihood of him turning out the born dramatist he claimed to be; and, indeed, it could easily be shown that even his power 'of conjuring up imaginary people in imaginary places and finding pretexts for theatrical scenes between them' (on which he plumes himself in the Preface to *Plays Pleasant*) is much more the novelist's dramatic knack than the playwright's, that his mere sense of the physically dramatic, taking that alone, is far from being the true sense of the theatre. But these initial, native deficiencies wouldn't have mattered so much if it hadn't been for that other element; the grim fact that the very circumstances which had made him dramatist had simultaneously robbed him of his best right to be one. Be one, that it to say, in his own high sense of it—a maker of works of art depicting she daily life of the world, phials filled with essence of actuality. A man of his wit and force couldn't, of course, fail to contrive stage-pieces with a good deal more pith and picturesqueness about them than the majority of plays turned out by the class of brains the stage deserves; but anything bigger, anything adequate to his own definition, he had already forfeited the faculty to produce. He was trebly disqualified—and the first of these three handicaps stares out at us so brazenly from the record of his life that the wonder is it never warned him off; so plain is it indeed that it has visibly stamped itself into the framework of his house, making an ominous writing on the walls of his home. '*They say. What say they? Let them say.*' These are the words (his biographer tells us) that Mr. Shaw has had carved above the fire-place in his study. They are sufficiently significant. Admirable enough as the motto of a callow rebel, the old contemptuous Border battle-cry amounts to a surrender of his sword when heard on the lips of a dramatist. For, being interpreted, it really means that 'I, the under-seated, owner of this hygienic hearth, boast a deliberate lack of that imaginative sympathy which is the chief credential of the interpreter of character.' And by sympathy, in this sense, one does not mean a slobbering pity; for pity can be as partial as contempt. By imaginative sympathy one simply means the jolly power of watching, with a chuckling absorption and delight, the doings of every sort and size of people; and of this happy gift, if ever he had it, Shaw by now has been wholly dispossessed. Sympathy is something hardly to be dis-cerned in a man who has deliberately made disdain a working prin-ciple; who has learned to study human nature in the spirit of an opponent; and whose idea of 'a generous passion' has become a 'passion of hatred' for all the 'accursed middle-class institutions that have starved, thwarted, misled and corrupted us from our cradles.' *Tout comprendre, c'est tout pardonner*: you cannot cut your enemy and know him too. That is a sort of vivisection that *is* fruitless. And Shaw really admitted his own incapacity for play-writing when he affirmed that the average audience was a set of soapy stupids, 'part of them nine-tenths chapel-goers by temperament, and the remainder ten-tenths blackguards.' For the stage at its best is only a mirror held up before the face of the watching house. The big play is composed of little players; it must comprehend them even when they don't compre-hend it.

That, then, is the first of Mr. Shaw's three acquired deficiencies; his socialism has made him unsociable: his confirmed habit of wiping somebody out, which he formed among the Fabians because it was so effective there, becomes here a disastrous obliteration of his model; he is like an archer (not William, though!) who has set up a target with care and then discovered it has used up all the wood meant for arrows. And now, on the top of it, driving it in further, comes acquired defect number two—one that limits still further his already narrowed range of subjects, and one that is all the more mischievous because it is masked by a quality that may have done much at the outset to convince him that drama was his line. All Shaw's early efforts as a writer were given, as we have seen, to the task of forming a medium of expression apt for physical utterance—a type of diction he could debate with and dictate with dogmatically, dealing it out from his hustings or stabbing it into his societies in successive sentences as pat and purposeful as neatly planted blows. Now, that meant good dialogue; and so, long before he had ever dreamt of turning dramatist, he had perfectly acquired the great trick which so many playwrights never do learn: the art of making all his words fit live lips and leap alertly off the tongue, as slick and natural as slang, fresh with the colours of actual intercourse. But whilst his platform-work thus taught him the acoustics of the stage and how to make his characters talk like human beings, it also confirmed him in a foible which reacted on those characters to make them human beings of one particular kind. For the essence of his own speeches had been their slitting, pelting salience: it had been his work to resolve the old vague rumblings of oratory into a rattle of definite drops—and nothing, he found, sped a period so well as a core of cute meaning, self-contained. With the result that a crisp statement soon became essential to his sentences: he could no more begin to write one without an assertion to maintain it than a cabby could go a drive without a fare.

But though this confirmed inability to ask a question, or to suggest, or appeal, or submit, or discriminate, or qualify, or use art as a means of evocation, summoning a wisdom deeper than the artist knew he controlled—although this limitation was an immense asset on a platform, it obviously became a fatal barrier to completeness when the habitual asserter set to work to write a play. For it meant that the stage-door of his theatre had to be shut in the faces of a throng of very necessary characters; all the dim folk and foggy folk, the puzzled and perturbed, the groping, hoping, helpless, humble, unassertive humans, who act by instinct instead of by reason and whose deeds speak so much more clearly than their words—all these he was compelled to turn away. He couldn't employ them, for he couldn't equip them with a part. His sympathies, we have seen, were already limited—but even if he were filled with a positive affection for such characters he couldn't take them on—no, not even to take them off; for although he understood them they did not understand themselves; and for people who don't know their own minds and can't communicate the knowledge clearly, Shaw has no form of speech that will do. He can write none but definite dialogue; and definite dialogue entails definite minds; and the result is that all the members of his cast seem members of one exclusive caste. *A specimen of the sensible, highly educated young English-woman; prompt, strong, confident, self-possessed. . . . A man of cool tem-perament and low but clear and keen intelligence, with the imperturbability of the accurate calculator who has no illusions. . . . A vigorous, genial, popular man of forty with a sound voice which he uses with the clean athletic articulation of the practised orator. . . . A dignified man, a born chairman of directors. . . . A strong man, with a watchful face. . . .* Pass them in parade, from Vivie Warren to Andrew Undershaft, and you find they have all had to be endowed with this rare faculty—a power of quick, precise, and ruthless calculation and self-confidence, the necessary adjunct to the way they'll have to speak. Each has a ready point of view, bright and finished as a rapier; and the drama has to resolve itself into the ring and rattle of these weapons, the multiplex duel we get when they all unsheathe their points and prettily proceed to cross opinions. What fun it is, how exciting it can be, we all, to our happi-ness, well know. But we have to admit that the mirror misses much. It is odd to reflect that his democracy is the cause of this exclusiveness.

Yet if these are serious handicaps I fear the third is even heavier. It was bad enough to be compelled to insist on his *dramatis personæ* all coming clearly provided with opinions; but what was worse was the fact that the exigencies of platform work had compelled him to add a pack of neat opinions to his own equipment, and that his haste and his innocence and the highly peculiar circle of his friends made the pack in many ways a faked one. '*To be set too early,*' says Meredith, some-where, '*is to take the work out of the hands of the Sculptor who fashions men. A character that does not wait for circumstances to shape it is of less worth in the race that must be run.*' Well, Shaw set too soon. The pressure of those early days of gleeful mutiny, the need for being dogmatic, precipitated his young ideas in a premature philosophy, to which ever since he has clung; and at the same time the material out of which he had to get his ideas, the personal experiences he turned into opinions, were quite unfairly lopsided, incomplete, artificial. The idiosyncrasy of his troupe he might to some extent have counterbalanced by picking their points of view with care and then arranging these so that they partly reproduced the pattern and poise of reality; but such ingenuity availed nothing whatever against the bias of his own point of view. He might (and he did) arrange his rapiers like spokes to look like a mimic Wheel of Life; but to no purpose, for the hub was out of truth. And it was out of truth because, quite literally, what he had taken as his centre was really eccentric, and what he had accepted in his innocence as a genuine axle was actually only a crank.

For remember, once more, where he was when he formed his views: remember the New Woman and *The Woman Who Did*, and the Ibsen Society and rational dress, and the general dank, indoor, stuffy, insincere atmosphere of devotees and defiance in which he formed his first impressions and made one. It was suburban in the worst sense—under the Town, shut in and overshadowed by its mass. 'I am a typical Irishman,' he once said, 'my family came from Yorkshire.' Actually, he is a typical Cockney: he came from the country before he had learned that Middlesex wasn't the middle; and what he ought to have said was: 'I am a true Metropolitan: my views are so very provincial.' Shut up in one pigeon-hole, he felt he was surveying the whole room; he took it for granted that the highly specialized existence he shared was a fair sample of reality: he got his ideas of human society from the members of his societies; and innocently accepted the New Woman as woman. He knew nothing of the working North, nothing of pastoral England, nothing even of the genuine suburbs or the actual provinces, or the places where life does expand with some serenity, repeating its comeliest delights. Morris had had Kelmscott to use as a base, his grey manor with its immemorial beauties was his hub; and when he looked out from it he realized that Shaw's little London was a mere dirty splash on one of the spokes. But though Shaw took a Hertfordshire house many years later, and though a healthy Hibernian longing for the open has no doubt always been mixed with his motives, yet he never let that longing take him to his true kingdom; and his work has been far more a product of indoor dilettantism than that of Mr. Henry James. For Mr. James has travelled tirelessly, shedding old shibboleths and learning the non-existence of horizons; whereas Shaw has always remained complacently satisfied that his early contact with life was remarkably complete. He is constantly pluming himself on the breadth of his experience: 'Like a greengrocer and unlike a minor poet, I have lived instead of dreaming and feeding myself with artistic confectionery.' 'Three times every week I could escape from artistic and literary stuff and talk seriously on serious subjects with serious people. *For this reason—because I persisted in Socialist propaganda—I never once lost touch with the real world.*' So does he point proudly to the bars of his prison and boast of how they keep reality before him. He honestly believed that a brisk debate with Mr. Belfort Bax brought him very near to the simple heart of human nature. He felt that he understood the democracy because he knew so many democrats.

It was as a Fabian meeting multiplied, then, that Shaw first beheld the race of man; and his views of life were largely formed to fit this fascinating vision. Let me give one example of the way he generalized, of the way he accepted a suburban experience as a symbolical episode and framed a law on the strength of it which he promptly applied to the rest of creation. Let it be his theory of the relation of the sexes—of woman as the huntress and man as the prey. It reappears constantly, for it is one of the several steelyard rules which he can handle easier than golden ones; but its first appearance is in *The Philanderer*. Now we have the assurance of Mr. Shaw's biographer that *The Philanderer* exhibits an attitude towards women induced in Shaw by 'unpleasant personal relations with women prior to the time at which the play was written. . . . The first act is a more or less accurate replica of a scene in Mr. Shaw's own life.' There you have it! The core of *Man and Superman* is simply a twisted point of view manufactured out of the shoddy and unreliable material circumstances brought him when he had to take what he got to make opinions. Not all the adroitness in Ireland could overcome that initial drawback. He may declare that 'Ann is Everywoman' as loudly as he will, and swear that her demonstration, that the initiative in sex transactions remains with women, is a piece of pure impartial drama, the result of 'a creative process over which I have no control.' We know better. Falsified from the commencement, the piece had to be a fantasy. It is one of the most delightful variety entertainments ever witnessed on the stage, but it holds no mirror up to life. What it reflects is an impatient youth of genius being impeded by a pack of spinsters who can't spin, the female intellectuals peculiar to a little patch of London (and a patch which has by now been ploughed and broken), and deciding that his predicament must be typical of Everyman's, that he has discovered a Universal Law which nobody before him has had the honesty to announce. . . .

Then his plays are an imposture? Pardon me, I never said so: what I say indeed is that he has acted with perfect sincerity, that all the errors in the result must be attributed to our time. It is because they are not a fair indictment that they do become a grave one. But then, on the other hand, it is when we realize their vices that we discover his true virtues. For the fine thing is this—and this the only use of critics' efforts—that once the limitations of the plays are realized they cease to possess any; once you see that Shaw has done the best he could for us under the circumstances, then his effort is seen in relation to those circumstances and its errors instinctively allowed for. Recognize that a passion for purity, gentleness, truth, justice, and beauty is the force at the base of all his teaching, and you will find his message one of the most tonic of our time. Realize further how he has limited himself by the philosophy he has expounded, and you will escape all danger of being hurt by its deficiencies. And instead of the irritation, the bewilderment, or (what was worse) the priggish complacency with which you regarded them, you find yourself turning to them with sympathy, with comradeship and eager friendliness, able to use all their strong medicine without being embittered by the taste. It is only when you regard them, in short (and this is the summary of the whole irony), it is only when you regard them with the very sympathy they doggedly deride that you receive the help which they hunger to offer.

PYGMALION

1913

Pygmalion was first presented at the Hofburg Theater, Vienna, on 16 October 1913. The first performance in England was at His Majesty's Theatre, London, on 11 April 1914, where it ran for 118 performances. A detailed history of the production is given in Richard Huggett, *The Truth about 'Pygmalion'* (1969). The temperamental differences between Shaw and the two principal players, Sir Herbert Beerbohm Tree and Mrs Patrick Campbell, made it little short of a miracle that the play was ever produced.

67. Unsigned notice, *Westminster Gazette*

14 April 1914, vol. XLIII, 6507, 3

In this notice, initialled 'E.F.S.', the critic began by referring to unsatisfactory features in the production of the play. Shaw himself was the producer of the play but the rehearsals were marked by serious differences between the producer and the leading actor, Sir Herbert Beerbohm Tree, and the leading lady, Mrs Patrick Campbell.

For some reason one has a feeling of surprise at seeing a 'Shaw' play presented at His Majesty's by Sir Herbert Tree, and it can hardly be said that *Pygmalion* at the moment is quite at home in the theatre, which, by the bye, has a stage and auditorium too large for a play of such an intimate character. Moreover, the actual production is by no means satisfactory. The name of the 'producer' is not given; still, one may assume that he has not enjoyed despotic power over Sir Herbert, for the piece is taken at a funereal pace, and in many scenes the characters work ill together, suggesting insufficience of rehearsal, and the business of Pygmalion's part sometimes appears to be improvised. I have also an impression that here and there his dialogue owed more to Sir Herbert's invention than his memory, particularly in the last scene, or, nicely speaking, the penultimate, where many of the phrases have little of the Shaw 'snap' in them. And how tactless this scene, with its bewildering and 'Shaw-rivandage'—if I may coin the word—at enormous length, very puzzling to an audience trying desperately to make out to what it is leading, and cheated at the end! For no one feels certain what the ending is. In order to give the play, a clever, interesting work, its reasonable chance of the substantial success desired by it, some skilful 'producer' ought to be called in and given autocratic power over everybody.

In the case of a playwright who does not use the drama merely as a vehicle for telling stories one feels curious as to what is the foundation idea of a new piece. Curiosity, in the present instance, remains unsatisfied. There are plenty of ideas, but none is predominant. The name, of course, suggests an old story, and probably was chosen mainly to anticipate charges of plagiarism, for there is little of the Pygmalion or Galatea element. The programme description, 'a Romance,' obviously is a joke, unless it is to be regarded as a hint that the enigmatic conclusion really indicates that Higgins was in love with Eliza, and they were going to make a match of it.

[The criticism tells the story of the play.]

Certainly *Pygmalion* is a puzzling work, but fortunately it has abundance of good qualities. Accepting without admitting the premises, the development of Galatea is very clever, particularly in the exhibition of the transition stage. The play has plenty of clever, typical 'G.B.S.' dialogue and some neat epigrams, such as 'It is time enough to think of the future when you have no future to think of.' Although the pace of the acting is exasperatingly slow, the play is interesting and diverting throughout, even if it drags somewhat towards the close. Moreover, there is one comic character not yet mentioned by me which delighted the audience; this is Eliza's father, a genial ruffian, navvy by calling, but dustman since the work is easier, a talkative scoundrel who boasts himself one of the 'undeserving poor.' When he finds that Eliza has gone to Wimpole-street, he comes to 'touch' the Professors, not as a wrathful parent, but as a father with something to sell, willing to take a 'fiver' for the mere loss of her society, but asking ten times as much if their motives are dishonourable. A quaint, droll dog, with a wonderful gift of the gab, and a great grudge against the middle-class morals which cause people to hamper him. He was diverting about his home affairs. Mr. Doolittle was not married to the 'lydy' with whom he lives; he was willing, not for the sake of morality; she was not, for the insecurity of tenure compelled him to treat her with an amiable consideration that would have been unnecessary, even ridiculous, if she had been his wife. On this theme the house roared with laughter, and the point was worked up neatly on his second appearance, when we found that a fortune had been left to him, and therefore the 'lydy' insisted upon marriage, being anxious to make sure of her tenure of the moneyed man. This character of Doolittle, the Dustman—the 'Golden Dustman'—in the last act is one of the most entertaining in the whole Shaw theatre. No doubt it is not such a closely realistic picture as some of the others, and the man expresses ideas for which he would hardly have found words. Yet it seems legitimate enough to permit him to find words for the ideas and sentiments of his class.

68. Alex M. Thompson on a 'potboiler', from signed notice, *Clarion*

17 April 1914, 5

Britain's most famous playwright has won his place at last on the stage of Britain's most famous playhouse. But it is characteristic of the British way in these things that while the great playwright's really significant plays, such as *Major Barbara, John Bull's Other Island, Man and Superman* were allowed to waste their brilliance on the desert air of Sloane Square, the play admitted to our classic shrine is one whose purpose, according to the author himself, is 'to boil the pot'.

On the lofty portals of the orthodox Temples of the Drama the golden legend blazons forth: 'Abandon aim all ye who enter here,' and the most devout of Shavians will be the most emphatic in accepting Mr Shaw's claim that he has conformed to the golden rule. Except to 'boil the pot' and evoke effects like 'the crackling of thorns under the pot,' there is no purpose visible in *Pygmalion*. But there is, of course, abundance of bold and startling wit, most of which probably no other author would have thought of, and much of which assuredly no other author would have dared to offer to any audience.

69. H. W. Massingham, in an initialled notice, *Nation*

18 April 1914, vol. XV, 3, 93

H. W. Massingham finds in *Pygmalion* further signs of the often observed defect in Shaw, that he observed too coldly and allowed his interest in the play of wit and argument to obscure beauty and affection.

There must be something wrong about it, said Mr. Shaw in one of a rather scandalous series of interviews with himself which preceded the appearance of *Pygmalion*, or all the world would not be going to see it. Mr. Shaw was right. There *is* something wrong about *Pygmalion*. To begin with, it is not in the right place. His Majesty's Theatre is too big, and Sir Herbert Tree is too slow. Mr. Shaw's art deals in hard, brilliant surfaces and quick reactions. Above all, his mind is tangential, shooting at everything that flies. These qualities do not consort with Sir Herbert's deliberate manner and the broad imposing stage to which it is set. Mr. Shaw should be played quickly and lightly, not magnificently and grandiosely. But there is a fault in the piece as well as in its production. Let me try and show what it is.

Pygmalion was a royal artist (the breed, save for the Kaiser, is extinct) who fell in love with a statue of ivory that his hands had made. In pity of his case Aphrodite breathed life into the beautiful creature, and Pygmalion duly married it. The story, like all good stories, had a meaning. Its inventor was well aware of the fact that the artist is first and most in love with his art; and Mr. Shaw, being in the same line of business himself, is also familiar with it. He knows, too, that this art-passion is an exclusive and cruelly exacting attachment, which de-humanizes its victim, so much so that the Greeks figured Pan as 'half a beast,' and Mrs. Browning, in a suggestive little poem, shows how the making of a poet usually involves the spoiling of a man. Not without a price does the reed which Pan hacks and trims for his piping become a divine instrument; its life with the other reeds has gone for ever.

This is what is the matter with Eliza Doolittle, of Covent Garden, who has fallen into the hands of Mr. Henry Higgins, Professor of Phonetics. Mr. Higgins's specialty has led him into the most daring experiment possible to a *virtuoso* of his type, the transformation of a Cockney flower-girl into a duchess. The feat was not quite so formid-able as it looked, for Mr. Higgins's task was merely to transmute one kind of slang into another—the lisping, drawling sing-song of the slum into the equally flat dialect of the drawing-room. As for the girl herself, all that was necessary was to devitalize and disembody her—to turn something into nothing. These tasks Mr. Higgins duly accom-plished. But he had forgotten one thing—that he was dealing with a human being, not with a cleverly constructed machine. So, when his flower-girl has passed the supreme tests of queening it at a dinner, a dance, and a garden-party, her awakening wrath, love, feeling, character, make him aware of the kind of metal which he has tried to fashion for his sport. Eliza Doolittle had passed her examination in fine-ladyship, but she has not ceased to be a woman. When she asks him for a share in life, and in his love and interest, for a future, an occupation, he would fling her back into the slums, or into the arms of the first husband that offers. He, Higgins, artificer in flesh and blood, has done with her. So the girl turns on her brutal trainer, and shows him the kind of man he is by way of inviting him to finish the job he began, and step out of his world of self-sufficing artistry to the common ways of mankind. This he half-consents to do, more, I am afraid, in the spirit of a blackmailed criminal than of a man of genius who has been caught out.

Now, this is assuredly a good subject, well suited to Mr. Shaw's fashion of holding romance upside down, and giving Truth an air of cold repulsion. Indeed, Professor Higgins is a little like the self that Mr. Shaw likes to show to the world, much in the spirit of a shy man who hides his spirituality or his tenderness under a mask of coarseness or of gruff demeanor. What I complain of is that with his reserves and ironies, and by a certain caprice and waywardness of thought, Mr. Shaw has failed to show his audience precisely what he meant. His Professor Higgins is not merely a bully, a ramping, swearing boor; he is such a gross vivisector, that the finer conception of the artist— a kind of scientific Rossetti—almost disappears. Perhaps this is what Mr. Shaw designed him to be. But this is surely a needless and painful defamation of the legend. The artist of the Greek fable is tenderly disguised as a lover; at his best, Pygmalion-Higgins is merely a diligent watcher of a test-tube. Is that a dramatic conception? It might have been; but it is not. Rather it points to the unguarded spot in Mr. Shaw's artistic armor. He observes too coldly; life's absurdity juts so sharply out from the mass as to obscure its beauty. He has hardly the patience even to chronicle affection; it is the clash of wits—the excitement of argument—that seems to interest him. Even then he lets one strain of suggestion cross another. He is as 'volatile' as Miss Mowcher. Conceiving *Pygmalion* in the proper spirit of serious comedy, he lets it slip into farce, stiffens it again with irony, and then jollies it up with a shower of verbal squibs and crackers. Thus, when Higgins and Eliza really come to business, it is to no fine issue. He becomes the average male brute, who has found a useful female drudge. She is well fitted to be his help-mate. But he wants no helpmate, only a slipper-warmer; he has his art. Or perhaps he does, in which case he is Higgins no longer. The audience must guess whether he loves her or she loves him, and what kind of blood flows in the veins of these queer, jangling creatures.

Equally wanting in firmness of conception and treatment is the minor key of Mr. Shaw's fancy. Eliza's father, Alfred Doolittle, is almost a masterpiece, save that, like Galatea-Eliza, he talks rather than is. He, too, stands for an admirable idea—the rude anarchic living of the workman exchanged by a turn of fortune for 'middle-class morality,' ending up in a dolorous, long-deferred wedding at St. George's, 'Anover Square. Here, again, Higgins has interfered in what was no business of his; he should have let this genial ruffian go his wicked ways. Is this what Eliza's transmogrification was meant to illustrate? Again, I failed to follow Mr. Shaw's line of thought, or to see it as dramatic development. Eliza was immensely amusing as she talked slum talk in primmest Lindley Murray, and answered Park Lane's courtesies with the terrible, if meaningless, adjective, bl——y. But

she talks like a gramophone, not like a woman. 'What hast thou
done with thy life?' asks the poet of himself. I ask Mr. Shaw what he
has made of the soul of Eliza. For here was the grand opportunity of
his drama—the coming to herself of this slip of the streets when she
realizes the crime which a cold-blooded brute of a scientist had committed against her. Mr. Shaw may have meant to show that the rich
can do nothing for the poor but leave them alone, and await the
judgment of God on both. That would have been a powerful piece of
criticism. Mr. Shaw hints but does not make it.

In structure, *Pygmalion* is often brilliant, daring, and gay; too
flippant, too long, and altogether too cheap. It would, as I have said,
have played better in a smaller theatre. Yet I am not sure that, so far
as the broad lines of character are concerned, Professor Higgins could
have been much more adequately presented than by Sir Herbert Tree.
Both he and Mrs. Campbell belong to the type of dramatic workers
who step out of their dressing-room in the same spiritual habit as the
one in which they entered it. No marvellous sea-change for them,
such as a Coquelin or a Duse was wont to put on. They are content
to be themselves; and as, in particular, Sir Herbert is a large, filling
personality, he does well for the blustering Professor, and is more
human, more sensitive, than is his set classical parts. Mrs. Campbell's
beauty is not the beauty of a London flower-girl; but she simulated it
with great skill and humor. Mr. Edmund Gurney's Alfred Doolittle
was quite perfect. Mr. Merivale was unfortunately given a character—
a scientific Indian colonel—created in order to provide a foil to
Higgins, and a chaperon for Eliza.

70. John Palmer on 'the popular legend of G.B.S.'

1915

John (Leslie) Palmer (1885–1944), author and dramatic critic, was assistant editor of the *Saturday Review* from 1910 to 1915 and later dramatic critic of the *Evening Standard*. In this article 'Mr Bernard Shaw: an Epitaph', which appeared in the *Fortnightly Review*, vol. 97, January–June 1915, 443, he noted 'the impulsive and just hostility of the British public to the recent articles and letters of one who is, perhaps, the most notable of the organically extinct, but galvanically active, authors to whose existence the Great War has definitely put a term'. This was Shaw, whom he called 'a very remarkable man—the only British author who has won for the British drama any sort of international recognition'. Palmer set himself to defend Shaw's true merits, without showing any approval of his recent statements about the war (in particular the pamphlet, *Common Sense about the War*) and he thought it necessary 'to destroy once for all the popular legend of G.B.S.'. This he did by examining what he called 'seven distinct fallacies'. The first fallacy was that Shaw was 'an immensely public person'. John Palmer thought that the public personality of Shaw was 'not an authentic revelation of the extremely private gentleman who lives in Adelphi Terrace'. The second fallacy was that Shaw was an original thinker. He, himself, had repeatedly denied this. Similarly, he had not made the extravagant claims for himself as a dramatist, attributed to him in the third fallacy. The remaining fallacies are discussed in the passage quoted below and the article ended with an examination of Shaw's views about the war.

The fourth fallacy is that Mr Shaw is an incorrigible jester. Almost the first thing to realise about Mr Shaw is his overflowing gravity. He has taken more things seriously in his career than any living and notable person. He has taken music seriously, and painting, and Socialism, and philosophy, and politics, and public speaking. He has taken the trouble to make up his mind upon scores of things to which the average heedless man hardly gives a second thought, and will give no thought at all in the future—things like diet, hygiene, photography, phonetic spelling, and vivisection. He has even taken seriously the English theatre, unlike virtually every other Englishman of letters who has had anything to do with it. It is only because he is so immensely serious that he has been able to give the impression of being so tremendously casual and brilliant. He is ready for anything because he has seriously considered everything. A first-rate impromptu usually indicates a mind richly stored and well arranged. Mr Shaw can extemporise on most subjects because he has thought seriously about them. The more brilliantly he sparkles upon a given theme the more sober has been his education in its rudiments. Unfortunately, many people have come to exactly the opposite conclusion. Because Mr Shaw has a rapid and vital way of writing, because he presents his argument at a maximum, seasons it with boisterous analogies, and frequently drives it home at the point of a 'foolborn' jest, he is suspected of sacrificing sense to sound. The dancing of his manner conceals the severe decorum of his matter.

The fifth fallacy has to do with the all-head-and-no-heart formula. It is said of Mr Bernard Shaw by some very excellent critics that he is an expert logician arguing *in vacuo*; that he has exalted Reason as a God; that his mind is a wonderful machine which never goes wrong because its owner is not swayed by the ordinary passions, likes, prejudices, sentiments, impulses, infatuations, enthusiasms, and weaknesses of ordinary mankind. Mainly this last superstition has grown out of the fact that Mr Shaw as a critic of music, art, and the drama was actually a critic. He took his criticism seriously, and found it necessary to tell the cruel truth concerning the artistic achievements of many sensitive and amiable young people. Later, when he came to write plays, there was more evidence of his insensibility, of his arid and merciless rationalism, of his impenetrable indifference to all that warms the blood of common humanity. We must really put all this aside. It is not fundamental. If there is one idea more than another that persists all through Mr Shaw's work it is to be found in his perpetual repudiation of Reason. Almost his whole literary career has been spent in adapting the message of Schopenhauer to his own optimism and belief in the goodness of life. Not Reason and not the Categories determine or create; but Passion and Will. Mr Shaw has always insisted that Reason is no motive power; that the true motive power in the world is Will; that the setting up of Reason above Will is a 'damnable error'. Life is the satisfaction of a power in us of which we can give no rational account whatever—that is his final declaration; and it corresponds with the temperament of its author. Mr Rudyard Kipling has described the rationalists as men who 'deal with people's insides from the point of view of men who have no stomachs'. Mr Shaw would agree. No one, in habit or opinion, lives more remotely than he from the clear, hard, logical, devitalised, and sapless world of Comte and Spencer.

The sixth fallacy is that Mr Shaw is an anarchist, a disturber of the peace, a champion of the right of every man to do as he pleases and to think for himself. This idea of Mr Shaw is altogether at fault. The practical extent of Mr Shaw's anarchism—as was instanced in the British Bluebook wherein a committee of the most respectable gentlemen of the British Bar and Church agreed with Mr Shaw that British divorce was unnecessarily expensive, inequitable, and humiliating—coincides with the anarchism of our judges and our bishops. Mr Shaw is so far from being an anarchist, that in *The Sanity of Art* he has written down one of the best defences of law and order—of the convenience and necessity of policemen, churches and all kinds of public authority—that has appeared in popular form within recent years. It is true that he pleads for liberty, and points out that it is better for a man to act and think responsibly for himself than to run to the nearest constable. But it is also true that he wants people to have no more liberty than is good for them, and that he very seriously distrusts the ability of the average man to think for himself. He knows that the average man has neither the time nor the brains nor the imagination to be original in such matters as crossing the road, or getting married, or determining whether marriage is justifiable. Nothing could be further from the mind of Mr Shaw than the philosophic anarchy of Godwin or John Stuart Mill. He is not an anarchist either in speculation or in practice.

The seventh fallacy is that Mr Shaw is a headlong, dashing, and opinionative writer, without technical equipment, who has succeeded by an impudent trust in his unassisted genius and brought off his best effects by sheer good fortune. This fallacy has stuck to Mr Shaw all through his career as a critic of music, painting, the drama, as a playwright, as a pamphleteer, as a public speaker. When Mr Shaw, as Corno di Bassetto, was writing about music for a London newspaper the public insisted that his appointment was a joke. Mr Shaw played with this popular legend of himself, as he has played with a hundred others. He was thought to be merely a rude young man who knocked the professors' heads together without the least idea of what they contained. Entirely the reverse was true. Far from being an irresponsible amateur with a literary knack, Mr Shaw, in all he has undertaken, has, if anything, erred from an excessive knowledge and interest in the expert, professional, and technical side of his subject. He knew years ago all about the enormity of exploding undiminished chords of the ninth and thirteenth on the unsuspecting ear, just as today he thoroughly understands the appallingly scientific progressions of Scriabin. Similarly he can tell the difference at a glance between real sunshine in an open field and the good north light of a Chelsea studio; or explain why 'values' are more difficult to capture when colours are bright than when they are looked for in a dark interior. As to the technique of the theatre—well, the subject is hardly worth discussing. Some of his later plays are nothing if they are not technical. The fallacy that Mr Shaw was a happy savage among critics and artists— ignorant and careless of form, unread in the necessary conventions, speaking always at random with the confidence that only a perfect ignorance can give—is particularly deplorable, because it necessarily blinds its adherents to his most serious defect. Usually he knows too much, rather than too little, of his subject. He is too keenly interested in its bones and its mechanism. His famous distinction between music which is decorative and music which is dramatic is quite unsound; but it is not the mistake of a critic ignorant of music. It is rather the mistake of a critic too keenly absorbed in the technique of music. If the professors in the early 'nineties had objected to Corno di Bassetto because he was liable to lapses into the pedantry of which they themselves were accused, they would have been nearer the mark than they were in foolishly dismissing him as an ignoramus. Similarly, as a dramatic critic, G.B.S. erred not by attaching too little value to the forms and conventions of the theatre, but by attaching too much. It is true that he did not make the absurd mistake of some of his followers, and regard Ibsen as a great dramatist on account of one or two pettifogging and questionable reforms in dramatic convention—such as the abolishing of soliloquies and extra doors to the sitting-room. But he certainly attached too much importance to these things—mainly because he knew so much about them; and this insistence of his as a critic has had its revenge in some of his own plays where his purely technical mastery of theatrical devices, his stage-cleverness, and his craftsman's virtuosity, have led him into mechanical horseplay and stock positions unworthy of the author of *John Bull's Other Island* and *Major Barbara*. Mr Shaw has continually suffered from knowing his subject too well from the angle of the expert. Far from being the happy and careless privateer of popular belief, he is usually to be found struggling for freedom under the oppression of things stored for reference in his capacious memory. The great critic, like any ordinary, unskilled spectator, should be able to look at a work of art without prejudice in favour of any particular form or fashion. It should not influence his judgment in the slightest whether the music he hears is symphonic or metrical, whether the thirteenth is exploded as a thirteenth or prepared as a six-four chord. He should be similarly indifferent whether a dramatist talks to him in a blank verse soliloquy or in conversational duologue. Preoccupation with manner, *apart from matter*—usually implying an *a priori* prejudice in favour of one manner over another—is the mark of pedantry; and of this pedantry—always the pedantry of a man who is expert and knows too much—Mr Shaw is not always free, though he is far too good a critic to be often at fault.

HEARTBREAK HOUSE

1919

Heartbreak House, written during the years 1913 to 1919, was first presented by the New York Theater Guild at the Garrick Theater, New York on 10 November 1920. It was given 125 performances. The first English production was on 18 October 1921 at the Royal Court Theatre, London. It ran for 53 performances.

71. Unsigned review in *Nation*, entitled 'The Philanderers'

27 September 1919, vol. XXV, 26, 770

In the preface to *Heartbreak House*, Shaw explained why comedy had to be 'loyally silent' during the war; 'for the art of the dramatic poet knows no patriotism; recognizes no obligation but truth to natural history; cares not whether Germany or England perish. . . . That is why I had to withhold *Heartbreak House* from the footlights during the war.'

Now that the Host of Satan (in which we do not include the British soldier) has been temporarily and partially 'demobbed,' see the advancing banners of the Army of the Lord. See the followers of Jesus emerge from their prisons, and his Church from her 'funk-hole.' Note especially the reappearance of the artists. It was inevitable that the war, which killed out whole nests of our younger singing-birds, should virtually silence the critical and imaginative writer. Modern Literature is international; the realm of the mind, as Mr. Shaw says, knows no frontiers. For the literary man, accustomed to the European tradition, the strife of nations cut off great tracts of his intellectual life and poisoned

others. Even when it yielded, as it did yield, the amplest material for
satire, pity or indignation or patriotic concern closed the satirist's
mouth. The destruction of youth in itself robbed art of its natural food,
no less than of its faculty of creation and renewal, and its joy in existence. Who, amid the agony of boyhood, cared to write of love? Who
could shoot at folly, when the world had become a madhouse, and
the critic's sensitive reason seemed even to himself to be shaken on its
throne? Thus the true man of letters, denied his habitual spiritual
pasture, and living a starved life on Nationalism of the better or the
worser kind, submitted to silence or to half-silence. Perhaps it was just
as well, for even if wisdom had spoken no man would have regarded her.

Now, however, the embargo on thought being removed, the thinkers
have in a measure come to their own again. Mr. Shaw's silence as a
dramatist, though not as a pamphleteer, has been only half voluntary.
His O'Flaherty, V.C., written during the war, was refused a licence by
the Censor, and our stage thereby closed to a pleasant drollery, well
suited to relax the grim face of war. The idea of the returned 'V.C.,'
afraid to meet his Fenian mother because he had told her he had gone
to fight the English, might have shocked an owl of a brigadier, but
it would have made the rest of the world laugh, including even the
Hun. In *Heartbreak House*, an unplayed (and perhaps unplayable)
comedy, and in a series of provocative prefaces to that and some
slighter dramatic work, Mr. Shaw comes to closer terms with his
subject. The best conducted war puts sense to school to folly, and evil
on the throne of good. Mr. Shaw's humor was not likely to overlook
the tragi-comedy of such a reversal. He is a rationalist, who, like
Voltaire, the greatest member of the school, sees life not as an image
of perfection, but through his vision of what a simple, 'business-like,'
and not even over-liberal application of good feeling, benevolence,
consideration for others, and understanding of their 'case'—a kind of
unidealized Christianity—could make it.

Viewed through this medium of common-sense, war will always
seem a monster. Nor can the rationalist console himself with the
thought that his country inflicts damage in sustaining it. 'To the truly
civilized man, to the good European, the slaughter of the German
youth was as disastrous as the English. Fools exulted in German losses.
They were our losses as well. Imagine exulting in the death of Beethoven
because Bill Sikes dealt him his death-blow.' The civilian mind, indeed,
showed itself incapable of nearly every kind of moral measurement.
In 1915 the slaughter of Gallipoli and Neuve Chapelle passed as average

incidents of war, though ship after ship sank, and the bodies of thousands of boys were torn to fragments. But the sinking of the *Lusitania*, or the discharge of a bomb on the heads of a mother and a child, roused a whole population to frenzy. That is the usual way in which man reacts under the complete mental disarray produced by war. But to the intellectual such a confusion of values seems almost the worst thing about it. His quarrel with war is that while it permits a low type of thinking, it puts the higher work of the intellect out of action. Thus the English dramatic revival of the two-pre war decades all but died away, playwrights and artists being mostly employed in cheering up Tommies from the front. That was a minor loss; but when German names were erased from the rolls of British science, and German professors expelled with insult from British schools, a good part of the stuff of civilization seemed to have been blown away. Law did no better than learning. It persecuted pacifists, and acquitted soldiers on proved indictments for murder. Religion having nothing to do on its own, (as usual) outdid militarism.

Mr. Shaw's indictment of war proceeds, as every considered impeachment of a state of culture (in the German sense) must proceed, from his view of the intellectual leadership of the nation. What *was* this England that got mixed up in the dreadful *mêlée*, or, at least, what was its ruling Society like? The answer is given in the more than half-symbolical *Heartbreak House*. There were two Societies. There was the Society of the Nice and the Futile; and there was the Society of the Horsey Barbarians. Save for an occasional love-affair, the two rarely mingled: but between them they made up 'influential' England. The first was by way of being advanced, free-thinking, but unreal, living for fiction and poetry, or its vision of personal refinement, and not a little for sex. Its real capital was in Capua, while that of the barbarians was Melton Mowbray. Both neglected the things that mattered, such as political and social science and international diplomacy. Nature let these innocent-guilty ones play on, till she struck them (or their children) down with the unimagined plague of the war.

This is the thesis. It is expounded in *Heartbreak House*, a British Abbey of Thelema, given up to a riot of talkative flirtation. The lovers are extremely explanatory and analytical of themselves and of each other, and as most of their hearts had been broken before, the catastrophe of the sudden removal of one of them (and a burglar) by a German bomb should not be irremediable. Nor do the personages really matter. The three women, Lady Utterword, Mrs. Hushabye, and Ellie Dunn, are in the line of the ensnarer-deliverers, the men of the tempter-victims, with whom Mr. Shaw's earlier and later plays have made us familiar, and they make an amusing and complicated play of their entanglements. But essentially they are symbols, and their purpose is to exhibit an embarrassment of society rather than of the individual soul. They are really too will-less, too undirected, to go on. And they have lost faith in their own right to existence, and their power to enjoy it. 'Either,' says Hector, 'some new creation will come to supplant us as we have supplanted the animals, or the heavens will fall in thunder and destroy us.' That is what the father of the family, the mad-wise Captain Shotover, contemplates, and what a German bomb all but effects. The church indeed is hit, and the rectory reduced to a 'heap of bricks.' The seculars live on, in 'the soul's prison called England,' or as Captain Shotover, the sea-farer, has it, as the crew of a ship on the rocks, her rotten timbers splintered, and her rusty plates torn to fragments.

Thus far *Heartbreak House* and its inhabitants. It is Mr. Shaw's intention, we imagine, to leave out of account what was capable in the later conduct of our affairs. Physical courage and energy, and their moral equivalent, devotion to the national life when in peril from foreign violence, were indeed abundant. But Mr. Shaw's dramatic picture is one of intellectual decadence, of life lived without courage and faith. The inmates of 'Heartbreak House' have a butterfly air, but their sentimentality grows round a pretty hard core of selfish indulgence. Ellie's father, the romantic, the man of the 'eighties, is all for the soul and the ideal. But Ellie herself is for the body, too. After all, soul and body are one, and a rich marriage will find the former in the stuff it wants for its subsistence—books, music, the drama, society, country life. Thus English materialism, refined on its outer skin, coarse at the heart, helped to make the war from which English pluck had to find a way out.

To the brilliant, if over-long, *Heartbreak House* Mr. Shaw adds some slighter dramatic work, *Great Catherine*, the amusing sketch of the Kaiser as *The Inca of Perusalem*, and *Augustus Does His Bit*.

72. Unsigned review,
Times Literary Supplement

2 October 1919, 924, 529

In this review, entitled 'The English Marivaux', the author, probably A. B. Walkley, compared Shaw to the eighteenth-century French writer of light plays of romantic fancy (1688–1763). He expressed the customary Walkley-ean doubt about the ability of the play 'to stand the glare of the footlights' but concluded with the opinion that the pamphleteer in Shaw was 'surpassed by the artist'.

After the war Mr Shaw comes back to us unchanged, like an *émigré* returning home after the French Revolution. He has learnt nothing and forgotten nothing. You take up the familiar squat volume in the familiar greenish-grey binding, and find the inside familiar, too: the old point of view, the old logic, the old people, and the old preface. After so much upheaval in the world at large it is comforting to have at least one antique way to stand upon. It almost looks as though Mr. Shaw had been entrusted to the Society for the Preservation of Ancient Monuments. He is in perfect condition.

And so it is with a delightful sense of putting the clock back, of rummaging in some old cupboard of the past, that one turns over the pages of this volume and tastes again the old Shavian flavour. The Shavian women, notably, are unaltered, as agreeably repellent as ever. There are four women in *Heartbreak House*, the first of the two unacted plays in the volume, and all four are vixens. There are two women in the second, *O'Flaherty, V.C.*, and both are viragoes. Nearly all of them are free lovers—provided you understand by love what Mr. Shaw, but nobody else, understands by it. Pascal wrote about *les passions de l'amour*,[1] but naturally failed to anticipate the Shavian variety, which is love without passion. It is not exactly platonic either, for it involves a good deal of hugging and kissing—what Mr. Shaw in an earlier play,

[1] The passions of love.

239

The Philanderer, called sweet-hearting—but otherwise assumes an air of innocence. There is no harm in it, one of the ladies remarks, if you know how to take care of yourself—a reflection that might have seemed more appropriate to one of M. Marcel Prévost's *demi-vierges*.[1] The truth is they try to fall in love but cannot manage it. Addy 'has never been in love in her life, though she has always been trying to fall in head over ears.' And the men are to match. Hector (who has been making love to Addy 'automatically') confesses that he can't fall in love and only gets landed in all sorts of flirtations in which he is not a bit in earnest. The lady says it must be quite understood they're only playing. In real life, one fancies, that remark would be the plainest of invitations. But in this odd Shavian world they really seem to mean it. Their love-making is recognized all round as automatic and not in earnest. The general effect is a kind of pseudo-eroticism which has 'the contortions of the Sibyl without the inspiration.' Well, one can only say that these heartless, and, rigorously speaking, sexless mock-amorists are familiar figures of the Shavian theatre, where a real flesh-and-blood animal would be even more out of place than in the theatre of Marivaux.

Indeed, it would be far less absurd to call Mr. Shaw the English Marivaux than the English Molière, a title bestowed on him apparently on the single and singular ground of his prejudice against the medical profession. True, the people who gave him that name (if they had only thought of it) might have justified it on the further ground of his eminently Molièresque cruelty, a certain harshness in his laughter. His treatment of death in *The Doctor's Dilemma* is an instance; there are others in the present volume, as at the close of *Heartbreak House*, when two men have been blown to pieces by a bomb and the wife of one of them cries 'Serve 'un right!' and the girl who has jilted the other simply hopes there will be another raid to-morrow night. But Molière, after all, is the great spokesman of the compact majority, the exponent of philistine common sense—in other words, the very antipodes of Mr. Shaw. Whereas Marivaux's atmosphere of artificial emotion is, as we have just been noting, characteristically Mr. Shaw's, and most of Mr. Shaw's dialogue is the purest *marivaudage*. Shavian *marivaudage*, of course, bad manners instead of good, but just as artificial in its exchange of the bluntest home truths as were the courtly compliments bandied between the Marquise and the Chevalier. In Marivaux, too, as in Mr. Shaw, the women have better brains than

[1] Semi-virgins.

the men, outwit them, turn them round their little finger, and finally put up with them because there is nothing else to put up with. Might not *Heartbreak House* be called *Le Jeu de l'Amour et du Hasard*?[1] Ellie is in love with Hector, masquerading as Marcus. When Marcus is revealed as Hector, and her hostess's husband, Ellie simply says 'damn' (which, to be sure, the Marquise would never have done) and remembers she is engaged to the capitalist Mangan. But Mangan has also his disguises. He first appears as the disinterested benefactor of Ellie's father, then as the capitalist exploiter of his industry, finally as no capitalist but the poor employee, on commission, of a syndicate. When he has thrown off all his disguises, Ellie jilts him and marries the Captain (an elderly pantaloon). A captured burglar proves to be the long lost husband of the nurse. All this is sheer Marivaux.

It would be tactless and probably misleading, to carry this comparison further. Students taking a first course of French will only be disappointed if they turn to Marivaux in the hope of finding in him the fun of G.B.S. No, Mr. Shaw invented his own fun as the White Knight invented his own helmet. Only he invented it some time ago, and we have got so used to it that it begins to look a little old-fashioned. Those managing, mothering, domineering 'catty' women of his! How well one seems to know every jerk of the queer marionettes! In *Heartbreak House* they still go on in their old sweet way, saying the nastiest things to one another while, parenthetically, they ruffle the nearest man's hair or pat his hand or order him off to bed. No wonder the men burst into tears, as they are frequently doing in this play, old and young. And here is our old friend the ridiculous *bourgeois*, the exploiter of our iniquitous capitalist system, as helpless as the village idiot among the crowd of clever people who make a butt of him. Mr. Shaw furbishes him up a bit for us by making him one of the 'business men' whom the Government brought in to win the war for it, and who doesn't know anything about his own machinery, but does know how to stick a ramrod into the other fellow's. For all that, we recognize him as one of the stock Shavian stage-properties and can generally guess what he is going to say before he opens his mouth. So with the rest, the men who waste their time in that *baroque* form of love imagined by Mr. Shaw which is made in the head and strictly confined to it—a variant, perhaps, of Professor Bellac's *amour psychique*,[2] after all. Nevertheless, the old Shavian bitter-sweet fun is still there, for those who like it, that is to say, for all sensible people who can enjoy a hearty laugh at their unreal

[1] The Play of Love and Chance.　　　　[2] Psychic love.

but not unthinkable selves. How the fun would stand the glare of the footlights is another matter; incoherent fun is apt to pall in that situation and the game of idea-chopping to prove an inadequate substitute for the interplay of live characters. Anyhow, there is no telling, for Mr. Shaw has 'withheld' *Heartbreak House* from the stage, because the war has completely upset the economic conditions which formerly enabled serious drama to pay its way in London.' Why call it serious drama? Apparently because the play is symbolical of 'cultured, leisured Europe before the war,' and is from the same shelf as Tchekov's *Cherry Orchard*. But *que de choses dans un menuet!*[1]

In his preface, from which we have been quoting, or rather his 'Fantasia in the Russian manner on English themes,' Mr. Shaw ranges through a variety of topics, from the wickedness of science during the half-century before the war and the absurdity of making so much fuss about the Lusitania and so little about Gallipoli to the 'mad election' and the muzzling by war of the dramatic poet. All amusing enough, but what one feels about Mr. Shaw's prefaces is that they tend to prejudice his plays. They show the idea-fabric 'in the piece' before it is cut up into dialogue and trimmed and festooned for the stage, so that with the play in front of you you think, 'Oh, this is only the same old mind-stuff of the preface—with frills.' But the fact remains that the play is generally the more amusing of the two, which shows at any rate that frills are something Mr. Shaw knows how to contrive. In other words (and against the current opinion), the pamphleteer in him is surpassed by the artist.

[1] Metaphorically—what a lot to get into a pint pot.

73. John Middleton Murry, review, *Athenaeum*

17 October 1919, 4668, 1028

Review initialled J.M.M., and entitled 'The Vision of Mr. Bernard Shaw'.

John Middleton Murry (1897–1957) was a leading critic and publicist of the period between the two world wars. At the time of the publication of this review, Murry had just become editor of the *Athenaeum*. In his book, *The Problem of Style* (1922), he referred to Shaw and Samuel Butler as 'masters of plain prose'.

There was, we believe, once a time when to the general public Mr Shaw's prefaces were infinitely more extravagant than the plays which they introduced, which in their turn were infinitely more extravagant than anything the general public could reasonably be expected to read. In those days the advanced critics, we seem to remember, felt a muffled and proportionate shock; they were never quite sure whether the whimsicality and the paradox were legitimate. Was Mr. Shaw serious or was he not? Was he perhaps really pulling—oh, ever so little—even their cultivated leg? And since it was felt (very wisely felt) to be rash to hazard a definite opinion—if you said he was not serious, Mr. Shaw had a way of writing to the papers and making you look a pompous ass; if you said he was, well what would your friends and above all your editor think of you?—a characteristic compromise was arranged. Mr. Shaw was declared to be a serious comedian with a gift for self-advertisement. He was serious, but he didn't mean anything; he was serious, but not to be taken seriously. His plays were comic. You couldn't help laughing at them; you couldn't, alas! help reading them. So in the prefaces Mr. Shaw took a mean advantage of the public. He had its head in chancery, and he pummelled it. They were a kind of high-spirited practical joke in a rather doubtful taste.

The question is, how long can the attitude be kept up? After all, it is a difficult piece of equilibrism at the best of times, distinctly more difficult even than the general alternative, which is to look hard at Mr.

Shaw and to declare that there ain't no sich person. Of late the simpler attitude has been the more popular, perhaps because the fatigue of the more complicated one was beginning to be felt. The division of mankind into patriots and pro-Germans came as a heaven-sent interlude, a pool of silence into which *Common Sense about the War* and *Peace Conference Hints* could most conveniently be dropped. But that interlude is now perceptibly nearing its end, and here, before the new division into patriots and Bolsheviks has been decently established, is Mr. Shaw again with his usual perverse aptitude for buttonholing public opinion when it is off one hobbyhorse and has not had time to get on to another.

Nevertheless, the odds are heavy that it will get away again, or at least that the greater portion of it will get away. But the effect of *Heartbreak House* upon the small remainder may be curious. Curious, because the last four years have left Mr. Shaw pretty much where he always was, while they have flung the majority of his audience catastrophically adrift from what little anchorage they may have had. Their position has changed and with it the angle of Mr. Shaw's impact upon them. Now the preface to *Heartbreak House* appears to them like a lucid and concise narrative of their common experience, while the play upon which it is to some extent a commentary seems fantastic farce. This is, in the main, a reversal of the old order. To our former sense the balance of reality and unreality lay the other way.

That is merely a constatation. To attempt to explain it might be interesting; it would certainly lead us too far from our subject. We can merely accept the change and endeavour to make more precise the character of our present impression. The play *Heartbreak House* appears half-procession, half-pandemonium; it is like one of those portentous American cinematograph films, in which a fat man kills hundreds of people at lightning speed with a mallet as big as a lamppost. As a matter of fact, only one or two people are killed in *Heartbreak House*, but the effect is of the same kind. All the characters seem to be scurrying about with the intense crazy logic of lunatics. Mr. Shaw, who knows what he is about better than any other English writer of his generation, must have intended this impression; and we must assume that he means it when he says that '*Heartbreak House* is not merely the name of the play . . . It is cultured, leisured Europe before the war.' All that we can reply is that we do not recognize it. Perhaps Europe may have presented some such spectacle to the eye of the Man in the

Moon; but it would have appeared very different if he had come close enough to see the faces and hear the speech of a real Heartbreak House. Its inmates were futile; but they were not futile in this way.

Moreover, we are haunted by a faint suspicion. Although there may be some unfairness in turning an author's confession against himself, the comparison with *The Cherry Orchard*, of which Mr. Shaw deliberately reminds us on the first page of his preface, could not possibly be escaped. It would, in any case, have leaped to the eye. Can it be that Mr. Shaw has tried directly to imitate that marvellous play?

Tchekov's plays [he writes], being less lucrative than swings and roundabouts, got no further in England, where theatres are only ordinary commercial affairs, than a couple of performances by the Stage Society. We stared and said, 'How Russian!' They did not strike me in that way. Just as Ibsen's intensely Norwegian plays exactly fitted every middle and professional class suburb in Europe, these intensely Russian plays fitted all the country houses in Europe in which the pleasures of music, art, literature and the theatre had supplanted hunting, shooting, fishing, flirting, eating and drinking.

It is probably true; but somehow a nuance of falsehood has crept in. *The Cherry Orchard* is typical, but not typical in exactly the sense Mr. Shaw would have us believe. His statement is inaccurate because it is downright. There is not, as the mathematical logicians would say, a one-to-one correspondence between the futility of the Russian *intelligentsia* and our own; therefore the formula by which the one is completely expressed cannot be used to express the other. The corresponding object has to be seen and studied in and for itself. Instead of this, we suspect that Mr. Shaw has projected the Russian formula on to English society. The result is chaos and pandemonium. We do not mean that *Heartbreak House*, when it is produced in the English theatre, will appear mere nonsense. Mr. Shaw is too great a master of verbal felicity of dialogue for that to happen. Quite probably it will be intensely amusing on the stage, and an English audience will surely appreciate the incoherencies of Captain Shotover better than they can the delicate inconsequences of the billiard-playing uncle of *The Cherry Orchard*.

What we do mean is that *Heartbreak House* cannot be made the foundation or even an illustration of any argument concerning English society. As a picture, it simply is not true. Were the idea not fantastic, we would charge Mr. Shaw with having as little notion of English society as his Englishman had of *John Bull's Other Island*. That is, of course, not credible. What has really happened, we believe, is that even

Mr. Shaw has fallen into the pit in which so many of our younger writers have ignominiously floundered. He has tried to transpose the Russians. Superior to his fellow-victims, Mr. Shaw has landed on his feet. He is immaculate, self-composed, master of the situation. But a pit is a pit; one can't see very much either in or out of it, after all.

Then we come to the crucial juxtaposition: this preface and that play. Two-thirds at least of the preface—all of it with the exception of one or two paradoxical pages on Churches and Theatres—are masterly. As a ruthless analysis and description of England during the war in prose that is really prose, that will follow a sinuous and subtle argument with no more apparent effort than a bee hovering about a flower-bed, the preface to *Heartbreak House* is incomparable. Here, if you like, is an anatomy of society. This Heartbreak House we know and recognize. To describe it with such concise fidelity the writer needed to stand well away from the reality. He needed not to be distracted by the disturbing emotions that attend the spectacle of individual heartbreaks and cata-strophes. And we suspect that it is precisely the faculty which enabled him to see true England and the war as a whole, which brought him to grief when he tried to focus a house-full of English people. One cannot accustom oneself to a change of spectacles in a day.

74. From an unsigned notice, *Daily Telegraph*

19 October 1921, 20749, 7

There are two ways of considering a play by Mr Bernard Shaw: (1) as a thing complete in itself and rounded off to a perfect end; or (2) in the light of a pendant to the explanatory preface which it is his custom to provide for the edification of readers. The second method has the disadvantage of suggesting an assumed superiority over the ordinary theatre-goer who, through want of opportunity or lack of ability to furnish forth the needful sum to obtain a copy of the published piece, comes to a performance forced to grapple, as best he may, with the subtleties and intricacies of the author's style. What precise moral he drew from last night's production of *Heartbreak House* at the Court, it would be interesting to discover. Possibly after witnessing the extra-ordinary behaviour of the various characters in the first two acts he would accept Hector Hushabye's dictum that 'one of two things must happen. Either out of the darkness some new creation will come to supplant us as we have supplanted the animals, or the heavens will fall in thunder and destroy us'. Or, distrusting that gentleman's sincerity, as he had every reason to do, he might agree with Ellie Dunn that 'there's nothing real in the world except my father and Shakespeare. Marcus's tigers are false; Mr Mangan's millions are false; there is nothing really strong and true about Hesione but her beautiful black hair; and Lady Utterword's is too pretty to be real'. Alas! she is not the first, or likely to be the last, to discover that this world we live in is a world of illusions, and woe betide her or him who is compelled to stand aside and silently see them subjected to an agonising process of disintegration. It takes Mr Shaw a portentously long time to arrive at either of these conclusions. His loquacity grows with the passing years, although happily his wit shows little sign of dimming brilliancy. True, there are in *Heartbreak House* lengthy stretches during which the interest is apt to dwindle, for the characters will be talking when they should be up and doing. With hardly an exception they bear, also, the true Shavian brand. They are the most elusive and contradictory creatures in the world. At one moment they are all sympathy and conciliation; at an-other they are fighting like cat and dog. One might expect that their creator would have some mercy upon them; but no, he merely uses them as puppets upon which to exercise his utmost diabolical skill as a marksman. At the beginning his heroine, Ellie Dunn, is the model of a timid, impressionable young English girl, only to develop a few hours later into a cold, pitiless, calculating woman. Captain Shotover, the patriarch of the family, is a hard-swearing, domineering, tetchy old man in whom, to your surprise, you suddenly discover there is a genuine vein of romance and gentleness. Boss Mangan, the apparently strong man of the party, unexpectedly reveals himself as a feeble trickster, who had not even the ability to feather his own nest. And so the talk goes on until you begin to ask yourself, 'Is life, in this the twentieth century, bereft of all sense of honesty, of true feeling, or of honour?'

Time, unfortunately, does not permit of any detailed account of last night's performance. The blame must be laid to the charge of the author, whose piece occupied four hours in representation, and to the fact that the Court Theatre stands at some considerable distance from Fleet Street. Better acting, however, it would be difficult to point to.

75. Naomi Royde-Smith, from an initialled notice, *Westminster Gazette*

19 October 1921, vol. LVIII, 8824, 6

Naomi Gwladys Royde-Smith (d. 1964), novelist and critic, was sometime literary editor and dramatic critic of the *Westminster Gazette* and the *Weekly Westminster*. In her notice, she emphasised the disadvantage of the publication of *Heartbreak House*, long before it was produced on the stage, thus reversing the situation at the beginning of Shaw's career as a dramatist when the publication of the plays was designed to evoke a demand for their production.

The first night of a new Shaw play at the Court Theatre might have been a renewal of the wonderful days of the Vedrenne–Barker management and the last horse-omnibuses and hansoms. But 'not twice in a life shall the gods do thus:' and last night's performance of *Heartbreak House*, though in many ways a great success, did not in any sense revive the ancient glory.

To begin with, the book of the words has been so widely read and so much discussed, both in print and in the houses where the people who attend first nights gather to talk of these things, that the real hush of expectation was absent. Indeed, the people in the stalls around me talked almost as much as the people on the stage, and at the same time, too, though not quite so loud. We all knew all about the eccentricities of Captain Shotover's household before ever the play began, and that it ended in an air-raid, and would last for four hours if we were quiet, and possibly for five if we dared to laugh or to applaud; and the knowledge did not exhilarate, nor, after the third hour, did it soothe.

In action, too, Mr. Shaw's prefatorial plea that *Heartbreak House* was a fantasia in the Russian manner evaporated in the first twenty minutes. Mr. Shaw's discursiveness has even less in common with the atmospheric subtlety of Tchekov's stage method than anyone who had only read the plays of either author can easily remark for himself. The English theme remains English; the Shavian treatment sharp, antithetical, agile, impish, is if anything more Shavian than ever; there is nothing new about that.

There is, indeed, very little new about this play at all. A great many whiffs from *Man and Superman*; the elderly theme of the girl who must marry to escape poverty (as if the difficulty with girls of Ellie Dunn's class nowadays was not to get them to marry at all); the submerged criminal from *Major Barbara*, and, far less welcome, the conversations of the last act of that interminable play; traces of *The Philanderer*; a character or so from *You Never Can Tell*, all returned to mind as the material for the three acts of this fantasia was displayed, so that there was no real sense of novelty in the play from beginning to end. The very touches which made the book topical when it appeared, such, for example, as Boss Mangan's reference to the Prime Minister who offered him a post in the Government in his capacity of business man 'without the trouble of an election to Parliament,' have faded to-day and were received by the audience without a sound of recognition.

[Comment on details of the staging and acting.]

The wonders of the evening were Miss Edith Evans as Ariadne Utterword and Mr. Brember Wills as Captain Shotover. Miss Evans, who never appears in any play without astonishing me by the range of her powers and the complete absorption of her personality in the part she interprets, was a soft and lovely and utterly materialistic and self-satisfied woman of the decadent world. If at times she did not quite convey the fineness of the atmosphere she was supposed to represent, the fault lay with Mr. Shaw's didacticism, not with her finished art. Mr. Brember Wills, for the first two acts, made Captain Shotover almost great. His surging entries, his fugitive disappearances, were all electrical and significant, and to watch him trembling over his drawing-board and delivering himself of gems from the depths of Mr. Shaw's mysticism was a delight and a lesson in acting. In the last act he did little except lend his white beard to intensify the colour scheme into which

Miss O'Malley's golden head fitted so charmingly beside him. His long tirade was lost in the rising tide of weariness which had half-emptied the stalls before it was over.

When the curtain fell at last there was a long applause and many calls for the author, to which Mr. Shaw did not reply.

76. James Agate, *Saturday Review*

21 October 1921

James (Evershed) Agate (1877–1947), literary and dramatic critic, was leading dramatic critic for the *Sunday Times* from 1923 to his death. Agate was never an unqualified admirer of Shaw, although he was able to appreciate many of his virtues. As he wrote in a letter to the actress, Vivien Leigh, on 1 November 1944, 'I do not deny Shaw's immense genius, but I can't and won't stand it in the theatre because I don't think that genius is dramatic' (James Agate, *Ego* 7, 1945, 235).

Four hours of persistent button-holing at the Court Theatre convinced the dramatic critics that as a simple entertainment *Heartbreak House* was a failure. But what else it might be they did not try to find out. They hurled at the author the quite meaningless epithet of 'Shavian'—as though it were his business to be Tchehovian or Dickensian or any-body-elsian except himself—and then ran away like children playing a game of 'tick'. What is there about Mr. Shaw that he should break so many heads as well as hearts? In and out of season, from his preface-tops, he has proclaimed that he is no leisurely horticulturist, pottering about Nature's garden and pruning it into trim shapes. The tragedy and comedy of life, he has shouted, come from founding our institutions —and in these he certainly includes our plays—on half-satisfied passions instead of on a genuinely scientific natural history. Well, here is natural history preached with all the fury of the Salvationist. With Shaw fanaticism means the blind espousal of reason, a marriage which, in the theatre, turns out to be something joyless. But what, this disciple would ask, in comparison with truth and reason are such petty virtues as good play-writing, good manners and good taste? Truth, like everything else, is relative; and what is truth to the sentimental, loose-reasoning playgoer is not necessarily truth to the unsentimental, logical playwright. 'A fool sees not the same tree that a wise man sees.' 'If a man can be partaker of God's theatre, he shall likewise be partaker of God's rest', says Bacon. But if truth be the thing which Shaw will have most, rest is that which he will have not at all. If we will be partakers of Shaw's theatre we must be prepared to be partakers of his fierce unrest.

But then no thinker would ever desire to lay up any other reward. When Whitman writes: 'I have said that the soul is not more than the body, And I have said that the body is not more than the soul, And nothing, not God, is greater to one than oneself is', we must either assent or dissent. Simply to cry out 'Whitmanesque!' is no way out. When Ibsen writes a play to prove that building happy homes for happy human beings is not the highest peak of human endeavour, leaving us to find out what higher summit there may be, he intends us to use our brains. It is beside the point to cry out 'How like Ibsen!' *Heartbreak House* is a re-statement of these two themes. You have to get Ibsen thoroughly in mind if you are not to find the Zeppelin at the end of Shaw's play merely monstrous. It has already destroyed the people who achieve; it is to come again to lighten the talkers' darkness, and at the peril of all the happy homes in the neighbourhood. You will do well to keep Whitman in mind when you hear the old sea-captain bellowing with a thousand different intonations and qualities of emphasis: 'Be yourself, do not sleep.' I do not mean, of course, that Shaw had these two themes actually in mind when he set about this maundering, Tchehovian rhapsody. But they have long been part of his mental make-up, and he cannot escape them or their implications. The difficulty seems to be in the implications. Is a man to persist in being himself if that self run counter to God, or the interests of parish, nation, the community at large? The characters in this play are nearer to apes and goats than to men and women. Shall they nevertheless persist in being themselves, or shall they pray to be Zeppelin-destroyed and born again? The tragedy of the women is the very ordinary one of having married the wrong man. But all these men—liars and humbugs, ineffectual, hysterical, neurasthenic—are wrong men. The play, in so far as it has a material plot, is an affair of grotesque and horrid accouplements. It is monstrous for the young girl to mate in any natural sense with a, superficially considered, rather disgusting old man. Shall she take him in the spirit as a spiritual mate? Shaw holds that she shall, and that in the theatre even spiritual truth shall prevail over formal prettiness.

It were easy to find a surface resemblance between *Heartbreak House* and *Crotchet Castle*, to transfer to our author the coat-of-arms Peacock found for his hero: 'Crest, a crochet rampant; Arms, three empty bladders, turgescent.' The fact that opinions are held with the whole force of belief prevents them from being crotchets. Nor would I agree to 'bladders'. You have seen those little carts piled with iridescent and splendiferous balloons, some delicately moored, afloat in thin air. So this play of wooden plot and inflated symbol. The cart may plough through ruts or sink axle-deep in mud, the balloons are buoyant still. Rude urchins may fling dirt—the owner of the cart is not averse, when the mood takes him, from bespattering himself—the balloons still soar or are made free of the ether. Their vendor is the old sea-captain, a hawker of ideals. As this world goes he is mad. With him we are to climb Solness's steeple all over again, to catch at 'harps in the air'. To ears not ghostly attuned he talks a jargon nigh to nonsense; yet through him booms the voice of that restless Force which is Shaw's conception of God. Happiness is the sleepy pear ripening to decay. This is pure Ibsen. So, too, is the hymn to appetite and rum, two things from which our author has held himself rigidly aloof. 'It is not drunkenness so long as you do not drift; they are drunkards who sleep in their cabins, though they have but drunk of the waters of Jordan.' I quote from memory. The old man with his soul divinely loose about him, has something of the moral grandeur of Job, the intellectual stature of Isaiah. There is pathos in him. 'I can't bear to be answered; it discourages me', is the plea of waning power. And still he talks, shunning, postponing severance from life, 'seeking to ward off the last word ever so little . . . garrulous to the very last'. I imagine this is the one portrait in all the long gallery which the author will 'ever with pleas'd smile keep on, ever and ever owning'—the one to which he, here and now, signing for soul and body, sets his name.

The play stands or falls exactly as we get or miss this spiritual hang. As an entertainment pure and simple it is dull and incoherent—even for Shaw. It has all the author's prolixities and perversities. It has the old fault of combining thinking on a high level with joking on a low one. There is the old confusion of planes. There is the plane upon which the old man and the young girl, spiritual adventurers both, after the manner of Solness and Hilda Wangel, are fitting spiritual mates; but there is also the plane upon which the girl says: 'I am his white wife; he has a black one already.' The play is full of the 'tormented unreticence of the very pure'. Spirituality chambers with lewdness revealed: beauty beds with nastiness which any but the nicest mind had instinctively avoided. On all planes but the highest these people induce nausea. Throughout the evening Stevenson's 'I say, Archer—my God, what women!' came to mind over and over again. 'What a captain!' one said in ecstasy, but in the next breath, 'What a crew!' This, however, was merely the expression of a predilection. Shaw is concerned with the salvation of all his characters. Nowhere in this play do I find him with his tongue in his cheek. I refuse to believe that his Zeppelin is an irrelevant joke, a device for waking the audience up. If I did not take the author to be perfectly serious I should dismiss the play as a senile impertinence. I found it quite definitely exhilarating and deeply moving, and it therefore ranks for me among the great testaments. When I saw it at the Court Theatre it was admirably acted. The old captain of Mr. Brember Wills was magnificently distraught—Ibsen and Shaw, Whitman and General Booth rolled into one.

77. Sydney W. Carroll, notice, *Sunday Times*

23 October 1921, 5141, 4

Sydney Wentworth Carroll (1877–1958), journalist and critic, was dramatic critic of the *Sunday Times* from 1918 to 1923.

This is an example of the unfavourable criticism evoked by *Heartbreak House*. Carroll was not alone in finding the play a good cure for insomnia. In a letter to his nephew, Richard Bennett, Arnold Bennett wrote on 19 October 1921: 'Last night I had to go to Shaw's play *Heartbreak House*, 3h. 50 minutes of the most intense tedium. I went to sleep twice, fortunately' (*Arnold Bennett's Letters to his Nephew* (1936), 65).

Homer nodded. Shall we deny to our one and only Shaw a similar concession? Need we deny it to ourselves? I devour political tracts daily. Sometimes they serve me for my breakfast, at others they are sufficient substitutes for lunch, tea, or supper, and your average political tract requires considerable digesting. The drier, the tougher, the longer and drearier they are the better I like them. They make me feel civically educated. When I read them I study the power that is slowly driving the world mad, the force that compels me to work for my living. They enable me properly to appreciate the comic songs about income tax and the poor man's beer that I have to listen to at revues. But shall I be condemned to four hours of a political tract in a theatre?—Never. Frenzied delights of that kind, delirious ecstasies compared to which the Egyptian ballet in *Cairo* is a Salvation Army meeting, are not for me. I prefer to keep my heart intact and my brain at rest in a comfortable bed at home. That, after all, is the best place for sleep.

It really was not Mr Shaw's fault that we slept. He made all his characters shout and roar, bluster and scream. His piece is a series of interminable harangues, discussions, interjections, ejaculations, observations, and verbal explosions dealing in a confused jumble with life, politics, ethics, manners and sex slavery. As a contribution to drama it

254

is negligible. He finishes it with a bomb. If he had not, probably one of the audience would have done the job for him. The piece did not appear concludable otherwise. The noise of the bomb exploding might have awakened the seven sleepers of Ephesus, but it did not awaken one old gentleman to whom Mr Shaw had administered a sleeping draught comparable to which doses of poppy and mandragora were as the blackest of coffee.

Heartbreak House is described by Mr Shaw as 'A fantasia in the Russian manner on English themes'. It has been said to follow the manner of Tchekov. That is a gross libel on the Russian. Tchekov always has an atmosphere, this play has only a smell. Tchekov always has distinct, intelligible and amusing characterisation. This piece is crowded with the stock figures of Shavian drama conventionalised to dullness. There is not one figure that has not danced itself to weariness, been pulled and buffeted about in every direction by Mr Shaw in his previous plays. They have sunk from creatures with a reasonable semblance of vitality to marionettism. Some people may label all these crazy folk, these garrulous inconsequent maunderers, drivellers and shouters of epigram, philosophy and balderdash as allegorical, but what possible parable can there be in such a mountain of rubbish? Talk by itself may make an interesting play. But the talk must be brilliant, witty, and dramatic. It must not have merely small bright patches, spots of wisdom. It must be consecutive, coherent, and lead to some definite objective. Talking for the mere sake of garrulity, talking in order to prove the devastating influence of loquacity turned on at high pressure, talk that embraces every subject, every moral, every ideal and every expostulatory or vituperative expression known to the language is merely elemental babbling, the philosophy of a second childhood, verbal froth that obscures all the issues it is intended to deal with.

There were moments when the old Shaw darted like a streak of lightning into this Sahara of conversation. Here and there an oddly humorous passage, a sentence pregnant with deep philosophy, a situation fraught with the essence of humour, lit up the damnable depression and gloom of this latest of Bleak Houses. What one's mental impressions might be if one were asked to absorb this product in smaller doses it is impossible to conjecture. At the moment, if any reader of this paper is suffering from chronic and incurable sleeplessness a visit to *Heartbreak House* should effect an immediate remedy.

I could not follow the idea that was evidently at the back of the acting, which to me seemed forced, unnatural, strident, and oppressive.

As was quite natural in such a verbose work, forgetfulness of the lines was noticeable. Miss Edith Evans, delightful in the quieter passages, was simply unbearable when she raised her voice and exaggerated her Society manner. Miss Mary Grey cut a statuesque and impressive figure. Mr Brember Wills made a picturesque, shouting marine philosopher, and Mr H. O. Nicholson's delicate finish was particularly interesting. The best performance came from Mr Charles Groves as a humbugging burglar, while the acting of Mr Eric Maturin as a Society 'rotter' and that of Mr James Dale as an exquisite lady-killer helped to beguile the tedium.

PS—Since writing the foregoing, I am told that Mr Fagan has succeeded in speeding up the play so much that, without removing a single line, it now plays from 8 o'clock sharp until 11.10. Should, however, the blue pencil be directed upon a very necessary curtailment an even better result might be obtained.

78. Desmond MacCarthy, from a notice, *New Statesman*

29 October 1921, vol. XVIII, 446, 103

Reprinted in *Shaw* (1951), 143.

Desmond MacCarthy thought that *Heartbreak House* was possibly Shaw's 'best-written play' but deplored what he considered his 'indifference to Art'. When Desmond MacCarthy saw a revival in 1943, he thought that when the play was well performed it was 'one of the most excitingly amusing and interesting of Shaw's plays' (*New Statesman*, 3 April 1943; *Shaw* (1951), 149).

Heartbreak House is one of the most interesting of Mr Shaw's plays, just as it is undoubtedly the queerest and subtlest of them, and perhaps (so far as the phrasing of the dialogue is concerned) even his best-written play. It has, however, defects which might confuse any audience, and, what is worse, it contains incongruities glaring enough to offer some excuse even for contempt, from such as are either too unobservant, too unemotional or too prejudiced against Mr Shaw himself, to perceive the acute profundity of his criticism of modern society or the noble desperation which inspired the play.

Mr Shaw's indifference to Art, or that side of it which deals with methods and form, has recoiled on his own head before, but never with such annihilating effect. He will merge the artist in the prophet, and the result is that as a prophet he does not get the hearing he deserves. Look at the Press criticisms of this play! They have been disgraceful, but it is not to be wondered at. Probably every night there are ten or twelve people in the Court Theatre who, with a blue pencil and a pair of scissors, could turn Mr Shaw's play into a masterpiece. Why, why, has he not respect for his own work? He has for his own mind, his own soul, and his 'function', but for each play as he writes it, he has as little as the most frivolous author who trims a story to catch the wind of favour.

Some years ago the Stage Society performed two plays of Chekov;

The Cherry Orchard and *Uncle Vanya*. (They are going to repeat *Uncle Vanya* soon.) Of *Uncle Vanya* I wrote in 1914, just before the war:

The current of the days is slow here, the air the characters breathe is sultry with undischarged energy, and broken only by unrefreshing nerve storms; it is an atmosphere of sighs and yawns and self-reproaches, vodka, endless tea and endless discussion. But we have no right to label this atmosphere 'Russian' and to regard it with complacent curiosity. Have you not felt that fog in your throat on English lawns, in English houses? Indeed, the main point of difference between this spellbound cultivated Russian society and the English variety is not in our favour. If Chekov's intellectuals are half dead, the other half of them is very much and painfully alive. They suffer more consciously, there is intensity in their lassitude; at least they torture themselves and each other, by displaying each his own bankruptcy.

Now Mr Shaw, too, was apparently struck by this resemblance, and he proceeded to write a Tchekov play about English society. The result was a very remarkable one—*Heartbreak House*. Of course, his subject-matter was slightly different. English people are not like Russian people, but the great difference between such a play as *Uncle Vanya* and *Heartbreak House* is due to the temperament of the author. Mr Shaw does not know what heartbreak is. He conceives it as a sudden disillusionment (*vide* his heroine), cauterising like a flash of lightning; as a sharp pain, but not as a maiming misery. Compared with the vital and restless inmates of *Heartbreak House* Chekov's characters are like dying flies in a glue-pot. He presents his play as an important diagnosis of real conditions, yet he allows his high spirits continually to turn it into farce, so that hardly one person in a hundred sees its relations to reality. . . .

Mr Shaw is gloriously an artist in his sense of the importance of ideas, and in his sense of a subject, but he is without artistic respect for unity of effect. It seems he does not care about it. He sows thistles for donkeys in his flower beds, and then wonders at the donkeys for munching them and trampling on the flowers. His high spirits are a wonderful gift, but they master and distract him, and they have seriously damaged this fine play.

BACK TO METHUSELAH

1920

Back to Methuselah was written from 1918 to 1920 and published in 1921. It was presented in New York at the Garrick Theater by the New York Theater Guild in February and March 1922. The first production in England was at the Birmingham Repertory Theatre in October 1923 and the first production in London was by the Birmingham Repertory Theatre Company at the Royal Court Theatre in February 1924. The play comprised five separate parts and was usually played on succeeding nights although sometimes two parts were played together.

79. Lady Gregory on Shaw's new play

1919

Diary entry, 3 March 1919, from *Lady Gregory's Journals 1916–1930*, ed. Lennox Robinson (1946), 204.

Augusta, Lady Gregory (1852–1932) was co-founder with Yeats and Synge of the Irish Dramatic Movement which led to the creation of the Abbey Theatre.

G.B.S. read me his play beginning in the Garden of Eden. The first act a fine thing, 'a Resurrection Play' I called it. The second, two hundred years later, an argument between Cain, Adam and Eve, the soldier against the man of peace. I told him I thought it rather monotonous, an Ossianic dialogue, and he said that he thought of introducing Cain's wife, 'the Modern Woman', or perhaps only speaking of her in the argument. I said that even that would be an improvement as Cain is unnecessarily disagreeable and one could forgive if he is put, by aspersions on his wife, in a passion, for one can forgive where there is passion. It is like drunkenness—'Ah, you can't blame him, he was drunk,' when a man has cut his head open. He laughed and agreed or seemed to.

80. J. C. Squire, review in *Observer*

26 June 1921, 6787, 4

Reprinted in *Books Reviewed* (1922), 122.

Sir John Collings Squire (1884–1958), poet and man of letters, was literary editor of the *New Statesman* when it was founded in 1913 and himself started a new literary magazine, the *London Mercury* in 1919, editing it until 1934. He wrote reviews of books for a number of other magazines and the review of *Back to Methuselah* was one of his regular signed contributions to the *Observer*. Squire was an extremely clever and amusing parodist and his *Tricks of the Trade* (1917) included a fragment in the style of Shaw, *Mahomet the Prophet* (39). The sub-title referred to is 'A Metabiological Pentateuch'.

It would have been a pity not to use it at the top of the page. I remember learning, when still young enough to think long words amusing, a poem about the adventures of 'an antediluvian man of sesquipedalian height' who met an ichthyosaurus. Mr. Shaw's sub-title recalls that; but he may be allowed his little jokes. He is far too shrewd a journalist to employ these terms for his main titles. No sub-editor on an evening paper ever had a better gift for pungent and arresting headlines. *Back to Methuselah* is one of the happiest conceptions he has had; it catches one at once, and has the added advantage of meaning something. This, however, is what the reader does not understand immediately: there is, as usual, a preface interposed between the title-page and the play.

It is a long preface and not in every respect one of Mr. Shaw's best.

The History of Evolutionary Thought is surveyed, with glances at the theatre, painting, politics, and theology. Mr. Shaw races along with fewer good witticisms than usual and fewer really provocative remarks. The sensation of speed is enjoyable at first. But after a while one tends to drowse; one ceases to notice the swift succession of passing objects, and is conscious only of the rhythmic rattle of the train. The upshot of it is that Creative Evolution is 'the genuinely scientific religion for which all wise men are now anxiously looking.' Our old friend, the Life Force, comes in (he always reminds me, by the way, of Gibbon's sneer about 'the science, or rather the language of metaphysics') as the motive power. The play that follows has a major and a minor theme. The major is Creative Evolution at work—mind conquering matter. The minor is a new instrument for accelerating the process. Men do not live long enough to learn anything. They are children—none more so than Mr. Asquith and Mr. Lloyd George. Lamarck teaches that if a species wants anything badly it will get it. Men should want to live to the age of Methuselah, instead of dying in their intellectual infancy. If they did the evolutionary movement would proceed much more quickly and win far more commendation than it does from Mr. Shaw.

Certain stages of it are presented in Mr. Shaw's five Acts. He begins with an allegorical picture of Adam and Eve in the garden, and the suggestions of the snake, whence came Death and all our Woe. We next come to the present day, when the theory of volitional survival is formulated to a pair of stupid and incredulous politicians, a curate and a hoyden with bobbed hair. Next, in 2170, we find a man actually surviving for three hundred years (persons of normal age, in spite of mechanical advance, remaining as foolish and greedy as ever), and finally we come to A.D. 31920. That is not Utopia; Mr. Shaw's only Perfect State is the Eternity of the Spirit. But people are now born from eggs, in a condition corresponding to our condition at seventeen; they outgrow mundane passions and affections in four years; and the more elderly are safely and consciously forwarding a further movement away from our present plight. Lilith, the *dea ex machina*, at the close proclaims the aim: 'I shall see the slave set free and the enemy reconciled, the whirlpool become all life and no matter.'

The drama itself occupies 267 pages. At the close of the preface Mr. Shaw says: 'I am doing the best I can at my age. My powers are waning; but so much the better for those who found me unbearably brilliant when I was in my prime.' The admission is so handsome and so unusual that it seems almost a pity that it was unnecessary. Mr. Shaw's powers do not seem to be waning at all. The only typically senile vice that he has is the vice of garrulity, and that in him, to use the jargon which so delights him, was rather an inherited predisposition than an acquired habit. His juniors would be perfectly prepared to believe that, like the people in his last act, he was born from an egg and began discoursing when no more than his head was through the shell. But that his powers are waning there is no evidence at all in this book. Those who creep back to him in the belief that he has become completely mild and tame will be disagreeably surprised. His life differs from his play in this, that it is not merely the ghost of the Old Adam that is appearing in the last act. Mr. Shaw is as clever, as vigorous, as cunning, as high-spirited, as flippant, as curious as ever he was. There are conspicuous faults in this book. The preface, for all its merits, is rather inconsecutive, and gives one the feeling that although Mr. Shaw habitually thinks, he seldom stops to think. His characters are mostly sticks; his appeal is almost continuously to the intellect; the text is overloaded with topical references; a few passages are in bad taste and many pages are tiresome. Most of the middle of the play might have been taken for granted; we did not want that endless silly talk between Mr. Lloyd George, Mr. Asquith, and the rest, to help us form a conception of the present limitations of humanity; some scene much shorter could have furnished the necessary symbol. But there is no reason to trace any of these things to senile decay.

Mr. Shaw's qualities and faculties are precisely what they were; the faculty of being very boring was always amongst them, and he may cheer himself with the reflection that there is no fault here, large or small, which cannot be paralleled repeatedly from his earlier plays. I at least feel that in places Mr. Shaw is here surpassing his previous best, and notably in the first and last scenes. The whole play may be no more actable than the second part of *Faust* or yesterday's *Times*, but the first act and part of the last would be as effective in the theatre as anything that Mr. Shaw has ever done. The craftsmanship of the Eden scene deserves the much-abused epithet, 'astonishing'; every sentence is revelatory, and moves the action forward; and the whole is a genuine re-creation of the legend. The illusion is perfectly imposed, and the temptation to cheap cleverness, which previous wits who have dealt with that story have not resisted, is avoided. Mr. Shaw's sympathy with the Serpent is scarcely veiled, but he does not obscure his intellectual conceptions with irrelevant jests as he has so often done, nor does he allow those conceptions, in their turn, to smother the dramatic progress of his story. In the last act he comes nearer to poetry than he has ever come, and in the last pages nearer to awe. An operation would have to be performed on him before he could actually write poetry or communicate awe; but the operation would cut something out, not put something in. There are elements in his composition which inhibit him from an even momentary abandonment to love or pity or æsthetic enjoyment, and he is incapable of fear. He is always 'all there'; he possesses his subject and cannot be possessed by it; his sense of humour is never in complete abeyance; the strain of argument is always present; he is too interested in things in general to give his natural sympathy for individuals much play—being, like Nature, careful of the race, but careless of the single specimen; he despises the senses and, in so far as Art appeals to the senses, he despises Art. When he uses the mechanism of Strephon and Amaryllis, temple and bosky glade and pastoral dance, in the last act, our constant tendency to lapse into enjoyment of the idyllic element is checked by the pervasive sense of Mr. Shaw's irony; we know he thinks that all nonsense. Even at the close where, as I have said, he does actually come near awe, he does not quite achieve it: for in the imagined presence of the very spirit of Nature, to whom he has dedicated himself, Mr. Shaw's self-possession and detachment remain: it is as it were a theoretical awe struggling to carry conviction. Nevertheless, that scene, from the procession of primæval ghosts to the last eloquent harangue of the symbolic Lilith, is conceived finely, and constructed with extraordinary skill. It leaves one with a sense of having had a glimpse of grandeur.

A cold and pagan grandeur; but there is Mr. Shaw's philosophy. He is unlike Mr. Wells in many respects, but he is like him in this, that so long as he can regard himself as a humble instrument of Evolution he is perfectly happy. His horizon is wider than Mr. Wells's, and the operation of his revered process more extensive. Mr. Wells, except for an occasional dash into metaphysics just to show that he knows they are there, usually keeps his eyes firmly glued on the earth, which was once a whirling ball of fire. Time is good enough for him, and if the upward climb from the amœba is going to end in a material calamity, collision or cooling, he prefers not to worry about it. He advocates our co-operation with the biological movement as a man advocates any other measure of practical reform. Mr. Shaw is not satisfied with that. He has always been interested in the physical details of current evolutionary science. He will talk about Darwin, Lamarck, and Weismann until all's blue, and in the present preface he very nearly does. But his Adam and Eve is only a metaphysical parable. He is not content to begin with the amœba, or to end with a race of very highly educated engineers who play billiards on board their smoothly-running trains or discover how to fly to the other planets. Vegetarian, teetotaler, anti-æsthete, he does not really long to increase material comforts or delights; he wants to abolish them and the means of enjoying them.

His final blissful dream is of man shedding one organ after another, the foot, the hand, the head, until he becomes pure spirit: Creative Evolution. I hold no brief for Mr. Asquith or Mr. Lloyd George, but I doubt whether they would be justified in taking it from Mr. Shaw that the democracy has given them a mandate for this. No doubt they look grotesque little objects when Mr. Shaw exhibits them in front of a background of æons. But it is a tough test. Even the majestic author of this preface might appear slightly ridiculous were he conceived as delivering his soul under the shadow of something no larger or more ancient than the Pyramids and the Parthenon. Nevertheless Mr. Shaw has attempted to formulate his view of things and his ideal; and the attempt must command respect. Even he, with all his desire, has not bridged the passage from Time to Eternity in his exposition: but the difficulty of relating two things, neither of which one can comprehend, is no new one. Mr. Shaw announces that he has done his best to provide mankind with the Bible of a new religion: a demand for which has just been made by Mr. Wells. It may be taken for certain that mankind at large, if it ever hears of them, will find his dogmas about life eternal as vague as it will find his dogmas on life temporal unappetising. Put it in another manner. Are you yourself quite happy with the notion of the Universe as an enormous theatre where one long Shaw play is being acted? I don't think Bibles are made this way.

81. Desmond MacCarthy, *New Statesman*

9 July 1921, vol. XVII, 430, 384

Reprinted in *Shaw* (1951), 134.

Desmond MacCarthy's review of the published play and preface is a careful consideration of the relationship between Shaw's treatment of ideas in his preface and his dramatic presentation. He found 'hardly a gleam of religious emotion' in the plays but thought that 'some profound things are said by the way and not a few absurd ones'. When he saw the play on the stage, he thought that the majority of the critics of the performance had been wrong in assuring him that he was not missing much. He said that '*Methuselah* is a tremendous effort of the imagination on the part of a man who in some directions has obviously deep insight, to express his sense of the meaning of life' (*New Statesman*, 11 October 1924; reprinted in *Shaw* (1951), 139).

There is one generalisation about Mr Shaw's works as they have appeared volume by volume which I have never seen made, though I have read many books and articles about them, namely, that there are a great many more ideas in his prefaces than ever get into his plays. This is only natural, but often the ideas which are most emphasised in those prefaces and make them impressive find only a subordinate or an indistinct expression in the dramas when the curtain goes up. This is not true of his early prefaces and plays, but it is true of most of the volumes he has published since *John Bull's Other Island*. The early prefaces were really aids to critics; but how few, for example, of the important ideas on education and family life ever got out of the preface into *Misalliance* and *Fanny's First Play*, or how little of that indictment of people's states of mind, and feeling during the war, which will make the preface to *Heartbreak House* live, was ultimately reflected in the dialogue or action of that play! This generalisation will not seem unimportant the moment its implication is grasped: that for the last fifteen years, with some exceptions, Mr Shaw has not written the plays which express directly his most important ideas on the subjects he dramatised. Of course, the plays have been the offspring of his ideas and have been influenced by them, but they have not (with a few exceptions like *Pygmalion*) been the embodiment of them. This time he is sure he has written in *Back to Methuselah* the play he ought to have written. Yet he is mistaken.

He has written an impressive preface insisting on the paramount importance of religion for the individual and for the race, but he has produced five plays, in which there is hardly a gleam of religious emotion, and in which the religion he believes in himself is never shown as inspiring or influencing anyone. True, Adam and Eve and Cain in the Garden of Eden talk a little about the Voice and what it says to them; but the essential thing about these figures is not their communion with anything without or within them, but that they are represented each as bundles of specialised instincts and aptitudes into which the Life Force has divided itself in order to achieve its ends. *Blanco Posnet* and *Androcles* are religious plays, so is *Major Barbara*. In them you see religion acting upon men and women. In these five plays we are given a series of glimpses of the course which, according to Mr Shaw, human progress ought to follow and of the goal it can attain, if men can be persuaded to believe in Creative Evolution. Some of the reasons for believing in it are given in the preface. You must believe first that the reason why a giraffe has a long neck is that for many generations certain beasts with short necks have willed to have long ones. Well, if you are not familiar with the idea of natural selection, which also fairly plausibly covers the phenomenon, that may not be hard. The point is, that once you have believed that the will is creative, you can then be happy about the future of mankind, because they can will themselves in the long run into a state of eternal perfection. Of course, willing is not a matter of taking up a Geruda stone like Mr Bultitude[1] and wishing you were a boy again; it is a state of perpetual effort, conscious and unconscious.

Now, there is a drawback to the universal acceptance by mankind of Mr Shaw's religion which has nothing to do with the evidence for or against it. It is this. It only meets the needs of a particular and rather rare type of man. Mr Shaw, no doubt, would deny this, but he can only do so from a mystical point of view, not from the evidence afforded by the way men behave. He would say, 'We are members one of another; all religions assert it, and even science, by giving us a com-

[1] A character in *Vice Versa* by F. Anstey.

mon ancestry, admits it. In that case the deepest and strongest passion in all of us must be a devotion to the whole race. What each of us cares most for is the fate of mankind. Therefore, the religion which would really satisfy us is one which would enable us to foresee the endless progress of mankind towards perfection.' It is true that we are concerned, when we are reminded of it, and some of us profoundly, about the future of the race. It is a detestable thought, when it is vividly put before us, that the cosmic process may wipe out mankind altogether. The most eloquent passage in Mr Balfour's *Foundations of Belief*, which is really a pamphlet of intimidation—believe or you will be unhappy—calls up the picture of a dead world. But so is the idea of our own death detestable, when we really envisage dying. Yet we manage partly by forgetting, and partly by staring death out of countenance now and then when we are feeling calm and powerful, to accommodate ourselves to the idea; and it is far easier to become reconciled to the death of the race some millions of years hence, of which we are not so often or so vividly reminded. In short the instinct which makes us take to heart the welfare of mankind is only one of many, and it is the only one which the religion of Creative Evolution satisfies.

In Mr Shaw himself it is the predominant one; even his instincts as an artist are subordinated to it. He has said again and again that he would not have written a line if he had not wanted to make men better and more sensible. (His impulse merely to amuse and excite them and make them admire is stronger than he thinks it is, but that is another matter, and he explains himself to himself in that respect by saying that 'every jest is an earnest in the womb of time', which is a doubtful generalisation.) In the last play in this book art is put in its proper place as the creation of dolls for children, since it can no longer illuminate the path of progress. The point is, that Mr Shaw is a born reformer and therefore he cannot see that the religion of Creative Evolution has any defects.

A born reformer must be an optimist; this religion affords a basis for optimism: 'We fail, we die, it does not matter; the ends we strive for will be attained at last by those who come after us. The individual is of no account.' Mr Shaw's religion gives him that assurance and he needs it urgently because, when he looks round him, he does not by any means take an optimistic view of mankind's chances of improvement. When he wrote *Man and Superman* he took refuge from disillusionment in the idea of eugenics. We are under the feet of the swinish multitude; even the educated are ignorant and petty idiots for the most part; we must breed ourselves into being a better race. In the preface to *Back to Methuselah* he confesses that

the circumstances of this catastrophe (the 1914 war), the boyish cinema-fed romanticism which made it possible to impose it on the people as a crusade, and especially the ignorance and errors of the victors of Western Europe when its violent phase had passed and the time for reconstruction arrived, confirmed a doubt which had grown steadily in my mind during my forty years' public work as a Socialist—namely, whether the human animal, as he exists at present, is capable of solving the social problems raised by his own aggregation, or, as he calls it, his civilisation.

In fact, he wants another injection of optimism to be able to go on with any heart. It has crossed his mind that life is short (he is not far off the end of his own), too short perhaps for any man to master facts and learn wisdom. As the whole of creation (remember the giraffe's neck) shows that where there's a will there's a way, let men, therefore, will to live for three hundred years, and afterwards for a longer period.

The idea looks silly, but I have been a close reader of Mr Shaw for many years, and often his ideas which first struck me as silliest were the ones which I subsequently found had modified my thoughts most. There is no reason why science should not discover how to prolong life. I do not believe it can be done in the way in which Mr Shaw seems to believe, and the late Mrs Eddy believed it could be done, but if men determine to find out more about the nature of growth and decay and of their own bodies, they may make the necessary discovery. In that case, a world full of vigorous men and women of much greater experience than we can ever have would certainly stand more chance of progressing rapidly towards a better civilisation. It is an idea worth storing in the armoury of hope.

Perhaps the most stimulating psychological idea which emerges from these plays is the suggestion that it is the consciousness of the shortness of life which makes men so scatterbrained and ready to snatch at all sorts of things which do not belong to their peace. So little else seems worth while. Longevity would steady them; it would then be worth while to look forward. In the last play, 30,000 years hence, the 'ancients' have ceased to care about anything that men now usually pursue. All the desires and experiences which make up the value of life for us are compressed into the first three or four years of existence, a brief childhood, starting from the stage which we regard as that of completed manhood. Just as in the womb now the child goes through all the stages of physical development which preceded man, so emotionally and intellectually the whole of experience as we know it, is telescoped into the first few years of human life after the new being has emerged perfectly grown from the human egg. They afterwards become 'ancients', immortal and *sans* everything, except the passion for contemplation and one practical preoccupation (Mr Shaw being a reformer cannot envisage a static state of bliss)—namely, how to get rid of the body altogether, and reach—what?—Nirvana. God or Life will at last, through the agency of man's brain, disentangle itself from matter completely. That is the goal of the cosmic process according to Mr Shaw.

What he has attempted to write is not a series of plays with religion for its theme as an agent working in the minds of men, but a kind of Hegelian cosmology in pictures, which plausibly approximates to what conceivably might happen, if it turns out to be true that a giraffe has a long neck because its forebears have willed to have one, or if a carrot is red for the same reason.

In the first play, he uses the myth of the Garden of Eden to indicate the relation of man to the cosmic process; in the second he gives us a snapshot caricature of the sort of men in whose hands the future of mankind resides; in the third the coming of the longer-lived men; in the fourth he contrasts the short-lived, ignominious, childish creatures we are with the tremendously superior beings who have each had hundreds of years' experience, and the last play takes us to the edge of the Absolute itself. It is an extraordinary imaginative effort, but not an artistic success; the proportions are wrong. Some profound things are said by the way and not a few absurd ones.

82. R. Crompton Rhodes, from an unsigned notice, *Birmingham Post*

13 October 1923, 20388, 10

R. Crompton Rhodes (1887–1935) dramatic critic of the *Birmingham Post*, wrote notices of the performances of the five parts and, on the whole, contented himself with sober accounts of the first four parts as they appeared. In the final article below, he summed up his impressions of the entire work. Shaw's curtain speech expressed delight but also surprise that the first English production of the play should have been in Birmingham, which he remembered 'when it was, dramatically and theatrically, the most impossible place in the world for work of this description'. The speech is reprinted in the *Bodley Head Bernard Shaw*, vol. V (1972), 704, and in J. C. Trewin, *The Birmingham Repertory Theatre 1913–1963* (1963), 75.

The last phase of *Back to Methuselah* is the most moving thing that it has been my fortune to see on the stage. It closes with a wonderful speech from Lilith, the mother of Adam and Eve, which for pure thought surpasses in beauty and profundity any words of John Milton. This is a bold saying, and yet while under its spell a bolder would be justified. Mr. Shaw has carried us thirty thousand years ahead. 'As Far as Thought Can Reach,' when men and women are hatched from eggs at the maturity of our present one-and-twenty, when their childhood—when they reach the perfection of the ancient Greek philosophers—lasts but four joyous years, when they live for a thousand years with the ecstasy of transcendental contemplation. It is not easy to reduce this last phase of Mr. Shaw's play into a few words, but for nearly three hours he enthralls us with his brilliant speculations. Sometimes his thought is too profound or too elusive for those of us who have studied his play for a long period, and only a fool would pretend to understand it all—or understand nothing. His cycle is an affirmation of his faith in the immortality of the soul, in his belief that this corruptible flesh of ours is the prison of a soul that is incorruptible.

And whether or not Mr. Shaw be accepted as a theologian or as a philosopher, as a playwright he is at his greatest in this last phase. Of course, his three capacities are truly inseparable, but one felt that the dramatic form was not merely the best, but the only possible form for his message. He had forgotten all the petty politics which disfigured the intermediate parts, and passed over to the grandeur, the elemental grandeur, which inspired and animated his first phase, the story of Eden. Indeed, when one heard the ghostly voices of Adam, of Eve, of Cain, of the Serpent, coming through the night and the silence there was a thrill of terrible intensity yet of ineffable peace.

And Mr. Shaw was served brilliantly by his actors, as he affirmed in a speech which, while he disparaged Birmingham as it was, had truly more honey than sting. But Mr. Shaw's opinions as a member of the audience are not of much moment, although he has an unusual faculty of detachment. First of all, praise should be given to Miss Margaret Chatwin as Lilith, who gave the wonderful speech with the quality it deserved; then to Miss Edith Evans as the She-Ancient, and Mr. Cedric Hardwicke as the He-Ancient. Mr. Scott Sunderland as Ozymandias and Miss Evelyn Hope as Cleopatra, the primitive man and woman, were also excellent. But it is no use transcribing the playbill—all were good. Mr. Paul Shelving's settings were beyond all praise, for the glade, which had an Arcadian peace until it was transformed to the whiteness of eternal snows, was exactly what was needed to give life to Mr. Shaw's dream. The whole play remains to be considered as a whole, but if the enthusiasm of a fine audience is to be considered the last phase of this cycle will, above all, be tremendously impressive.

83. James Agate, from a notice, *Sunday Times*

24 February 1924, 4

This play-cycle was exhaustively reviewed in these columns when it was produced at Birmingham, and I do not propose to enlarge now upon what I said then. It remains one of the faultiest productions which has ever issued from a great mind, and its performance, for those who deem the theatre to be a place of theatrical entertainment, is a mystery and a mistake. There are, we know, a number of people to whom dramatic action and romantic acting are antipathetic, for whom the theatre as lecture-hall and the actor as lecturer suffice. These have enjoyed this cycle; all others have suffered almost intolerable tedium. It has been held that a great play is an acted story which is told best in the theatre, and will, in fact, bear telling in no other medium. If that be true, then *Back to Methuselah* is at the opposite pole from great play-writing. It is a reading, not more and certainly not less. Its thought is logically preposterous, and unwarrantably pessimistic, and much of its expression is, alas! cheap.

Yet that the series has been conceived in passion and carried out in dignity one would not deny. The preface remains one of the noblest pieces of writing of our time, and no performance of the cycle can spoil the sincerity which obviously informs it. We should do ourselves dishonour in subjecting this writer to jeers and futility. The failures of a great mind are worthier things than lesser successes.

84. Ashley Dukes on 'the most consistent of the moderns'

1923

Extract from a chapter on 'Forerunners' in *The Youngest Drama* (1923), 44.

Ashley Dukes (1885–1959), dramatist, critic, author and theatre manager, who opened the Mercury Theatre in 1933 for the presentation of experimental plays. He wrote a short handbook *Drama* (1926) for the Home University Library, in which he called Shaw 'more Ibsenite than Ibsen' and said that the positive quality of his plays lay in 'the passion of moral, political and social indignation with which they are infused'.

Mr Shaw is not only the sincerest, but the most consistent of the moderns. A dispensation of Nature, he declares, endowed him with the 'normal vision' that is shared only by a tenth part of mankind, while the remaining nine-tenths enjoy the illusions or the blessings of abnormality. Such a man cannot be other than 'advanced', to use the idiom of Jack Tanner; and our confidence in him rests on the knowledge that he will never be reactionary. He is not the kind of author who 'goes red' at twenty-five and turns true blue by forty. Were all the world afflicted by abnormal vision, his perceptions would still be normal. He was advanced in the eighteen-nineties, when he so gloriously mistook Ibsen for a borough councillor with feminist leanings. He was advanced in the nineteen-hundreds, when he sought to reconcile the Puritans to the theatre by the simple means of writing them plays. He was advanced in the nineteen-tens, when he abjured the errors of Darwinism and discovered the basis of a new theology in the theory of Lamarck. He is still advanced in the nineteen-twenties, when Chekhov moves him to *Heartbreak House* and the glandular hypothesis (*alias* creative evolution) inspires *Back to Methuselah*. He has outlived two generations of younger writers and is still the youngest of them.

Such is the rejuvenating quality of a pure intelligence. 'I declare', says Jack Tanner, in a line that will one day give pause to the commentators, 'I declare that according to my experience moral passion is the only real passion.' There is the creed in a phrase. Moral passion spells indignation against an immoral world—against hypocrisy and lying, prostitution and slavery, poverty and dirt and disorder. Social indignation underlies *Mrs Warren's Profession* and *Major Barbara*, political indignation is the divine spark of *Man and Superman* and *Heartbreak House*, moral indignation gives life to the scientific persiflage of *The Doctor's Dilemma*, religious indignation burns in *The Shewing-Up of Blanco Posnet* and again in *Methuselah*. We are reminded of some otherworldly and incredible phenomenon, like a snow-clad volcano in eruption. But for this solitary passion, all is frozen thought.

Yet how sincerity shines through this rarefied and mistless air! There were once people who thought Mr Shaw trivial because he was witty, and shallow because he was paradoxical. They were the victims of his intellectual feat of necromancy, which is that of showing the reverse side of everything—the rusty obverse of the romantic shield, the worm-eaten frame of the Old Master, and the back garden of the suburban villa on washing-day with the clothes hanging out. It was thus that he approached the glamour of warfare in *Arms and the Man*, the dignity of history in *Caesar and Cleopatra*, or the romance of sex in *Getting Married*. The gesture is a moralist's, impish though it be. These unromantic heroes, of whom Bluntschli with his 'ten thousand knives and forks and the same quantity of dessert spoons', must be accounted the chieftain, have a significance that goes beyond their own age. They challenge the received opinion not only of to-day, but of yesterday and to-morrow. They have the *Ewigkeitszug*.[1] Their voice echoes from the corridors of some far Utopia of the intellect; and what matter if the goal is never reached?

[1] Trend to eternity.

SAINT JOAN

1923

The first production of *Saint Joan* was by the New York Theater
Guild at the Garrick Theater, New York, on 28 December 1923.
It was given 213 performances. The first British production was at
the New Theatre, London, on 26 March 1924, where it ran for
244 performances.

85. Alexander Woolcott, notice, *New York Herald*

29 December 1923, 3

Alexander (Humphreys) Woolcott (1887–1943), New York
writer and critic, in a gossipy and hastily written notice of the first
performance, nevertheless saw more point in the Epilogue than did
many later critics in their more carefully considered judgments on
the play.

The Theater Guild produced the new Shaw play last night. An eager
and an uncommonly silent audience followed it from the rising of the
first curtain on the stroke of 8 to the fall of the last one a little past
11.30 o'clock.

They had seen a dramatic portrait of Joan of Arc set forth in a play
that is beautiful, engrossing and at times exciting. They had seen certain
scenes grow groggy for want of a blue pencil. They had seen others
falter and go raucously astray for lack of a strong director with a true
ear and a sure hand—or perhaps merely for lack of the seasoning which
enough rehearsals give.

But it would be captious criticism and fraudulent reporting to give emphasis to such reservations when the outstanding thing is that a deathless legend came to life again on the Garrick's stage, quickened by the performance of a play that has greatness in it. That certain fragments were clumsily and stingily staged is a thing one does not forget in the light of the greater fact that the role of the Matchless Maid fell to one who rose magnificently to her occasion.

As Shaw wrote the role and Winifred Lenihan plays her, Jeanne d'Arc steps forth on that stage just such a simple, hearty, forthright, good humoured, utterly convinced girl as you know in your heart she must have been. The actress lives to the full the girl from Domremy that it was given to the Sage of Adelphi Terrace to imagine. And we predict that for most of those who see *Saint Joan* this will be their image of her. The Maid as De Monvel painted her, the Maid as she walks her orchard or lifts her sword in the bronze or the marble that a thousand and one French villages could afford will give way insensibly to this brisk, friendly, boyish lass, with her hair tossed back, her lips twitching at the nonsense of all the great folk, her clear brow shining, her eyes alight. Shaw could ask no more. Nor could any of us.

When Shaw left Adelphi Terrace and went strolling back to that courtroom in Rouen nearly five hundred years ago it was almost inevitable that he should have looked at the Maid, verified his instinct as to what she must have been and then studied with a greater curiosity and a livelier interest the men who jostled around her, the Warwicks whom she made uneasy, the pious Bishop of Beauvais who sentenced her to the flames, the lesser clerics who itched to lay their hands upon her. He knew that they could not have been a bad lot. Why, they were just such a baffled, legalistic, dogmatic set of dunderheads as the play *Saint Joan* is likely to find out front in any chance theater where it may be playing.

It is the scenes in which the playgoer is permitted to orient himself in the shifting map of political and social and theological thought of the fifteenth century that the legend itself is made to mark time in the wings. It is these scenes which Shaw will cut when he sees the play outrun itself in London, especially that final scene which says the same thing several times.

And yet without that last scene *Saint Joan* would hardly be a Shaw play. The deed has been done. They had dragged the Maid from the gloomy courtroom to the square in Rouen. You have heard the murderous jabber of the waiting mob, the shrieks of those who saw too late how cruel and how bestial a thing was done that day in the name of God. You even have heard the executioner return complacent to the waiting Warwick and speak as ironic a line as ever playwright put on paper. 'You have heard the last of her,' he says.

And then suddenly the scene shifts to a vision of a later day and Joan's spirit walks the earth to learn with mingled feelings what has become of the France she served and what great mirations of herself the world had made. It is the implication of that scene that the very generation which has canonized Joan would burn her like at the stake again if her like were to come again on earth. It is as though Shaw were to step out into the audience and shake the fat fellow in the front row whom the play has worked up into such a glow of sympathy, such a flutter of easy pity—shake him and whisper in his ear: 'If you had been in Rouen that day are you sure you would not have voted with the Bishop of Beauvais and run with the witch-burning mob to see the torch applied!'

86. From an unsigned notice, *Stage*

10 January 1924, 2234, 20

This notice of the New York production was written by the New York correspondent of the *Stage*, London.

At the Garrick, New York, on December 28, 1923, the Theatre Guild presented for the first time on any stage, Bernard Shaw's chronicle play, *Saint Joan*. It became clear early in the performance that Shaw respected the dignity of his subject, aimed high, and gave from his best. Those who thought that he might treat the Jeanne d'Arc chapter of history facetiously or as an historical travesty as in *Great Catherine* had their fears quickly set to rest. He indulges in little flippancy; there is, if anything, too little comedy matter instead of too much; and his attitude towards the Maid is sober, almost reverential. The criticism of the mediaeval Church and its ministers—and indeed of the

Church militant at all times—is clear, clean, straight from the shoulder. It will doubtless in some circles arouse indignation; but its honesty can hardly be challenged at any important point. And the task Shaw set himself in writing *Saint Joan* is a noble one. Here is no simple biographical play built round an engaging and romantic figure, but an attempt, it seems, to dramatise the importance of the Maid in the world's history as pioneer in a great nationalist and religious movement. That the play falls short of the theme was perhaps inevitable. The really great Joan of Arc play will probably be written by one who is more of a poet, and possibly more of a mystic, than Bernard Shaw. But Shaw's effort does great honour to his finer self; and his achievement is considerable.

[Detailed account of the action of the play.]

If the scene in Warwick's tent is the old Shaw at his best, the Epilogue is the later Shaw at his most discursive. He uses his characters even more frankly than usual as his mouthpieces—turns them from vital beings into puppets for the sake of holding a debate upon all that had gone before. In the whirl of argument the personality of the Maid is lost. Perhaps that was what Shaw intended. If so it did not make for dramatic effectiveness.

The study of the Maid and her beatification, showing how a simple, mystical peasant girl, thought to have performed a miracle because somebody's hen had laid abundant eggs, becomes through martyrdom a legend, and from a legend a monster of saintliness so holy that her return to earth would be intolerable, is rather unevenly developed. The play is verbose. It contains a good deal of fustian, much that is noble, fine and sage, a little that is cheap, and, on occasions, flashes of true beauty and poetry. The character of Joan is drawn with much delicacy and simplicity. The trial scene is finely handled. But the social and religious movement behind, which caused such visible alarm to English, French and clerics alike, is not too effectively brought out. We accept it largely because we are told it is a fact; but we do not always feel it. And the extraordinary mixture of archaic language, modern English and current slang in which many of the scenes are written also has an ill effect, for it detracts from the dignity of the play without appreciably promoting intimacy and ease.

87. Luigi Pirandello, notice, *New York Times*

13 January 1924, 7 (magazine section)

Luigi Pirandello (1867–1936), Italian dramatist and novelist, was invited to write a notice of *Saint Joan* for the *New York Times*. The notice was printed under the headline, 'Pirandello distills Shaw' and given the sub-title, 'the Italian playwright discovers the Puritan poet idealist sublimated in *Saint Joan*.' The translator is not known.

The audience bewildered me.

At the premiere of *Saint Joan*, by George Bernard Shaw, I felt myself a real foreigner, suddenly brought face to face with this mysterious America of yours. Though it was not altogether bewilderment, I felt, as I went home from the play, that I had learned something interesting and unexpected about the psychology of the American.

During the first three acts of *Saint Joan* I noted with great satisfaction the rapt attention, the shrewd and intelligent smiling, the hearty laughter and the sincere applause with which every shaft of wit or irony in this admirable and inimitable Shavian dialogue was welcomed by an audience keenly aware of the artistic treat that was spread before it. But then came the fourth act, which seemed to me the best in the whole play—the trial and condemnation of the Maid—where Shaw's dramatic power rises to its height, and where he really succeeds in awakening a deep and intense emotion. I had been expecting, in view of the preceding cordiality of the audience, to see people jump to their feet and break into unrestrained applause. Nothing of the kind! I looked around the theatre in surprise. It was as though I had been suddenly transported into a world wholly unknown and incomprehensible to me. The spectators sat for the most part in silence.

For a moment or two I was oppressed with a sudden sense of mortification at my own incompetence. But then my own feelings were so great that I could not help asking a question that was a question half of protest to the friends about me. Had that scene been a failure? Had no one been moved by that almost divine explosion of passion in the Maid just before she was dragged away to the stake? I received in reply a suggestion that few had applauded for the very reason that the emotion in the audience was so great. And then, indeed, I was more surprised than ever.

I am sure that, had an act as powerful as the fourth act of *Saint Joan* been produced on any one of the numerous Italian stages, all the people present would have jumped to their feet, even before the curtain fell, to start a frenzied applause that would have called the actors, and possibly the author, to the footlights, not once, but many times, to receive the gratitude of the audience for the anguish it had suffered, and its joy for having witnessed such a triumph of art. But here, on the other hand, a certain sense of modesty seemed to be uppermost. A certain sense of shame at being deeply moved, a need of hiding emotion, and of getting rid of it as soon as possible. To applaud would have meant confessing this emotion to one's self and then publicly to others; and few seemed willing thus to betray themselves.

But then, to tell the truth, I was not as well satisfied as I had been at the applause during the three preceding acts, though these, in a somewhat different way, were just as deserving. As an Italian, I could not think it fair that an author should be applauded when he makes us laugh, and rewarded with silence when he brings tears to our eyes. Perhaps the reason is that it is harder to make an Italian laugh than it is to make him weep.

At any rate, I have a strong impression that for some time past George Bernard Shaw has been growing more and more serious. He has always believed in himself, and with good reason. But in a number of plays, after his first successes, he did not seem to believe very much in what he was doing. This, at least may properly be suspected, since it cannot be denied that in his eagerness to defend his own intellectual position against the so-called 'bourgeois morality', he not infrequently abandoned all pretensions to seriousness as an artist. Now, however, he seems to be believing less in himself, and more in what he is doing. From the epilogue of this drama on Joan of Arc we may gather almost explicitly the reason for which Shaw wrote it. This world, he seems to say, is not made for saints to live in. We must take the people who live in it for what they are, since it is not vouchsafed them to be anything else.

In fact, as we look carefully and deeply at this work of Shaw, taken as a whole, we cannot help detecting in it that curious half-humorous melancholy which is peculiar to the disillusioned idealist. Shaw has always had too keen a sense of reality not to be aware of the conflict between it and his social and moral ideals. The various phases of reality, as they were yesterday, as they are today, as they will be tomorrow, come forward in the persons who represent them before the ideal phantom of Joan (now a Saint without her knowing it). Each of these type persons justifies his own manner of being, and confesses the sin of which he was guilty, but in such a way as to show that he is unable really to mend his ways—so true is it that each is today as he was yesterday, and will be tomorrow as he is today. Joan listens to them all, but she is not angry. She has for them just a tolerant pity. She can only pray that the world may some time be made beautiful enough to be a worthy abode for the saints!

This new tolerance and pity rise from the most secret depths of poetry that exist in Shaw. Whenever, instead of tolerating, instead of pitying, he loses his temper at the shock of reality against his ideals, and then, for fear of betraying his anger—which would be bad mannered —begins to harass himself and his hearers with the dazzling brilliance of his paradoxes, Shaw, the artist properly speaking, suffers more or less seriously—he falls to the level of the jeu d'esprit which is amusing in itself, though it irremediably spoils the work of art. I may cite in point a passage in the second act of *Saint Joan* where the Archbishop expatiates on the differences between fraud and miracles. 'Frauds deceive,' says he. 'An event which creates faith does not deceive, therefore it is not a fraud but a miracle.' Such word play is for amusement only. A work that would do something more than amuse must always respect the deeper demands of art, and so respecting these, the witticism is no longer a witticism but true art.

In none of Shaw's work that I can think of have considerations of art been so thoroughly respected as in *Saint Joan*. The four acts of this drama begin, as they must begin, with Joan's request for soldiers of Robert de Baudricourt to use in driving the English from 'the sweet land of France'. And they end, as they must end, with the trial and execution of Joan. Shaw calls this play a chronicle. In fact, the drama is built up episode by episode, moment by moment, some of them rigorously particular and free from generality—truly in the style of the chroniclers—though usually they tend to be what I call deliberate 'constructiveness'. The hens have not been laying, when suddenly, they begin to lay. The wind has long been blowing from the east, and suddenly it begins blowing from the west. Two miracles! Then there are other simple, naïve things, such as the recognition of the 'blood royal' in the third act, which likewise seems to be a miracle.

But these moments are interspersed with other moments of irony and satire, of which either the Church or the English are the victims. However, this attempt to present the chronicle inside what is really history does not seem to me quite as happy as it was in *Caesar and Cleopatra*. In *Saint Joan*, history, or rather character historically conceived, weighs a bit too heavily on the living fluid objectivity of the chronicle, and the events in the play somehow lose that sense of the unexpected which is the breath of true life. We know in advance where we are going to come out. The characters, whether historical or typical, do not quite free themselves from the fixity that history has forced upon them and from the significant role they are to play in history.

Joan herself, who is presented to us as a fresh creature of the open fields, full of burning faith and self-confidence, remains that way from the beginning to the end of the play; and she makes a little too obvious her intention not to be reciting a historical role and to remain that dear, frank, innocent, inspired child that she is. Yes, Joan, as she really was in her own little individual history, must have been much as Shaw imagined her. But he seems to look on her once and for all, so to speak, quite without regard for the various situations in which she will meet life in the course of the story.

And she is kept thus simple and unilinear by the author just to bring her airy, refreshing ingenuousness into contrast with the artificial, sophisticated—or, as I say, 'deliberate' or 'constructed'—complexity of her accusers. There is, in other words, something mechanical, foreordained, fixed, about her character. Much more free and unobstructed in his natural impulses, much more independent of any deliberate restraints, and accordingly much more 'living' (from my point of view) is the Chaplain, de Stogumber, the truly admirable creation in this drama, and a personage on which Shaw has surely expended a great deal of affectionate effort.

At a certain moment Joan's faith in her 'voices' is shaken. And this charming little creature, hitherto steadfastly confident in the divine inspiration which has many times saved her from death in battle, is suddenly filled with terror at the torment awaiting her. She says she is ready to sign the recantation of all that she has said and done. And she does sign it. But then, on learning from her judges that the sentence of death is only to be changed into a sentence of life imprisonment, she seizes the document in a sudden burst of emotion and tears it to pieces.

'Death is far better than this!' she cries. She could never live without the free air of the fields, the beauty of the green meadows, the warm light of the sun. And she falls fainting into the arms of the executioners, who drag her off to the stake.

At this moment Shaw carries his protagonists to a summit of noble poetry with which any other author would be content; and we may be sure that any other author would have lowered the curtain on this scene. But Shaw cannot resist the pressure and the inspiration of the life he well knows must be surging in such circumstances in his other character—the Chaplain. He rushes on toward a second climax of not less noble poetry, depicting with magnificent elan the mad remorse, the hopeless penitence of Stogumber, thus adding to our first crisis of exquisite anguish another not less potent and overwhelming.

Rarely has George Bernard Shaw attained higher altitudes of poetic emotion than here. There is a truly great poet in Shaw; but this combative Anglo-Irishman is often willing to forget that he is a poet, so immersed is he in being a citizen of his country, or a man of the twentieth century society, with a number of respectable ideas to defend, a number of sermons to preach, a number of antagonists to rout from the intellectual battlefield. But here, in *Saint Joan*, the poet comes into his own again, with only a subordinate role left, as a demanded compensation, to irony and satire. To be sure *Saint Joan* has all the savor and all the attractiveness of Shaw's witty polemical dialogue. But for all of these keen and cutting thrusts to left and right in Shaw's usual style of propaganda, *Saint Joan* is a work of poetry from beginning to end.

This play represents in marvellous fashion what, among so many elements of negation, is the positive element, indeed the fundamental underpinning, in the character, thought and art of this great writer— an outspoken Puritanism, which brooks no go-betweens and no mediations between man and God; a vigorous and independent vital energy, that frees itself restlessly and with joyous scorn from all the stupid and burdensome shackles of habit, routine and tradition, to conquer for itself a natural law more consonant with the poet's own being, and therefore more rational and more sound. Joan, in fact, cries to her judges: 'If the Church orders me to declare that all that I have done and said, that all the visions and revelations I have had were not from God, then that is impossible. I will not declare it for anything in the world. What God made me do, I will never go back on; and what He has commanded, or shall command, I will not fail to do, in spite of any man alive. That is what I mean by impossible. And in case the Church should bid me do anything contrary to the command I have from God, I will not consent to it, no matter what it may be'.

Joan, at bottom, quite without knowing it, and still declaring herself a faithful daughter of the Church, is a Puritan, like Shaw himself— affirming her own life impulse, her unshakable, her even tyrannical will to live, by accepting death itself. Joan, like Shaw, cannot exist without a life that is free and fruitful. When she tears up her recantation in the face of her deaf and blind accusers, she exemplifies the basic germ of Shaw's art, which is the germ also of his spiritual life.

88. A. B. Walkley, unsigned notice, *The Times*

27 March 1924, 43611, 12

On the day of the first production of *Saint Joan* in England, 26 March 1924, A. B. Walkley, writing as 'Our Dramatic Critic', contributed a special article to *The Times* (43610, 12). He began by referring to the play about Joan of Arc that was to be presented that night and he hoped that it would 'not be disfigured'. He had been rereading Anatole France's life of Joan and, because that moved him so deeply, he was nervous about Shaw. He went on to say that 'the usual sort of "Shavian" pleasantry about this heroine would be unspeakably odious; I can only hope my misgivings will prove to have done him an injustice.' He ended his article by saying that it was Shakespeare's 'bad luck' to have lived at the wrong time to have done Joan justice, whereas 'Mr Shaw is more fortunate in his moment, and one must devoutly hope he will be found to have used it worthily.' This article seems to have been written without Walkley's having any knowledge of the play, but this did not apparently prevent his writing in such an unenthusiastic way. His notice, printed below, is an attempt to make amends and stands as the last record of the ambivalent attitude towards Shaw's plays that had shown itself in his notice of *Widowers' Houses* (No. 6) and almost all Shaw's subsequent plays. When Walkley reviewed the printed version of *Saint Joan* (*The Times*, 9 July 1924, 43699, 12), he concentrated on the preface and said that 'there is never the slightest token in Mr Shaw of misgiving, of intellectual doubt, of that humility which is forced on most students by the clearer perception of the inevitable limitation to their own knowledge of the cosmos.' He commented on what he called Shaw's 'usual gibe at the critics' in the closing pages of the preface.

At the close of the penultimate scene, when Joan had been led off to the stake, we breathed again. We thought that our fear about the 'Shavianization' of the story had proved unfounded, or, at any rate, excessive. There had been regrettable lapses into the slang of to-day—

'howler,' 'military dug-outs,' 'deliver the goods'—there had been some cheap jokes, e.g., the King's complaint that the sacred oil at the Reims coronation was rancid ('Oh, that oil!'), and Joan's habit of addressing him as 'Charlie'; there had been one rather too long debate in the Earl of Warwick's tent on the precise character of Joan's offence against the Church and the Nobility, respectively; there had been too many gibes against the Anglicanism of the English as exhibited in the Chaplain de Stogumber—all these were typical but minor 'Shavianisms,' blemishes rather than gaping wounds on the fair face of the story.

But never halloo till you are out of the wood! Mr. Shaw, having kept himself in hand for six scenes, let himself go in the last—a sort of epilogue, where the ghosts of all the characters visit Charles VII in his bedroom a quarter of a century later, all saying their little 'tag' like the personages at the end of a Christmas pantomime, and are followed by a frock-coated cleric of to-day who announces Joan's latest promotion in the Roman Calendar. This epilogue—which seems a dramatic analogue to the orthodox final chapter of a literary biography, headed 'Influence'—is an artistic error, because it lets the play down, robs it of its naivety, and imports (in the frock-coated cleric) an incongruity, not only to the ear but, what is more serious on the stage, to the eye. Frock-coats seem to have a morbid attraction for Mr. Shaw. There was the old gentleman in *Back to Methuselah* whose clothes struck the Long Livers as so funny. Here is the same joke repeated with the quattrocentists. A stale joke, then, which never was a good one.

Apart from that, we think the play one of Mr. Shaw's finest achievements. It is a nuisance that he is so obsessed with the present period as to drag it into every period, however remote, that he dramatizes. Nevertheless, he does dramatize pretty faithfully this Joan of Arc period. Indeed, we are inclined to think that he has stuck too rigorously to his 'documents,' and has been too anxious to explain to us the true history of his heroine. Thus it is a recorded fact that Joan's comrades, for military reasons, deceived her by bringing her, not to the Orleans side of the Loire, as she expected, but to the opposite side. This is faithfully reproduced in the play, where it is an incident without dramatic significance. It is a recorded fact that Joan's advance to Compiègne, where she was taken, was contrary to the advice of her own side. But what is the point of making the Bastard of Orleans lecture Joan in advance of the Reims coronation on this possibility? Only that Mr. Shaw has got in another chunk of history. It is good historical exegesis to explain why the Church regarded Joan's offence as heresy, and why technically it was not the Church that burned her, but the secular arm: but in the theatre who cares about such technicalities? So, too, with Joan's replies to the Bishop of Beauvais (whom, by the way, Mr. Shaw is inclined to whitewash) and the Inquisitor; they are historically correct, but they are neither dramatic nor poetic. An ounce of poetry here would have been worth a pound of history.

When all is said, however, the great figure of the story remains a lovely thing, lovely in simplicity, lovely in faith. There are no heroics; only a little limelight now and then, which no one will grudge her. Her rusticity of speech is, we think, a superfluity. Joan spoke the speech of Lorraine; you cannot represent that in an English play by making her speak the speech of an English peasant. Miss Sybil Thorndike plays her quite beautifully, rather like a headstrong boy (we do not hint at any horrible likeness to a 'principal boy'); she has the very face and voice for it; she has a keen intelligence, too, without which a great Shaw part would surely become a great infliction. Mr Ernest Thesiger's Dauphin is as farcical as Mr Thesiger and Mr Shaw between them can make it. You don't believe in this Dauphin, cowering before his Archbishop of Reims and his Constable of France, but you laugh at him heartily enough. . . . The costumes designed by Mr Charles Ricketts were a separate ecstasy. The house followed the play throughout with tense excitement, and called for the author at the curtain-fall. Miss Thorndike said they were looking for him, but whether they found him or not we could not wait to see.

89. James Agate, notice, *Sunday Times*

30 March 1924, 5268, 6

Reprinted in *Red Letter Nights* (1944), 214.

In this signed notice, James Agate tempered his general appreciation of the play by deploring what he thought its excessive length and asked, 'Will Mr Shaw never learn to distinguish between length and significance?' He repeated this criticism in a review of the printed play (29 June 1924) and renewed his attack on the epilogue, saying that it was 'for those who are hard both of hearing and understanding'.

The thing to do with a new work by Mr Shaw—and, indeed, with any new work—is to find out its particular quality of interest, enlightenment, ecstasy, and provocation, to discover the exact kind and degree of emotion which that particular work, and not some other contains. The point is to get at an author's meaning, and not to attempt to discover corroboration of your own conceptions. What like is Mr Shaw's *Joan*? For the moment, nobody else's matters. You are not to find yourself aggrieved because her memorialist has not seen fit to bathe his subject in the sentimental mysticism of M. Anatole France, or to make her the central figure of some romantic melodrama, all gilt armour and mellifluence, unfurling her replies to her judges in words silken as the banner of France. Incidentally, if ever you saw Sarah's Maid, half angel and half bird—who, to the charge of being a witch, retorted 'Si je l'étais, je ser-r-r-ais déjà loin!'[1] with a gentleness and ineffability unknown to celestial choir or cooing dove—incidentally, if you remembered this most pathetic impersonation, the thing to do was to forget it and put it out of consciousness altogether.

You are not, I suggest, to 'worrit' because in this play Joan is not really the principal personage, nor yet because the drama does not pan out quite as you would have it. Let me admit that it is a trifle disconcerting to see Joan plunged at the rising of the curtain into so very much the

[1] If I were, I would already be a long way away.

288

middle of things, ordering a noble lord about as though she were one of Mr Arnold Bennett's 'managing' young women. It would have been pleasant and romantic to find Joan tending sheep in her native fields of Domremy, hearing her 'voices', and rejecting some loutish suit. It is, to the conservative playgoer, distressing to have no glimpse of the coronation in Rheims Cathedral—what a 'set' they would have made of it in the old Lyceum days!—and to be fobbed off with the less important cloisters, and what for a time looks like mere desultory chatter. But I must not waste space in describing what the play is not, but rather try to make plain what it is.

Saint Joan seems to me—and I stand open to any amount of correction—to be a history of privilege. It is in seven scenes.

[A summary of the action of each scene follows, with comments on, among other features, Shaw's habit of informing old speeches with present-day meaning which 'must obviously be at some cost of authenticity' and the great length of the fourth scene in which there was danger 'of both physical and intellectual cramp'.]

There is a faintly jovial, quasi-satirical, and wholly unnecessary epilogue, conceived in a vein of lesser exaltation. Mr Shaw excuses this on the ground that without it the play would be 'only a sensational tale of a girl who was burnt'. Do not believe it; Mr Shaw does himself injustice here. There is not an ounce of sensation anywhere in his piece, and the epilogue is implicit in all that has gone before. It is the greatest compliment to this play to say that at its tragic climax every eye was dry, so overwhelmingly had its philosophic import mastered sentiment. None in the audience would have saved Joan, even if he could.

The production was beyond any praise of mine. The scenery, designed by Mr Charles Ricketts, was neither frankly representational nor uncompromisingly expressionistic, but a happy blend of the two. The dresses made a kind of music in the air, and at the end Joan was allowed to stand for a moment in all that ecstasy of tinsel and blue in which French image-makers enshrine her memory. As Joan Miss Thorndike had three admirable moments: when she said 'They do!', when she listened in the Ambulatory to the pronouncement of desertion to come, and when she listened to the reading of her recantation. May I beseech Mr Shaw to allow her to drop her dialect? Whatever the quality of Lorraine peasant-speech, it cannot have been Lancashire, and there was too much the smack of Oldham about such sentences as 'Ah call that muck!' and 'Th'art not King yet, lad; th'art nobbut t'Dauphin!' Apart from these eccentricities, which were not of the actress's seeking, Joan was excellent—boyish, brusque, inspired, exalted, mannerless, tactless, and obviously, once she had served her turn, a nuisance to everybody. The part is one which no actress who is leading lady only, and not artist would look at. But Miss Thorndike is a noble artist, and did nobly.

90. Hubert Griffith, notice, *Observer*

30 March 1924, 6931, 11

Hubert Griffith (1896–1953), playwright and dramatic critic. In this signed notice, he explained that he was disappointed with the play because, taking an unusual view, he thought that 'Shaw, with all his intellectual gifts, sees deeper into the hearts and emotions of people than any writer living, and that this will be his ultimate claim to fame.' He regretted that Shaw had given so much attention to intellectual argument and so little to Joan herself.

I have so passionate an admiration for Mr Shaw that I am among the few critics who do not, as a rule, seek to tell him how he ought to write his plays or how he ought to have written his plays. Others, freely admitting his genius, find him occasionally tedious, at times paradoxical and perverse, at times maddeningly argumentative, at times, they say, in bad taste. I experienced none of these things. I have never found him tedious, because all he has ever said has interested me. So far from being paradoxical and perverse, it seems to me he has fought with extraordinary clearness and consistency for his beliefs. I never find him too argumentative, for I see the bearing of his arguments on the matter in hand. And as for bad taste, it seems to me that where anyone of Mr Shaw's heightened delicacies and susceptibilities of mind is accused of bad taste, the taste and sense of humour of the accuser should be looked into. Add to this another thing that is not usually said about Mr Shaw, who is commonly regarded as a brilliant intellect, a whirlpool of pure intelligence; I don't believe in the whirlpool of pure intelligence. I think that Mr Shaw, with all his intellectual gifts, sees deeper into the hearts and emotions of people than any writer living, and that this will be his ultimate claim to fame. I say this before going on to say, not that *Saint Joan* should have been written otherwise, but to explain why I personally was disappointed that it was not written otherwise.

Mr Shaw, in writing *Joan*, has been interested in two points—Joan; and the fact that her first trial was a fair trial, with the accusers and judges actuated by as sincere a faith as their prisoner. I, and I think the audience, was interested in one thing only, Joan.

[There follows an examination of the treatment of Joan in the play.]

What was it besides faith and simplicity and common sense, besides enthusiasm and besides bravery—besides what a thousand peasant girls might have had, and remained for ever obscure—that Joan had, and that made her immortal? Was it the driving force of personality? The magic of genius? A play on Joan of Arc stands or falls by its answer to this question, not its portrait of the knowable, but its insight into the unknowable. And from Mr Shaw, who has made Julius Caesar live for us as a man of genius, and has put the souls of early Christian martyrs on the stage, in spite of all the dignity and beauty of his new play, we get an evasion.

It will be observed that I am finding fault with Mr Shaw on two grounds alone; that he has not wrought a miracle, and that he did not give himself time to, by diverting attention to unimportant people. We wanted the miracle and nothing less. With Miss Thorndike I find no fault at all. A performance of the sheer beauty of hers deserves untempered praise.

[Further comments on the acting.]

A last point may sum up what I feel about the play. The essential thing about Joan's trial is that it was a long one. The girl had been in captivity a year, sometimes in chains. The trial lasted, with intermissions, nearly three months, with menaces of torture, with the insistent threat of the stake, with daily cross-examinations; and to almost the end she was answering her accusers gallantly and even gaily. Mr Shaw could not have given us the whole of the trial, but he could have given us some hint of this marvellous feat with all the revelation of faith and character it contains. He could have given up two scenes to the trial, an early phase and a later one, or used any other recognised stage device to bring home to us the length of that martyrdom and the splendour of spirit in which it was done. But there is only one trial scene, and half of this is the theology of Bishop Cauchon.

91. T. S. Eliot, an unsigned article, from *Criterion*

October 1924, vol. III, 9, 4

This paragraph, from an item entitled 'Commentary' and signed 'Crites' is by Thomas Stearns Eliot (1888–1965), poet and critic, who was editor of the *Criterion* from 1922 until it ceased in 1939. In a review of *Mr Shaw and 'The Maid'* (1925) by J. M. Robertson, Eliot wrote in the *Criterion* (April 1926, vol. IV, 389) that there was a danger with *Saint Joan* of Shaw's 'deluding the numberless crowd of sentimentally religious people who are incapable of following any argument to a conclusion. Such people will be misled until they can be made to understand that the potent ju-ju of the Life Force is a gross superstition; and that (in particular) Mr Shaw's *Saint Joan* is one of the most superstitious of the effigies which have been erected to that remarkable woman.' In 'A Dialogue on Dramatic Poetry' (1928), reprinted in *Selected Essays* (1932), 51 Eliot wrote that 'Shaw was a poet—until he was born, and the poet in Shaw was stillborn.' There are numerous references to Shaw, the majority of them unfavourable (usually on the grounds of what he considered the shallowness of Shaw's thought) in Eliot's other writings on drama, but he admitted in *Poetry and Drama* (1951) reprinted in *On Poetry and Poets* (1957), 81 that in the use of colloquial prose in the speeches of the knights in *Murder in the Cathedral*, 'I may, for aught I know, have been slightly under the influence of *Saint Joan*.' In the same lecture, he said that 'our two greatest prose stylists in the drama—apart from Shakespeare and the other Elizabethans who mixed prose and verse in the same play—are, I believe, Congreve and Bernard Shaw.'

The true 'dominant' of our time (with 'the inevitable price of diminished progress') is Mr. Bernard Shaw. Mr. Shaw stands in fact for 'the great middle-class liberalism' (I am not now quoting from Professor Gamble) 'as Dr. Newman saw it, and as it really broke the Oxford movement.' St. Joan has been called his masterpiece. I should be inclined to contest this judgment in favour of *Man and Superman*, but certainly (unless we owe our clairvoyance solely to the lapse of time) *St. Joan* seems to illustrate Mr. Shaw's mind more clearly than anything he has written before. No one can grasp more firmly an idea which he does not maintain, or expound it with more cogency, than Mr. Shaw. He manipulates every idea so brilliantly that he blinds us when we attempt to look for the ideas *with which he works*. And the ideas with which he works, are they more than the residue of the great Victorian labours of Darwin, and Huxley, and Cobden? We must not be deceived by the fact that he scandalised many people of the type to which we say he belongs: he scandalised them, not because his first principles were fundamentally different, but because he was much cleverer, because his thought was more rapid, because he looked farther in the same direction. The animosity which he aroused was the animosity of the dull toward the intelligent. And we cannot forget on the other hand that Mr. Shaw was the intellectual stimulant and the dramatic delight of twenty years which had little enough of either: London owes him a twenty years' debt. Yet his Joan of Arc is perhaps the greatest sacrilege of all Joans: for instead of the saint or the strumpet of the legends to which he objects, he has turned her into a great middle-class reformer, and her place is a little higher than Mrs. Pankhurst. If Mr. Shaw is an artist, he may contemplate his work with ecstasy.

92. Robert de Flers, notice, *Le Figaro*

11 May 1925, 2

Robert de Flers (1872–1927), dramatist and critic, for some years editor of *Le Figaro*, was a friend and correspondent of Marcel Proust. In this passage from a signed notice of the first production of *Saint Joan* in France, he showed warm appreciation, mingled with considerable surprise that a dramatist from abroad had been able to present so eminently acceptable a picture of France's great saint.

The English burned Joan of Arc and it is an Englishman who has just consecrated to her the most elevated and most tender work that has ever been written in her honour. It may be that this is her final miracle. It is true that the Englishman is an Irishman and that he is a genius. We are indebted to Bernard Shaw for a Joan of Arc, at last free from the insipidity of colour prints and the idiocy of the painted statuettes that are on sale in the small shops in the Saint-Sulpice district of Paris for those who wish to make generous gifts to country churches. We are indebted to him for a simple and straightforward Joan who does not count the syllables of her hexameters as she used to count her sheep, and who seeks neither pretty images nor pretentious metaphors, a Joan shorn of great verbal elegance and who is poor in speech as she is poor in her garments, but who is so rich in courage and faith; moreover, she is a Joan who never shows any signs, as we have seen in other works, all the more irritating for being worthy of her, of expecting to receive delegations or choirs in her honour and to take part with great enthusiasm in her own commemoration.

What beauty and what sweetness! Here we have a Joan of Arc who is heroic and familiar, full of life and the clear light of day and who goes forward to her destiny, human and divine at the same time, filled with ecstasy and wisdom, beneath the great pardon of the sky of France and the bright sunshine of God. I am sure that this tragedy which is certain to become immortal, will be carefully analysed for years most zealously, and that great efforts will be made to discover the inspirations and to understand the tendencies and influences of the work. For the present, however, it is enough—and, indeed, it is essential—to realise that this play brings tears to the eyes of the audience each evening and it revives in our hearts the most admirable figure in our whole history which learning and piety, between them, were beginning to freeze over.

It is quite amazing that in England and America this play should have given rise to such strong feelings that sharp controversies have resulted. One of the criticisms has been that the supernatural element has been neglected. This is a strange comment. May it be because Bernard Shaw has not made us hear the ineffable voices of the Saints Catherine and Marguerite and that of the archangel Saint Michael? Yet, it is not we who should hear them, but Joan herself. We see her at all times guided and influenced and borne up by their heavenly echoes. In this way, the mystery retains its intimacy, the grace that actually saves. The mystery, indeed, is the mystery of the soul.

Bernard Shaw has found the power and the originality of his play in the arresting contrast between his heroine and the environment on which she sheds her radiance and where all the intrigues of interest and ambition are being carried on. He has depicted, with incomparable colour and movement, all the actors in the drama, squire Baudricourt, the Archbishop of Rheims, the Dauphin, Dunois, the Earl of Warwick, Peter Cauchon, Bishop of Beauvais and all the judges of the court. He has presented each one of them, not with the detail of laboriously documented facts, but animated by the deep feelings and the dominating passions that directed their actions. This is living history. We guess, indeed we feel sure that this has not been dredged up out of books, but that it has been brought to life by the imagination of a visionary spirit.

93. Rebecca West compares Shaw with Thomas Hardy

1924

Signed article, with the title, 'Interpreters of Their Age' in the *Saturday Review of Literature*, 16 August 1924, 41.

Rebecca West (Cicely Fairfield) (b. 1892), novelist and critic, found that, when compared with Hardy, Shaw, for all his virtues, lacked poetic power and a true sense of tragedy.

I once met a lady in New York who afterwards expressed herself as being deeply disappointed with the meeting, on the ground that I had a childish mind. As evidence she gave the fact that I had said in her presence that Thomas Hardy was a greater man than George Bernard Shaw. The incident gave me a severe shock, not only because one naturally expects to be loved by all, but because till that moment I had never realized that any fully literate person could possibly place Mr. Shaw above Mr. Hardy; and I still do not think that any artist could do so. Nevertheless, when I try to find precise justifications for my certainty, I find it hard to do so. Mr. Hardy has attained absolute beauty again and again in his prose and his verse, but there is a great deal to be said against him. His novels are of extremely unequal merit, and some of them (as *The Well-Beloved*) have practically no aesthetic quality. Both they and his poetry are perpetually at the mercy of a certain comic lugubriousness, which at any moment may transform him from a vehicle of the Tragic Muse into an imaginative mortician. Moreover he has had very little practical effect on the life of his time. I can think of no social or political problem that is any nearer its solution because of any illumination given by Mr. Hardy. Indeed I imagine that Mr. Hardy rarely approaches the intellectual side of life save through the avenue of history, which he treads in a mood of intense romanticism and very vague and untutored philosophic enquiry.

Mr. Shaw, on the other hand, has a natural turn for perfection. The changeless climate of his work is beauty, because he cannot write prose that is not inhabited by radiance like crystal. When you have heard his wit you have heard as much as would pass him into immortality, and even then—to use an American music-hall tag that seems to me to rise to the realms of poetry in that its content is so much greater than the mere logical meaning of its words—'you ain't heard the half of it, dearie.' He is learned in the wisdom of the heart as well as the head. Only fools think his genius brain-bound and solemn, for he has written of love as wisely as any living man in *Candida* and *Heartbreak House*, and so of religion in *Androcles and the Lion*; and there was never a play of lighter laughter than *You Never Can Tell*. Moreover he has had the most enormously salutory influence on his day. He has proved by his interventions on social and political discussions that no matter how fast the earth may whirl on its axis the pace is never so quick that one cannot talk sense. I do not believe that the young people of to-day could have borne the war, and this changeling that has been slipped into the cradle of the new Europe instead of peace, had it not been that Mr. Shaw had been proclaiming in their ears all their youth long that life was of course a muddle, but that there is no sport like reducing muddles to order. Incontestably a great, a very great man.

Nevertheless, I am sure that Thomas Hardy is the greater man. Contemplating him, I feel awe that one does not feel for the other. But I find it difficult to justify that emotional conviction. One must so certainly admit that Mr. Shaw is greater in the sphere of the conscious. Perhaps that indeed is the secret of the minute dissatisfaction with him that gives the advantage to Mr. Hardy in the comparison. Mr. Shaw has mobilized all his forces in the sphere of the conscious; he has left no energy for the use of his sub-conscious mind. Now Mr. Hardy has as immense an energy, but he has spent very little of it in the sphere of the conscious. He has sat apart from things, brooding on reality, and he has become saturated with a sense of a certain aspect of reality that is characteristic of our day. A certain change has come over the race—or, rather, the white races—in the last century or so. If you turn to the portraits of our recent forebears, by Gainsborough, or Romney, or Reynolds, you will find there is something lacking in their faces which is present in those of nearly all men and women of to-day. That quality is indeed something sombre; yet its absence cannot be ascribed to prettyfication on the part of artists, for even Raeburn—who was as sternly realist as Mr. Sargent or Mr. Augustus John—gives no hint of it. Were I to try to analyse it I should perhaps call it the power to accept tragedy: to recognize that tragedy is not always punishment from above for wrongdoing, nor a temporary hitch that can be mended, if a brisk prayer is forthcoming, by sleight of the omnipotent hand, but simply and finally tragedy; and that nevertheless life is a god to be served. It is true that this has always been among the secrets of the artist, but not before has it been common knowledge. Every man is no longer certain that the night will not swallow him, even if he has offered up sacrifices; but he feels that if it does the triumph will not be with the night. But whether or not it can be defined in a sentence, it is certain that it is completely expressed in the works of Thomas Hardy? It is the core of each of them that is considerable. In *Tess of the D'Urbervilles*, in *Jude the Obscure*, in *The Dynasts*, one looks on the face of modern man, shadowed and fortified by this new knowledge.

94. William Archer on the psychology of Shaw

1924

In this signed article, 'The Psychology of G.B.S.', *Bookman*, December 1924, vol. LXVIII, 399, 139, Archer surveyed Shaw's character, paying particular attention to his defects. He recognised the extent of Shaw's achievement—it was the year of the production of *Saint Joan* in London—but concluded that despite his successes, his total effect was limited. Archer died on 27 December, shortly after the article appeared and in a letter to Shaw, dated 17 December, he had said that the operation he was about to undergo gave him the excuse to say 'that though I may sometimes have played the part of the all-too candid mentor, I have never wavered in my admiration and affection for you'. Shaw thought Archer 'incorruptible as a critic' (*Pen Portraits, 1*).

The death of Anatole France leaves Bernard Shaw the Grand Old Man of literary Europe. Thomas Hardy, indeed, is an older man; but his fame is comparatively insular. Mr. Shaw, though he has made no great mark in the Latin countries, has conquered Central Europe and even Leninland; and his renown has reached round the world to Japan, where I myself have seen *The Man of Destiny* acted in the idiom of the country.

Never has a more baffling character, a talent harder to define or classify, appeared on the world-stage. Among writers of the past, Voltaire is perhaps his nearest analogue. Voltaire, like G.B.S., was a wit, a dramatist and an inexhaustible pamphleteer. But how normal—one might almost say how commonplace—was Voltaire's character in comparison with Shaw's! And in virtue of that very normality, how incomparably greater was his influence! He was born, it is true, into a smaller and far less puzzling world. The intellectual problems with which he dealt were comparatively simple. But the radical difference between the two men was one of temperament. Voltaire's mind was a plane, undistorting mirror; Shaw's is concave, convex, corrugated, many-faceted—anything you like except plane and objective. Voltaire, with no more genius or eloquence than Shaw's, revolutionised the world; Shaw, a professed revolutionist, will revolutionise nothing.

For many years it was impossible to mention the name of Bernard Shaw without being confronted with the question 'Is he ever serious?' or 'Does he expect people to take him seriously?' The question was not inexcusable, for he has said countless things regarding which he himself would have been puzzled to decide what element of seriousness lurked beneath the surface of reckless, irresponsible humour. But a very small acquaintance with his writings ought to have assured any discerning reader that at bottom he is intensely in earnest. I am tempted to call him the most uncompromising, not to say fanatical, idealist I have ever met. His life has been dominated by, and devoted to, a system of interwoven ideals to which he is immovably faithful. His sense of right and wrong is so overmastering that he carries it into regions—such as that of personal hygiene—which most people are apt to regard as morally indifferent. And his ideals, if sometimes a little crankish, are for the most part high and humane. He sometimes fights for them with a ferocity that appears like unscrupulousness: but this appearance is due to the fact that his perceptions are warped by the intensity of his feelings: the mirror of his mind does not accurately image the external object. His will is always intent on the good as he sees it; and that I take to be the essence of a high morality. Having known him for forty years, I say without hesitation that his greatest moral failing, in my judgment, is (or was) a certain impishness, a Puck-like *Schadenfreude*, to which he would sometimes give too free play. Apart from this, there is no man for the fundamentals of whose character I have a more real respect. I own myself deeply indebted to him for many lessons taught me in the years of our early intimacy; though he never succeeded in imbuing me with his inflexible devotion to ideals.

The paradox of his career is, it seems to me, the extraordinary disproportion between his fame and his influence. It is hard to think of anyone who has made so great noise and so little mark. There would be no difficulty in accounting for this if he were anything in the nature of a windbag. But that is the last thing that can be said of him. Mere whimsicalities apart, there is hard and solid thought behind his every utterance. Nor is his thought, like that of Mr. Chesterton, the product of an uncontrollable excess of cerebration. It is always animated by a sincere desire to see and to express the truth. Not in its essence original

—for the main ideas of the Shaw philosophy are borrowed from a dozen different quarters—it is always presented in clear and sometimes truly luminous form, with great originality of argument and illustration. Though not a creator of verbal beauty—not a Conrad nor an Anatole France—Mr. Shaw is a superb literary craftsman, habitually expressing himself with unsurpassed lucidity and force. How comes it, then, that the world at large has always answered in the negative the question, 'Ought we to take him seriously?'

The key to the riddle lies, I think, in the before-mentioned abnormality of his temperament. He has devoted his whole life—in his plays no less than in his disquisitions—to the Art of Persuasion; and he is himself so unique, so utterly unlike the overwhelming majority of his fellow-creatures, that he has never mastered the rudiments of that art. And the worst of it is that he considers himself preternaturally skilful in making people dance to his piping. I do not say that this is an entire illusion. He has sometimes succeeded where success was least to be expected. Long, long ago, when he was on the staff of the *World*, the editor, Edmund Yates, took umbrage at something he had done, and wrote him a rather cutting little rebuke. At once G.B.S. dashed at his typewriter and hammered out a long, witty, impudent rejoinder, which he showed to me. I said: 'All right—if you want your connection with the *World* to end suddenly and catastrophically, you can't do better than send this.' Two days later he showed me triumphantly a note from Yates, apologising for his little spurt of temper, and saying that his only reason for not regretting the incident was that it had procured him such a delightful letter. In other cases, too, I have known his bravura method of handling a situation come off with marked success. But on the other hand, one could cite many failures of tact, blunders in the art of manipulating human nature. His progress as a dramatist was seriously retarded by the falling through of his first great opportunity, when *You Never Can Tell* was actually accepted and put in rehearsal at the Haymarket Theatre—and then dropped again. Mr. Cyril Maude lost the finest part that ever came in his way; and (what was much more serious) G.B.S. was thrown back for years upon the side-show theatres, in which he was free to obey his every whim, and was exempted from the discipline by which all the great masters of drama have profited—that of having to make their appeal to a natural, unaffected, non-cliquish public. It is improbable, indeed, that G.B.S. could ever have been anything else than an incorrigible self-pleaser; but there is always the off-chance that an early success might have worked wonders. Again, when he appeared in 1909 before the Select Committee on the Censorship, his fantastic misreading of the mentality of that body led to a regrettable incident, and injured the cause he was eager to advance. These flagrant errors in method of attack are not exceptional but characteristic. The orator who miscalculates his audience may amuse, but will never convert.

'Have not facts,' it may be said, 'negatived this diagnosis of the case? Has not Mr. Shaw, by your own showing, been wonderfully successful in gaining the ear of the world? He is not even, in these latter days, the proverbial prophet without honour in his own country. Has not *Saint Joan* been one of the great successes of the past season? Have not even the critics, hitherto so grudging in their valuation of Mr. Shaw's genius, fallen down and worshipped his latest masterpiece?' It is very true that Mr. Shaw has got at the ear, and even at the brain, of great multitudes of people: but has he got at their will? Has he influenced their motives? Has he shaped their actions? No! The great Victorian sophists, Carlyle and Ruskin, though men of far less brilliant intellect, stamped themselves on their time much more effectually than he. His one or two attempts to get into public life (for which his marvellous readiness in debate seemed eminently to qualify him) have been baffled by his inability to adapt his method of attack to the human nature of a body of electors.

The reason is again to be sought in his peculiar, his unique, temperament; but the same fact can be looked at from another aspect and expressed in different terms. Mr. Shaw is the most complete and instinctive apriorist of recorded time. He does not live in the real world, but in a world of his own construction. No doubt this is in some measure true of all of us, but it is the inmost secret of Mr. Shaw's whole psychology. His perception of fact is absolutely at the mercy of his will. The world without has no existence for him, except in so far as it can be, and is, fitted into the pre-existent scheme of his world within. The result is that he can seldom or never make a perfectly accurate statement of fact. The most honourable of men, the most incapable of telling a falsehood for his own advantage, or even in furtherance of a cause or an argument, he is equally incapable of seeing, reflecting, expressing things as they objectively or historically are. He sees them through the distorting, systematising medium of his own personality; whereas the man who is to be an effective force in this world must either have the clearest insight into things as they are, or, if he sees them awry, must do so by reason of a common and popular obliquity of vision. Between

these two stools Mr. Shaw falls to the ground. The plain common
sense of his world-wide audience tells them that there is something
indefinably but fundamentally wrong with his statement of things.
He presents a vivacious distortion of life at which they laugh consumed-
ly; but, having done so, they go on their way, unconvinced and
uninspired.

95. Robert Lynd on Shaw as classic
and myth

1924

From a signed article in the *Bookman*, December 1924, vol. LXVII,
399, 141.

Robert Lynd (1879–1949), journalist, critic and essayist, was a
regular contributor to the *New Statesman*. The title of the article
was 'G.B.S. as G.O.M.'. Robert Lynd said that Shaw had been
engaged in a fight with the public and with *Saint Joan* he had
delivered the knock-out blow.

Mr. Bernard Shaw is at the present moment in danger of becoming
the Grand Old Man of European literature. Mr. Hardy is the Grand
Old Man of English literature but, at a considerably earlier age, Mr.
Shaw has had the pleasure of seeing his fame spreading to the ends of the
earth. It is one of the ironies of fate that an author who once owed his
limited fame to the fact that he was a novelty, now owes his world-
wide fame to the fact that he has ceased to be a novelty. His shock
tactics no longer shock because the public has grown accustomed to
them. He now writes as the public expects him to write, whereas he
used to write as the public expected and hoped that nobody would
write. The public likes to get what it expects even from a writer of

paradoxes. It begins by trying to make the writer of genius give it what it expects, and it ends by learning to expect what he gives. In such conflicts, indeed, it is always the public that has ultimately to give in. It has given in to Mr. Shaw, and he is now among the accepted authors.

Mr. Shaw, it must be confessed, did very little to make his acceptance by the public easy. He has consistently taken the view that the inevitable dispute between the great artist and the great public is one that can be settled only by a fight to a finish, and he set himself early in life to study the methods of the leading boxers, in order presumably to discover the most effective means of making an opponent see stars, of punching him in the ribs, and of finally getting home with the 'knock-out.' The fight that resulted has been one of many rounds and, while the public has seen stars and seen red in nearly every round, Mr. Shaw himself has been on the floor two or three times. He got such a hammering from the public at the time of the appearance of *Common Sense About the War* that one enthusiastic spectator, feeling certain that no man could survive such punishment, hurried off home and wrote his epitaph. Mr. Shaw, however, has more lives than a cat, and even when some of his old admirers were saying 'He's done!', as they did on the publication of that excellent play, *Heartbreak House*, Mr. Shaw refused to admit that the public was one too many for him, and he rose with a smile for the still more trying round associated with *Back to Methuselah*. With this, the longest acting play in the English language, he wore the unfortunate public completely out. The public by this time was limp, exhausted and without heart for further fighting. It only remained for Mr. Shaw to deliver the knock-out blow with as little humiliation to the vanquished as was possible, and this he did with *Saint Joan*. The British public is admittedly a good loser, and since that day Mr. Shaw has justly been applauded as a classic.

[There follows an examination of some features of Shaw's character and public personality: Robert Lynd thinks that Shaw will, in a measure 'survive as a great national myth, like Dr Johnson,.]

Mr. Shaw is a great controversialist as well as a great artist, and the literature of controversy seldom survives its own generation. Swift too was a great controversialist, but 'The Conduct of the Allies' is now dead except for scholars, while *Gulliver's Travels* is a book for children. This is not to suggest that Mr. Shaw has not performed a great service to his age with his discussions of politics, religion, marriage, education, vivisection and medicine. He has often I think been wrong-headed in his affirmations, but like Socrates he has been a useful gadfly to his time with his interrogations. Even today, however, when we read *The Doctor's Dilemma* again or go to see a new performance of *Getting Married*, we find ourselves enjoying them as comedies of situation rather than as what are called comedies of ideas. We can enjoy them, I mean, even if we regard many of Mr. Shaw's opinions on contemporary problems, or the contemporary shapes of problems, as grotesque. Comedy, indeed, is in its essence an exaggeration, and it is utterly impossible for a comic writer to speak as a Solomon to the sons of men. Mr. Shaw is a writer of comic imagination and serious intellect, and of the two, I think, his comic imagination is the gift of the most serious importance to mankind. He himself probably over-emphasises the importance of convincing people by argument, as he attempts to do in his prefaces. His real genius, it seems to me, is that of a comic writer who sets the imagination at play, as he does in the theatre. I have heard that he considers his *Androcles and the Lion* a mere pot-boiler but, just because he gave rein to his comic imagination in it, I am not sure that it will not turn out to be his masterpiece. It showed incidentally that he could touch the heart as well as make us laugh. But who can decide which is Mr. Shaw's masterpiece? He has written at least half a dozen masterpieces from *Caesar* and *John Bull's Other Island* to *Androcles and the Lion* and *Heartbreak House*.

96. Émile Cammaerts on Molière and Shaw

1926

From a signed article, entitled 'Molière and Bernard Shaw' in *Nineteenth Century*, vol. C, September 1926, 413.

Émile Cammaerts (d. 1953), Belgian-born writer and scholar, who became a Professor in the University of London, made a sustained comparison between Molière and Shaw. He considered that, despite many differences, they were alike in that they were 'obsessed by the idea of preserving sincerity in individual and social relations'. The article, written for one of the most distinguished critical magazines, tends to overlook the lighter sides of both writers.

The prominent part played by the works of Bernard Shaw in contemporary literature is no longer in question, and we need not apologise for coupling his name with that of the great French classic. It is within the range of possibilities, even of probabilities, that the *Plays Pleasant and Unpleasant* will be acknowledged in the future as the most important contribution to comedy writing in Europe since *Tartuffe* and *Le Misanthrope* were produced in Paris. The best plays of Shaw and Molière are essentially character studies stripped of all poetical incidents, and must therefore be distinguished from the so-called 'comedies' of Shakespeare, in which imagination and psychological observation are closely associated; they are still more remote from the realistic play of the modern type, whether or no it attempts to solve some social or philosophical problem.

To the superficial reader the analogy between the two writers cannot be carried any further. The familiar and sometimes racy language of Shaw is very different from Molière's polished style; the age of wigs and panniers stands far from that of bobbed hair and jumpers, the ways of thinking, the modes of expression, of the seventeenth century seem remote from our customs and utterances, so that we are apt to forget certain constant features which belong to civilised mankind, quite apart from time and country, and to the art of writing character comedies, whatever language or style is used. . . .

It would be absurd to pretend that Shaw's outlook on life is similar to that of Molière. The most superficial comparison between the latter's *Don Juan* and the strange episode which interrupts *Man and Superman* would show the gulf which separates the master of paradox from the master of common sense. Too much, however, ought not to be made of this difference, which is one of method rather than of principle. Molière uses the weapon of reason, which is to oppose current ideas and fashions to older and firmer traditions based on experience—what we are accustomed to call common sense or popular wisdom. Shaw uses the weapon of paradox, which is to contend that if such and such an idea is sound, another idea, which ought to horrify the defenders of the first one, is just as sound in the light of their arguments. The first weapon may be likened to a shield and is most effective in the defence, the second may be likened to a sword and is most effective in the attack. Confronted with the social prejudice of modern progress, for instance, Molière would no doubt have opposed the vices of modern times, the waste and ugliness of modern industry, to the material advantages derived from it. Shaw prefers to oppose what he calls the clumsiness of constructive industry to the skill and perfection of destructive industry, and to show that the arts of peace are not nearly so beneficent as the arts of war are harmful. They would both tend, by different methods, to achieve the same aim and shake the dangerous and somewhat ridiculous conceit which blinds so many people to the errors of their time.

It would be no doubt interesting to know to what extent Shaw may have been influenced by Molière, and whether, for instance, the idea of having his *Fanny's First Play* criticised on the stage by the critics of the day was derived from *La Critique de l'Ecole des Femmes*. The relationship between the two writers, however, is much deeper than such analogies of detail may reveal. It springs from the nature of their art, from the very essence of character comedy whether written in Greek, Latin, French, or English. Shaw would have taken Molière's attitude towards the world and society even if he had never read a line of the French classic, merely because, like Molière, he is a great writer of character comedies and because these comedies deal mainly with the exposure of all hypocrisies and the tearing off of all masks. Molière attacks doctors and religious hypocrites; Shaw attacks doctors and politicians. The best mediæval comedy, *La Farce de Patelin*, is a scathing satire on lawyers. There has always been, and there still is, a popular prejudice against the so-called 'professional classes.' The manual worker looks askance on the clever fellow who is supposed to make a good living without any physical exertions—that is, without 'decent' work. This suspicion, sprung from ignorance but too often confirmed by experience, is strengthened by the fact that the same people who use their brains instead of their hands wield a mysterious power over their fellow-citizens. Blackmore, in *Lorna Doone*, alludes to an old English saying according to which 'the doctor mangles our bodies, the parson starves our souls, but the lawyer must be the adroitest knave, for he has to ensnare our minds'. The bitterness of the attack of the comedy writer is in proportion to the influence of his character's profession: a bad farmer only spoils a farm, a bad doctor may harm a whole town, a bad statesman may ruin a whole country.

We may safely assume that if another great comedy writer attempts, in the twenty-second or the twenty-third century, the task which Molière and Shaw have fulfilled in the seventeenth and the twentieth, the same people will come in for a fair share of criticism. The relative importance of the characters may vary to a certain extent, but the fact remains that whoever is in a position to do the greatest amount of good is also able to do the greatest amount of harm—and must necessarily become the butt of the attack of those who, according to Molière's definition, must show all the failings of mankind and specially those of their contemporaries.

97. T. E. Lawrence on Shaw and 'the most blazing bit of genius'

1928

From a letter dated 14 April 1928 to William Rothenstein, in *The Letters of T. E. Lawrence*, ed. David Garnett (1938), 582.

Thomas Edward Lawrence (1888–1935), 'Lawrence of Arabia', archaeologist, military leader and writer, became a friend of Shaw and his wife and was the model for the character of Private Meek in *Too True to be Good*. In this letter to the painter, William Rothenstein, he comments on Shaw as a subject for a portrait and then as a writer.

It is interesting that G.B.S. sits again to you. He is beclouded, like Hardy and Kipling, with works which tend to live more intensely than their creator. I doubt whether you can now see him: you know too much. His best chance would be to find some foreign artist who did not know his face; and to be painted by him as 'Sir George Bernard'. So perhaps we would know what he would have been if he had not written. Lately I've been studying *Heartbreak House*: whose first act strikes me as metallic, inhuman, supernatural: the most blazing bit of genius in English literature. I'd have written that first, if I had choice.

98. Winston Churchill, from an article, *Pall Mall*

August 1929, 16

Winston Churchill (1874–1965), English politician, Prime Minister from 1940 to 1945 and from 1951 to 1955, wrote at the beginning of this article that Shaw was one of his 'earliest antipathies'. This extract shows that, despite political differences, Churchill appreciated Shaw's skill as a writer. The article was reprinted in *Great Contemporaries* (1937), 47.

It was not until the late 'nineties that real, live, glowing success came, and henceforth took up her abode with Mr. Bernard Shaw. At decent intervals, and with growing assurance, his plays succeeded one another. *Candida*, *Major Barbara*, and *Man and Superman* riveted the attention of the intellectual world. Into the void left by the annihilation of Wilde he stepped armed with a keener wit, a tenser dialogue, a more challenging theme, a stronger construction, a deeper and a more natural comprehension. The characteristics and the idiosyncrasies of the Shavian drama are world-renowned. His plays are today more frequently presented, not only within the wide frontiers of the English language, but throughout the world, than those of any man but Shakespeare. All parties and every class, in every country, have pricked up their ears at their coming, and welcomed their return.

The plays were startling enough on their first appearance. Ibsen had broken the 'well-made play' by making it better than ever: Mr. Shaw broke it by not 'making' it at all. He was once told that Sir James Barrie had completely worked out the plot of *Shall We Join the Ladies* before he began to write it. Mr. Shaw was scandalized. 'Fancy knowing how a play is to end before you begin it! When *I* start a play I haven't the slightest idea what is going to happen.' His other main innovation was to depend for his drama not on the interplay of character and character, or of character and circumstance, but on that of argument and argument. His ideas become personages, and fight among themselves, sometimes with intense dramatic effect, and sometimes not. His human beings, with a few exceptions, are there for what they are to say, not for what they are to be or do. Yet they live.

Recently I took my children to *Major Barbara*. Twenty years had passed since I had seen it. They were the most terrific twenty years the world had known. Almost every human institution had undergone decisive change. The landmarks of centuries had been swept away. Science has transformed the conditions of our lives and the aspect of town and country. Silent social evolution, violent political change, a vast broadening of the social foundations, an immeasurable release from convention and restraint, a profound reshaping of national and individual opinion, have followed the trampling march of this tremendous epoch. But in *Major Barbara*, there was not a character requiring to be redrawn, not a sentence nor a suggestion that was out of date. My children were astounded to learn that this play, the very acme of modernity, was written more than five years before they were born.

THE APPLE CART

1929

The Apple Cart was written for the first Malvern Drama Festival in 1929. Barry Jackson, the Birmingham impresario, who expected to present the play at Malvern, was disappointed when Shaw allowed the first production to be in Poland. It was presented at the Teatr Polski, Warsaw, on 14 June 1929. The Malvern production was on 19 August 1929, when it was given four performances. It was transferred to the Queen's Theatre, London on 17 September 1929, where it ran for 258 performances.

---

99. Ivor Brown, in an initialled notice, *Manchester Guardian*

20 August 1929, 25887, 12

Ivor (John Carnegie) Brown (1891–1974), author and dramatic critic, was a regular critic for the *Manchester Guardian* and in 1928 was appointed dramatic critic of the *Observer*. In an article entitled 'The Spirit of the Age in Drama' in the *Fortnightly Review*, vol. 128, July–December 1930, Ivor Brown considered the innovations in dramatic technique that he thought Shaw had made in *The Apple Cart*.

After Warsaw, Malvern; then Birmingham and London. That is the order of *The Apple Cart*'s progress as a stage-play. Yesterday's private performance was the curtain-raiser of the Malvern Shaw Festival and afforded us our first glimpse of a comedy in which Mr. Shaw has cast himself, in the opinion of any democrat, as the devil's disciple. The scene is England thirty years on, and the main point of the play is to show a rather melancholy but sombrely ambitious King Magnus defending a royal veto and authority against his 'democratic' Cabinet Ministers, who are, with the exception of a young ex-schoolmistress who appears to take her new office of power-mistress seriously, a company of clowns fancy dressed in green and gold. There is Boanerges at the Board of Trade; he shouts and disports himself in Russian blouse and boots and is in general a hearty, amiable fraud blown out with childish vanity. A choleric toper runs the Home Office, a whiskered nanny-goat is in charge of the colonies, the Prime Minister is a touchy, hysterical, and pompous gas-bag, who is given the job on the ground that he couldn't be fitted in anywhere else, and so on. As this troupe of oafs and pantaloons was brought on parade one naturally wondered what the leading lights of the Fabian Society, who are now ruling the country, would make of it. The democratic Chancellor of the Exchequer of the Shavian parable beamed at us from the stage in a state of silvered senility. Unfortunately Mr. Philip Snowden and Mr. Henderson had engagements at the Hague . . . and one looked in vain among the audience for Lord Passfield.

So much for democracy, whose curious champions are presenting an ultimatum to King Magnus, a slim gentleman in middle age, who wears a neatly waisted, frock-coated uniform of dark blue, such as was once favoured by officers of the Guards. Magnus, it seems, represents superior intelligence, but it needs little of that quality to make game of the Cabinet clowns who stand up like ninepins for his dialectical bowling. There are two interludes in the story of Magnus and the ultimatum, and these will be discussed later. It is enough to say that the King upsets the Cabinet's apple-cart by threatening to abdicate and stand as M.P. for Windsor, where, of course, he might have a little backstairs influence. Terrified at the prospect of an ex-king diddling them in the Commons by superior brainwork, the Prime Minister collapses and tears up his ultimatum. Magnus has won.

But won for what? For dictatorship? Scarcely. For there is nothing grandiose or Napoleonic about the courteous and witty monarch who preserves a nice graciousness of manner while pulling the whiskers of his nanny-goat Ministers. He fights urbanely to keep a right of veto, but mere veto is nothing to a Mussolini; he believes that he can prevent his politicians from making absurd blunders, and so, no doubt, he could, since the politicians, as we have seen, are conceived in the image of Joey and Pantaloon. That is one strange thing about the play. Mr. Shaw's thinking is generally constructive as well as mischievous. But here he is strangely negative. We hear nothing of the King's positive opinions, of his nation-saving policy, or of a cure for people sick with self-government. He does, it is true, expound with eloquence and skill a reasoned defence of monarchy as a simple method of rule. Democracy, he points out, has made much use of the phrase 'responsible government,' but under Parliamentary conditions responsibility becomes slippery. When a muddle has occurred Ministers can be evasive, shuffle replies on to other or junior Ministers, refer back to the Civil Service, play for time with 'inquiries,' and so wait until something else turns up to sidetrack attention. The monarch or autocrat does, quite literally, stand up to be shot at; he may browbeat, but he cannot squirm. He has chosen the cloak of responsibility and he must wear it, and not slip it over another man's neck.

That is true, and the slipperiness of Ministerial responsibility is a possible weakness of Parliamentary government, which, incidentally, is only one form of democracy. Mr. Shaw has continually confused the idea of democracy with any form of it which happens at the moment to be vulnerable, and his defence of autocracy, if it is intended to be taken seriously, turns out to be feeble, negative stuff the moment you look below the pleasant, dialectical virtuosity with which he can so easily clothe it. To cartoon your elected persons until they are mere gargoyles and to idealise your unelected monarch is a pitiful approach to political philosophy. The case for autocracy is nearly always limited to throwing missiles at a travesty of democracy, and Mr. Shaw has wheeled up a barrow load of crab apples in order to join the game. There is no disappointment awaiting those who look for good marksmanship in this form of sport. Time and again he hits poor Joey bang between the eyes. The only objection is the fundamental one that Joey doesn't exist outside the world of Shavian caricature.

Another point. Are the democratic clowns republicans? Apparently. But their republicanism bears no relation to any contemporary English opinion. They are back in the time of Charles I, and jealous of royal right. In so far as there is republicanism in Britain to-day it is not in the least concerned with prerogative; it merely distrusts the atmosphere of a Court which it regards as a fountain of snobbery and as keeping the popular attention from essential matters by its tinsel parades of musical-comedy splendour. That and the humane distaste for condemning any man to the slavery and boredom of the Crown may or may not be sound arguments against monarchy, but they are the only ones which concern intelligent people to-day. The muttering about regal usurpation is beside the issue. Consequently the whole result of Mr. Shaw's sniping at democracy is trivial; the targets are not real.

The two interludes to which reference was made are of a different order. The first, occupying the whole of a short second act, shows King Magnus dallying with a charmer called Orinthia, who would like to be rid of the homely Queen Jemima and take Magnus over as a promising royal concern. She is another type of autocrat, imperious, empty, vain, delightful, ambitious, idiotic, and, as the history of the world shows, often immensely powerful. Magnus is fascinated, but remains free; he will push his own apple-cart and not allow her to equip it with pineapples and have it driven by a team of milk-white palfreys. The second interlude shows the arrival of an American Ambassador asking for America to be reunited with the British Empire as one of the Dominions. America has conquered the world financially and socially; why should it not crown the jest by running the British Empire from within as well as from without? Here Mr. Shaw's political raillery is at its best. The incident is purely fantastical, and the wit abounds. Had the whole play been skittish in this way it would have had not only a superficial unity but a far stronger appeal. It is by asking us to take King Magnus seriously that Mr. Shaw upsets his own apple-cart. Magnus is allowed to speak his mind, but the Opposition is only allowed to perform exercises in slap-stick. Had it all been a lark, had it all been the buffoonery of politics in which Mr. Shaw can be so nimble, how much better! The suits and trappings suggest a Nonsense Land in which all should be drolls and dreams and puppets, instead of all but one.

Of course it is rich in entertainment. Mr. Shaw can, it is true, sink to jokes of the 'I-am-a-plain-man' order, with the obvious pantomime retort, but his ingenuity in the cut-and-thrust of dialogue is as slick as of old. Contemptuous as ever of shape and form, he continues to demonstrate that pattern does not matter if the word be quick and the fancy fresh. The democratic playgoer will have ample ear-tickling to alleviate any vexation of the mind.

100. H. W. Nevinson, notice, *New Leader*

23 August 1929, vol. XVI, ns, 148, 9

Henry Woodd Nevinson (1856–1941), writer and journalist. The article is an outstanding example of the criticism that *The Apple Cart* evoked from many who had looked on Shaw as a leader of Socialist thought. See also No. 106.

Malvern has long suffered the unfortunate reputation of being a health resort—unfortunate because invalids, idlers and people of independent means have occupied it. The place is the established home of modern comfort, combined with the nursery of real or imaginary diseases. I need not say the political atmosphere is intensely Conservative, and it is significant that when I drove through it five years ago with the present Prime Minister during his first term of office, it was here alone out of all England that he was received with boos and cries of execration.

Yet this was the place fixed upon for a Festival Week in honour of Bernard Shaw. It was fixed upon by Sir Barry Jackson, I suppose, as being convenient for the Repertory Theatre at Birmingham, which he has supported with the lavish generosity of his wealth. The week began on Sunday with a private performance of Shaw's latest play, *The Apple Cart*, given for the first time in England, but given a few months ago in Warsaw.

It amused me to see the distant interest of the Malvern population watching our large party as we emerged from the London train. 'So these are the intellectuals,' they seemed to be saying. 'Those are the authors, dramatists, critics, actors and the rest. What a queer looking lot!' But when I looked at the sanatoriums, the substantial villas, the gardens and carefully-trimmed lawns, the big hotels, and other evidences of smug prosperity, it was not of the intellectual crowd that I was thinking.

I seemed to see again a tall, slim figure, who came to London from Dublin nearly 50 years ago, and, like myself, was hanging on to the skirts of literature and journalism. He was a striking figure, tawny from

317

head to foot, his hair and beard tawny, his clothes tawny, his shirt tawny, and I have little doubt his boots were tawny, though I think he never wore sandals. Keen and alert he ranged about the British Museum Reading Room, studying music, I suppose, studying Karl Marx, preparing for his early book, *An Unsocial Socialist*, for his early Fabianism, and his musical and dramatic criticism. A few years later he began to emerge with *Widowers' Houses*, and since then he has emerged indeed!

I have long considered his the finest critical mind in Europe. No other critic on religion, politics, science or society has been so acute, so courageous, so sincere. One after another his plays and the prefaces to his plays have laid bare the falsities and hypocrisies and boastful pretensions of our country and our time. I can think of no modern prophet who has swept away so much accepted rubbish and cleared the air of so much cant. In some forty years he has affected a revolution so vast that political revolutions and changes of Government are dwarfed in comparison, and last Sunday we witnessed the revolution's outward and visible sign.

By his own sheer genius, by courage and persistence, that active and tawny figure has raised himself to such a fame and has influenced the mind of the country so deeply that we were holding a Festival Week in his honour, and the festival was to be held in a model centre of self-satisfaction and comfortable torpor. To myself that was the miracle. That was the wonder revealing the powers of an unconquerable mind and the ultimate reasonableness of the human spirit.

But for the play itself, I do not like to upset the apple-cart, and I wish with all my heart I could put it on a level with Shaw's noblest work —such dramas as *Mrs Warren's Profession*, *John Bull's Other Island*, *Androcles*, *Fanny's First Play*, or *Saint Joan*. I am sorry; I think most of us present were sorry, but *The Apple Cart* is not on that level. It seemed to me badly constructed in its dramatic form and pernicious in its moral.

It seemed badly constructed in that each of its three acts ran upon a separate idea with hardly any connection between them. In the second act this want of connection is glaring. We are there shown the King of England some thirty years hence, engaged in a lover's quarrel with Orinthia, whom one would without hesitation describe as his mistress, if we were not most strangely informed that their relationship is 'strangely innocent.' I am not narrowly sceptical, but there are some things I cannot believe, no matter how strongly asserted.

However, though the innocence has no face value whatever, let us leave it at its face value, as we leave the King and Orinthia rolling together in a struggle upon the floor, while one of the King's secretaries pulls the door open and discreetly retires. I had hoped that Orinthia (played by that exquisite actress, Edith Evans) would have taken some part in upsetting the apple cart. No such luck. She never appears and is never mentioned again. In her place we are shown the virtuous Queen Jemima, who knits and listens quietly, as every virtuous Queen should, and, apparently, has no notion that her royal husband leads a strangely innocent life elsewhere.

The other episode in the play which has little, if any, connection with the main theme is the sudden appearance of the American Ambassador, dressed in the stars and stripes of an old-fashioned caricature of Uncle Sam, bringing a message from the President, in which he proposes the reunion of the United States with the British Empire.

And he shows that owing to America's money and power it would be very difficult for the English King to refuse the offer, even though it might entail the removal of the Empire's capital from London to Washington or Dublin. The offer is, in fact, a demand, and the poor conscientious and strangely innocent King is thrown into the second great perplexity that confronts him during the play. He does not resolve this perplexity, nor does he resolve the main question that the play suggests.

That question is whether a benevolent monarchy is not a better form of government than a democracy in which the citizens share through the franchise. This is where I call the moral of the play pernicious. Shaw throws all the weight of his dialectic on the side of benevolent monarchy. He shows us the wise, considerate and thoughtful King, highly educated, a master of argument (acted, by the way, with incomparable skill by Cedric Hardwicke), and he confronts this modest and gentlemanly person with a gang of fools and knaves who represent the Cabinet. Such an impossible set of duds I have never seen. No, not in Trafalgar Square or the House of Commons.

If Shaw chooses to represent monarchy by a man of singular charm and wisdom, and democracy by such a herd of imbeciles, of course, the triumph of monarchy or benevolent despotism is assured. In one of the too few really witty sayings in the play, he describes a Cabinet as an overcrowded third-class carriage. It is a good description of these uniformed duds. To make the parallel complete two women have been crowded in, one apparently, better suited for the comic opera stage, the other the only serious member of the Cabinet, but hysterical and silly beyond feminine nature. Of course, monarchy wins hands down, though the actual position is left nominally unchanged at the last.

To myself, who try to retain a belief in democracy, freedom and the popular Government, this, the main doctrine of the play, appears pernicious. All the worse, at the present time when despotism has raised its head again in most European countries. All the tyrants in Europe will delight in the play.

It is about a year I suppose since Shaw first turned his admiration to Mussolini and his form of benevolent tyranny. Can it be that a brief experience of modern comforts in Italy has so changed his whole outlook upon society and politics, that he is now ready to abandon those principles for which we have battled so long? Or is this, after all, only the natural result of the old Fabian doctrine of government by 'experts?' It was a doctrine that always depressed and terrified me, but even an 'expert' is to some extent responsible to the people who appoint him and keep him in office. King Magnus, the despot, would be responsible to no one, and his benevolence must be taken on trust— a trust all the more shaky because his despotism is hereditary.

If Shaw's despot turns out to be neither wise nor benevolent, the only way is to cut off his head, a violent and almost obsolete measure in this country. As to Shaw's burlesque of Boanerges, the Labour member of the Cabinet, that sort of person is as obsolete as Charles the First's head, and should be kept out of any play by a man of Shaw's genius.

101. W. B. Yeats on the reception of *The Apple Cart*

21 August and 16 November 1929

Extracts from letters to Lady Gregory, from *The Letters of W. B. Yeats*, ed. Allan Wade (1954), 767 and 770.

Philip Snowden was the Chancellor of the Exchequer in the Labour government whose policies, then and later, won him more support from the Conservatives than from his own party.

---

21 August 1929 The *Irish Times* to-day has a leader on the production of *Fighting the Waves* and *The Apple Cart* as both 'produced amid such stir of attention as seldom gratified the most notable of dramatists' which is of course nonsense so far as my play is concerned but friendly. However they abate the compliment by thinking the first but 'an interesting experiment' and the second as 'no more than a skit'. I saw the chief English papers yesterday at the club. Shaw has had an exclusively party reception—the Conservative papers, especially the *Morning Post*, enthusiastic and the Labour papers abusive. All agree that the play was enthusiastically received. I imagine that Shaw has made the sensation of his life, and can join Snowden in the Carlton Club.

16 November 1929 I caught the cold that undid me at *The Apple Cart* and perhaps it was the cold coming on, but I hated the play. The second act was theatrical in the worst sense of the word in writing and in acting, and the theme was just rich enough to show up the superficiality of the treatment. It was the Shaw who writes letters to the papers and gives interviews, not the man who creates.

102. St John Ervine, notice, *Observer*

25 August 1929, 7213, 11

John St John Greer Ervine (1883–1971), Irish dramatist and critic, was a close friend of Shaw for forty years. This signed notice was entitled 'Mr Shaw's Superb Pantomime'. St John Ervine wrote a long biography of Shaw, *Bernard Shaw: his Life, Work and Friends* (1956), in which the warmth of his admiration for Shaw as a playwright was offset by his lack of enthusiasm for many of Shaw's opinions.

The Apple Cart is a superb medley of pantomime and morality play, in which Mr. Shaw has nicely mingled the manner of *Everyman* with that of *Ali Baba and the Forty Thieves*—the second act might be called a sequel to *The Sleeping Beauty* after that lady has been aroused from sleeping—and I know of nothing in contemporary comic writing which equals it in brilliant buffoonery, exhilaration of spirit, audacity of idea, and provocative and disconcerting good sense. There are passages in the play which will provoke some persons, as they provoked Mr. H. W. Nevinson, that incorrigible romantic whose love of peace is continually shattered by his love of soldiers, into violent dissent, but those who are provoked can scarcely complain that they have been bored. Any person who asserts that *The Apple Cart* bored him publishes his own shame: he acknowledges that he is fit only to sell beet-root. The intellectually-bankrupt and the spiritually-damned will yawn their fat heads off while this piece is being performed, but that precisely is what we would wish them to do. Fat heads ought to be off! It will be sufficient, perhaps, for the discerning if I say that a thousand persons, drawn from every part of these islands, and including visitors from foreign countries, of whom less than a hundred were what may be called professional playgoers, witnessed the performance with interest and delight.

The Apple Cart, which is as disconnected as a revue, is not, of course, a play, but who cares whether it is or not? Mr. Shaw has spent a long life in writing plays which are not plays, and has persuaded people all over the world to prefer them to plays which are plays. It opens with a discourse on ritualism which has as much relevance to the rest of the play as the old-fashioned overture had to the rest of the opera. This discourse is added to the play in exactly the same spirit in which the gargoyles were added to cathedrals, out of sheer exuberance and overflow of genius. The second act is almost an independent piece, and might, with little alteration, be performed by itself. The end is more or less in the air. But what an entertainment! How easily, and with what verve, it runs through the rules and flattens them out.

[Summarises the story of the play.]

That, baldly, is the play. Too baldly. But how can I or anyone hope to put into a column and a half a fair measure of the brains that are in it? To produce such a piece of high farce, fantastic wisdom and brilliant discourse at the age of seventy-three is a feat of which men half the age of Mr. Shaw might be envious, and I feel impatient with the paltry yammerers who complain that its author is out of touch with life. What life? Whose life? Are we to believe that gentlemen whose days are spent in running from the keyhole of the stage-door to the typewriter in the newspaper office know more about life and are abler to pronounce judgment on it than this great man who has more intelligence in his little finger than they have in their entire bodies?

103. Harold J. Laski on Shaw and Democracy

1930

Extract from signed article, 'Is Democracy Breaking Down?' in the *Listener*, 31 December 1930, 1081.

Harold J. Laski (1893–1950), Professor of Political Science at the London School of Economics, considered the views put forward in *The Apple Cart*, in a review of the printed text. Following the passage quoted, he examined Shaw's political remedies, 'equality of income, and . . . a reorganisation of constitutional machinery' and concluded by asserting that 'if every listener were to digest the lesson of his Preface and then write to his member of Parliament about it, we should have, even in this democracy, an irresistible demand for that overhaul of institutions, which is the essential condition of our political future.'

If it is true that the younger generation has deserted Mr. Shaw for Mr. T. S. Eliot, then the publication of *The Apple-cart* will, I hope, recall them to a better frame of mind. For the 'Preface' to his too-much-discussed play shows all his great qualities at their very best: it is direct, incisive, realistic, with a pungency of immediate value which makes at least one reader thump his desk with admiration. I hope Mr. MacDonald will make it compulsory reading for his Cabinet colleagues during the Christmas vacation; then they might bend their minds to that institutional reconstruction which is the surest need of modern democracy.

Of the play itself, despite its often brilliant wit, I do not think much needs to be said. Mr. Shaw's own preface seems to me a tacit admission that, in the dialogue at least, he has weighted the scales extravagantly against poor Proteus and his colleagues; the second act is still an irrelevant and not very amusing interlude; and though there is brilliant comedy in the episode of the American Ambassador, I would gladly have sacrificed it all to know more of what Mr. Shaw really thinks of the place of 'Breakages Ltd.' in modern society, and what we can do about it. In a word, by contriving what he quite fairly describes as an extravaganza, Mr. Shaw has been able to evade a problem, or series of problems, the importance of which no living thinker has seen more clearly or more profoundly.

But the preface is a different matter. In it Mr. Shaw demonstrates, in that prose which is the best instrument for its purpose since Swift's, that if by democracy we mean a social system in which there is equal consideration for all, the institutions by which this is attainable simply do not exist in the modern community. He tilts, quite fairly, at the futility of the method by which we choose our political leaders. He shows, again quite fairly, that a Parliament which is overwhelmed, and a Cabinet so pressed as never to be capable of coherent thought, cannot possibly perform the tasks of modern government in a reasonable way. He shows decisively how much the treatment a man receives is a matter of the property to which he is annexed. Quite rightly, in my judgment, he makes the pivot of administrative power in the modern State depend upon the views of the civil service. And he exhibits, in all its futility, the sheer fantasy that the whole of the people can ever hope to occupy itself with the business of State.

TOO TRUE TO BE GOOD

1931

Too True to be Good was first produced by the New York Theater Guild at the National Theater, Boston, Massachusetts, on 29 February 1932, for fourteen performances. It was then produced at the Guild Theater, New York, on 4 April 1932 for fifty-seven performances. After performances at the Teatr Polski, Warsaw, beginning on 4 June 1932, the first British production was on 6 August 1932 at the Festival Theatre, Malvern, where it was given eight performances. It was first presented in London at the New Theatre on 13 September, where it was played forty-seven times.

104. Charles Morgan, unsigned notice, *The Times*

8 August 1932

Charles Langbridge Morgan (1894–1958), novelist, essayist and dramatist, became dramatic critic of *The Times* in 1926, when he succeeded A. B. Walkley, and held the post until 1939. He was a fastidious writer who, in general, felt himself out of sympathy with Shaw's entire approach to the theatre. In *Everyman* on 18 August 1932, C. B. Purdom defended Shaw against Morgan's criticisms in an article entitled 'Shaw Needs No Defence'. In the article, Purdom wrote, 'The form of the play, it seems, displeases Mr Morgan. He does not object to the prophecies but to the way in which they are presented. I wonder! Could Mr Morgan really stand a prophet in the theatre? For do not all prophets denounce their age? The play lacks style, that is what Mr Morgan really means. And he is right in the sense that it has no style in the conventional sense. The play makes its own rules. As for style in the essential sense, it has plenty. Mr Shaw's own style, which, good or bad, is sufficient.'

Mr. Shaw's present work has, as a document, the interest and, as a play, the tedium, of an undigested notebook. Being formless, it produces neither dramatic illusion nor intellectual tension; in that sense it is dull; but, though without form, it is not void, for the alternate wisdom and childishness that give to the word 'Shavian' its meaning inform it all, and, by virtue of their incongruousness, grant to it the salvation of style. When Mr. Shaw is scribbling in his notebook, now a fragment of a sermon, now the patter of a pierhead clown, it is never disappointing to look over his shoulder unless one is foolish enough to expect a work of art, or even the exposition of an idea, with beginning, middle, and end. His badness, like his goodness, is unique. None but he would allow a colonel, who enjoys sketching, to say: 'the water-colours have saved me by keeping me on the water-wagon,' and expect an adult audience to laugh. When one puppet has exclaimed: 'Medea! Medea!' no one but Mr. Shaw would condemn another to reply: 'It isn't an i-dea; it's the truth!' To such depths can the arrogance of humour descend, but they are distinctively Shavian depths; and it is true also that none but Mr. Shaw could have written the footnote to Bunyan which does, for a glorious instant, make one feel that genius is about to spring. . . .

An atheist has lost faith in his atheism. A colonel, doubting the sanction of his authority, is envious of a private soldier of genius, Private Meek, who commands without the responsibility of command. A clergyman-burglar, whose ideas we are expressly forbidden to identify with Mr. Shaw's own, is sure of nothing but the world's need to affirm something—but what? All, all are gone—the old familiar faces of duty, of faith, of belief in convention. What shall replace them? What 'shining light' shall man pursue, and whither shall he flee to escape from his nakedness and from the wrath to come?

There, indeed, is a theme for a great sermon. The problem may not be as new or as directly a consequence of the militaristic bee in the Shavian bonnet as Mr. Shaw supposes. It was not in 1914 nor in 1918 that man asked for the first time: How shall I learn to pray who have lost my belief in God? But whether it be new, as Mr. Shaw pretends, or very old, as we believe, this spiritual paradox, this particular aspect of man's search for a way of life that shall fulfil him is a subject for the grapple of genius. Mr. Shaw may have his pitiful stale quips about soldiers, his clown's umbrella, his medical wit from *The Doctor's Dilemma*, his stage-chase from *Charley's Aunt*; he may have even the grosser jests, surprising in him; he may have them all, if he will culti-

vate them elsewhere than in the pulpit, and all the licence to preach
that he can desire, if he will but pursue his theme. Whither shall man
flee to escape from his intolerable nakedness? What way of life shall
he choose and how maintain himself in it? There need be from a
dramatist no final answer. It is not an artist's business didactically to
award first, second, and third prizes to the saints. He need not answer;
but he must ask with diligence and passion, that the minds of those who
hear him may, by the singleness of his inquiry and the energy of
aesthetic form, be newly impregnated with the seed of perception.
This, if any, is the link between art and philosophy. A few notes in a
wilderness of fantastic irrelevance will not forge it.

Mr. Shaw has a congregation that no other preacher can command.
For ugly frivolity he has now himself only to blame. If he has questions
to ask touching the soul of man, if they are to him vital questions and
not merely a sage's cloak thrown over the motley of a buffoon, let him
ask them straightly. His position assures him audience in a world that
has need of prophets; for that reason the less is he entitled to waste a
great theme as ballast for a leaky farce.

105. H. W. Nevinson on Shaw and universal fame

1932

Nevinson's signed article, entitled 'Shakespeare's Rival' in the *Spectator*, 25 November 1932, vol. 149, 5448, 758, was a review of Archibald Henderson's biography, *Bernard Shaw, Playboy and Prophet* (1932).

You remember that in the epilogue to *Fanny's First Play* we are given a long discussion upon the possible authorship. Various names are suggested—Granville Barker, Barrie, Pinero, and so forth. At last someone suggests Shaw. 'Rubbish!' 'Rot!' are the retorts of the other critics present. 'I have repeatedly proved that Shaw is physiologically incapable of the note of passion,' says one. 'Intellect without emotion,' says another; 'I always say myself,' or 'A giant brain, if you ask me; but no heart.' So the controversy goes on, till one of them says wearily, 'And naturally we are all talking about Shaw. For heaven's sake let us change the subject.' But the protest is useless. They all go on prating about 'Shaw, Shaw, Shaw!'

The scene and the protest are still true. Wherever you go you will find a controversy raging about Shaw. He is a figure in the eye of the human race. We are now told that he is off this winter for a tour of the world; that will not help him to escape from the Dartmoor of notoriety. The bloodhounds of curiosity will everywhere dog his track. Wherever he goes—by ship or train or camel or elephant—he will be recognized and debated. I saw it last August at the Malvern Festival, when all the people of town and village crowded together, waiting to see him pass. Pointing or nodding to each other, they would say, 'That's him!' The swimming matches were neglected, the illuminations paled, the audience in the theatre rose and faced about to watch him take his seat. Shakespeare never excited such interest either in Southwark or Stratford, and on all sides the old, old criticisms re-echoed: 'Shaw's characters are all himself. Mere puppets stuck up to spout Shaw.' 'Incapable of passion!' 'A giant brain, if you ask me; but no heart.' And then we would all settle down in joyful expectation to witness *Too True to be Good*, one of his greatest and most unpopular plays, just as we had settled down some months before to witness *The Apple Cart*, his worst and almost the most popular.

So it is. In vain the bright young things assure me that Shaw is a back number. In every civilized land I have heard the cry of 'Shaw, Shaw, Shaw!' Only among the savages of Central Africa and the Middle West of the United States have I been free of it. His fame is almost what is called universal, and to myself the only drawback is that when he speaks from the Fabian platform, for instance, the audience begins to laugh so idiotically before he has uttered a single sentence that I cannot hear what he wants to say. It is a change from the distant age when, in the Reading Room of the British Museum, I used to encounter a tall, lithe, energetic figure, tawny all over from head to foot but for the clear blue eyes, and enwrapped in the study of Wagner and Karl Marx. Or, again, when, in the old Browning Society, I heard him asserting amid the scornful derision of Furnivall and the other Browningites that 'Sludge the Medium' was the poet's greatest work.

There has been no bushel on his light, but with a fine self-confidence he has taken care to place it on his own candlestick. Thirty-four years ago, he wrote, 'For ten years past, with an unprecedented pertinacity and obstination, I have been dinning into the public head that I am an extraordinarily witty, brilliant, and clever man. My reputation is built up fast and solid, like Shakespeare's, on an impregnable basis of dogmatic reiteration.' Like everyone who cares for the high purposes of the drama, I have followed his course on the stage from *Widowers' Houses* up to the comparative failure of his last great play, admiring all but one, and especially admiring *Mrs. Warren's Profession*, *Arms and the Man*, *Androcles*, *Fanny's First Play*, *St. Joan*, and *John Bull's Other Island*, which, I suppose, set the seal on the playwright's fame in Society because Edward VII saw it and invited Shaw into his box, a command disobeyed.

But to myself his highest value has always been the passionate and indignant seriousness with which he has thrown himself into all the most controversial questions of the time, always, in my view, on the right side, and the scorn, the wit, and ironic laughter with which he has compelled the world to listen. I may here mention only three— his condemnation of the Denshawai atrocities, his advocacy of Woman

Suffrage, and his share in our vain endeavour to save his compatriot Roger Casement from the gallows.

In this vast volume, running to 850 pages, with numerous illustrations, Mr. Archibald Henderson has erected what will be called a monument, but is not at all a tombstone, to the great personality whom he has long known intimately and for whose fame he has laboured for thirty years almost as persistently as Shaw himself. Here may be found a full and accurate record of all the amazing examples of vitality displayed in a life which must now, unhappily, be described as long. Shaw may endeavour to suppress his passionate emotions—what is called his heart—as he will. In the whole of this record one feels the pulse of generosity, and one marvels at an entire freedom from the envy, hatred and malice which so easily beset writers, artists, and dramatists of lesser mould.

106. George Orwell's attack on Shaw

1933

From letter to Brenda Salkeld, 10? March 1933, printed in *The Collected Essays, Journalism and Letters of George Orwell*, ed. Sonia Orwell and Ian Angus (1968), vol. I, 143.

George Orwell (Eric Blair) (1903–50), novelist, journalist and publicist, was an unorthodox Socialist who was deeply concerned about, among other things, simplicity and directness of style. It is surprising, therefore, that he seems, in much literary journalism, not to have written at any length on Shaw who, according to a recent biographer, was a formative influence (George Woodcock, *The Crystal Spirit* (1967), 247).

Have you seen any more of your friends who worship Bernard Shaw? Tell them that Shaw is Carlyle & water, that he ought to have been a Quaker (cocoa and commercial dishonesty), that he has squandered what talents he may have had back in the '80s in inventing metaphysical reasons for behaving like a scoundrel, that he suffers from an inferiority complex towards Shakespeare, & that he is the critic, cultured critic (not very cultured but it is what B meant) that Samuel Butler prayed to be delivered from. Say that Shaw's best work was one or two early novels & one or two criticisms he wrote for the *Saturday Review* when Harris was editor, & that since then it has got steadily worse until its only function is to console fat women who yearn to be highbrows. Say also that he has slandered Ibsen in a way that must make poor old I turn in his grave. Also that Shaw cribbed the plot of *Pygmalion* from Smollett & afterwards wrote somewhere or other that Smollett is unreadable.

107. Osbert Burdett on Shaw's popularity

1933

From signed article in *London Mercury*, June 1933, 136.

Osbert Burdett (1885–1936), author and literary critic, called his article, 'A Critical Stroll through Bernard Shaw' and surveyed the whole of Shaw's work. After the passage quoted here, in which the general tone of the article was set, he went on to examine in some detail the plays and other writings. His conclusion was that 'Shaw's writings are the brilliant mirror of a shallow time'; he ended by saying that 'were journalism, applied not fine literature, our subject here however, it would be a critical pleasure to praise the variety of forms, the wonderful skill, which G.B.S. has imported into the fresh, and hitherto sacred, fields that his journalistic genius has boldly invaded.'

Contemporarily successful writers reflect the spirit of their time, and Bernard Shaw's popularity is appropriate to an age of newspapers. In Fleet Street his opinions are always considered to be 'news,' even though often suppressed there. The chief of living journalists has made his reputation by annexing the theatre to propaganda and debate; but he has not won the poets, nor critics able to distinguish between journalism and literature, a point-of-view and a person, an argument and a drama, an effective staccato and a rhythm of life. Moreover, people who can make these distinctions, yet who can enjoy one form of entertainment without confusing it with another, feel ungrateful when, confronted with so much fun, generosity and good temper, criticism forces them to insist that the best journalism is to literature what the best applied art is to fine; and that, among the hundred topics on which Mr. Shaw's work invites discussion, literature and drama are small talk. His and Blake's are opposite extremes, which by contrast reveal the limitation of each other. A brilliant surface is not beauty. Cerebration is not depth; and the Rodin bust shows a high impressive mask—to a head that has no back to it.

The style is as effective, and unquiet, as that of Macaulay, another brilliant journalist, who appropriated History to propaganda very much as Mr. Shaw has appropriated pen, platform and stage. Both are efficient, plausible, and successful in the highest degree; both are personalities; and both have won unbounded admiration from philistines. The bulk of Bernard Shaw's followers consist of earnest folk, often women, who, accepting his leadership (or enjoying his fun) on one or more of his current topics, confuse their pleasure and his personal popularity with the pleasure of art and the reputation of a great author. Our incapacity for art and our appetite for journalism, like a taste for tonics and indifference to wine, explain the nature, and the extent, of this success. Why, then, do the critics enjoy him? The young Shaw who reproached himself for indulging in light opera when he knew that Bach would have been better for his soul is the counter-part of the critic who cannot resist a Shavian book when the Muses should be beckoning him.

108. Lillah McCarthy: the view of an actress

1933

From *Myself and my Friends* (1933), ch. VI, 65.

Lillah McCarthy (Lady Keeble) (1875–1960), was the first wife of Harley Granville Barker. She appeared with him in many productions of Shaw's plays and created the leading female roles in *Man and Superman*, *The Doctor's Dilemma* and *Androcles and the Lion*. This passage occurs at the end of a chapter devoted to the Court Theatre in her book of reminiscences. She states that 'Shaw restored the English theatre to its rightful place in national life' and says that Ann in *Man and Superman* was a 'new woman' and 'she made a new woman of me.'

Shaw is his own worst enemy. He so provokes men by his unorthodox pronouncements, carries them away so completely by his realism, that he gives them no time to observe the beauty of the language which he uses. Yet those who read his plays and prefaces know that he stands as one of the lordly company—to be numbered on the fingers of one hand—of present-day writers who are masters of the art and craft of prose writing. Towards the end of *Man and Superman* there is a love scene between Ann and Tanner. It is of a beauty which no words of mine can describe. Beauty of characterisation, beauty of story, beauty of ideas, all woven together into a fabric so fine as to obscure the exquisiteness of the material—the words—which are used in it. At the climax of the scene Tanner takes Ann in his arms and says: 'I love you. The Life Force enchants me. I have the whole world in my arms when I clasp you . . .' And, as the play closes, Tanner sums up all things with words that sound like sighs, 'Ann looks happy; but she is only triumphant, successful, victorious. That is not happiness, but the price for which the strong sell their happiness.'

At one of the rehearsals, Louis Calvert, touched by the scene, turned to me and said: 'You would be a great dramatic actress—a great tragedienne—away from plays like this'. Maybe! but away from plays like that I should never have developed as a woman.

ON THE ROCKS

1933

On the Rocks was first presented at the Winter Garden Theatre, London, on 25 November 1933, for forty-one performances. It was presented at the Abbey Theatre, Dublin, on 9 July 1934.

109. From an unsigned notice, *Morning Post*

27 November 1933, 12

He has made politics amusing. Such is the triumphant achievement which Mr Bernard Shaw, in his 78th year, but a playboy still, undoubtedly brings off in this new 'discussion' of his. A triumph it is. All the flood-lit mediocrity which bores us on the political stage of real life is here transmuted into a sparkling farce of ideas.

Mr Shaw is, of course, happy in not having, like the cartoonists, to drag in the 'old, familiar faces'. His characters are topical and typical; but they are creations, not caricatures. His own wit and nearly always clever jugglery of themes, and the admirable acting of a brilliant cast, do the rest. In three hours of desultory talk in a scene never stirring from the Cabinet Room at No. 10 Downing Street, and with only one interval, few could be conscious of a dull moment.

110. Kingsley Martin, signed notice, *New Statesman and Nation*

2 December 1933, vol. VI, 145, ns, 694

(Basil) Kingsley Martin (1897–1969), journalist and author, editor of the *New Statesman and Nation* from 1931 to 1961. Kingsley Martin was a personal friend of Shaw and a lifelong admirer, although he differed from him on many occasions. There are many comments on Shaw in Kingsley Martin's writings, notably in his two volumes of autobiography, *Father Figures* (1966) and *Editor* (1968), and in an essay, 'G.B.S.', contributed to *Shaw and Society*, edited by C. E. M. Joad (1951). In *Father Figures*, Kingsley Martin recalled that 'the very first piece of journalism that I ever did in my life . . . was a short article about *Arms and the Man*, which was published in the *Cambridge Magazine*.' This was when he was an undergraduate. Shaw wrote to a friend that the article seemed to him 'to be very good stuff' and that the writer had 'talent enough to make six ordinary theatre critics and leave a good deal to spare; but that is not saying much; it is not really an exacting profession'. Kingsley Martin did not become a theatre critic but his notice of *On the Rocks* is of interest because, while he was primarily a political journalist, he was nevertheless able to assess the play as drama and not simply as political comment.

At the Reichstag trial last week Van der Lubbe remarked that he thought the trial had lasted long enough: there had been enough talk and he wanted a sentence, preferably of death or twenty-one years' imprisonment. Mr. Shaw feels a similar impatience: he has watched the democratic farce long enough, and tells us in *On the Rocks* that it is time we cut the Parliamentary cackle and took our punishment like men. It would be idle to pretend that the intellectual quality of this play is equal to the best of Shaw. If one compares it with one of the earlier long discussion plays—and this is one of the longest and it is made up wholly of discussion—it is obvious, for instance, that there is more jocularity and less wit than in *Getting Married* or *Misalliance*. One finds with some surprise that the rather obvious joke about Guy Fawkes as the one man who really knew what to do with Parliament —a joke which made, I believe, its first appearance in this paper two years ago—is repeated and underlined in this play. This ragging of democracy is amusing enough, but it is easy money—and so would the ragging of dictators be if ragging were allowed under dictatorship. Mr. Shaw uses a very broad brush; and the rare moments when his touch is subtle remain in one's mind when most of the fun is forgotten. Left alone in the room, the Prime Minister, a worn-out shell with a lovely voice and a memory for the accustomed phrases, sits down and rejoices that he has a minute's 'peace.' A few seconds later his reverie turns automatically into a rehearsal for a speech about world peace to be delivered before the assembled clergy at the Church House. The tragedy of a man who never has time to think and who always has another engagement could scarcely be better conveyed. In that momentary touch of genuine drama Shaw does more to get over his point about the damage of public life to men who once had minds than in several hours of declamation. The proportion of such drama is certainly smaller than it used to be in Shaw, and it is to be noticed that in this play he actually allows some characters to carry off the honours of argument without exploding their pretensions in the moment of triumph. The excellent Mr. Hipney, the Captain Shotover and the best character in the play, is not shown up as being dependent on a supply of rum in the background. He is allowed to be solid all through, the 'one politician who has learnt anything from experience'—what he has learnt being that Parliament was well enough until we had adult suffrage and now would be better abolished; that liberty is 'twaddle'; that the coming revolution must be led by a man who believes in it with his heart, not only with his head; that the right system would be not to abolish democratic choice altogether, but to give people the pick of several trained and qualified dictators; and that the revolution must be socialist and yet not Marxist, since the working classes are hopelessly divided amongst themselves. The conclusion of the play is that any strong man who can make people believe that he can give the unemployed work may do as he likes. The remedy for our ills is socialism, but an English socialism. The unemployed who break the windows as the curtain falls sing not 'The Red Flag' but 'England Arise.'

Most of the play is devoted to rubbing in the hopelessness of democracy and the characters are admirably chosen for that purpose. The Prime Minister (an enormous part admirably played by Mr. Nicholas Hannen) is shown by a woman healer (Miss Fay Davis) that he is suffering not from overwork, as he and others imagine, but from underwork—from the effects of always talking and never allowing his brain time to think. (The Russians, according to Mr. Shaw, have a special Cabinet for thinking). He leaves his secretary (the part is particularly well played by Miss Phyllis Thomas) and his wife and family and the Cabinet, and the House of Commons and the deputations and public meetings, and goes into a retreat for a fortnight, armed with the works of Karl Marx whom, curiously enough, he had never heard of at Oxford. He returns to confront the Cabinet with a full-blown Socialist programme which, however, include bribes for the various departments. The Cabinet Ministers are well cast: Lawrence Hanray is a terribly convincing Duke of Doomsday, Norman MacOwen a very canny vote-catching President of the Board of Trade, while Mr. Charles Carson as Sir Dexter Rightside, the leader of the Conservatives in the Coalition, is deliciously supported at the critical moment by the beet-root faced Admiral Sir Bemrose Hotspot, the First Lord of the Admiralty, who sheds a tear when he remembers that 'Dexy was at school with me' and on that ground supports him in breaking up the National Government. Significantly enough, the one really effective person in this Cabinet is not a politician but the Chief Commissioner of Police—a dapper, definite and determined young soldier, played with great success by Mr. Walter Hudd.

It has been said that this is a 'Fascist' play. That, I think, misstates Mr. Shaw's intention. It warns rather than advocates. Make up your mind, he says, that Parliament, as you now know it, cannot be the instrument of salvation. Devise a constitution which gives scope to personal and national loyalty, but do not imagine that it can succeed without transformation of the social order. The one good element in democracy—the safeguard it offers against inefficiency and cruelty on the part of a particular dictator—can be secured by a system (of intelligence tests perhaps?) which would ensure that the ruler had at least the necessary qualification for governing. Go boldly ahead with your revolutions and do not stop for any thought of liberty. People want to be told what to do. They want rulers; they do not mind losing liberties they have discovered to be valueless. At this point Mr. Shaw seems to feel a momentary chill. Must we, he asks, throw out the baby with the bath-water? Let us put Mr. Shaw's question more explicitly.

Can we effect the necessary economic changes without setting up a form of government which will stop Mr. Shaw writing plays, and which may indeed outlaw all the free life of the mind?

111. From an unsigned notice, *Irish Times*

10 July 1934

If there is one thing we have learned to expect from Mr Shaw, it is stagecraft, yet in *On the Rocks*, which is being performed for the first time in Ireland at the Abbey Theatre, stagecraft is the one quality that seems to be missing. The author develops his theme slowly—too slowly, perhaps—in the first act, but the first half of the second act treats us to as brilliant a display of Shavian fireworks as we have any right to expect! Then what happens? He leaves his subject flat for half an hour to talk to us at great length about something else, and only comes back to his real theme, as if by an afterthought, a few minutes before the final curtain. *On the Rocks* is delightful in parts, but in others it is just dull.

[Summarises the story of the play.]

Up to the stage when the author abandons both democracy and the play to their fate, the second act is almost as good as anything he has written in the last five years, and closely packed with a number of good things. He is just as adept as ever at leading his audience along one line of argument, and then puncturing the whole affair with a sudden shaft of wit. His logic is as sure and unexpected, his irony as remorseless, and his irreverence for the *status quo* as marked, as in former years. Added to this, the play is very topical and, although he deals with England, some of the lines have an application to this country which is quite surprising. Yet it is not a satisfactory play; one feels that the real Shaw was writing it only part of the time.

112. H. G. Wells questions Shaw's view of the theatre

1934

From *Experiment in Autobiography* (1934), vol. II, ch. 8, 540.

Wells refers to his first acquaintance with Shaw and goes on to comment on their differing views of life and the theatre.

I want to get hold of Fact, strip off her inessentials and, if she behaves badly, put her in stays and irons; but Shaw dances round her and weaves a wilful veil of confident assurances about her as her true presentment. He thinks one can 'put things over' on Fact and I do not. He philanders with her. I have no delusions about the natural goodness and wisdom of human beings and at bottom I am grimly and desperately educational. But Shaw's conception of education is to let dear old Nature rip. He has got no further in that respect than Rousseau. Then I know, fundamentally, the heartless impartiality of natural causation, but Shaw makes Evolution something brighter and softer, by endowing it with an ultimately benevolent Life Force, acquired, quite uncritically I feel, from his friend and adviser Samuel Butler. We have been fighting this battle with each other all our lives.

. . . Shaw like James and like his still more consciously cultivated disciple, Granville Barker, believed firmly in The Theatre as a finished and definite something demanding devotion; offering great opportunities to the human mind. He perceived indeed there was something very wrong with it, he demanded an endowed theatre, a different criticism, a different audience than the common 'Theatre-goer' we knew, but in the end he could imagine this gathering of several hundred people for three hours' entertainment on a stage becoming something very fine and important and even primary in the general life. I had no such belief.

113. Bonamy Dobrée on Shaw's immortality

1934

From a signed article, 'The Shavian Situation' in *Spectator*, 13 July 1934, vol. 153, 5533, 46.

Bonamy Dobrée (1891–1974), English literary critic, was Professor of English at the University of Leeds from 1936 to 1955. His article, a review of Shaw's *Collected Prefaces*, is an example of the growing tendency in the last two decades of Shaw's life to praise him above all for his literary style, rather than for the content of his work.

If you ask haphazard acquaintances what they think of Mr. Shaw, they will almost certainly answer, irritatingly, with phonographic regularity, 'Oh, Shaw. Well, damned clever, of course—but then, of course, he isn't serious; of course he's an Irishman . . .' The bombardment of 'of courses' represents the Englishman's profound suspicion of the intellect. But what is most astonishing about this string is that the average man will end up with a remark which is, though he does not know it, of the flagrantly 'You're another' kind: he will say, 'Of course, he's irresponsible.' Now that is the one thing Mr. Shaw has been continually saying to us, for if you were to try to sum up in one phrase what his teachings, preachings, exhortations, and denunciations are all about, you would say that his text has invariably been 'For heaven's sake realize your responsibility, and shoulder it.' His superman, as defined in the preface to *The Sanity of Art* (1907) is one who will accept new and heavier obligations; his preface to *On the Rocks* (1933) is a notification to rulers to be responsible or to get out. In nearly all his prefaces you will find that he is urging people to face the implications of their acts, or of their lethargic failure to act, and to take up the burden of their responsibilities.

The fact that Mr. Shaw is an Irishman gives him the advantage that foreigners always have of being able to see us clearly, and of not being tarred with the brush that he so easily discerns blackening us; he is thus in an admirable position to exercise that noble faculty of 'cynicism,' as seeing through pretensions is called by those who bluff themselves, a faculty usually very salutary. It gave Farquhar, in many respects Mr. Shaw's forerunner, his bite; Mandeville also had the advantage of being a foreigner, and there is a good deal of Mandeville also in Mr. Shaw. Moreover, there is another thing which gives Mr. Shaw the advantage—distance in time as well as in space; for he belongs to the eighteenth century, firstly in his romantic idealization of women, which he combats and deplores but cannot get over; and, secondly, in his conviction that the only virtues worth bothering about are the social virtues. Even his metaphysics are social metaphysics: the urge of creative evolution is towards producing better citizens.

But his metaphysics do not permit him to dwell quite happily in the eighteenth-century rationalism which is also his home: looking out from his happy distances he cannot accept mankind as it is, nor tolerate its infuriating inability to manage its affairs. He cries out to his deity —Creative Evolution—'O God, give them more intelligence, make them grow up!' Himself supremely endowed with intelligence, he sees the monstrous folly of those systems on which we pride ourselves, the thinness of the screen which divides us from barbarity, the lunacy of our financial system, the horror of our wars, the criminality of our legal codes, the hideous cruelty of our most cherished morals. He would help to create a new religion for mankind, a new civic order, and in his last stage has become so impatient of human inertia that he sees nothing for it but to provide us with dictators who will not hesitate to shoot. Yet he has not altogether abandoned Fabianism, and still seems to believe that you can abolish poverty by abolishing the rich. The reason for abolishing the rich is that they are irresponsible, while the poor have not the means to responsibility. For he has, ultimately, in spite of his Caesarism, no belief in a society created by force: 'All communities must live finally by their ethical values: that is, by their genuine virtues. Living virtuously is an art that can be learnt only by living in full responsibility for our own actions.' Thus the object of his plays and his prefaces is to bring conviction of guilt to every man-jack of us: and our crimes are cant, mugwumpery, hypocrisy, cruelty, and an obstinate refusal to face issues.

Our greatest pamphleteer since Swift, master of impeccable prose, wielder of a style which is original because he has something to say, added to a supreme gift of the gab, he represents, for the first three or

343

four decades of this century, the great exploder of complacency. The difficulty is to discover why he has not had more effect on his time; a great deal of effect he certainly has had, but not one comparable to to that of, say, Voltaire. Yet he is as serious, as genuinely comedic, as great a master of vituperation. The answer perhaps is that he is too generously endowed with the Irish faculty for logic, a faculty notoriously abhorrent to Englishmen. Besides, he urges with as great moral fervour as he does important debatable ones, issues which seem to most men already settled in a direction repugnant to Mr. Shaw, settled it seems to them by common sense, common usage, common appetite, and this has made Mr. Shaw appear frivolous to them. He cannot be serious, they say, about vaccination or vegetarianism, though they may give him the benefit of the doubt on vivisection; therefore, how can he be serious about other things? 'Of course' (again) 'he does not mean what he says.' And further Mr. Shaw does not allow enough for the weaknesses of mankind: you never feel that he would be capable of enjoying sin as Voltaire might have enjoyed sin. Or, to put it another way, his Puritanism has served him badly: for never having sinned, he has no sense of sin, a sense which gave Bunyan, whom he so much admires, such power over his readers. Moreover, the ordinary human being wishes that Mr. Shaw would sometimes exhibit rancour, and attack persons instead of institutions. They accuse him of pride, whereas really he is kindly; they convict him of arrogance, whereas he is modest enough, feeling only that unless the point is driven home it is not worth while driving it at all. Therefore, a slight aroma of self-righteousness clings about him, a fate which is undeserved; but men may be excused for sniffing it. This may be because, though he has sometimes changed his mind, as all intelligent men do, he will never admit to an inconsistency: the brilliant debater takes charge, and suggests that you are a fool not to have seen that the inconsistency is only apparent. The only thing he lacks as a controversialist is the trick of conceding points to his opponent that he may more convincingly smash him later on.

If in his plays he has in the main used the comic method to awaken men's consciences, in his prefaces he has always adopted a more direct method. This volume is a noble apologia. Unlike his contemporaries, he has not timidly attacked or tinkered at isolated abuses, but rushed upon the whole group of conceptions upon which our tottering society rests. Though he has added nothing to philosophy, but taken it ready-made where he could find it, he has been original in applying it in such a wholesale fashion, so logically, to life. Some of his ideas, as he knows, are already outmoded, partly because we have accepted them; but he is assured of immortality because he has always dealt with the things that matter at the moment in the most effective language of the moment. Though he cares nothing for style as such, it is for his style that future ages will read him, secure in a civilisation where the problems of this one will seem fantastic, because the work of a great craftsman, who is also passionately sincere, will always fascinate others who practise that craft.

THE SIMPLETON, THE SIX AND THE MILLIONAIRESS

published 1936

114. Unsigned review, *Times Literary Supplement*

28 March 1936, 1782, 267

This review was published under the title 'The Encirclement of Mr Shaw: Social Doctrines in a Dilemma'.

Three plays, each with a preface, make up the present volume. The first is *The Simpleton of the Unexpected Isles* which was performed at Malvern last July; the second, which appeared in Regent's Park a year earlier, is *The Six of Calais*, a brief riotous opportunity for Edward III to lose his Plantagenet temper and afterwards, to exhibit his Plantagenet guile; and the third, *The Millionairess*, is an elaborate cartoon, embellished with farce and of a woman who is, in common with Bonaparte and Lenin, a born boss. 'A born boss is one who rides roughshod over us by some mysterious power that separates him from our species and makes us fear him; that is, hate him.'

This play, considered with its preface, is the most interesting that Mr Shaw has written since *The Apple Cart*. The drawing of the minor characters is, even within the play's unnaturalistic convention, perfunctory, and the anecdote though ingenious, is told with a Shakespearean carelessness for loose ends; but the millionairess herself is precisely what she is intended to be—not a woman to evoke any kind of sentiment favourable or unfavourable, but an extraordinarily active puppet dancing to a recognisable intellectual pattern. It is not a play for those who, in the theatre, wish to feel, or imagine or be exalted;

it has, in this respect the same determined aridity as all Mr Shaw's later work; it is as fertile as a diamond. But unlike its immediate predecessors, it does perform the function of a diamond. It is not blunt and cloudy; it cuts and shines; for which reason it might well succeed in the theatre as an adornment for an actress who knows how to show it off.

Its special value at the present time is as a pointer—the first direct pointer that has lately been given us—to the processes of Mr Shaw's mind. One who did not see *The Simpleton* performed, and so has not discussed it, may remark impersonally that a single difficulty underlay all seemingly hostile criticism of it—not dislike of Mr Shaw and certainly not, as he ungenerously says, a fear that critics might lose their bread and butter if they agreed with him. There have been honest men in the trade of criticism since Mr Shaw left it; and there are still newspapers with more integrity and less personal rancour than he supposes. The difficulty seems to have been, simply, that no-one could make out what, in this play, he was driving at. Having something to say, he failed to make it understood. 'Failed?' he may answer, 'And whose fault was that? Were the parables understood?' As narrative they were. Those who heard them were at least permitted to carry away a lucid and complete story; the special instance was clear enough; over this their imagination—and it was the purpose of a parable to fluidify imagination, not to freeze it—was at liberty to move. It is the defect of Mr Shaw's parable of *The Simpleton* that by a destructive spiritual pride it is obscured in its narrative essence.

It is now revealed as a plea for the right of men of one party to 'liquidate' men of another. Mr Shaw does not wish to be considered an advocate of 'punishment or cruelty'; enough of his old humanitarianism survives in him to forbid that; but 'social responsibility' is to be inculcated at school in such a way as 'to make every citizen conscious that if his life costs more than it is worth to the community the community may painlessly extinguish it'. Hence a preface on Days of Judgment and a play exhibiting judgment in progress, which enables Mr Shaw to hurl into nothingness those of whom he disapproves. Aware that his proposition as it stands has an arbitrary air, he recognizes as its consequence a demand for codification.

The citizen will say 'I really must know what I may do and what I may not do without having my head shot off'. The reply 'You must keep a credit balance always at the national bank' is sufficiently definite if the national accountancy is trustworthy and compulsory unemployment made impossible.

In form, it is definite enough; but has it, or the play based on it, any pertinent meaning either in philosophy or in politics?

'Credit at the national bank' must mean one of two things—either a credit exclusively material and economic or a credit that includes the imponderabilia of human activity such as unremunerative art or speculative thought. If Mr Shaw's phrase has the latter meaning, the right to exterminate is not logically defensible, for no contemporary judgment, no 'national accountancy' is equipped to estimate imponderable values that have their substance in the future. If the credit he intends is material only and so, perhaps, measurable, his proposal becomes simply that a man must die who does not produce from day to day the material equivalent of what he consumes. This, in fact, appears to be his intention, for throughout this preface he lays great emphasis on the social wickedness of living 'on other people's earnings'—that is, on income from invested reserves. He himself does so, he says, to an extent which more than compensates him for the depredations of which he is the victim; but this does not lead him to approve the system.

The moral, then, is that 'the community must drive a much harder bargain for the privilege of citizenship than it does now'. This 'involves an Inquisition'—such as the Tcheka. The Inquisition will 'furnish the material for a new legal code', codification will follow, and the hard bargain be enforced thereafter by 'an ordinary court of law'. The Tcheka, in brief, which Mr Shaw believes must in the process disappear, will have perpetuated itself, and the curse or blessing of the new system will still depend upon the set of values from which the original 'hard bargain' was derived. In all the play and preface nothing has been said except that at the price of bloody tyranny, we might achieve a set of social values different from those now held. This—if we omit, as Mr Shaw omits, all inquiry into the spiritual validity of the new values—is common ground. Those who were baffled by the play are to be blamed only for their failure to perceive that their quest of constructive originality in it was a waste of time. It was the attempt of Samson to bring the house down.

In contrast with *The Simpleton*'s, the fable of *The Millionairess* is clear; and in its preface, amid all the bombast of assertion incidental to its author's style, we are permitted to watch Mr Shaw feeling his way towards new territory and to understand the nature of his present confusion. It has long been plain that he has outgrown his faith in the rigid gradualism of Fabian Socialism. He has flirted with dictators to Left and Right. By the mouth of King Magnus he has delivered a genuinely constructive criticism of the excesses of democracy. Lately he has appeared not simply as a critic of the methods of Geneva but as an advocate of the civilizing virtues of aggressive imperialism. No one knew where he stood or, indeed, in what maze he had lost himself.

At last, he has defined his *impasse*. 'The most complete Communism and Democracy can only give to Epifania her chance far more effectively than any feudal or capitalistic society'. Now, Epifania is Mr Shaw's chosen example of the money-making boss and 'the supremacy of the money-maker is the destruction of the State'. It follows that Epifania and the other bosses political and military 'who ride roughshod over us,' must be restrained, and that, since Communism and Democracy give her rein, Communism and Democracy will not do. Yet there is merit in them. 'One of their highest claims to our consideration, and the explanation of the apparently paradoxical fact that it is always the greatest spirits from Jesus to Lenin . . . who are communists and democrats' is, precisely, that they do give 'bosses' their chance. The circle is complete. The whiting has his tail in his mouth, and Mr Shaw, still encircled, is looking for a way out.

We must have bosses but must not be boss-ridden. 'Clearly we shall be boss-ridden in one form or another as long as education means being put through the process'—the process, as defined by Mr Shaw, of our existing schools and universities. 'The remedy is another Reformation in the direction and instruction of our children's minds politically and religiously'; and, lest we should sleep in our beds upon that comfortable platitude, Mr Shaw bravely adds: 'We should begin well to the left of Russia, which is still encumbered with nineteenth-century superstition'. Another suggested remedy is that we should 'develop the Vril imagined by Bulwer-Lytton which will enable one person to destroy a multitude,' and will be therefore, when available to everybody, 'an infallible preventive of any attempt at oppression.' Vril is elsewhere given as a name to the bosses' 'power of domination which others are unable to resist.' The remedy, therefore, for the excesses of Hitlerism is that we should all become Hitlers. The whiting's tail is still in its mouth.

At the end of the preface, Mr Shaw makes one last struggle to escape:—

I say cheerfully to the dominators 'By all means dominate: it is up to us to so order our institutions that you shall not oppress us nor bequeath any of your precedence to your commonplace children.

What more does this mean than death-duties and an autocracy limited by a rule of law? It might have been said more simply. But, except when he reverts for a sentence to a contrast between Communism and Creative Evolution—'only a creed of Creative Evolution can set the souls of the people free'—Mr Shaw is entangled by his attempt to apply economic remedies to spiritual evils. Not death and poverty, but the fear of death and poverty, are the curses of the world and the cause of war and oppression. The man that casts them off need not await the conversion of others; he is as invulnerable as the lilies of the field. But Mr Shaw still believes that something more than a name is shared by the communism of Lenin and the communism of Jesus, and so long as his doctrine of Creative Evolution, which is a spiritual doctrine, retains the poison of this error, his genius will be barren. The duty of man is not to his neighbour alone, whether by assassination or by service.

115. Edmund Wilson on Shaw as an artist

1938

From an article on 'Bernard Shaw at Eighty' in *Atlantic Monthly* CLXI, February 1938, 198. Reprinted in *The Triple Thinkers* (1938), 1952 edn, 158.

Edmund Wilson (1895–1972), American literary critic, examined Shaw's political career at the time of his eightieth birthday, with particular reference to his development as 'the type of the critic, who, by scolding the bourgeoisie, makes good with it and becomes one of its idols'. He found many shifts in Shaw's position on political matters and likened his various changes of character to different characters in a comedy, 'each of whom he can pick up where he has dropped him and have him go on with his part'. This led Wilson to see that the conflicts in Shaw and 'his intellectual flexibility' were well suited to the writing of comedies for the theatre. The two passages quoted are from the closing part of the essay, in which Wilson considered Shaw as an artist.

There are other references to Shaw in Wilson's works of criticism, notably an essay written in 1951, 'The Last Phase of Bernard Shaw', reprinted in *The Bit between my Teeth* (1965), 34.

One of the prime errors of recent radical criticism has been the assumption that great novels and plays must necessarily be written by people who have everything clear in their minds. People who have everything clear in their minds, who are not capable of identifying themselves imaginatively with, who do not actually embody in themselves, contrary emotions and points of view, do not write novels or plays at all—do not, at any rate, write good ones. And—given genius—the more violent the contraries, the greater the works of art.

Let us consider Shaw as an artist.

Bernard Shaw's great role in the theatre has been to exploit the full possibilities of a type of English comedy which had first been given its characteristic form during the seventies of the nineteenth century in the comedies of W. S. Gilbert. The comedy of the Restoration, which had culminated in Congreve, had been the product of an aristocratic society, which depended for its ironic effects on the contrast between artificial social conventions and natural animal instincts, between fine manners and fine intelligence, on the one hand, and the crudest carnal appetites, on the other. The comedy of the nineteenth century—setting aside Oscar Wilde—depended on the contrast between the respectable conventions of a pious middle-class society and the mean practical realities behind them, between the pretension to high moral principles and the cold complacency which underlay it. As with the dramatists of the Restoration, it was always the pursuit of pleasure that emerged from behind the formalities, so, in the comedies of Gilbert which preceded his Savoy operas and of which the most famous and successful was *Engaged* (1877), it is always the greed for money that extrudes from behind the screen of noble words and discreet behaviour. 'Dear papa,' says the Victorian young lady in one of the scenes of *Engaged*, when she has just heard of the failure of a bank in which the fortune of her fiancé was invested, 'I am very sorry to disappoint you, but unless your tom-tit is very much mistaken, the Indestructible was registered under the Joint Stock Companies Act of '62 and in that case the stockholders are jointly and severally liable to the whole extent of their available capital. Poor little Minnie don't pretend to have a business head; but she is not quite such a little donkey as that, dear papa!' The characters of Gilbert's comedies, who talk the language of Victorian fiction, are never for a moment betrayed by emotion into allowing themselves to be diverted from the main chance; and the young men are perfectly ready, not from appetite but from sheer indifference, to make equally passionate professions to any number of young ladies at the same time. It is not far from the Symperson family and Cheviot Hill of *Engaged* to Shaw's *The Philanderer* and *Widowers' Houses*.

But neither Gilbert nor Dickens nor Samuel Butler—those two other great satirists of the money-minded English, to whom, also, Shaw is indebted—could teach him to analyse society in terms of economic motivation or to understand and criticize the profit system. This he learned to do from Karl Marx, whose work during his English residence, the period when *Das Kapital* was written, was itself of course a product of and an ironical protest against English nineteenth-century civilization. Bernard Shaw thus brought something quite new into

English imaginative literature. His study of economics had served him, as he said, for his plays as the study of anatomy had served Michael Angelo. And with economic insight and training he joined literary qualities of a kind that had never yet appeared in combination with them—qualities, in fact, that, since the century before, had been absent from English literature entirely.

The Irish of Bernard Shaw's period enjoyed, in the field of literature, certain special advantages over the English, due to the fact that, since Irish society was still mainly in the pre-industrial stage, they were closer to eighteenth-century standards. If we compare Shaw, Yeats and Joyce to, say, Galsworthy, Wells and Bennett, we are struck at once by the extent to which these latter writers have suffered from their submergence in the commercial world. In their worst phases of sentimentality and philistinism, there is almost nothing to choose between them and the frankly trashy popular novelist; whereas the Irish have preserved for English literature classical qualities of hardness and elegance.

Bernard Shaw has had the further advantage of a musical education. 'Do not suppose for a moment,' he writes, 'that I learnt my art from English men of letters. True, they showed me how to handle English words; but if I had known no more than that, my works would never have crossed the Channel. My masters were the masters of a universal language; they were, to go from summit to summit, Bach, Handel, Haydn, Mozart, Beethoven and Wagner. . . . For their sakes, Germany stands consecrated as the Holy Land of the capitalistic age.' Einstein has said that Shaw's plays remind him of Mozart's music: every word has its place in the development. And if we allow for some nineteenth-century prolixity, we can see in Shaw's dramatic work a logic and grace, a formal precision, like that of the eighteenth-century composers.

Take *The Apple Cart*, for example. The fact that Shaw is here working exclusively with economic and political materials has caused its art to be insufficiently appreciated. If it had been a sentimental comedy by Molnar, the critics would have applauded its deftness; yet Shaw is a finer artist than any of the Molnars or Schnitzlers. The first act of *The Apple Cart* is an exercise in the scoring for small orchestra at which Shaw is particularly skilful. After what he has himself called the overture before the curtain of the conversation between the two secretaries, in which the music of King Magnus is foreshadowed, the urbane and intelligent King and the 'bull-roarer Boanerges' play a duet against one another. Then the King plays a single instrument against the whole nine of the cabinet. The themes emerge: the King's disinterestedness and the labour government's sordid self-interest. The development is lively: the music is tossed from one instrument to another, with, to use the old cliché, a combination of inevitableness and surprise. Finally, the King's theme gets a full and splendid statement in the long speech in which he declares his principles: 'I stand for the great abstractions: for conscience and virtue; for the eternal against the expedient; for the evolutionary appetite against the day's gluttony,' etc. This silver voice of the King lifts the movement to a poignant climax; and now a dramatic reversal carries the climax further and rounds out and balances the harmony. Unexpectedly, one of the brasses of the ministry takes up the theme of the King and repeats it more passionately and loudly: 'Just so! . . . Listen to me, sir,' bursts out the Powermistress, 'and judge whether I have not reason to feel everything you have just said to the very marrow of my bones. Here am I, the Powermistress Royal. I have to organize and administer all the motor power in the country for the good of the country. I have to harness the winds and the tides, the oils and the coal seams.' And she launches into an extraordinary tirade in which the idea of political disinterestedness is taken out of the realm of elegant abstraction in which it has hitherto remained with the King and reiterated in terms of engineering: 'every little sewing machine in the Hebrides, every dentist's drill in Shetland, every carpet sweeper in Margate,' etc. This ends on crashing chords, but immediately the music of the cabinet snarlingly reasserts itself. The act ends on the light note of the secretaries.

This music is a music of ideas—or rather, perhaps, it is a music of moralities. Bernard Shaw is a writer of the same kind as Plato. There are not many such writers in literature—the *Drames philosophiques* of Renan would supply another example—and they are likely to puzzle the critics. Shaw, like Plato, repudiates as a dangerous form of drunkenness the indulgence in literature for its own sake; but, like Plato, he then proceeds, not simply to expound a useful morality, but himself to indulge in an art in which moralities are used as the motifs. It is partly on this account, certainly, that Bernard Shaw has been underrated as an artist. Whether people admire or dislike him, whether they find his plays didactically boring or morally stimulating, they fail to take account of the fact that it is the enchantment of a highly accomplished art which has brought them to and kept them in the playhouse. It is an art that has even had the power to preserve such pieces as

Getting Married, of which the 1908 heresies already seemed out of date twenty or thirty years later but of which the symphonic development still remains brilliant and fresh. So far from being relentlessly didactic, Shaw's mind has reflected in all its complexity the intellectual life of his time; and his great achievement is to have reflected it with remarkable fidelity. He has *not* imposed a cogent system, but he has worked out a vivid picture. It is, to be sure, not a passive picture, like that of Santayana or Proust: it is a picture in which action plays a prominent part. But it does not play a consistent part; the dynamic principle in Shaw is made to animate a variety of forces.

[Reviews Shaw's writing for the theatre against the development of his political ideas and the changing background of events.]

Here it cannot be denied that Bernard Shaw begins to show signs of old age. As the pace of his mind slackens and the texture of his work grows looser, the contradictory impulses and principles which have hitherto provided him with drama begin to show gaping rifts. In his *Preface on Bosses* to *The Millionairess,* he talks about 'beginning a Reformation well to the left of Russia,' but composes the panegyric on Mussolini, with the respectful compliments to Hitler, to which I have already referred.

Yet the openings—the prologue to *The Simpleton,* with its skit on the decay of the British Empire and the knockabout domestic agonies of the first act or two of *The Millionairess*—still explode their comic situations with something of the old energy and wit; and the one-acter, *The Six of Calais,* though it does not crackle quite with the old spark, is not so very far inferior to such an earlier trifle as *How He Lied to Her Husband.* It is interesting to note—what bears out the idea that Shaw is at his best as an artist—that the last thing he is to lose, apparently, is his gift for pure comic invention, which has survived, not much dimmed, though we may tire of it, since the days of *You Never Can Tell.*

And he has also maintained his integrity as a reporter of the processes at work in his time—in regard to which his point of view has never been doctrinaire but always based on observation and feeling. He has not acted a straight role as a socialist; a lot of his writing on public affairs has been nonsense. But his plays down to the very end have been a truthful and continually developing chronicle of a soul in relation to society. Professionally as well as physically—he has just turned eighty-one as I write—he is outliving all the rest of his generation.

Nor can it be said that the confusions of his politics have invalidated his social criticism. Of his educative and stimulative influence it is not necessary today to speak. The very methods we use to check him have partly been learned in his school.

GENEVA

1938

Geneva, described by its author as 'a fancied page of history' was first presented at the Festival Theatre, Malvern, on 1 August 1938, for four performances and was first produced in London at the Saville Theatre on 22 November 1938. The run, which continued at the St James's Theatre from 27 January 1939, lasted for 237 performances.

116. Alan Dent, notice, *Spectator*

5 August 1938, vol. 161, 5745, 232

Alan (Holmes) Dent (b. 1905), English dramatic critic, edited *Bernard Shaw and Mrs Patrick Campbell: their Correspondence* (1952).

The Malvern audience only needs a little more intelligence to make it all that a festival audience ought to be. The opening play, Mr Shaw's long-awaited *Geneva*, called on that intelligence and found it lacking. Over and over again it let out indiscriminate whoops of laughter at things which Mr Shaw obviously meant for serious statements. The shrug with which this political exposition concludes is a genuinely despairing one, and the sallies which lead up to this are food only for thoughtful laughter, if laugh we must at the exposure of our plight.

The first two acts of this play were written long before the third, are far more frankly farcical, and serve as mere ante-chambers to the final court of justice. They are much less urgent and important in their matter, though full of quips and definitions that have the lighter Shavian ring. Sanctions, for example, are defined by a brace of pleasing instances: 'Take oil. Motor-oil is a sanction if you withhold it; castor-oil is a sanction if you administer it'. But the point and essence of

357

Geneva is the very long third act, in which three easily recognisable trouble-makers, two of them dictators, and the other a militant general, are arraigned for destroying the liberty of Europe. The author has allowed each to state his own case with a striking fairness, though he seems to have least tolerance of Herr Battler whom we last see whimpering about the fate of his dog when the end of the world is threatened. Signor Bombardone is made to expound sincerely the belief that war preserves courage, which he calls the noblest of man's attributes, and General Flanco supports an ingenious case for government by gentlemen as opposed to government by cads. The judge, a model of serenity who is said to be Dutch but has much of the detached logic and integrity to which the author himself has arrived, suddenly dismisses the court at the end, and with it the wrangling world it represents. Christianity, Semitism, Communism, Soviet Russia, two rather ineffectual ladies who seem respectively to stand for Camberwell and the Unexpected Isles, and England in the presence of a pig-headed aristocrat—all these have been contributing to the welter of argument, and all these are dismissed with the leaders. We are a hopeless world, and man as a political animal is a total failure. Mr Shaw, in short, is here seen and heard washing his hands of us; and he uses a good disinfectant soap and the coldest clear water in doing so.

117. Brooks Atkinson, notice,
New York Times

31 January 1940, 15

(Justin) Brooks Atkinson (b. 1894), dramatic critic and essayist, literary and dramatic critic for the *New York Times* from 1922 to 1960. In *G.B.S. and the Lunatic* (New York, 1953), Lawrence Langner (1890–1962) gave an account of his relationship with Shaw, which was largely concerned with the production of Shaw's plays by the New York Theater Guild, that Langner had founded in 1918. Langner wrote that the Theater Guild did not produce *Geneva*, even after Shaw had removed some 'anti-Semitic' speeches to which Langner had objected. He said (on p. 170) that 'it seemed to us a dull conversation piece, despite the importance of the issues which it discussed but did not dramatize. . . . The play opened in New York on January 30, 1940, and met with the complete failure which we had anticipated, although it ran for several months in London.'

Mr Shaw is not improving in his playwriting. In *Geneva*, which was acted at Henry Miller's last evening, he makes logic and wisdom about great matters very difficult to listen to. It is his fiftieth play, first produced at the Malvern Festival in 1938 in another era before war broke out. As a drama, it does not differ radically from the philosophical inquisitions he has been restlessly turning out for the past ten years. But it is even a little more static than *On the Rocks* which was well acted in New York in 1938.

An English company, led by Maurice Colbourne and Barry Jones, has brought *Geneva* here after an adventurous tour across Canada. Out of respect for one of the world's great men and out of courtesy to a visiting company from overseas, it would be pleasant to salute *Geneva* as at least a lively conversation piece. But in this theatregoer's opinion it is dull. For all his agility of mind, Mr Shaw, now 83 years of age, can make the intellect seem extraordinarily futile.

IN GOOD KING CHARLES'S GOLDEN DAYS

1939

In Good King Charles's Golden Days, subtitled 'A History Lesson in three scenes: a true History that never happened', was Shaw's last play before the Second World War. It was first presented at the Festival Theatre, Malvern, on 12 August 1939, for six performances. It was performed eight times at the Streatham Hill Theatre from 15 April 1940 and twenty-nine times at the New Theatre, London, from 9 May 1940.

---

118. James Agate, notice, *Sunday Times*

13 August 1939, 6070, 17

Almost it begins to look as though his eighty-odd years had succeeded in whipping out of Mr Shaw some at least of that offending Adam whose offendingness has been the English theatre's chiefest glory and delight throughout two—or is it three—generations. Mr Shaw has shed his Shavianism, which needs a word of explanation. Here, then goes!

A Shavianism is something which today we accept as commonplace, but which, when it was promulgated by Mr Shaw yesterday, was regarded as a piece of witless and even tasteless buffoonery. Now Mr Shaw's new play, *In Good King Charles's Golden Days*, produced this afternoon at Malvern before a crowded house, and with enormous success, contains nothing to which the most conservative playgoer could refuse assent. Wherefore Mr Shaw has desisted from Shavianism. Q.E.D. But let us go warily; old leopards are no better at changing their spots than young ones.

Let us see who it is that is uttering these witty and tasteful commonplaces. Is it Mr Shaw? Hardly. Or if it is, it is Mr Shaw predicating this and that through the mouths of Isaac Newton, the philosopher, George

360

Fox, the Quaker, Godfrey Kneller, the painter, Catherine of Bra-ganza, Charles's Queen, Nell Gwynn, his mistress, and a cloud of fair, and sometimes unfair, ladies. And, of course, Charles himself.

Now let us expand 'this' and 'that'. These limited pronouns here have unlimited greatness thrust upon them. They cover the case for Protestantism and the case for Popes; the function of Art, the function of Science and the point where the two join issue; the theory of modern Kingship and how it differs from the ancient; the principles of government, the objections of the English to be governed, and how badly they compare with Catherine's docile, not to say sheep-like Portuguese.

'Is this all?' asks the reader. Well, it is what the little word 'this' covers. 'That' is more personal, having to do with the individuals seated on, pushed off and hanging around the throne of England during fifty troubled years; with Charles himself; with Titus Oates and the advisability of tieing him to the cart tail and whipping him —actually this was done and the burly brute survived; with unpopular James; with Charles's royal helpmate, Catherine; with French Louis and that fascinating go-between, the Duchess of Portsmouth; with the erstwhile fair, the seldom chaste and now wholly inexpressible nuisance, the Duchess of Cleveland. 'Any more?' asks the reader. The reader is greedy.

Was it easier to tie Oates to the cart tail than to tie up the foregoing with the Shavianism we pronounced Mr Shaw to have discarded? Not much easier. All that is said in this play is the essence of Mr Shaw and therefore of Shavianism, only thrown back in time. Are Charles and Isaac and Godfrey, all being wise and witty men, wise and witty enough to realise that the curves of Hogarth and Einstein, whom they oddly foresee, are the same curve viewed from another angle, art and science being two facets of the jewel which is consciousness? The answer is Yes, they are wise and witty enough, because they are good Shavians born two hundred and fifty years before their time.

Is this a good play? The answer depends neither on Mr Shaw nor on his actors. It depends entirely on the playgoer. If you find the perihelion of Mercury more interesting than the perimeter of Lady Castlemaine. Yes. If not. No. For the ladies are but ornaments; this play's business is the affair of the men. Is it long? Yes. Too long? No. Should it be cut? Not by so much as the teeniest, weeniest preposition used to end a sentence with. Is there any action? No. Will anybody miss the lack of action? Yes, the witless and the idle.

Is the play worth preserving? It will preserve itself, if only because of that magnificent passage in which Mr Shaw, using Kneller as his mouthpiece, praises the Creator in that He has seen fit nowhere to repeat Himself; since there are no two things—suns, moons, fishes, birds, beasts, flowers, landscapes, consciences—alike and not to be differentiated in the entire created universe.

Mr Shaw can always be relied on for one purple passage. This play has at least six, two in each act. And the body and bulk of it is the best warp and woof that has come from the Shavian loom since *Methuselah*. That the resulting web is not audaciously new need not distress us. Mr Shaw has had his whack at the 'Splendide audax'[1] business. If he is now thinking of taking in sail—and that would be understandable —what better way than by re-affirming all he has taught about art, science, politics, religion, kings, queens, men and women?

This play embodies the re-affirmations of a great man, of one who, in our theatre, has been and will remain a giant. And that should be considered handsome, for I am not, by nature, a Shavian.

[1] Splendidly audacious.

119. Salvador de Madariaga on the paradox of Shaw

1940

From a signed article, *Listener*, 29 February 1940, vol. XXIII, 581, 411.

Salvador de Madariaga (b. 1886), Spanish statesman and scholar, considered Shaw as an Irishman by race and Englishman by choice. At the beginning of the article, which was entitled 'G B S: Domestic Mephistopheles', de Madariaga looked at Shaw's racial origins and his allegiance to his chosen country. At the end he referred to England's ability to 'afford the luxury, in the middle of a war, of keeping a domesticated Mephistopheles to stop her from losing, even in her hour of danger, that most British of all virtues —a sense of humour.'

Success soon made Shaw one of the most prominent men of English public life; and I say English, because this Irishman by race is an Englishman by nationality or by choice, since he lives in England and has identified himself with her. It would be difficult to judge the influence which in the long run the leaven of his ideas has had on the evolution of contemporary English society, and in particular, on the evolution out of the Victorian era. By her very nature Conservative England always drags about a dead weight of mental, moral and social forms, even when those forms have lost all meaning with the lapse of time. This Victorian dead weight might well have been a serious obstacle to the country in adapting itself to the more rapid rhythm of the twentieth century. Shaw was one of the men who most successfully served England in liberating her from the dead weight of a past which had become useless, although it does not follow that the idea of producing this effect with his works entered consciously into his way of thinking either as an artist or as a writer.

This service was typically Shavian in its negative and destructive character, because the genius of Bernard Shaw is Mephistophelian, that is to say, not only negative, but negation itself. Set down by fate in the heart of a people with a sign opposite to his, Shaw quickly adopted an attitude of antagonism which soon became a permanent feature distorting his mind for good and all. This attitude of contradiction, so much in harmony with his innate tendency to indulge in paradox, leads him to stereotype dialectic inversion as a method not only of expression, but even of thought. And so, for some time now, the opinion of Bernard Shaw has been in effect, invariably, the opposite of the balance of opinion in the country.

In a free country, where public opinion is the result of a bombardment of contradictions, opposition, far from being harmful, is both salutary and natural, provided that it is always objective, that it always sticks to the facts and to the circumstances, and so preserves its vitality. Now the opposition of Shaw does not always conform with this condition. With excessive and growing frequency, Bernard Shaw passes from opposition to contradiction and from contradiction to a merely formal and topical inversion. And so, as his attitude becomes more mechanical, more automatically opposed to the general trend of opinion, it loses its stimulating force and comes to be dismissed as a feature, picturesque and amusing, but without much weight in the thought of the nation. The average Englishman has finally come to think that he is always sure of finding in Bernard Shaw his own thought . . . turned upside down. Bernard Shaw has ceased to be unexpected, unpredictable, incalculable. Bernard Shaw is now the same as the average Englishman, only just the reverse. Nothing is so like plus one as minus one.

Further, it is clear that in order to play these tricks with them, ideas must be lightened as much as possible, till their bare bones are stripped of the flesh of experience which gives them their weight and, incidentally, their value. This also fits in with Bernard Shaw's natural tendency to play with air and fire, forgetting earth and water, and to enjoy thought for thought's sake. Now to the average Englishman, ideas for the sake of ideas are pure self-indulgence; mental pleasure without any justification in concrete facts is as sinful for him as carnal pleasures unjustified by procreation are to the Church. Here also Bernard Shaw withdraws himself from his surroundings in abstract intellectual exercises which the empirical Englishman regards as merely arbitrary. . . .

The fact is that, for all his genius, Bernard Shaw is not a self-radiating luminary emitting light from a centre constant and consistent with itself; he is rather a pole of negative electricity set in a people of positive electricity, so that the sparks which come from him are not of his own light, but the result of the mutual reaction between him and his surroundings; flashed off on the spur of instant situations and passing tensions and, therefore, without any sense of continuity. Bernard Shaw offers no consistent philosophy, but a series of lightning flashes of opposition to the north, to the south, to the east or to the west, according to whichever side of him happens to feel the approach of the metal of Britain.

120. Harold Hobson on Shaw's wit

1940

From a signed article in *English Wits*, edited by Leonard Russell (1940), 281.

Harold Hobson (b. 1904), dramatic critic of the *Sunday Times* from 1944 to the present day. After somewhat sweeping observations on various aspects of Shaw, the article concluded with a statement of the 'two cardinal features of Shaw's wit'.

The disturbance of complacency is one of the two cardinal features of Shaw's wit. Loose, conventional, lazy thinking upon any subject was abhorrent to him, so that it is not merely aristocratic or bourgeois institutions which come within the scope of his criticism. Trade Unions equally with the training of a gentleman are objects of his satire. Boanerges, the working man Cabinet Minister of *The Apple Cart*, asserts confidently that the workers will never throw him over.

[Quotes speech by Boanerges from Act I of *The Apple Cart*: from 'No king on earth' to 'the right men in the right place'.]

The second cardinal feature of Shaw's wit is its good-nature. It has been agreed down the ages that ill-will is a fundamental part of wit.

In the midst of the fountain of wit, says Lucretius, something bitter arises, which poisons every flower. This ill-nature is entirely absent from Shaw. The very exuberance of his condemnation, as in the instances of Shakespeare and the Fabian lecturer, is only the overflow of extravagant high spirits. He satirises marriage; but he does not hate it, like Strindberg. He ridicules theories of medicine in *The Doctor's Dilemma*; but he does not hate them, as Chesterton, for example, hated them in the figure of Dr. Warner in *Manalive*. He finds men and women and their associations and activities absurd and foolish and inefficient, but he neither despises them nor would rejoice in their final failure. He makes wit as good-humoured as humour.

121. H. G. Wells, letter to Shaw

1941

Letter, dated 16 April 1941, reprinted in *G.B.S. 90* (1946), 55.

The performance of *Major Barbara* was of the film version, produced by Gabriel Pascal in 1940 and first shown in 1941.

My dear G.B.S.,

I was going to write to you to-day—our minds move in sympathy. I saw *Major Barbara* on Monday and I found it delightful. You have given it fresh definition. Andrew Undershaft might have been better cast with a more subtle face. As it is he seems to be astonished at himself throughout. The house was packed. Moura and I got the last two seats and you could not have had a more responsive audience. They laughed at all the right places. Mostly young people in uniform they were. That old Fabian audience is scattered for evermore. I firmly believe that we are getting the young. We shall rise again sooner than Marx did and for a better reason.

Pavlov was invincibly like you. You will probably be confused by posterity. He talked almost as well. But he wrote damnable prose. I was never educated by any sort of schooling. I left school at thirteen. Afterwards I did biological work at the Royal College of Science, but the nearest I came to 'Materialistic Mechanistic Science' was a half-year in the Physics course at Kensington. It bored me so much that I learnt Latin and German and matriculated while it was going on. It is a pity you never had a sound dose of biology. Still, you do pretty well as you are.

This getting old is tiresome. I don't feel old in my wits but my heart seems to falter and I have phases of brain anaemia when I forget names and all that small print stuff. I've written a *Guide to the New World Order* and I am writing a novel. So get on with your play.

Whatever happens now we have had a pretty good time.

Yours as ever,
H.G.

122. J. B. Priestley on Shaw and 'playgoers of our grim time'

1946

Extract from a signed article, 'G.B.S.—Social Critic' in *G.B.S. 90* (1946), 50.

John Boynton Priestley (b. 1894), novelist, dramatist, essayist, identified two main ideas in Shaw's social criticism. The first was 'that theory and practice must correspond' and the second was 'the conception of the community as a living whole'. The passage quoted is the closing paragraph of the essay. Other references to Shaw are to be found frequently in Priestley's writings. In 1956, he wrote an essay, 'Thoughts on Shaw' for the Shaw centenary issue of the *New Statesman* (28 July 1956, vol. LII, 1324, 96: reprinted in *Thoughts in the Wilderness* (1957), 181) and there are some pages of criticism in *Literature and Western Man* (1960), 277. Priestley found Shaw in some ways intellectually dishonest but neither this nor the 'lack of any deeply personal emotional commitment to many of his ideas' prevented him from creating comedy, the best of which was 'clear of sourness, ill-temper, hysterical injustice'.

Already some of his early plays have lost their challenge as social criticism, or at least as topical social criticism, and are now enjoyed as pieces of excellent stage-craft in the all-too-rare comedy of intellectual high spirits. I wish he could see these delighted audiences (who arrive at the playhouse tired and worried and hungry, not like the well-fed easy-going folk for whom he wrote originally) and could hear their shouts of laughter, for that would be the best birthday present of all. These playgoers of our grim time who enjoy his wit, his stage-craft, his philosophy, may still be unfamiliar with nine-tenths of what he has meant them to understand; but nevertheless I think that most of them have already absorbed or have even been conditioned by a good deal of his social criticism. They bring it with them to the playhouse, like another and much vaster programme. Much of what now seems to them common sense was once considered merely a part of Shaw's 'paradoxical clowning'. (And the critics who denounced him for it now seem quaint period figures.) Some of the air we breathe now has G.B.S. in it, a little mountain oxygen that has somehow penetrated the fog. And where this mountain air comes from there is nothing small, nothing mean, nothing vindictive and cruel; it knows the sun of wit and wisdom and great cleansing winds of doctrine.

123. Val Gielgud on Shaw and the radio

1946

From a signed article, 'Bernard Shaw and the radio' in G.B.S. 90 (1946), 171.

Val Gielgud (b. 1900), writer and broadcaster, brother of Sir John Gielgud, was Head of Radio Drama and Director of Sound Broadcasting at the British Broadcasting Corporation for thirty-five years. In the article from which this passage is taken, he considered Shaw both as an author of plays for sound broadcasting and as a speaker on the radio.

It is impossible to imagine that, had the flowering of Mr Bernard Shaw as a playwright coincided with the achievement of maturity of broadcasting, Mr Shaw would not have been radio playwright number one and *par excellence*. Of all modern playwrights Mr Shaw has shown himself least inclined to be trammelled by conventions purely theatrical or by the cramping 'unities' of the stage. Of all modern playwrights Mr Shaw has proved himself a master of words, of dialogue, and of the stage-play as a medium for the verbal expression of opinions and points of view. He has confessed that he has made use of dramatic form for the 'putting-over' of opinions which the average man or woman will not bother to read in books. He has, I think, implied that he is more interested in conveying his opinions to mankind, and in converting numbers of mankind to these opinions, than in what is commonly called 'commercial success'. In plays specially written for broadcasting, Mr Shaw would have found an unrivalled medium for the handling of language to give dramatic expression of points of view; for the achieving of the largest audiences possible for such plays. Unfortunately, when Radio was born, Mr Shaw's allegiance had already been given. Not that he proved unwilling that his plays should be broadcast. But he has been adamant on the point that they should be broadcast precisely as they were written for the stage.

There has been a curious contrast in this connection between the attitudes of Mr Shaw and Mr Somerset Maugham. The latter, while expressing a certain mild surprise that anybody should feel inclined to transfer to one medium what has originally been conceived in terms of another, has never shown the least objection to the adaptation of his work to the exigencies of broadcast presentation. Mr Shaw has repeated with unwearying consistency that what he has written he has written; that every word must be broadcast—or the play left to the theatre for which it was designed. It hardly needs pointing out to people at all familiar with the difficulties of broadcast programmes planning that this has raised a barrier in many cases insuperable to presentation of Mr Shaw's plays at the microphone. The problem of the quart and the pint pot is commonplace at Broadcasting House. It is exemplified most vividly in the problem of fitting almost any full-length play of Bernard Shaw's within the confines of an evening's broadcasting, particularly when that programme is already, to some extent, 'in irons', owing to such immutably fixed points as the Nine o'clock News and Parliamentary Report.

On the other hand, again unlike Mr Somerset Maugham, who having given permission for his works to be translated takes no apparent interest in the result, Mr Shaw has given typically striking evidence of being by no means the least attentive listener, whenever his plays have been broadcast. One of his famous postcards invited the producer responsible for an early broadcast of *Captain Brassbound's Conversion*, towards the end of 1929, to borrow a revolver and use it upon himself! I received—and value highly—letters of most pertinent criticism and comment upon productions respectively of *Saint Joan* and *The Million-aires*. Indeed, in writing of *Saint Joan*, in which Miss Constance

Cummings gave what I thought to be a notably brilliant performance —one which, incidentally, made history from the broadcasting point of view as it was given without a script—Mr Shaw showed for the first time a tendency to withdraw from his absolute standpoint. He admitted that certain references, such as those to the Visions in the last act, could have been cut as being aurally ineffective, and that certain other emendations—which he specified—in the text would have been desirable. It is one of my most cherished hopes that, when the time comes for the B.B.C.'s third programme to swing into active operation, giving programme time unlimited by fixed points, a series of Mr Shaw's plays will be prominent amongst the programme's activities. If that hope should be realized I hope it may also be possible to persuade Mr Shaw to make emendations and cuts along the lines which he suggested with regard to the *Saint Joan* performance. Dramatic broadcasting, no less than the cinema, could not fail to profit immensely from the active co-operation 'on the floor' of the most remarkable and vital literary figure of our age.

124. Dean Inge on Shaw's contradictions

1946

From a signed article entitled 'Bernard Shaw: Socialist or Rebel?' in *Listener*, 10 October 1946, vol. XXXVI, 916, 471, originally a talk broadcast on the BBC Third Programme.

William Ralph Inge (1860–1954), Dean of St Paul's Cathedral, London, writer and controversialist, a close friend of Shaw's, considered the contradictions in Shaw's thought as shown in his plays and other writings. He found Shaw's 'lay Christianity' as expressed in the notion of the Life Force 'of good omen for the future'. Dean Inge contributed an article on 'Shaw as a Theologian' to *G.B.S. 90* (1946), 110.

He has paid the English the great compliment of knowing that we are willing to laugh at ourselves. This is an English, not an Irish, virtue. An Irish friend of mine was unwise enough to make fun of his fellow-countrymen. He no longer lives in Ireland. But in England satire, with a pretended lightness of tone, has long been a favourite weapon. Butler in *Hudibras* says subversive things comically; *Gulliver*, which we treat as a book for children, is a savage and morose attack upon human nature. Shaw's favourite, the modern Samuel Butler, cuts very deep in his account of the manners and customs of *Erewhon*. We are not a witty people like the French, but we have a sense of humour, which means that, though life may be a tragedy for those who feel, it has a large element of comedy for those who think, and that legitimate differences of opinion should be accepted with toleration and not with hatred. . . .

There is one other possible development of Shaw's thought which interests me. He does not call himself a Christian, because he thinks that the Christians, that is to say the Churches, have never tried Christianity. He says somewhere that the Holy Ghost is the only survivor of the Christian Trinity, which means that for him mysticism which the Quakers call 'the inner light' and others call 'personal religion' is

372

the religion of the future. It includes, he says, faith, hope and love; and is not this essential Christianity? I have noticed a strong movement in this direction among independent thinkers, such as H. G. Wells, Aldous Huxley, whose new book, *The Perennial Philosophy*, I strongly recommend, Walter Lippmann, Laurence Housman and Joad. It is a welcome reaction against the materialistic view of reality which seemed to be imposed upon us by nineteenth-century science.

Shaw disliked Darwinism because he thought it denied all purpose in the world; Lamarck, he thought, made room for it. I do not agree that Darwin's evolution excludes purpose; events, perhaps, cannot be causes, but there may be purpose behind them; what no science can tolerate is the theory of occasional intervention.

This lay Christianity is, I think, of good omen for the future. I would only ask its advocates to remember two things. First, that the identification of the indwelling Spirit of God with the historical Jesus of Nazareth—'the Lord is the Spirit', as St Paul says—was already made in the lifetime of many who could remember the Galilean ministry; and second, that the natural language of faith is unconscious symbolism, which to those who do not need its traditional forms has the appearance of uncritical acceptance of myth. We can, none of us, do without symbols, as Plato knew, and St Paul tells us in his famous hymn to Love. 'Miracle', says Goethe, 'is faith's dearest child; the child not the parent, but a child still beloved by many good people'.

Shaw's 'Life Force' in *Man and Superman*, after working unconsciously, and moving men and women about like puppets, wishes to know what he, or it, is doing. Well, for the Christian, 'God moves in a mysterious way, His wonders to perform'. But we think that the Life Force is more intelligent and beneficent than the Spirit Sinister of Hardy's *Dynasts*; things do not happen anyhow.

BUOYANT BILLIONS

1948

Buoyant Billions, Shaw's last full-length play, was first presented at the Schauspielhaus, Zürich, on 21 October 1948. The title in German was *Zu viel Geld* (Too Much Money). It was presented at the Festival Theatre, Malvern, on 13 August 1949, for six performances and first presented in London, at the Prince's Theatre, on 10 October 1949, when it ran for forty performances.

125. Jakob Welti in an unsigned notice in *Zürcher Zeitung*

22 October 1948, 5

Jakob Welti (1893–1964).

It is clear from this notice that the first production of a play by Shaw was a very important event in the theatre of a Continental country, possibly more so than in England.

For the third time, Bernard Shaw has allowed Zürich to give the world premiere of one of his plays. In 1926, it was the one act play about Kaiser Wilhelm II, *The Inca of Perusalem*, and in 1934 it was what the author called 'a comediettina for two voices', *Village Wooing*. Number three is called *Too much Money* and is divided into four conversations or acts. In the preface Shaw calls the comedy 'trivial', while in the subtitle of the German version of the play by Siegfried Trebitsch that has already been published, there is the description, 'A Comedy of No Manners'. As a ninety-two year old, so worthy of respect and admiration as Shaw, should never be contradicted—it is well known that he is

374

always right—one should guard against disputing his own opinions of his new play. When compared with the whole rich corpus of his dramatic work, *Too much Money* seems to weigh neither less nor more than many other plays he has written in the last two decades.

Essentially we are presented with a repetition, admittedly in a somewhat milder tone than in the past, of well-known themes of the Irish Methuselah, to whom debating and writing are the elixir of life. The preliminary, long-drawn out encounter between father and son illuminates the situation of civilised humanity today, from the standpoint of the two generations, in which GBS, of course, brings up the atombomb. For the old capitalist, who opens the debate, it is an invention of the devil; for the son it is a possibility of improving the world, blessed by God. He wants to go—with his father's money, for he neither has nor earns any of his own—on a journey to the tropics to discover how the atom-bomb may be used to exterminate mosquitoes, tse-tse flies and migratory locusts. In Panama, however, he meets another rich man's daughter who has withdrawn from civilisation; something happens that cannot be prevented; the two fall in love. They return to England where their situation is discussed frankly and with Shavian thoroughness at a family council and finally brought to a mutually satisfactory solution.

Reason in love and marriage is what Shaw preaches. In addition he looks, from the point of view of the rationalist, at the new situation of those people who formerly belonged to the possessing class. How the descendants of the rich Mr Buoyant-Upontop—*Buoyant Billions* is the original title of the play—are to come to terms with the fact that, after the death of their father and provider, the state will leave them next to nothing of his great fortune, is exhaustively discussed in a Chinese temple room fragrant with incense, which serves the old money-maker Buoyant as a place of repose and meditation. There are more excursions into exotic fields and not simply in externals. Shaw reminds us once again of the mature wisdom of ancient Asia. A Chinese priest and his assistant provide the religio-philosophic content in this Anglo-Irish comedy of love, marriage, money and politics. 'The future belongs to those who learn' is Shaw's conclusion this time.

Berthold Viertel, one of the old guard of the great ones of the Berlin theatre, is the guest-producer. For his debut, one might have wished him a more thankful task than the presentation of this play, so full of speeches, in which the words are so much more witty than the action. An introductory mark of respect to Shaw was well devised; passages from the preface to the play were spoken before a large projected picture of the white-bearded master. In the play itself, for which Tec Otto has created a picturesque jungle hut together with a snapping crocodile straight out of a Punch and Judy show as well as a light, decorative temple setting, Viertel emphasises the light-hearted, English-parody note rather less than was the practice in earlier presentations of Shaw's comedies. A great deal is rather drawn out and perhaps even treated too heavily. This is perhaps also due to the actors. Not all of them show polish and desirable precision in the dialogue. Maria Becker on her return gives the weight of a real personality to the millionaire's daughter whom the elderly Shaw has endowed with a surprising tenderness and the magic bloom of love. Will Quadflieg is her equally lovable, clever and constant admirer. In the family reunion, conversation is carried on, to the great delight of the audience, by the other sprigs of the Buoyant family, very different in nature, and their spouses, characteristically presented by Mesdames Giehse, Arndts and Vita and Messrs Schürenberg, Parker and Witzig, with Wilfried Seyferth, the dignified solicitor who adapts himself gradually to this foolish, open-hearted company. Whereas at the beginning of the play, Hermann Wlach as the conservative capitalist, has the ear of the audience, in the Buoyant family circle Erwin Kalser is the pleasantly smiling, old and wise object of everyone's respect, with the nickname, 'E.P.', standing for 'Earthly Provider'. Messrs Richter and Beneckendorff embody the exotic element with tact and taste. The applause which after the first two acts was moderate only, grew considerably in the rest of the play and was very loud at the end.

126. Unsigned notice, *The Times*

15 August 1949, 51460, 7

Mr. Shaw making his bow as a nonagenarian dramatist, exhibits all the old intellectual gaiety—the quality by virtue of which the Shavian scourging of a muddle-headed, sentimental, pleasure-seeking society became fashionable entertainment. It has outlasted the power to produce fresh ideas for social and moral reform. Mr. Shaw says nothing now that he has not said before, and said more memorably, but the familiar admonitions, comic paradoxes, calculated impertinences, verbal incongruities, and oddly characteristic simplicities float buoyantly on sparkling stretches of talk. This 'comedy of no manners,' if you will, is a superfluous postscript to Shavian drama; yet there can be no sort of doubt that it is the most entertaining of the festival's new plays.

If there is a general conclusion to be drawn from the discursive discussions it is that the profession of 'world betterers' has become overcrowded. There are too many hot-headed sentimentalists believing that in their hands absolute power would not corrupt absolutely, too few 'learners' with the will and the capacity to study how they may adapt themselves to the ever-changing demands of life. The future is for learners; in them is mankind's only hope. Mr. Shaw makes the point lightly, almost casually. If he insisted on it overmuch he might find himself speaking again through the lips of the native survivor of judgment day on the Unexpected Isles: 'I, Prola, shall live and grow because surprise and wonder are the very breath of my being and routine is death to me.' In those isles of 1935 more importance was attached to the faculties of surprise and wonder than to the intellectual virtues of the omniscient Ancients of the Metabiological Pentateuch; and Mr. Shaw is seemingly of the same opinion still.

He launches Junius (who as the seventh son of a seventh son should have second sight) on a career of world bettering which is shattered by the Life Force almost before it has begun. A woman who has built herself a hut in a jungle clearing and can charm snakes and alligators by playing the 'Londonderry Air' on a saxophone knocks his professional ideas endways simply by being biologically irresistible to him. He pursues her to Belgrave Square. She is the daughter of old Bill Buoyant, a man of one all-sufficing talent. He is an infallible judge of what stocks and shares will rise and which will fall. The lovers arrive in time to take part in a brilliantly amusing discussion of this, that, and everything else which could conceivably arise from the problem of how an utterly dependent family are to fend for themselves when death and its duties dry up the source of their father's fabulous wealth. Bill Buoyant decides that a candid fortune hunter is as likely to make a good husband as any other, and his favourite daughter perforce agrees with him. She is at the mercy of the Life Force and she can no other, though she remains acutely conscious of the irrationality of her uncontrollable impulses.

For good Shavians the most rewarding passage of the comedy is perhaps that in which a native of the jungle discusses eternal values in the language of an enlightened Victorian bishop, so reducing the status of the 'pink man' to that of a superstitious savage. Mr Kenneth Mackintosh is the suavely patronising native. Another excellent passage is that in which Mr Denholm Elliott expounds with sudden passion the faith of the world betterer. And then Miss Frances Day is allowed three or four surprising sentences which reveal that somewhere in the odd Shavian female she plays so amusingly there is the heart of a woman in love. Mr Shaw seems a little ashamed of the human feeling which has momentarily got loose, and he is careful to balance things with an eloquent tribute to mathematics, the giver of ecstasy surpassing all all other ecstasies. The discussion is admirably staged by Mr Esme Percy and voiced with tact, measure, and point by the company.

127. H. N. Brailsford on Shaw and Shelley

1949

From a reprint of a broadcast talk, *Listener*, 21 April 1949, vol. XLI, 1056, 663.

Henry Noel Brailsford (1873–1958), journalist and political writer, in a review of Shaw's autobiographical *Sixteen Self-Sketches* (1949). The greater part of the article was a consideration of Shaw's life, character and personality.

And now if anyone doubts that the real Shaw, under all the posing, is a deeply modest man, let me quote what he tells us of Sidney Webb. He describes him as 'the ablest man in England', and goes on to confess that when G.B.S. seemed most original, he was simply 'an amanuensis and a mouthpiece' for Webb and his Fabian colleagues. This is, I am sure, a generous exaggeration. Certainly Webb was a very able man, and he had what Shaw lacked at this time, a minute knowledge of social and economic history and an intimate acquaintance with the technique of government, acquired as a Civil Servant. It is true that Shaw's literary brilliance and dramatic instinct would have been much less effective than they were without Webb as his prompter and coach. But with all his industry, his shrewdness and his disinterested devotion, Sidney Webb's was not an original mind, and Shaw's mental horizon was by far the wider. Webb's guiding idea that government must be raised to the level of a science was derived from Herbert Spencer. His political judgment was sadly at fault and many a year was wasted by the illusion with which he infected Shaw, that socialism could be won by permeating the Liberal Party and pulling wires behind the scenes.

Shaw tells us in these sketches with delightful humour how he trained himself as a public speaker, and there are some entertaining pages about the ten years he devoted to weekly journalism. In these ways, as also in his interpretation of Ibsen and in his own early plays with a moral, he served his day and generation. As a politician, he tells us, he was always helping a lame dog over a stile which he believed to be insurmountable. But the Shaw who will fascinate posterity was concerned with something more fundamental. It is in *Man and Superman*, above all in the entrancing Dialogue in Hell, and again in *Back to Methuselah* that he stated his ultimate philosophy. How did he reach it? He tells us how he reacted against the neo-Darwinians. He acknowledges his debt, first to Lamarck and then to Samuel Butler, for his doctrine of creative evolution. Bergson contributed something to his mythology of the Life Force, which proceeds by trial and error in its age-long drive to attain self-understanding. But my guess is that the starting-point of this train of thought lay in Shelley. Shaw tells us that he read the whole of Shelley, verse and prose, at the end of his teens, and that it was Shelley who made him a socialist and a vegetarian. I can hear echoes of Shelley and his teacher Godwin on some of the most moving pages of Shaw—in his horror at the cruelty of imprisonment, and above all in his belief in the fundamental equality of all living things. Shaw's perpetual insistence that 'equality is essential to good breeding', that we must evolve a democracy of supermen, was not a typical Fabian attitude; it was his own faith and Shelley's. The idea on which all the inspiring mythology of his Methuselah legend is based, that we can create ourselves by willing—that also was one of Shelley's beliefs, which he drew from Godwin's doctrine of perfectibility. Even Shaw's Ancients, who had got rid of sleep, were anticipated in that enthusiastic vision. Shaw's glory is that after the neo-Darwinists, he brought back mind to the universe and with it, to use his own words, 'justice, mercy and humanity'. With all his daring and originality, he belongs to the true Catholic Church of the humanist tradition. His last word is to be found in Lilith's speech at the end of *Back to Methuselah*. The greatest gift of the Eternal Mother was curiosity and her message to mankind was this: Let them dread of all things stagnation. That is Shaw's way of saying what was Goethe's last word to his generation:

> Wer immer strebend sich bemüht
> Den können wir erlösen

Salvation comes to him who never ceases to strive.[1]

---

[1] The last line of the article is a translation of the German.

128. Terence Rattigan on Shaw and the play of ideas

1950

From a signed article, 'Concerning the Play of Ideas', *New Statesman and Nation*, 4 March 1950, vol. XXXIX, 991, 241.

(Sir) Terence Mervyn Rattigan (b. 1911), English dramatist, considered the effect on the contemporary theatre of Shaw's theories and practice. Following the opening paragraphs quoted below, he went on to examine what he thought the consequences of 'the Shavian-Ibsenite victory', that his brother playwrights and himself were daily 'exhorted to adopt themes of urgent topicality, and not a voice is raised in our defence if we refuse'. The article was the first of a series and in subsequent contributions, Shaw was defended by James Bridie (11 March 1950, 270), Benn W. Levy (25 March 1950, 338) and Sean O'Casey (8 April 1950, 397). According to Kingsley Martin (in *Shaw and Society*, edited by C. E. M. Joad, 1951, 37), Shaw 'had written to say that when the other dramatists had done their worst he would come in if necessary and "wipe the floor with the lot of them" '. Shaw's reply appeared on 6 May 1950 (*New Statesman and Nation*, vol. XXXIX, 1000, 510: reprinted in *Shaw on Theatre*, edited by E. J. West, 1958, 289). He referred to Rattigan's contention that his plays were 'not plays at all, but platform speeches, pamphlets and leading articles. This is an old story!' He defended his plays against the old charge that they were 'all talk' and asserted that talk had to have ideas behind it because 'without a stock of ideas, mind cannot operate and plays cannot exist. The quality of a play is the quality of its ideas.'

I believe that the best plays are about people and not about things. I am in fact a heretic from the now widely held faith that a play which concerns itself with, say, the artificial insemination of human beings or the National Health Service is of necessity worthier of critical esteem than a play about, say, a mother's relations with her son or about a husband's jealousy of his wife.

I further believe that the intellectual *avant-garde* of the English theatre—or, rather, let's be both brave and accurate, and say of the English-speaking theatre, since in my view, the Americans are the worst offenders—are, in their insistence on the superiority of the play of ideas over the play of character and situation, not only misguided but old-fashioned.

It was in 1895 that Shaw began his battle in the *Saturday Review* on behalf of the 'New' theatre, the Ibsenite theatre, the 'theatre as a factory of thought, a prompter of conscience and an elucidator of social conduct'. In what single respect have the present-day proponents of 'sociologically significant' drama advanced one step beyond the standpoint taken up in 1895 by a man whose only aim, as he himself admits, was, by his vituperation of the existing theatre, to 'cut his own way into it at the point of his pen'?

That he succeeded brilliantly in that ambition, and that he is still a vital and, happily, living force in our theatre should not blind us to the fact that fifty years of completely stagnant thought and theory concerning the drama is a depressing concept, if not to the *avant-garde*, at least to me. For the history of artistic endeavour is surely the history of change, and our painters are not still urged to paint like Burne-Jones, nor our poets to compose like Swinburne. Why then should our dramatists still be encouraged to write like late Ibsen or early Shaw?

Let us examine Shaw's campaign of the 'nineties and see where it has led the modern theatre.

Nowhere at all, is my belief.

OBITUARY NOTICES AND TRIBUTES

Shaw died on 2 November 1950

---

129. Unsigned leading article, *The Times*

3 November 1950, 51839, 5

Bernard Shaw became, and at the end of a life prolonged far beyond the common span he remains, the most famous of twentieth-century writers. He was a polemical writer by choice, an artist by inner necessity. In speech, pamphlet, or play he has treated almost every public theme of the past sixty years, and his gay and trenchant opposition to whatever was contrary to the dictates of Shavian reason leaves the world with what has been described as a 'chaos of clear opinions.' Many attemps have been made to disengage from that chaos the positive and lasting content of his contribution to the age, but there is still excess of offered light. All that his contemporaries can do, while recognizing that his thought is inextricably entangled with their own, is to hazard the belief that in the long run his genius will be judged not as that of a preacher with a mission to revolutionize the values of society but as that of an artist whose truly creative work appears in his plays.

The influence of SHAW outside the theatre has been strikingly incommensurate with his enormous fame. As the dominating voice of the anti-Victorian reaction he, himself a Victorian, found eager acceptance for his attacks on unworkable, obsolete and cramping ideals. In this strenuous and brilliantly effective phase he taught the art of civilized 'de-bunking.' His way of examining accepted ideas without reverence, but with complete candour and a scrupulous regard for what was inherently sound in them, made many easy-going people realize that whatever they believed they must defend by hard, realistic argument or they would be sapped, mined and blown up. From him the young and receptive learned that truth was many-sided and no dogma sacrosanct. In the early years of the century SHAW could justly claim that he was colouring the mind of a whole generation.

Later he sought no less strenuously, with dialectic no less brilliant, to communicate his own passion for social justice and to insist that every man is morally responsible for his own deeds, which are irrevocable, and that his life depends on his usefulness. This somewhat self-consciously unsentimental idealism made few converts. The ship's navigators were entertained rather than enlightened by SHAW's lectures on navigation, and the world continued to drift in spite of his dogmatic iteration. Meanwhile the artist in SHAW, driven like every other artist by the need for self-expression, was contriving, in defiance of critical orthodoxy, a new type of comedy for the enrichment of English drama.

The originality of this comedy is shown not only by its wholly characteristic triumphs but also by the exactness with which it conforms to its creator's natural limitations. SHAW, though his nature was intensely histrionic and his platform manner remarkable for ease, was never a man of the world. He was a man of ideas, at home only in the realm of the intellect and inhabiting a mansion in that part of it where it is difficult to observe life as a whole, but comparatively easy to draw deductions from it. To call attention to his deductions he invented for the world's stage the outrageous 'G.B.S.,' so vital a gladiatorial figure that it was suffered to outlive its *raison d'être* by many years, and part of the pleasantness of first meeting SHAW lay in the discovery that he was not 'G.B.S.' Ideas did SHAW's bidding with so rare a felicity because there was no idea that he could not express with vigour, lucidity, wit, and charm. He was too much in earnest to be a mere virtuoso, and even in his Fabian days he used this power less to advance a particular orthodoxy than to weave together strands drawn from diverse political philosophers. This habit of thought—the artist's habit—was innate, and the orthodox of all parties and creeds have had occasion to regard him as something of a Trojan horse in their camps.

As a man of ideas SHAW had the defect of his quality. He was inclined to ignore or to underrate the instinctive side of human nature and to leave out of account all the inexplicable things that are as much part of our true selves as the things we can explain. The strongest impulse unable to explain itself in lucid terms, working without visible means of subsistence to heroic or evil ends, baffled his dialectic. He could write it off only as a fresh manifestation of human stupidity and believe as long as possible that it was too unreasonable to be true. A wicked man taxed SHAW's credulity almost as much as a good man. This defect of human understanding led him to suppose that the battle was never between virtue and vice or between duty and inclination but always between intelligence and stupidity. It perpetually handicapped him in his effort to purge society of that inarticulately tenacious strain which GALSWORTHY named Forsyteism; it should have been his ruin as a dramatist, but so vital was the dramatic impulse within him that he was able to make a virtue of his powerlessness to people his plays with men and women and he peopled them instead with ideas.

As a playwright he put into the expression of an idea that extra half-ounce of creative energy which brought it to an immediate and seemingly fresh fullness of life. The thing assumed personality, as though it had suddenly come by its birthright. There was no less of energy in the expression of the opposing idea, for though SHAW had little imaginative sympathy with men and women he viewed all ideas with the kindling eye of genius. Towards them his duty was to reveal as the sun reveals, impartially, unemotionally, veraciously, and to withhold the life-giving rays from none, not even the clowns and the dwarfs. The conflict of these ideas, each producing momentary conviction in the audience, is the essence of Shavian comedy, and demonstrably it can produce tension every bit as dramatic as that produced by the clash of personalities. However well or ill the plays wear on the stage, Shaw dies with his position as a great comic dramatist established. His work has passed into English dramatic literature. In it there is the play of intellect with its leaven of wit and fun; there is the wisdom richly mixing with the entertainment; there is the prose dialogue, so easy for the actor to speak, which, for all its strict attention to the business in hand, could not have been composed except by a writer who was at heart a musician; and there is, above all perhaps, a superb gaiety of spirit which seems strangely at home alike in the heart of controversy, in the depths of intellectual despair and on those austere heights 'as far as thought can reach'.

130. Unsigned leading article,
Manchester Guardian

3 November 1950, 32463, 5

With the death of George Bernard Shaw England has lost the greatest figure in contemporary literature and the world has lost its best-known dramatist. The young Irishman who came from Dublin to London more than seventy years ago gained only six pounds for the first nine years of his literary labour. Now for a longer period than any writer in our history he had been an international figure. As no English writer since Byron, he had captured the Continent and America so that the 'first night' of one of his plays might be held in New York or Moscow, in Vienna or Warsaw. This eminence he had created by his own genius and by his unceasing insistence that his powers should be recognised. Ruskin once remarked that civilisation had now given way to the art of bill-posting. Very early in his career Shaw realised this truth, and determined that it was his own name that should be on the poster. He familiarised the public with every detail of his person, his character, and his opinions from his beard 'like a tuft of blanched grass,' his giant forehead and erect figure, and his diet of vegetables to the intimacies of his correspondence with Ellen Terry and Mrs Patrick Campbell. No one discussed himself in public more copiously or with more apparent candour, yet he himself has confessed, that behind all this seeming self-exposure the secret of his personality may still be hidden. 'The celebrated G.B.S.,' he once wrote,

is about as real as a pantomime ostrich. The whole point of the creature is that he is unique, fantastic, unrepresentative, inimitable, impossible, undesirable on any large scale, utterly unlike anybody that ever existed before, hopelessly unnatural, and void of real passion.

Many a young writer can testify that his superficial ruthlessness was only his inadequate protection against his teeming compassion: his kindliness to Wilde in his exile and his attempt to champion Casement in his ultimate distress showed a loyalty that had no regard for popular or national verdicts, while even his much-debated attack on vivisection

386

arose from such a passion against cruelty that, as Chesterton once said, even the dumb animals themselves might walk in his funeral.

The diversity of Shaw's activities multiplies the difficulty of an assessment. In recent years his reputation has rested mainly on his achievement as a dramatist, for even when he was well over eighty he continued to write plays which, if they lacked the 'unbearable brilliance' of his prime, remained original and effective. As a dramatist he may be best remembered, with *Candida* and *Saint Joan* and perhaps *Heartbreak House* as the peak of an achievement which will enter the permanent repertory of great English plays. But in the drama of life he had cast himself for so many parts that their mere enumeration is difficult: the language reformer, one of the earliest of his rôles and one that may be found to have occupied him more than is generally known in his later years; the musical critic and the champion of Wagner; the Shakespearean iconoclast and the propagandist for Ibsen; novelist, Socialist, philosopher, theologian, and London vestry man. The degree to which he was an original thinker is probably negligible, but he was so admirable a verbal artist, so brilliant in controversy and satire (the greatest master since Swift), so ready to invert the conventional view and trust to what might happen, that there can be few forward-thinking minds for two generations that have not been at some period affected by his influence. Those who knew him only in these last decades cannot be fully aware of his power, for the flaming young revolutionary of the eighties and the nineties had subsided somewhat into the venerated St Bernard of Malvern. The causes for which he fought had become outmoded or won, the paradox had grown into the platitude, and the 'jest in the womb of time' a reality. The major irony of his career was that in his earlier days, when he had something new and important to say, he was regarded too often as the intellectual comedian free-lancing the universe, while in these later days, when his views were caught into the headlines of the world's press, he had less that was significant to offer. In the life of his time his activities during the thirty years before the first European war were of greatest importance. Through the Fabian Society, with Sidney Webb as a sober and statistical supporter, he helped to convert English Socialism from street-corner anarchy into effective and constitutional penetration of municipal and national government. The historian of the future may see in that crucial change the reason why in England changes in society revolutionary in their nature were effected without a calamitous recourse to violence.

The world between the wars left him in a greater degree of uncertainty.

He felt that England was in danger of going 'on the rocks' through inefficiency and inanition, while democracy was substituting verbiage and stagnation for effective action. His early interest in pugilism was prophetic of his later tolerance towards dictators, and in his prefaces he appeared to admire almost equally the achievements of Rome and Moscow. He seemed almost to view with a tolerant eye the methods of violence which the totalitarian States have employed. But the violence which he condoned in others he could never have practised himself. If he had carried into life a physical recklessness equal to his mental daring he might have ended his life in the dock or even on the gallows as a revolutionary leader instead of with the veneration of the middle classes whom he execrated and who in return rewarded him with affluence. Even in his intellectual equipment one quality separated him from the fanatic. He was, as he himself wrote, 'the victim of an unsleeping and incorrigible sense of humour'. His sharp Irish voice would punctuate his conversation with a wit of continuous spontaneity, and this gay weapon in his armoury was the sole 'sword of common sense' against every stupidity, corruption, and vested interest that he found in an unjust world. Of death the humorist can seldom speak, and death Shaw contemplated but rarely in his work. It was the brightness of life that he valued, and those who have watched him in these later years have felt the pathos that the fire was dying gradually within him. 'I want,' he once wrote,

to be thoroughly used up when I die, for the harder I work the more I live. I rejoice in life for its own sake. Life is no 'brief candle' for me. It is a sort of splendid torch, which I have got hold of for the moment; and I want to make it burn as brightly as possible before handing it on to future generations.

As human calculations go, his moment of life was a long one. It has passed. He enters that shadowy immortality which is the afterlife of all whom the on-coming generations will not willingly let die.

131. James Bridie on Shaw as playwright

1950

Signed article in *New Statesman and Nation*, 11 November 1950, vol. XL, ns, 1027, 422.

James Bridie (Osborne Henry Mavor), Scottish dramatist, often thought to have written very much under the influence of Shaw. In an essay on 'Shaw as Dramatist' in *G.B.S. 90* (1946), Bridie made comparisons between Shaw and Molière, with particular reference to *The Doctor's Dilemma*. In this obituary tribute, he tries to place Shaw in the English theatre and emphasises the view that Shaw lacked 'purely dramatic gifts' but compensated for this with 'unflagging eloquence and a knowledge of human nature'. He ends with the unusual observation about Shaw that 'no writer was ever less heartless.'

When a man of letters dies, it is safe enough to praise or to disparage his work, because most men of letters are forgotten well within the century. There is little chance that the critic will become a laughing-stock to posterity—an uneasy and ridiculous ghost. When a great writer dies, it is another matter. We suddenly become posterity ourselves, and posterity in its infancy is seldom very clever.

I think we may assume that Shaw was a great dramatist. Although we are rightly proud of the English theatre, he is one of the three or four men of that theatre in the four hundred years of its existence who have attracted attention all through the civilised world. It is necessary to make some sort of groping attempt to discern in what his greatness consisted.

To begin with, we have no points of reference. He appears to be big enough to rank with Marlowe, Jonson and Dryden (when we look at British dramatists as trees walking); but he is not in the least like any of them. This is not to say that he discovered a new way of writing plays. Even in his great conversation pieces he seldom strayed far from the conventions of the theatre of the 'nineties in which he served his apprenticeship as a dramatic critic. Apart from their content, his purple patches were not unlike the purple patches of Pinero and Jones; his comic passages derived remarkably from Gilbert and Wilde in their method of presentation; and the construction of his 'straight' plays closely followed the contemporary masters.

His new and sensational contribution to the theatre was that he said what he thought instead of saying what the audience was supposed to think. The theatre of the 'nineties reflected a section of a very highly organised society indeed. This section consisted of those who were able to pay for stalls. The pit and gallery were placated by the ultimate triumph of a stereotyped sort of virtue. The stalls were fashionable. This means that both their thoughts and their manner of thinking them were very strictly defined. In spite of its apparent variety and a good deal of brilliance in expression, the late Victorian theatre was a very formal sort of theatre indeed.

His enthusiasm for Ibsen taught Shaw that it was possible, within the bounds of theatrical ritual, to express individual ideas and to make the audience like them. He rediscovered the fact that it is possible to interest and edify audiences as well as to hypnotise and entertain them. It is well known that a man will lay down the most interesting detective story to listen to an argument in a third-class railway carriage. Shaw made use of this observation in the theatre. He had few of the purely dramatic gifts of Ibsen which enabled that author to keep a sure grip on the emotions of his auditors. But he had unflagging eloquenc and a knowledge of human nature which enabled him to hold attention when even Ibsen was driven to casual pistol shots and screams to keep the stalls awake.

Shaw advanced to the conquest of the English theatre when he was close on his forties. He began by terrorising the mandarins from the pages of the *Saturday Review*, and went on to help to organise a coterie theatre and to write plays. His effort to liberate the theatre—and it was essentially a liberation—was not immediately successful from the material point of view. It is difficult to realise at this date that there were twenty years in the series of comic masterpieces before Shaw conquered the West End of London with his first long run. *Fanny's First Play* ran for nearly two years at the Little Theatre in 1911. By that time Shaw was a famous enough dramatist to hit the town with a parody of himself; and yet hardly a handful of people had ever seen his plays. Even today the West End theatre has not quite forgiven him for the *Saturday Review*. He is still a dramatist for the repertories and the

festivals, although eighty per cent of his plays are quite formal in shape and have no difficulty in holding the most ordinary of gatherings.

I have an Agag-like delicacy in approaching the discussion of the quality of these plays. Not long ago, in these columns, there was a symposium on the Play of Ideas. [See No. 129.] The closing essay was by Mr Shaw in person. He said, I think, that none of the respectable tradesmen who took part in the symposium gave the least evidence of ever having produced, written, or even seen a play. This was unfortunately true. It was not true of Mr Shaw's own contribution. While the others talked as clergymen tend to talk of their particular mystery, as if it were a succession of what a leading statesman called clitches and in a high-pitched artificial voice, Shaw got down from the rostrum and ranged about in the market place. He loved the theatre. It was his church. But he looked on his church as a part of life and not as a thing apart. His plays, with all due respect to his critics, borrow their vivid colours from life.

It is said that he lacks sentiment. This is an odd thing to say about one who had a passion, even as a critic, for what he called 'feeling'. His stage is peopled with quarrelsome, aspiring, frightened, courageous, argumentative creatures. We certainly miss the stock characters who, temporarily in real life, but permanently on the stage, are under the influence of erotic insanity. Shaw was rather afraid of them and, when he did attempt them, seldom handled them very cleverly. In any case, whatever makes the world go round, it is certainly not love; and we should be grateful to a dramatist who can now and again tear himself away from its exclusive contemplation. Religion, business, history, biology, philosophy, art and all non-libidinous human relationships are interesting too and, in the hand of a great craftsman, can be made exciting.

There is this to be said for the critics. Shaw wrote three tragedies— *Saint Joan*, *The Doctor's Dilemma* and *Major Barbara*. After a tragedy we expect to come out into the pulsating darkness with our souls purged, as they say, with pity and terror. Shaw gave us the pity and terror; but, like his own Stogumber, he was horrified by what he had done. He had none of the brutal egotism of the great poets. He could not destroy hope. Even in his pessimistic plays (*Geneva* and *Too True to be Good*) he dissolved his fantastic Day of Judgment in laughter. No writer was ever less heartless. His Mrs Alving would have given Oswald the sun. From the beginning to the end of his life he gave us the sun.

132. 'Sagittarius' on Shaw, 'the universal man'

1950

New Statesman and Nation, 18 November 1950, vol. XL, 1028, 449.

'Sagittarius', writer of satiric verses for the *New Statesman and Nation*, the *Guardian* and other papers, was an admirer of Shaw and a vice-president of the Shaw Society. Her verse tribute was entitled 'The Dean's Dilemma'.

Where shall Shaw's honoured ashes rest?
  Who owns the universal man?
Two Pantheons the right contest
  To claim this controversial man.
    This deathless, this tremendous man,
    This perfectly stupendous man
Provokes once more a wordy war for Englishman and Irishman.

Westminster and St Patrick's Deans
  Hold arguments prelatical,
Both chapters mass behind the scenes
  In attitudes dogmatical.
    Both press a disputatious plan,
    Both chide a most audacious plan,
Shaw lived and died as England's pride although he was an Irishman.

Westminster's Dean, they say, proclaims
  'I deprecate your shabby plan,
Since Ireland's most illustrious names
  Are laid within the Abbey, man.
    In London they'll be buried, man,
    Like Goldsmith and like Sheridan,
Though they may be no less than he were everyone an Irishman.'

St Patrick's Dean, they say, replies,
　'Why can't you cease your troublin', man,
For all can see who use their eyes,
　He was indeed a Dublin man.
　　Descent is there for all to scan,
　　Our registers can trace the clan,
You waste your breath; in life and death, he always was an Irishman.'

Though by the accident of birth
　St Patrick's has the prior claim,
Since here he passed his days on earth
　Westminster has the higher claim.
　　This ageless, this immortal man
　　In England passed his mortal span,
Which makes it clear his heart was here though he was born an Irish-
man.

The Doctors of Divinity
　An ultimate decision ban—
Which land has his affinity?
　There can be no partition plan.
　　He did not end where he began,
　　He did not choose—now no one can;
　　The situation's Shavian,
He's at the last, as in the past, an enigmatic Irishman.

133. Allan M. Laing, 'G.B.S. in Heaven'

1950

New Statesman and Nation, 18 November 1950, vol. XL, 1028, 456.

Allan M. Laing (1888–1970), journalist. In 1949, he edited an anthology, *In Praise of Bernard Shaw*, a short collection of brief comments on Shaw. In an article, 'The Only Man for Me', contributed to the centenary commemoration number of the *Shavian*, vol. I, no. 7, July 1956, 27, he wrote of his uncritical admiration for Shaw and said that 'it will always be one of my proudest boasts that I, though less than the dust beneath his chariot wheels, was able to persuade him once or twice to change a sentence or a word in his books, and that for this willing service he rewarded me with an appointment in form as his Honorary Proof-Reader.' He was a vice-president of the Shaw Society.

Who that knew Shaw's tireless zest
Credits his 'eternal rest'?
If there's Heaven beyond our sky,
A lazy Shaw is all my eye.
Angels fair, your peaceful lives
Will not last when he arrives.
Wings and harps and songs of praise
He will damn with pungent phrase;
Idlers on a cloud who sit
Will be shamed with biting wit;
He'll, for mansions pearl-bedecked,
Chaff the heavenly architect;
He will kick the tender shins
Of angels who record our sins,
And insist their dreadful book
Be revised, by hook or crook,
With a preface to express
The contempt of G.B.S.

He may even at the Throne
Cast the contumelious stone.
Wigs, in short, will strew the floor,
Heaven be Paradise no more,
But a place on progress bent,
Loud with Shavian argument . . .
Thus, unless to break the spell,
Shaw is sent to stir up Hell.

134. Thomas Mann on Shaw as 'mankind's friend'

1951

Signed article in the *Listener*, 18 January 1951, Vol. XLV, 1142, 98; reprint of script of broadcast talk on BBC Third Programme. Thomas Mann (1875–1955) was the leading German novelist and man of letters of the twentieth century. This obituary tribute was entitled 'He was Mankind's Friend'. Mann gave special emphasis to Shaw's interest in German culture and Germany's interest in him and singled out as an essential quality in the man and the writer, his emancipation 'from tragedy and gloom'.

Les Dieux s'en vont—'The Gods pass'. With George Bernard Shaw another of Europe's old guard has departed, the Nestor of that great statured generation, gifted with enduring vitality, productive to the last, leaving behind what must be called in comparison, a race, not without interest but frail, sombre, endangered and withered before its time. He was preceded in death by Gerhart Hauptmann, of whom G.B.S. scarcely took note, though plays like *The Weavers* and *The Rats* should have greatly pleased him, and by Richard Strauss, whom he knew quite well and in whom he admired the great tradition as well as the brash, revolutionary efficiency of a man born under a lucky star.

Still among us are the octogenarians André Gide, Shaw's kinsman in capricious genius and protestant morality, and the aged Knut Hamsun, now merely vegetating, a man broken by politics, though still the quondam creator of highly discriminate narrative works that yield nothing in richness and charm to Shaw's dramatic works. Shaw, judging by his writings, was sublimely unconcerned with this compeer and it is true that in many respects the two of them were counter-poets, especially in the matter of socialism. The brunt between them in the personal sphere was a sense of obligation towards Germany, well founded in either case, though it spelt Hamsun's political doom, while in the more intelligent Shaw it maintained the character of a well-tempered gratefulness, which, for the rest, laid little claim to any very extensive intimacy.

There is a certain meaningfulness in allowing a German to speak in Shaw's honour, for Germany—and more particularly the Austrian cultural dependency of Germany, in the person of Siegfried Trebitsch, who, with curiously unerring instinct, staked his cards on translating Shaw's plays into German—Germany recognised his importance to the modern stage, indeed to modern intellectual life as a whole, earlier than the English-speaking world. His fame actually reached England only by way of Germany, just as Ibsen and Hamsun conquered Norway, and Strindberg Sweden, by the same roundabout route, for London's independent theatre fell short of doing for Shaw's reputation—soon to grow to world-wide dimensions—what men like Otto Brahm and Max Reinhardt and their actors, and with them Berlin's dramatic criticism, were able to accomplish, for the simple reason that at that time the German stage was ahead of its British counterpart. Moreover, less frozen in the bourgeois mould, more receptive to new things, better prepared to view the Anglo-Celt as the new spear-shaker, the great dramatic, intellectual and mischief-maker, the mighty wielder of words, twinkling with exuberance, the creative critic and dialectician of the theatre of our age. He never denied his indebtedness to Germany, and repaid it in a highly amusing essay, 'What I Owe to German Culture', going so far as to declare that his own culture was to a very considerable degree German. This is a vast exaggeration, at least regarding the influence of German literature on him, which was meaningless. He himself very humorously described the fragmentary and casual nature of his knowledge of this sphere, which indeed enjoys a great popularity anywhere. In his childhood, he relates, he had once read a story by a certain Jean-Paul Richter and *Grimm's Fairy Tales* as well, adding that he still regarded Grimm as the most entertaining German author. Strange that he should not have mentioned Heine or Hoffmann, usually accounted the most entertaining Germans. Stranger still that he should have regarded Grimm as a single individual, possessed of the un-German quality of being entertaining. He seems to have been unaware that this Grimm consisted of two persons—the brothers Jakob and Wilhelm, romantically inspired lovers of German antiquity, who listened to their fairy tales from the lips of the people, and collected them conscientiously. This, apart from the fact that the two planned a gigantic etymological dictionary of the German language, with which they were never done, and which German scholars are now again engaged in rounding out. In point of fact, this work of many volumes makes the most entertaining reading in the world for anyone as interested in the German tongue as Shaw was in the English.

'Everyone ought to learn German', Shaw said, and he himself was determined to do so. But since he was only fifty-five there was no hurry. He never did learn it, and when Germans who knew no English visited him he would let them talk until they ran out of breath. Then he would put his hand to his heart and say, '*ausgezeichnet*'. He did not quite know what this word meant, he said, tongue in cheek, but it always made the Germans happy. I myself would have been quite apt to speak a little English with him, but I never visited him, for purely humanitarian reasons, for I am convinced that he never read a line of mine and this might well have been a source of some embarrassment to him. True, we might have avoided that plight by shunning literature altogether and turning at once to a subject that concerned us equally—music. It was German music Shaw had in mind, and nothing else, when he spoke of German culture and his debt to it. He made that very plain, and declared frankly that all the western culture he had acquired was as nothing compared to his intuitive grasp of German music from its birth to its maturity.

Shaw, the son of a mother who was a singer and singing teacher, left a body of dramatic writing that is the epitome of intellectuality. Yet the music of words is part and parcel of it, and he himself stressed that it was constructed on the model of thematic development in music. For all its sober brilliance, its alert and derisive critical judgment, it strives deliberately for musical effect. No reaction to it pleased the author more than that of a British colleague whom he held in high esteem—Harley Granville Barker—who exhorted the actors at a Shaw rehearsal: 'For God's sake bear in mind that this is not a play but an opera—deliver every speech as though you expected to give an encore'. In truth, Shaw, like every important dramatist before him, created his own idiom. The language of the theatre at bottom, as unrealistic as the chanted passion of the opera—exalted, exaggerated, pointed, terse and striking, no wit less rhetorical than Corneille's verses or Schiller's iambic measures, and, strange as it may sound, no less pervaded with pathos, a term not here meant to imply unctuousness and bombast, but the ultimate in expression—an eccentricity of speech, steeped for the most part in humour, full of *esprit*, challenge, effrontery, the reigning paradox.

In his preface to *Saint Joan*, which is so good that it almost makes the play superfluous, he stripped bare the scientific superstition of our times, insisting that the theories of our physicists and astronomers and the credulity with which we accept them would have dissolved the Middle Ages in a roar of sceptical merriment. That sets the style. Yet not only does Shaw, the essayist, speak in this way. He often, indeed for the most part, has his characters speak in similar fashion, and it should be noticed in passing that his figure of speech about 'dissolving an audience in a roar of sceptical merriment' precisely describes his own effect on his spectators.

When William Archer, in 1885, first met the young Dubliner, only recently come to London, in the library of the British Museum, he found Shaw preoccupied with two works which he studied in turn for weeks on end. They were *Das Kapital* by Marx, and the score of Wagner's *Tristan und Isolde*. Here you have the whole of Shaw— here is Shaw, the radical socialist, zealously addressing meetings, going beyond the teachings of Henry George, who aimed only at the reform of land holding, demanding the nationalisation of capital in every form; Shaw, the guiding spirit of the Fabian Society, who wrote *The Intelligent Woman's Guide to Socialism and Capitalism*, a book Ramsay MacDonald went so far as to call 'the world's most valuable next to the Bible'; Shaw, beginning his career as a playwright with *Widowers' Houses*, a tract about middle-class pseudo-respectability, about the social evils of slum ownership; Shaw, who remained for ever a man of social contentions, who called his plays, sometimes a little condescendingly, 'dramatic conferences', and Shaw, the born Thespian utterly lacking Wagner's sultry eroticism, with its out-heavening of Heaven, yet Wagner's true pupil as a maker of intellectual music and also as his own apostle and tireless commentator. He wrote a book about Wagner, *The Perfect Wagnerite*, a work of shrewd lucidity that compares most favourably with the burrowing flim-flam of German Wagner exegetists, nor is it mere coincidence that close beside this book stands another treatise of critical gratitude and homage, *The Quintessence of Ibsenism*, for Ibsen, about whose trait, his kinship to Wagner, I once attempted to write, was Shaw's other teacher and his case is an interesting demonstration of the extent to which an altogether different temperament can utilise, for its own purposes, like-minded experiences, once they had been fully encompassed; creatively melting them down into something totally new and personal.

Ibsen is supposed to have said once that each of his plays might just as well have become an essay. Shaw, for one, never forwent the essay, which inhered in his every play—letting it stand beside the play, or rather embodying it in a preface often as long and as eloquent as the play itself, calling things by their names with a critical directness unfitting in the play proper. I, for one, find fault, for example, with the unhappy scrambling of essay and drama that allows Cauchon and Warwick, in the fourth scene of *Saint Joan*, to concoct the terms 'protestantism' and 'nationalism', in definition of Joan's heresy and of heresy in general. Factually, these terms may not have been anachronisms in the fifteenth century, but as formulations they have an anachronistic effect which breaks up form and style. They belong to the essay, where indeed they are to be found. The play should have shunned them, should have been content with an interpretative formulation. Neither this, nor even the fact that in *Saint Joan*, as in other plays of Shaw, the aria sometimes turns into an editorial, can keep this dramatic chronicle from remaining the most fervent thing Shaw ever wrote—the play that is poetically the most moving, that comes closest to high tragedy, a work inspired with a truly elating sense of justice; a work in which the mature rationality of an *esprit fort* that has outgrown the confines of the eighteenth and even the nineteenth century, bows before sanctity; a work fully deserving its world fame.

There is but one other play I would put beside it, or perhaps even ahead of it. That is *Heartbreak House*—creative fruit of the first world war—a play of which neither Aristophanes nor Molière nor Ibsen need have been ashamed; a play that belongs in the foreground of comedy, a play of sparkling dialogue and a fanciful cast of characters, supremely humorous, yet filled with things cursed and condemned, pitched in the mood of a doomed society. When all the one-act plays are included—enter among them such as *Great Catherine* and *The Shewing-Up of Blanco Posnet*—it turns out that Shaw wrote more plays than Shakespeare, and if they are of uneven weight, like those of his great predecessor, against whom he liked to match himself so gaily, if some of them have withered, their problems growing outdated, as he foresaw, they do include, beside those already named and singled out for praise, such things as *Caesar and Cleopatra*, *Man and Superman*, *Androcles and the Lion*, and the stunningly clairvoyant political satire *The Apple Cart*, things that have withstood and will long continue to withstand the onslaught of time, in part because of their wisdom and their profoundly edifying message; in part because of the winged wit of their poetic idiom. When we add the floodtide of essays, commentary, and amplifying criticism, embodying an all-embracing encyclopaedic knowledge that draws equally on the natural sciences, theology, religious and general history, and especially the social economic sphere, always artistically leavened, full of aesthetic charm and unfailingly entertaining—when we add all this we find ourselves face to face with a lifework of astonishing scope, apparently the fruit of continued inspiration, unceasing merriness, and of an indefatigable will to work.

Like Ibsen and Wagner, Shaw was first and last a hard worker. In the words of Zarathustra, 'His goal was not his happiness, but his work'. To him, idleness was, above all, a crime against society and utterly foreign to his nature. He said once that he had never been young in the sense that the average person sows his wild oats. For that very reason he remained everlastingly youthful in his work, frisky as a colt, even in his old age. Anti-bourgeois to the core, a Marxist fond of a revolutionary slogan, 'Enemies of the bourgeoisie—unite', he was yet in his own moral convictions and mode of life middle-class through and through, indeed puritanical. He could have retired from literature tomorrow, he said, and become a respectable cheesemonger without changing one iota of his domestic habits. For him, the counterpart of the bourgeois was not the bohemian, but the socialist. The world of people, he said, who spent their evenings over champagne suppers, with actresses, models and dancers—that world was unknown to him, and he wondered how its hapless victims endured it, indeed, he often doubted that it actually existed, for all the actresses and dancers he had known were decent, hard-working women. He himself was a man of rigorous and sensible work habits. He did not burn the midnight oil, tossing off his plays on the spur of inspiration: he performed his intelligently planned literary labours between breakfast and the noonday meal, and he went to bed regularly before midnight, so that he might tackle them in the morning with freshness, lucidity and poise.

Dissolute bohemianism revolted him—he simply had no practical use for it. Vice bored him, and as for intoxication, he put these words into the mouth of the old captain in *Heartbreak House*: 'I dread being drunk more than anything in the world. To be drunk means to have dreams; to go soft; to be easily pleased and deceived; to fall into the clutches of women'. Clearly, intoxication was meant to include pre-eminently erotic ecstasy, an experience unknown to Shaw. This does not mean that he was a misogynist. On the contrary, like Ibsen, he may well be described as an extoller of women. The women in his plays are generally superior to the men, in common sense, and sense of humour, usually at the expense of the men. But he was fond of quoting Napoleon, who said that women were the business of idlers; adding, on his own, that no man with any serious mission in the world could spare time and money for affairs with women. St. Anthony he was not, for that saint was beset by temptations, while Shaw, with his vitreous nature, evidently found continence of the flesh as easy as abstention from meat. He made no dogma of vegetarianism; one man's meat, he said simply, was another man's poison. But, the rebellion against the tyranny of sex—his own expression—was part of his social, moral and aesthetic credo, and there is nothing in his plays of passion, infatuation, sensual abandon, that *Come può esser ch'io non sia più mio*[1] of Michel-angelo, and indeed these qualities would seem strangely out of place there.

One is tempted to ask him, as the prince importunes the queen in Schiller's *Don Carlos, Sie haben nie geliebt?* ('Have you then never loved?'). The answer would probably have been a laughing 'No'—laughing, but a 'No', none the less. Of that same vitreous character, a Marienbad elegy, with its passion-brimmed sorrow—indeed, any-thing like the experience of the septuagenarian Goethe underwent with Ulrike von Levetzow would have been unimaginable in the case of Shaw, and he prided himself more on it than do we on his behalf. His was a magnificent durability, yet it somehow lacked full-blooded-ness, so much so that, despite the grandeur of his life, it detracted from his stature.

I am quite fond of the massive meals that delighted Luther, Goethe and Bismarck, and I rather fancy Churchill's drinking and smoking as well. In the picture of Shaw, not merely his physical presence, but also his intellectual stature, I find a certain quality of gauntness, vegetarianism and frigidity that somehow does not quite seem to fit

[1] How can it be that I am no longer master of myself?

my idea of greatness. That idea implies a degree of human tragedy, of suffering and sacrifice. The knotted muscles of Tolstoy bearing up the full burden of morality, Atlas-like. Strindberg, who was in hell; the martyr's death Nietzsche died on the cross of thought; it is these that inspire us with the reverence of tragedy; but in Shaw there was nothing of all this. Was he beyond such things, or were they beyond him? He called one of his own plays 'A Light Play about Difficult Things'—he might well have given that title to all of his writings, and I am not so certain whether this very definition will not apply to all art to come, and whether Shaw may not turn out to have been the smiling prophet of generations, emancipated from tragedy and gloom. Yet I ask myself whether his facility was perhaps not a little too facile; whether he was ever the man to take grave matters with their full gravity. Let the future determine his weight in the scales to the last ounce. This much is certain—his sobriety, like his diet of greens, was necessary to his particular brand of clear-headedness and constraint and liberating ebullience, and nothing could be more erroneous than to mistake his coolness for an actual incapacity for love. He may have laughed at everyone and everything, but he was anything but a Mephistophelian nihilist—thrusting the Devil's chill fist in the face of the powers of creation.

Again, it is his Captain Shotover in *Heartbreak House* to whom he gives these words to say: 'Old men are dangerous: it doesn't matter to them what is going to happen to the world'. Shaw did care what was to become of the world, right down to the age of ninety-four. The clergyman who intoned the prayers at his death-bed was quite right when he said, 'This man was surely no atheist'. He was no atheist, for he reverenced the vital force that is conducting so noble an experiment with man on earth, and was sincerely concerned lest God's experiment become a failure.

Convinced that the aesthetic element, creative joy, is the most effective instrument of enlightened teaching, he tirelessly wielded the shining sword of his word and wit against the most appalling power threatening the triumph of the experiment—stupidity. He did his best in redressing the fateful unbalance between truth and reality, in lifting mankind to a higher rung of social maturity. He often pointed a scornful finger at human frailty, but his jests were never at the expense of humanity. He was mankind's friend, and it is in this role that he will live in the hearts and memories of men.

135. Eric Bentley on 'Shaw Dead', *Envoy*

February 1951, vol. 4, 15, 8

Reprinted in *In Search of Theater* (1954), 251.

Eric Bentley was born in Bolton, England, in 1916, but has worked as University professor, dramatic critic and producer chiefly in America. He wrote on Shaw in *The Playwright as Thinker* (1946), republished in England as *The Modern Theatre* (1948), concluding the chapter on Shaw with the comment that 'William James's statement that Shaw's genius is much more important than his philosophy is true, if by it we understand that genius is a synthesizing power which obliterates barriers between thought and technique and gives evidence of both in a particular mode of presentation. The Shavian mode is drama.' He wrote a full-length study, *Bernard Shaw* in 1950.

What one really feels at the news of a death is seldom easy to say; one knows only what one is supposed to feel. The sole emotion I felt when someone said: 'Shaw died last night,' was incredulity. Though on the face of it the death of a man of 94 is anything but incredible, I realised that I had expected the old man to live forever. At any rate I had never thought I myself might live in a world from which Bernard Shaw was absent. He had always been there. When I was born he was already, with his snow-white beard and his periodical messages to the chosen, like enough to God the Father. From my adolescence on, he was the patriarchal companion of my whole intellectual development—like God, never present in the flesh (perhaps I was the first to write a book on Shaw without ever having met him).

In the first half of the 20th century, I should be tempted to say, no event was complete until it had been commented on by Bernard Shaw. His creative work spilled over into letters to the paper, interviews, and postcards. He missed nothing. Three years ago when a college theatre programme in the Middle West wrongly attributed a comedy to Shaw, a telegraphic repudiation from Ayot Saint Lawrence arrived the following day.

We have lived in a great taskmaster's eye, and to learn that such an eye is closed forever is a shock. At the death of a god nature seems empty and mankind alone. We who have lived with Bernard Shaw find it a come-down to be left with ordinary mortals. In a word, it is sad to think that this admirable and ingratiating man is no longer *there*.

When I reached for the first newspaper that was full of Shaw and Shaw's death, in a sudden rush of feeling I felt the correct funereal grief which up to then had refused to come. Shaw's death was horrible and the world a vale of tears. I read on, however, and the unreality of journalism brought me back to life's reality with a jerk. What I was reading made me sick. It was praise of Shaw, but what praise, and from whom! One would have thought the deceased was a bishop who had lived down his youthful wild oats by endearing himself to the best people in the diocese. Such mourning for Shaw was a mockery of Shaw. The mourners were busy agreeing that he believed in a Deity and would go to heaven, and, as to what he stood for, in so far as it differed from what *they* stood for, they forgave him! Grasping the first occasion when Shaw was powerless to come back at them, the bourgeoisie brayed and Broadway dimmed its lights.

Those who take Shaw seriously will read in his solemn death rites the third and latest phase of a disaster that began years ago: the acceptance of Shaw *at the expense of* all he stood for. The disaster began when Shaw gave them something to accept—'GBS' the irresponsible clown. It entered a second phase when he grew old. The deference that is refused to genius is freely enough accorded to senility. You have an old man pretty much where you want him. A corpse even more so. Honour the corpse all you whom the living body embarrassed and annoyed!

Let us hope that this phase of the disaster is the last. It will be so if we take Shaw seriously, and say: 'Bernard Shaw's death is a liberation. We are now free of the old, old man of Ayot Saint Lawrence, we cannot be held prisoners of his corpse, all Shaw's utterances are now the same age, and we shall attend to those that have most life in them, whatever their date. Shaw's old age led only to his death, but his death can lead us back to his life, and his works.'

The dead man is a link with our past and, in self-pity, we grieve over the death. The man's life and works are either nothing or they belong to the future. Mr. Priestley had a sense of this fact when he remarked that Shaw was not merely the last of the giants but the first really civilized man. I take his statement also as a good attempt to define something about Shaw which has never yet been properly defined, though it is perhaps his quintessence. 'Civilized,' says Mr. Priestley, and we hear Shaw's voice again, so beautifully modulated, warm, yet not enthusiastic, soft, yet not without edge. He was aristocratic without being snobbish, and urbane without being worldly—the gentleman of the future (let us hope so, for the future's sake).

But Shaw's character was remarkable beyond all connotations of the word civilized. For instance, he was good without being pious. Though his theology was by no means as orthodox as some clergymen now think, he embodied that human purity which has ever been the aspiration of the religious, and combined it with the hard-headed wit of the unregenerate. When we reflect how few of the religious ever achieve such purity even by holding themselves aloof from the world, how much the more remarkable was it as the achievement of one whom the world fascinated and preoccupied.

A purity at the centre came radiating outwards in Shaw's more obvious virtues, notably kindness and its dialectical partner, bravery: virtues not merely commendable in themselves but which give the distinctive quality to Shaw's talent. Many people are kind and brave, and some have talent. But how many of half Shaw's talent have had a quarter of his kindness or his bravery?

Was there ever a man who could be so devastating and yet manage to be never insulting? The combination indicates something more than tact: it presupposes an amazing and boundless kindness. Think of satire and polemics in general, think of the politicians and the literati in general, and then think of this polemicist, satirist, this man of politics and letters who, on his own confession, never learned to hate. In a world practically submerged in hatred for communist or capitalist, Nazi or Jew, he never learnt to hate! And then we wonder that, when he joined in a discussion, his words had a distinctive tone!

When I speak of Shaw's bravery I am not thinking of the courage it takes to attack established ideas and institutions. To do this comes so naturally to a brilliant man, and flatters his ego so much, that very little courage is required. I mean a bravery in the face of life itself. Life never got Shaw down, and this too makes him an unusual phenomenon, especially in our time.

Like his kindness, Shaw's bravery comes to us in the tone of his writing. Read any passage. What marks it unmistakably as Shaw? The opinions? The epigrams? The rhetoric? Is it not a certain tone and tempo, jaunty, if you will, springy, high-spirited, and at the same time almost dainty—the tone of the undefeated, of the undefeatable, the tone of a defiance quite un-Prussian, quite un-20th century—the tone of the 'civilized,' of the pure, the kind, the brave.

Shaw's kindness came of itself; his bravery had to be created, because he was by nature timid; his famous pugnacity being a deliberate device by which he helped himself to be brave. Now just as his kindness would have little significance for us except as linked to his brilliance, so his bravery derives its special force as being wrested from his timidity. It is in conflict with its dialectical opposite, and as such is in a state of tension. A tension which is felt in all Shaw's writings.

And so it is also with Shaw's good humour. A man cannot be a great writer without knowing the breadth of the gap between the ideal and the real. Can we believe that a man as cheerful as Shaw did know it? The more we read him the more we realise that his happiness was wrested from his unhappiness. It was a moral achievement, the pressure of which is felt in his prose. As Nietzsche observed, we feel the calm of the sea the more when we sense its potential turbulence.

What Bernard Shaw stood for was not limited to what he advocated; his writings stand as a constant reminder of what he *was*. He was perhaps the happiest great writer who ever lived. He did not preach happiness. On the contrary! He *was* happy, and I can think of no better tidings for us to-day than the fact of his joy in living. For if Bernard Shaw was pure, kind, brave, and, by consequence, happy, we live in an age which is corrupt, cruel, cowardly, and, by consequence, miserable. Corruption, cruelty, cowardice and misery are influential; they draw all things into themselves. But their opposites are influential too, they flow outwards, they are fruitful and multiply. A life like Shaw's is that much gain written up on the credit side of history's balance sheet, capital that remains and increases at compound interest. It is productive and therefore good. It helps to create a better future as surely as vice, weakness, and despair help to create a worse.

When I insist that this is a moment to transfer our attention from death to life, from the past to the future, you may retort that it all depends whether death to-day lies more behind than ahead, whether there is to *be* a future. If Bernard Shaw is to be not merely the first civilized man but the only one, was not his happiness misplaced and the moral significance of his career, to say the least, limited? Was he not a ridiculous Don Quixote tilting at windmills?

To this I can only reply that a future is something we have to assume, even though the assumption turn out to be wrong. And even if the worst happens, and the load of misery and hate prove too heavy, and our civilization goes under, historians will have to record that there was one who gaily refused to add his weight to the load and who left his works to prove that even in the 20th century happiness was not extinct; a fact which will have its importance for future civilizations. If the worst does not happen, we shall have time to read beyond the opening chapters of Cervantes' book and discover that Sancho Panza's philosophy is not enough, and that the Don, in his sweet and undaunted temper, in his high innocence and utter commitment, in his fine unreasonable refusal to accept the severance of the real and the ideal, was a worthy predecessor of George Bernard Shaw.

Bibliography

The following is a short list of the works about Shaw which may be most useful in showing the development of the critical response to his plays.

BOOKS

BROAD, C. L. and V. M., *Dictionary to the Plays and Novels of Bernard Shaw*, London, Black, 1929.

COLBOURNE, MAURICE, *The Real Bernard Shaw*, London, Dent, 1949. Includes a chart of the plays, with brief factual notes on the productions.

GIBBS, A. M., *Shaw*, Edinburgh, Oliver & Boyd, 1969. This brief volume in the 'Writers and Critics' series contains a chapter in which the critical response to Shaw's work is surveyed, and a bibliography.

HENDERSON, ARCHIBALD, *George Bernard Shaw: Man of the Century*, New York, Appleton-Century-Crofts, 1956. This immense centenary biography incorporates and replaces previous biographies of Shaw by this indefatigable author. The book is valuable as a mine of information rather than as a coherent biography or criticism, but it is indispensable for detailed study of Shaw's life. There is a long appendix, 'Shaw around the World', by Lucile Keeling, which contains the largest available amount of information about the production and publication of Shaw's plays in many countries.

LAURENCE, DAN H. (ed.), *The Collected Letters of Bernard Shaw*, London, Reinhardt. This edition is to consist of four volumes. The first two, covering the years 1874–97 and 1898–1910, were published in 1965 and 1972 respectively.

LAURENCE, DAN H. (ed.), *The Bodley Head Bernard Shaw*, 7 volumes, London, Reinhardt, The Bodley Head, 1970–4. This edition includes, together with the plays and prefaces, much previously unbound material, such as 'interviews' and programme notes by Shaw, commenting on the response to his work.

MANDER, RAYMOND and MITCHENSON, JOE, *Theatrical Companion to Shaw*, London, Rockliff, 1954. The book is called 'a pictorial record of the first performances of the plays of George Bernard Shaw'. It gives details of first performances and cast-lists of revivals. There are chapters on Shaw's methods as a producer, by the editors; on acting in Shaw's plays by Dame Sybil Thorndike; and on Shaw at rehearsal by Lewis Casson. Appendices include notes on productions of Shaw by different companies, lists of foreign translations and productions and details of the first publications of the plays.

MEISEL, MARTIN, *Shaw and the Nineteenth Century Theater*, Princeton University Press, and London, Oxford University Press, 1963. A detailed examination of the development of Shaw's drama as a continuation of the nineteenth-century dramatic tradition.

NICOLL, ALLARDYCE, *English Drama 1900–1930*, Cambridge University Press, 1973. This volume contains a study of Shaw in a chapter entitled 'J. M. Barrie and G. B. Shaw' and an entry for Shaw in the 'Hand-list of Plays'.

PURDOM, C. B., *A Guide to the Plays of Bernard Shaw*, London, Methuen, 1963. A Shaw handbook, which includes chapters on 'The Man' and 'The Dramatist' and a long section consisting of factual information about each play—a summary of the story, notes on the characters, views on the type of production that the editor considers appropriate, and brief information on the history of the play in the theatre. There is also 'A Note on Printing the Plays'.

RATTRAY, R. F., *Bernard Shaw: A Chronicle*, Luton, Leagrave Press, 1951. A record of the facts of Shaw's life, as man and writer, in strict chronological order.

VALENCY, MAURICE, *The Cart and the Trumpet*, New York, Oxford University Press, 1973. A thorough study of the whole of Shaw's dramatic work.

WARD, A. C., *Bernard Shaw*, London, Longman, 1950. Published for the British Council and the National Book League, this is an essay in the bibliographical series of supplements to *British Book News*. It contains a select bibliography and a list of first performances of the principal plays.

WARD, A. C., *Bernard Shaw*, London, Longman, 1951. This is a book-length survey of Shaw's work in the 'Men and Books' series. It includes a bibliography.

WEINTRAUB, STANLEY (ed.), *Desmond MacCarthy's The Court Theatre 1904–1907: A Commentary and Criticism*, Coral Gibbs, Florida, University of Miami Press, 1966. A new edition of the original publication by Desmond MacCarthy.

WEINTRAUB, STANLEY, *Journey to Heartbreak*, New York, Weybright & Talley, 1973, and London, Routledge & Kegan Paul, 1973. An indispensable survey of Shaw during the 'crucible years', 1914–18. It examines in detail the relationship between Shaw the dramatist and Shaw the public and political figure, with much information on the effect of his attitudes to the war on the response to his writing.

WEINTRAUB, STANLEY, article on Shaw in *Encyclopaedia Britannica*, 1974.

WEINTRAUB, STANLEY (ed.), *Saint Joan: Fifty Years After, 1923–24 to 1973–74*, Baton Rouge, Louisiana State University Press, 1973. This collection of twenty-five reviews and other articles about *Saint Joan* is edited, with an introduction, by Stanley Weintraub.

WEINTRAUB, STANLEY, *Shaw: An Autobiography*, London, Reinhardt, 1970, 1971. In two volumes, Stanley Weintraub has skilfully arranged Shaw's writings about himself.

PERIODICALS

Drama, London, Autumn 1956: the journal of the British Drama League, Shaw and Archer centenary number. Contains letters from Shaw to Gilbert Murray and extracts from a lecture by Archer on Galsworthy, Barrie and Shaw, given in New York, 1921.

Modern Drama, Lawrence, Kansas, University of Kansas, September and December 1959. The September issue was a special Shaw number and included fifteen essays on different aspects of Shaw and the first part of a selected bibliography of Shaw, 1945–55. The second part appeared in the December issue. In the absence of a full bibliography, this is one of the most valuable lists that have yet appeared.

World Theatre, Brussels, Elsevier, Spring 1957. Published by the International Theatre Institute with the assistance of Unesco, this edition was devoted to 'the classics of tomorrow, Ibsen and Shaw'.

SHAW PERIODICALS

There are three current periodicals devoted to Shaw and his work. The *Shavian* is published by the Shaw Society in Great Britain; the *Independent Shavian*, which is more a newsletter, is published by the New York Shavians Inc.; and the *Shaw Review*, a journal of more academic weight, is published by the Pennsylvania State University Press.

Index

II SHAW'S THEMES AND CHARACTERISTICS

III GENERAL

THE CRITICAL HERITAGE SERIES

GENERAL EDITOR: B. C. SOUTHAM

Volumes published and forthcoming